Acclaim for *The Future of the Past*

"A smart and engaging work . . . You can take your pick of strong essays in *The Future of the Past* as they unexpectedly engulf you in subjects ranging from pollution of the sacred Ganges to cultural memory and survival in the South Pacific to the political role of spoken poetry in Somalia to . . . the double-edged role of libraries, computerization, and literacy itself in the loss or preservation of history. His book serves as something of a counterpoint, a hopeful sign about the level of discussion possible in American culture."

—*The New York Times Book Review*

"This book is worth reading for its chapter on the Sphinx alone . . . Lively."

—*Harper's Magazine*

"[A] fascinating meditation on the ways we remember—and pave over—history."

—*The Commercial Appeal* (Memphis)

"[Stille] never slides into an academic tone. Each chapter moves briskly from a gripping opening scenario to a well-researched contextualization and onto an appropriately sobering concluding meditation. . . . remarkable."

—*South Florida Sun-Sentinel*

"A thoughtful look at how technology and other forces of modernity may be obliterating our past . . . [A] sobering and lucid tour of our disappearing past . . . highly recommended."

—*Library Journal*

"Stille is an indefatigable reporter, remarkable especially for his willingness to stray off the beaten path, whether into the complexities of a Latin text or the rivalries among Mogadishu's warlords. . . . Stille's book is far more than just a litany of loss and woe. He is passionately interested in why all this is happening, and in the larger patterns that emerge; his eye is keenly trained to pick out the threads that link, say, the death of a lemur and the loss of a manuscript."

—*Preservation Magazine*

"[An] absorbing book."

"The accumulative impact of this absorbing collection may surprise even those who've already read any individual piece."

"Exemplary."

"Fascinating and troubling."

"Splendid . . . Stille, a lovely storyteller, brings to life the passionate and forceful personalities of preservationists, dedicated scholars, bald opportunists, looters, and other key players. . . . A powerful narrative, rich with anecdote, detailed description, and lively dialogue. This is a must read."

The Future of the Past

Alexander Stille

The Future of the Past

PICADOR

FARRAR, STRAUS AND GIROUX

NEW YORK

www.picadorusa.com

Picador® is a U.S. registered trademark and is used by Farrar, Straus and Giroux under license from Pan Books Limited.

For information on Picador Reading Group Guides, as well as ordering, please contact the Trade Marketing department at St. Martin's Press.
Phone: 1-800-221-7945 extension 763
Fax: 212-677-7456
E-mail: trademarketing@stmartins.com

Grateful acknowledgment is made to the editors of the periodicals in whose pages slightly different versions of the chapters of this book first appeared:

Chapters 1-4, 6, and 9-11 appeared in *The New Yorker.*
Chapter 7 appeared in *Granta.*
Chapter 8 appeared in *The American Scholar.*

Library of Congress Cataloging-in-Publication Data

Stille, Alexander.
  The future of the past / Alexander Stille.
    p. cm.
  ISBN 0-312-42094-3
  1. Historic preservation—Philosophy. 2. Technological innovations—Social aspects. 3. Social change. 4. Globalization—Social aspects. 5. Nature—Effect of human beings on. 6. Environmental protection. 7. Antiquities—Collection and preservation. 8. Cultural property—Protection. 9. Twenty-first century—Forecasts. I. Title.

CC135.S76 2002
303.4—dc21   2001054348

First published in the United States by Farrar, Straus and Giroux

First Picador Edition: April 2003

10 9 8 7 6 5 4 3 2 1

To the memories of
Michele Cordaro and Leonard Boyle

Contents

Introduction

IN THE CITY OF ROME the physical remains of the past are every-where—a living palimpsest where the many layers of twenty-seven hundred years of history exist side by side in strange juxtaposition. As cars whiz by the ancient Republican temples and the art deco theater in the Largo Argentina, you wait for the bus near the spot where Julius Caesar was assassinated. A few blocks away, faces of long-dead Romans stare out from the facades of modern buildings decorated with old sar-cophagi, and a block of twentieth-century shops curves gently, con-forming to the shape of the ancient amphitheater on whose foundations it stands. In the basement of a modern pizzeria there is a large sundial that kept time when the emperor Augustus ruled the world. I found these remnants of the past, living so gracefully and casually in the midst of everyday life, strangely comforting. They change your sense of time and your place in the world, making the ups and downs of the present seem smaller, while also making you feel a part of a much larger contin-uum. The city has seen every possible form of human glory, folly, and depravity—has witnessed emperors who declared themselves gods and holy men dressed in sackcloth who crawled up marble staircases on their bare knees. It has been ravaged and rebuilt numerous times and survived with something of its soul intact. Amidst the din of tourists, street vendors, quarreling neighbors, *motorini* gunning their engines, women putting out their laundry, children playing soccer in the square, the massive, harmonious forms of the Pantheon and St. Peter's Basilica loom in the background. And as you bathe in the happy, noisy confusion of the present, the great pagan temple and the central church of Christianity remind you that the important things in life are few, diminishing the sting of the ephemeral worries that crowd our minds from day to day. There is nothing fussy or museumlike about the city: the past coexists comfortably and gives way to the needs of the present. The city's extravagant, crumbling beauty is so abundant that it lies about you everywhere in pieces: you take a wrong turn and stumble on an exquisitely carved Corinthian column lying on the pavement at the end of an alley, abandoned to the care of a family of cats. As you are walking on a summer evening through the city center, someone having a party casually opens the shutters of the upper window of a grimy sixteenth-century building in order to let some air into the room and smoke a cigarette; you look up and see a perfectly preserved Renaissance fresco on the ceiling—a scene of angels and a winged cupid floating on clouds against a sky of lapis lazuli—and hear the tinkling of glasses and the sound of laughter. Then the shutters close again. It is just another private home in Rome, like hundreds of others, one you have never seen before and will probably never see again.

While living in Rome I began to work on a story about Father Reginald Foster, senior Latinist to the pope, a man engaged in a quixotic but highly compelling attempt to keep the Latin language alive. The story first suggested the idea for this book and became its eighth chapter. Foster, who was born in 1937, came of age during the 1950s, when Latin was still very much alive: it was the language used for teaching in Catholic seminaries from Buenos Aires and Sydney to Crakow and Rome. And Foster, son and grandson of plumbers from Milwaukee, speaks Latin more fluently than most people speak their own languages, and works in what is perhaps the only office in the world where Latin is spoken. He walks through and sees a different city from the Rome the rest of us know. For Foster the city is a vast text, interwoven around the monuments, running along the tops of doorways and the bases of monuments, statues, and burial sites, recounting tens or hundreds of thousands of stories—of slaves and emperors, of soldiers fallen in long-forgotten campaigns, of husbands and wives, of popes, cardinals, saints, and courtesans or simply men and women wealthy enough to leave their mark on the city. The correspondence or ironic juxtaposition between a monument's origin and its current status and all the layers of meaning that have accumulated between them give the city a kind of symphonic quality, whose music most people are no longer able to hear.

The status of Latin changed drastically in the mid-1960s when the Church struggled to modernize itself. Since then, Foster, despite his own superhuman efforts, has seen its use gradually fade within the Church. In a sense, the death of Latin is paradigmatic of a larger dilemma of our age. It may be entirely reasonable for a society to decide that Latin is no longer an essential part of school curriculum and that other needs—computer skills, knowledge of Spanish, Chinese, or English—should take precedence. Things change, and today English, the language of the Internet, plays the role of lingua franca that Latin served until the eighteenth century. Every major historical change involves, by necessity, enormous loss. Without adopting a Luddite, antitechnological stance, I think it is important to acknowledge that our society is in the midst of a fundamental rupture with the past, which involves loss as well as gain. The benefits of the information revolution—instant worldwide communication and universal access to infinite amounts of data—are plainly evident and have been justly celebrated. Nevertheless, we should, I think, at least acknowledge and examine what we are losing as well. The experience with Foster raised an interesting question for me: what does it mean to have a living relationship with the past? And what happens when some of those links are broken?

And yet to characterize our era as one purely of loss would be to miss some of the most exciting developments in human history. As I began to think about this project, I saw my first example of virtual reality, a three-dimensional reconstruction of the tomb of Queen Nefertari—the favorite wife of Ramses II—in the Valley of the Queens in Luxor, Egypt. The virtual reality was the centerpiece of an exhibition held at the Palazzo Ruspoli in Rome, dedicated to the tomb, which had been discovered by an Italian explorer in 1904 and was closed to the public in the 1970s after it had fallen into a state of dangerous dilapidation. It was then carefully restored, recovering much of its faded glory, by Italian art conservators with the financial backing of the Getty Conservation Institute in California. Scientific studies had demonstrated that the greatest threat to the long-term future of the tomb was the presence of tourists, whose breath and sweat would introduce moisture and accelerate the process of salt crystallization that has been corroding its brilliantly painted surfaces. So the Getty commissioned an Italian software company to create a virtual reality simulation of the tomb that could be set up in an underground chamber in the Valley of the Queens as a substitute for the real thing. After all, the famous cave paintings at Lascaux—among the first artistic expressions of our ancestors—have been closed to the public for many years and tourists visit an artfully made copy that, in turn, has undergone so much wear and tear that it, too, has been restored. "Moving" through the shadowy chambers of a virtual reality simulation of an ancient Egyptian tomb—sponsored by a California foundation, executed by an Italian software company, displayed inside a Renaissance palace in downtown Rome decorated with trompe l'oeil paintings (the Renaissance equivalent of virtual reality)—was a strange end-of-millennium moment that seemed to contain many of the odd contradictions generated by the future of the past.

Space radar, computer models, infrared photography, carbon dating, magnetic resonance imaging, DNA and chemical analysis, and CD-ROMs offer us unprecedented opportunities to study and preserve the past. At the same time, the by-products of accelerating technological change—industrialization, population growth, and pollution—threaten to destroy in a few generations monuments and works of art that have survived thousands of years of war, revolution, famine, and pestilence.

Scholars are creating a virtual Pompeii, so that anyone anywhere can explore the Villa of the Mysteries and other wonders, but the actual Pompeii is deteriorating markedly, its gorgeous wall frescoes fading visibly or being chipped off and sold by clandestine looters. Orbiting satellites gather radar images that penetrate underneath the sands of the Sahara desert and tell us what the topography of Egypt looked like thirty thousand years ago. But the monuments of ancient Egypt, which stood remarkably preserved in dry sand for thousands of years, are crumbling because of the rising water of the country, a result of the Aswan Dam and widespread irrigation. We are faced with a dramatic paradox: soon we may have virtual realities of the tombs of the Valley of the Kings in classrooms around the world—a genuine democratic advance—but the tombs themselves, most of which looked almost new when they were discovered in the late nineteenth and early twentieth century, may no longer exist. In fact, when I traveled to Egypt to write the first chapter of this book, I found that the Egyptian government had, against the Getty's advice, reopened Nefertari's tomb to tourists. And it is not hard to understand why: it is the most expensive single attraction in Luxor costing some $34 for a ten-minute visit. Yet the government has had to close other tombs—once equally glorious—whose condition has deteriorated to a perilous state. "In another twenty years, most of the archeology of Egypt is going to be in museums," Fred Wendorf, an archeologist at Southern Methodist University who has worked in Egypt for nearly forty years, has said, perhaps overstating things a bit. "Everything else is going to be covered by water or plowed up in fields or coated with asphalt."

The vanishing of the physical record is a metaphor for the larger question of our tenuous connection to the past. As we hurtle into the information age—where it appears more urgent to master software programs than to learn ancient or foreign languages—it is legitimate to wonder what relationship we will have to the ancient world or the preindustrial civilizations of the Middle Ages and the Renaissance. Will classical studies continue to fade from the curriculum or will they be revived by brilliant new technology that makes it possible to explore the digitally reconstructed cities of antiquity? The Internet gives us the potential of instant access to infinite amounts of information, but there is also a genuine risk of our becoming a society with little historical framework in which to set all the information we have access to. Will a wired world be better informed than any other, or will information crowd out knowledge as we struggle to sort through the flood of messages and images with which we are bombarded each day? Globalization may well raise the standard of living and introduce democratic reforms to countries around the world, but it is also bringing about an unprecedented homogenization of culture and will almost certainly accelerate the disappearance of thousands of regional dialects, languages, and distinct cultures. Paradoxically, the rootlessness of contemporary society has created a tremendous yearning for a connection with ancient or vanished civilizations. The New Age preoccupation with Atlantis, Stonehenge, ancient Egypt, and pre-Columbian Mesoamerica and the nostalgic historical emphasis of Disney theme parks are all manifestations of this deeply felt need.

The loss of historical memory is hardly unique to our age. The agricultural revolution—which replaced many small hunter-gatherer communities and nomadic pasturalists with the first cities and empires—arguably changed our lives more deeply than the information revolution will. Alexander the Great and the Macedonian Greeks conquered Egypt, and the Romans, in turn, subjugated the Greeks. The spread of Latin itself wiped out scores of local languages and cultures, from the Etruscans in Italy and the Gauls in France to the Lydians in Turkey and the Thracians in Bulgaria and northern Greece—peoples of whom we have scant traces. The triumph of Christianity saw the destruction of much of pagan civilization, the smashing of statues, and the loss of hundreds of thousands of other works of antiquity. The builders of the modern Rome we now admire happily flattened entire medieval neighborhoods to make way for their great Renaissance palaces and Baroque churches. The spread of Europeans throughout the Americas destroyed the Aztec and Incan empires and hundreds of other indigenous cultures that had developed over thousands of years. Certainly the destruction of the past has been just as great in previous ages and certainly more violent. Is our sense of loss, then, merely the nostalgia that every generation feels for its own immediate past?

I think it can be demonstrated that the rate of change has increased markedly during the past two hundred years and has continued to speed up during our lifetimes. In a number of ways, fundamental aspects of life changed relatively little from antiquity until the nineteenth century. In the first century A.D., it took about twenty days to go by boat from the eastern end of the Roman Empire in Turkey or Lebanon to its western extreme in Spain or North Africa. In the 1830s, before the invention of the railroad and the telegraph, it took about two weeks to get news from New York to Chicago. Sailing boats traveling from Europe took about as much time to reach the United States as it took Columbus to find the New World. The telegraph, introduced in 1841, cut the time it takes for news to travel to the speed of light. The telegraph—the beginning of electronic information technology—may have been an even more revolutionary change than the Internet is for us, but it also marked the beginning of a phase of change whose rate has only continued to accelerate: it took thirty-eight years for radio to reach fifty million American homes; television reached that level in thirteen years, cable TV in ten, and the Internet in only five. Now we are ruled by Moore's Law, which states that the speed and power of a computer processing chip will double approximately every eighteen months.

Similarly, human population and the average life span changed very little from the time of Christ to the early nineteenth century. It is estimated that the population of the world at the time of the Roman Empire was about a billion, and it changed relatively little for the next sixteen hundred years. In the premodern era, population rose and fell and rose and fell, alternating periods of growth and prosperity with times of plague and famine, making human life seem an endless cycle of renewal and decline—very far from our modern sense of history as a gradual but ineluctable march of continual growth and progress. It took homo sapiens about a hundred thousand years to reach one billion and another eighteen hundred years to reach two billion. Now we are at six billion, and it took just ten years to produce the last billion.

In the Roman world, perhaps 5 percent of the population lived in cities, the other 95 percent in the countryside, tilling the earth. In the United States a majority of the workforce still made its living through agriculture until the 1870s. Now just 2 percent of the population feeds 280 million Americans and exports food to the rest of the world as well.

Many of these changes, of course, were extremely welcome. Until the beginning of the nineteenth century, most people died in childhood and a staggering number of women died giving birth; the average life span was about thirty. Modern medicine has doubled the average life expectancy and advances in agriculture have allowed us to feed a vastly greater number while freeing most of us from backbreaking labor.

These changes have also had significant cultural consequences. The massive growth in population and industrialization led to the exploration and colonization of much of the world by European peoples. The late nineteenth and early twentieth centuries saw a period of global trade not unlike today's. But the first wave of globalization—the age of the railroad, steamship, and telegraph, of the big empires of iron and steel—still left vast pockets of the world relatively undisturbed. Until quite recently, the majority of humanity still told time by the sun, organized their lives by the slow rhythms of the seasons, and lived by the traditional knowledge and beliefs of their ancestors, accumulated slowly over the course of centuries and millennia.

Today, there is hardly a corner of the globe where Coca-Cola is not sold or people do not wear Nike sneakers. A few years ago, CNN ran a program entitled "Broadcasting Live from the Great Mosque at Mecca!" (In the nineteenth century, the adventurer Richard Burton, dressed in Bedouin garb and speaking fluent Arabic, had snuck into the Great Mosque, perhaps the first European to do so.) China's Forbidden City has now opened its first Starbuck's coffee outlet. Until quite recently, there were landscapes that remained unexplored and uncataloged. And there were cultural spaces—the Great Mosque, the Forbidden City, the sex lives of American presidents, the hills of Papua New Guinea, the source of the Nile, the inner dynamics of the British royal family—that remained private and inaccessible. Those spaces have been reduced to virtually none in the age of media that, for good and ill, break down all barriers and leave no doors unopened.

Indeed, the loss of historical memory may be directly related to our thirst for knowledge and information. "In physics, we have the Heisenberg uncertainty principle, which says that we change what we observe. Something similar happens in archeology: 'You study it, you kill it,'" says Egyptologist Mark Lehner, who is the main subject of chapter I. His observation is particularly obvious in the case of Egypt, where our knowledge has increased exponentially since explorers began prying open pharaonic tombs and digging up temples but where doing so has also exposed the monuments to the elements. The example of archeology, however, may be emblematic of something larger. And the principle that Lehner refers to applies to a number of other areas: to our knowledge of other cultures as well as of nature itself. For example, no age other than our own has so thoroughly and respectfully documented the remote cultures that were referred to as "savage" only a few decades ago, and yet, of the six thousand different languages spoken around the world—each a distinct culture and mental universe—half are expected to die out during the next century. As Hegel wrote, the owl of Minerva—goddess of wisdom—flies at dusk.

In writing this book, I set about trying to show the double-edged nature of technological change in a series of different contexts and from a number of odd angles. The first three chapters, set in Egypt, China, and Sicily, all deal with monuments. In the China chapter, I contrast Western and Asian attitudes toward monuments, conservation, and the past, while in the Sicily chapter I write about the Western passion for collecting. One of the principal ways we now relate to the past is through the objects that collectors and museums have chosen to acquire and the commodification of artifacts is very much part of the modern sensibility.

Chapters 4 and 5, set in India and Madagascar, deal with different aspects of the environment since in our modern world we treat the environment and rare species much as we treat ancient objects—as relics of our biological past that need "preserving." Indeed, species today are information, laid out chromosome by chromosome by DNA-sequencing computer programs. In Madagascar, I had originally wanted to do a story that explored the following paradox: on the one hand, we are gaining enormous amounts of knowledge about the natural world through technology—recovering the DNA of long-extinct species from mosquitoes fossilized in amber or reconstructing the family trees of entire species going back millions of years—but on the other hand, species are disappearing at an increasingly rapid rate because of the consequences of human development. This is one of the most exciting times in the history of science, in which we are discovering new species, yet an estimated fifteen thousand species of plants and animals are listed as highly endangered. Madagascar seemed a perfect setting for this story, since it is a naturalists' paradise, with 80 percent of its species found nowhere else in the world, but it is also an extremely poor country where the pressures of human development pose serious risks to the environment and threaten the habitats of many of the unique species found there. As I began to do reporting and research, however, the story shifted beneath me. I discovered how much more complex the issues were than I had originally supposed. In my naïveté I had never stopped to think that there could be anything wrong with trying to save a rain forest. In a country where people live a bad harvest away from starvation, nature conservation suddenly appeared much more problematic. The issues of technology and preserving species were perfectly valid, but they were embedded in a social context of incredible moral complexity.

Madagascar also forced me to see that some of our notions about nature were deeply related to issues I was dealing with in the chapters on monuments and museums. In fact, the first early museums, the cabinets of curiosity of the Renaissance, collected natural wonders—strange species and fossils turned up by travelers—together with ancient works of art. Moreover, my own idea of nature as something to be preserved was very much a product of modern Western urban culture. The movement to create national parks began in the United States in the late nineteenth century, precisely at the time when industrialization was transforming our country. Thus the idea of pristine nature is the flip side of mechanization and in some ways the park is to nature what the museum is to the art of previous centuries, a backward glance at something that is understood as past. Indeed, it is significant that Theodore Roosevelt was both the champion of our national park system and an important benefactor of the American Museum of Natural History in New York (of which his father had been a founder).

My interest in natural history went hand in hand with an interest in ethnography and the study of "primitive" people, who have been regarded in effect as our living ancestors and whose societies have been regarded as contemporary vestiges of our own distant past. It has been one of the principal impulses of modern anthropology both to preserve as well as to document these cultures. Of course, one of the central ironies of the field is that the arrival of the anthropologist has generally been part of the process of extending Western influence. In the chapter called "The Man Who Remembers," I describe the career of Italian anthropologist Giancarlo Scoditti, who has spent most of the past twenty-six years studying and documenting the culture of a tiny island off the coast of Papua New Guinea. Some of the elders of the community, master carvers and oral poets, welcomed him, the first anthropologist ever to live on the island, because they understood the value of documenting a series of traditions and customs that they felt were destined to disappear. Now when he returns to the island, some of the younger people ask him what the meaning of a particular ceremony or song was, or the right step in a traditional dance. Thus Scoditti's written work has become the principal repository of some of the island's traditions yet, at the same time, writing—in the form of the Christian Bible and as transmitted by missionary schools and the state educational system—has discouraged and replaced these traditions. The vehicle of the first great information revolution, writing, is itself a tool both of memory and of loss.

The last third of the book deals with the technology of writing and the role of libraries in the transmission of cultural memory in the ancient world (the ancient library of Alexandria), the Renaissance (the

Vatican Library), and the contemporary world (the National Archives in Washington). Electronic technology would seem to be the philosopher's stone or the Holy Grail that the librarians of Alexandria and Rome were looking for: a means of preserving almost unlimited amounts of knowledge in a highly compact space in a form that would be invulnerable to the little insects that worm their way through even the toughest animal hide parchment in the Vatican stacks. As it turns out, electronic data is surprisingly fragile. It can be counted on to last on tapes or compact discs for about twenty years before it tends to become corrupted. Thus, if the data is not copied and recopied onto new storage media regularly, it is likely to become unreadable. Not only are the electronic signals themselves likely to become damaged or corrupted but, because software and hardware are changing so rapidly, we will probably not be able to access much of the data produced in recent decades. The first computers I owned, in the 1980s, were a small Radio Shack model that recorded data signals onto a kind of tape recorder device and then a large, heavy desktop machine with 5¼-inch floppy disks. What are the chances of anyone's being able to read these devices if someone comes upon them in an attic fifty years from now? Thus, Moore's Law—that the speed of personal computers will double every eighteen months—works both ways. The constant improvements and changes in the computer industry mean that we are producing more and more information every day but also that we are bound to lose more information now than at any time in the past.

In tackling this project, I chose to avoid arguing a particular thesis, which, I felt, would push me to write a more tendentious book—for or against technology or change. Moreover, the changes we are experiencing are so complex and profound, their final shape still so molten and unclear, that any judgments and predictions we make are almost doomed to prove simplistic or mistaken. I wanted instead to immerse myself in a small but representative number of specific situations where I felt I had a better chance of capturing the complexity, strangeness, and contradictions of transformation. The beauty of journalistic reporting is that things rarely go the way you plan; life has a way of surprising you, derailing your most cherished assumptions and showing the inadequacies of your favorite theories. Nevertheless, I felt it was important to hazard some provisional conclusions in the final chapter about the broad implications of the changes we are experiencing, knowing full well that many of them may prove wrong.

The Future of the Past

The Sphinx—Virtual and Real

SITTING AT A computer terminal in Santa Monica, California, I watched the Great Sphinx of Giza take shape before my eyes as a scholar's careful measurements were transformed into an elaborate wire-frame model, then grew a "skin" that showed not the half ruined statue that now lies in the sands of Egypt but the Sphinx as it may have looked at the time of its creation forty-five hundred years ago, with its nose, royal beard, and headdress intact.

Just a few miles away at the Getty Conservation Institute in Marina Del Rey, technicians have compiled data from a fully automated, solar-powered monitoring station placed behind the Sphinx, measuring wind direction and velocity and relative humidity in order to study erosion patterns of the ancient world's greatest surviving colossal statue. In the basement of the institute, men in white lab coats were testing perfect airless environments for the preservation of the body of King Tutankhamen and his fellow mummies at the Egyptian Museum in Cairo, and the institute has sponsored the virtual reality reconstruction of the tomb of Queen Nefertari so that anyone with a ten-thousand-dollar Silicon Graphics computer can "walk through" her final resting place sixty-five hundred miles away in the Theban necropolis in Luxor.

Although these technological marvels are helping to transform the way we study and preserve the historical past, the reality on the ground in Egypt looks rather different. When I first saw the Great Sphinx in 1996, it was covered in scaffolding as Egyptian conservators worked to protect its lion body by encasing its bottom half in newly cut limestone blocks—the latest in a series of attempts to save the Sphinx. Several years earlier, a two-ton chunk had fallen off the chest of the Sphinx, and the soft middle portion of its body continues to flake and chip in pieces that turn to a dust as soft as talcum powder when you rub them between your fingers. Slowly and relentlessly, its body is being eaten at by wind and moisture, aided by the smog of Cairo, which now rivals Mexico City's as the worst in the world. Behind the rump of the Sphinx, the Getty's solar-powered monitoring device stood disconnected, tangled up in its own wiring, looking like a space-age music stand alone on a stage without an orchestra. The Sphinx still stares impenetrably across the millennia but instead of contemplating the mysteries of existence its gaze is now trained at the Pizza Hut and Colonel Sanders Kentucky Fried Chicken restaurants that have opened just two hundred yards in front of it. The urban sprawl of Cairo—which has grown from two to seventeen million people in the last forty years—has reached the feet of the Sphinx and the Pyramids, bringing with it cars, sewage, air pollution, and fast-food culture.

"You have arrived in Cairo at a very bad time," an Egyptian voice explained to me in an ominous tone over the phone the day of my arrival at the Nile Hilton. "There has been a theft at the Egyptian Museum. They have just fired the head of the Supreme Council of Antiquities. I'm not sure very many people will be willing to speak with you." A thief had hidden inside a sarcophagus, snuck out after closing time, stolen several gold objects from the collection of King Tutankhamen, and hidden them in the bathroom. He was arrested trying to smuggle something out the next morning. The incident was seized upon by the minister of culture as an excuse to sack the director of antiquities, who was considered an open, likable person who had worked well with foreign archeologists in Egypt. His successor asserted his power by revoking many recent decisions and thundering against foreigners using their work in Egypt to "give their students Ph.D.'s." But how else, the archeologists wondered, are we supposed to train a new generation of Egyptologists?

As I was to discover in the next few weeks, the deterioration and conservation of antiquities is an extremely delicate subject in Egypt, and nowhere more so than at the Sphinx—national symbol of Egypt, tourist attraction, and world icon, in which almost everyone feels they have a stake and a say.

I headed out to Giza with Mark Lehner, a scholar who teaches at the University of Chicago and who may know more about the Sphinx than anyone else alive. We started in the confusion and traffic of downtown Cairo, crossed the Nile onto its west bank, and drove about seven miles south and a couple of miles inland from the river. "This all used to be farmland when I first came here in 1972," Lehner said as we drove along the Pyramids Road. Now the road is lined with cheaply built cement high-rises that are already badly dilapidated and black with soot. Although they are less than twenty years old, they are in considerably worse shape than the Pyramids, which begin to appear, majestic as ever, over the roofs crowded by satellite dishes.

Not only has the population nearly doubled in the twenty-five years Lehner has been coming to Egypt, it has become infinitely more cosmopolitan. "When I first came, I recall people collecting outside storefront windows where you had a few imported things, silk ties maybe from Italy or a little can of Nescafé," Lehner said. "Now we have McDonald's, Pizza Hut, satellite dishes, CNN, and David Letterman." As Egyptian society has opened up on some fronts, it has turned inward on others. Just in the last several years, there has been a sudden proliferation of the chador—the veil traditionally worn by Islamic women—which had been gradually disappearing from the streets of Cairo in recent decades.

During the 1980s, Lehner was the field director of something called the Sphinx Mapping Project, the first full-scale attempt to scientifically survey and record the colossus with photogrammetric cameras that record and measure the volume of objects with mathematical precision.

The data and images from the Sphinx Mapping Project became the basis for the computer reconstruction of the Sphinx that I had seen in Santa Monica.

For five full years, Lehner worked full-time studying, tracing, photographing every inch of the Sphinx. "I spent weeks on top of the back of the Sphinx just doing hand mapping of the outlines," he said. "I spent weeks on top of the paws, mapping all the stones in that area. I knew the Sphinx so well at that time I could go home at night and run all of this detail in my head like a video and think about it."

When we met, Lehner was forty-six, a relatively short, slightly built man with round, thin tortoiseshell glasses, and thinning grayish hair that gave him a scholarly air. But he moved around in his blue jeans and boots with the light and agile step of someone who has spent years working outdoors, clambering in and out of excavation ditches, climbing up and down pyramids with surveying equipment, crawling in and out of narrow passageways. He wears a somewhat rakish green felt hat with a leather band that his academic colleagues kid him about, saying he is trying to look like Indiana Jones in *Raiders of the Lost Ark*. Despite twenty-five years in Egypt and in academe, Lehner has retained his flat, plain North Dakota accent and the colloquial informality of someone who grew up in the 1960s.

During his years mapping the Sphinx, Lehner would eat a stale cheese sandwich in the shade of the south side of the monument and watch as large potato chip–sized chunks of limestone flaked off and fell to the ground. The flaking is due to salt crystallization. Dew condenses on the Sphinx in the cool of the night and early morning. Salt within the stone is drawn to the surface by the moisture and dissolves. When the dew burns off during the day the salt crystallizes again, expanding greatly in size and pushing at the surface with explosive force. Sometimes as the morning dew evaporates in the sun, you can actually hear a popping sound as the salt hardens, pushing off layers of stone that then blow off in the wind. The Sphinx as it exists today, Lehner said, is in many ways no longer the same monument as it was when he began working on it: "So many of the details have changed." The surface modeling has suffered not only from erosion but, in large areas, from the cement, mortar, and limestone that have been added to support and protect the statue.

The Sphinx, part lion, part pharaoh, part god, stands guard over the entrance to the pyramid complex in the valley of the Giza plateau. Although gigantic for a work of sculpture—some 66 feet tall and 240 feet long—when seen from a distance it is dwarfed by the three massive pyramids that loom over it in the background, lined up in a row. Throngs of tourists thread their way along the road between the Pyramids down to the Sphinx as Egyptians in long robes follow alongside selling Coca-Cola, postcards, Egyptian papyri, T-shirts, and camel rides. Bobbing above the crowd are the brightly colored umbrellas of the tour guides trying both to ward off the desert heat and to prevent their charges from becoming separated from the group.

As you face the Sphinx, the first and largest pyramid, known as the Great Pyramid, appears over its left shoulder. Standing almost five hundred feet tall, nearly eight times as big as the Sphinx, it was built by the pharaoh Khufu in about 2600 B.C. The other two pyramids, built by his son and grandson, sit on a diagonal line in diminishing size along the ridge, creating an architectural complex that is of unprecedented scale yet surprising harmony. It is thought that these enormous mountains of stone built in the desert were meant to symbolize the ancient Egyptians' creation myth, according to which life came into being as a mound of earth rising out of the waters of chaos, like the land reappearing after the flooding of the Nile. Originally cased in hard granite—almost all of which has been stripped off and reused in recent centuries—the Pyramids were meant to glitter in the sun, evoking perhaps the association in ancient Egypt between the pharaohs and the sun god Ra. In fact, it was during the fourth dynasty, when the Pyramids were built, that the pharaoh assumed the title of Son of Ra, a god on earth.

The Sphinx lines up in the middle of the three pyramids, leading most scholars to believe that the Sphinx was built by Khafre, the pharaoh of the "second pyramid." Khafre's Valley Temple—which served as the gateway to his pyramid—sits right next to the Sphinx's own temple, as if in a pair. At the time of the summer equinox, the setting sun falls between the corner of Khafre's pyramid and the right shoulder of the Sphinx.

This view of the Sphinx has not changed since pharaonic times. When you face the Sphinx and look out beyond the Pyramids, the only thing you can see is the Sahara desert stretching all the way to Libya. But to your back—in an area that used to be wilderness—are the fast-food franchises on the main street of the town of Nazlet-el-Saman. The village sprouted up on the edge of the archeological site in the middle of the nineteenth century as Giza became a major tourist stop. The "village" is now a city of 300,000. Since it was an improvised, illegal community that sat on what was officially archeological land, it had no proper drainage system and its sewage seeped into the ground a few hundred yards from the Sphinx. The Egyptians (with American foreign aid money) have put a sewage system into the area, but in doing so they have tacitly acknowledged that the village is there to stay. With hundreds of thousands of people already living in shantytowns that have mushroomed within the cemeteries of Cairo, the government is unlikely to displace the people here in order to respect the original boundaries of the archeological site.

A few years ago, the Egyptian government was planning to build a ring road about two miles from the Pyramids to relieve traffic congestion in Cairo, but the road would have destroyed what is left of the desert panorama around the Sphinx. "That would have been the end," Lehner said. "It's the last refuge. If they put in the road, then there will be an exit ramp, and a gas station will follow, and stores and a city. Then the Sphinx and the Pyramids will be like the Acropolis in Athens, an island in a city." Since the Sphinx and the Pyramids are one of UNESCO's official World Heritage Sites, there was an international hue and cry about the highway and Egyptian president Hosni Mubarak canceled the project, on which billions of dollars had already been spent.

While the Sphinx seems small when seen at a distance against the background of the Pyramids, it actually stood more than ten times our height. As we entered the site, the Egyptians working on the scaffolding of the Sphinx greeted Lehner like a long-lost friend and began animatedly discussing their work in Arabic. As we stood there talking, another handful of workmen arrived carrying a half-ton limestone block tied up with rope suspended from a long wooden plank that rested on their shoulders. Seeing them skillfully maneuver this massive piece of stone up the levels of the wooden scaffolding with the simplest possible technology, I felt briefly as if we were back in the pyramid age.

The struggle to conserve and control the Sphinx goes back thousands of years. "The Sphinx has been a political football from ancient times to the present," Lehner said. Still propped up in front of the Sphinx is a black stone slab erected in 1401 B.C. by a pharaoh of the New Kingdom, King Thutmosis IV, taking credit for the first major restoration of the Sphinx. Its hieroglyphs tell the story of how, as a young prince, Thutmosis stopped and took a nap near the Sphinx, which then spoke to him in a dream, promising that he would be king of Egypt if he would clear away the sand and restore its damaged body. Some scholars believe Thutmosis may have killed his older brother in order to ascend to the throne since he was not first in line to become king. Whatever the case, one thing is certain: Thutmosis restored the Sphinx and put up his plaque in the first year of his reign to show that the Sphinx, who was considered both a god and a symbol of kingship, had given his blessing to the new pharaoh. Thutmosis clad the Sphinx in large limestone blocks to protect it from wind erosion—a strategy the Egyptian workmen we saw hoisting the huge limestone block were trying to follow thirty-four hundred years later.

The Sphinx is so old that it forces us to reconsider our notions of what is ancient and what modern, what is an original work of art and what a restoration. Even for Thutmosis, living in 1401 B.C., the Sphinx was already an extremely ancient monument: it was for him older than the cathedral at Chartres is for us today.

The Greeks and Romans visited and restored the Sphinx in the same spirit of wonder at the achievements of a vanished ancient civilization as we do now, and left graffiti on the walls of monuments like many modern tourists. The Romans cleared the sand from the Sphinx in preparation for a visit by the emperor Nero—for whom the Sphinx was far more ancient than Nero's Rome is for us. They also dragged numerous obelisks back to Italy as symbols of their imperial power, a feat later imitated by Napoleon. Louis Farrakhan, the leader of the Nation of Islam, announced at the Million Man March that Napoleon had knocked the nose off the Sphinx because he could not stand the idea that a work of such greatness was created by black people. Napoleon, while guilty of much looting and plunder, is innocent of this particular crime: eighteenth-century engravings of the Sphinx show it already missing its nose. Arabic documents from the fifteenth century recount that Egypt's Islamic leaders felt it necessary to deface the great statue because ordinary Egyptians of the period were still paying homage to it a millennium and a half after the collapse of the pharaonic dynasties. (A similar spirit may have motivated the Taliban of Afghanistan who in 2001 systematically destroyed giant stone sculptures that testified to the country's ancient Buddhist past.)

As Farrakhan's remark makes clear, the need to appropriate these iconic monuments and their history continues up to today.

While the monuments are on Egyptian soil, the vast majority of the people visiting them are Western tourists who consider them part of world cultural heritage, and Giza has become a cultural battlefield where East meets West. The modern field of Egyptology was a direct product of Napoleon's invasion of Egypt in 1798 and the Egyptian antiquities service was directed by Frenchmen until 1952. For most of the twentieth century, Egyptians were actively discouraged from working on their own monuments. The fields of archeology and conservation are very young among Egyptians and they are acutely sensitive to anything they perceive as a slight to their national pride. On conservation projects, the Egyptians are eager to have foreign money and expertise but are understandably anxious to maintain control over their own monuments.

They were stung by international criticism and a flurry of newspaper stories when large chunks of the Sphinx fell off both in 1981 and in 1988, and each time the government responded by firing the director of the Egyptian antiquities service—although neither man was directly responsible for the monument's troubles. To allay public fears, the Egyptian government has undertaken major restoration work on the Sphinx, some of it doing more harm than good.

Islamic fundamentalists have also used the monuments in their war on the current government. Several years ago, fundamentalists killed several tourists visiting the Sphinx and the Pyramids, and in 1997 they struck at Hatshepsut's Temple in Luxor, slaughtering sixty-two people. The attacks appeared designed both to send Egypt's economy into a tailspin as well as to damage the prestige of the government by showing it unable to protect the symbols of national pride.

At the same time, the Egyptian government is contending with various New Age movements that believe that the Sphinx and the Pyramids are not Egyptian monuments at all but the legacy of a much older and more sophisticated civilization that left them there 12,500 years ago as a kind of coded message containing the deepest secrets of the universe. They are bombarding the Egyptian government with requests to drill and probe in hopes that the sands of Giza will soon yield the answer to the riddle of the Sphinx.

A sizable segment of modern American culture seems fixated on ancient Egypt. One of Las Vegas's big new hotels is the Luxor, built in the form of a pyramid with a copy of the Sphinx as its entrance. A pyramid is the symbol of the Internet provider America Online, illuminated by a bolt of lightning every time a customer logs on. In any New Age bookstore you can find a shelf full of books on "pyramid power" and the Sphinx. There are hundreds of Web sites on the Internet dedicated to ancient Egypt. Many of the pharaohs whose tombs have long been raided have achieved in digital form a measure of the immortality they sought. While some of these sites contain valuable information, an astonishing number are dedicated to bizarre theories about ancient Egypt, making it difficult for the uninformed browser to untangle fantasy from reality.

One Web site purports to "establish" the connection between the monuments of ancient Egypt and the planet Mars. With the help of "computer-enhanced photographs," its author perceives a lion-shaped figure on the surface of Mars that resembles the Sphinx. Another site, called "The Pyramid's Amazing Chronography," insists that the Giza complex was built by the God of the Old Testament because "the Bible makes it abundantly plain that Noah's son Ham was the father of Egypt." Hollywood takes up the theme in *Stargate*, which portrays the Pyramids and the hieroglyphs as the key to a hidden passageway through space and time created by powerful extraterrestrials. Many identify the true creators of ancient Egypt as the inhabitants of the island of Atlantis mentioned in Greek mythology.

These notions recently received a surprising assist from the world of science. A geologist at Boston University, Robert Schoch, announced that the Sphinx's weathering patterns led him to revise the date of its creation from 2600 to 5000 B.C. or earlier. Schoch, who had no previous experience with the geology of Egypt and who based his conclusions on a three-week visit, had been recruited by John Anthony West, one of the main proponents of the Atlantis theory and a popular mystical author who leads tours of Egypt. West has produced a film promoting this "discovery," narrated by actor Charlton Heston. Best-selling books like *The Message of the Sphinx*, by Graham Hancock and Robert Bauval, have given these ideas a mass audience, finding a ready market among gullible people inclined to believe that a lost civilization buried its secret to life under the sands of Giza.

"Is it possible that men and women of great wisdom and learning cast a 'glamour' over the Giza necropolis at some point in the distant past?" the authors ask rhetorically. "Were they the possessors of as yet unguessed-at secrets that they wished to hide here? And did they succeed in concealing those secrets almost in plain view? For thousands of years, in other words, has the ancient Egyptian cemetery at Giza veiled the presence of something else—something of vastly greater significance for the story of Mankind?" Hancock and Bauval answer with a resounding yes, arguing that the monuments of Giza are a kind of astronomical code containing the secret to "the science of immortality . . . the quest for eternal life."

As the foremost American expert on the Sphinx, Lehner has found himself in the middle of this latest controversy. *The Message of the Sphinx* dedicates an entire chapter to attacking him. What makes Lehner a particularly able critic and a bête noire of New Agers is that he himself is a former believer: the son of a preacher from Minot, North Dakota, Lehner came of age in the late 1960s when he fell under the sway of the writings of a Christian visionary named Edgar Cayce, known to his followers as "the sleeping prophet." Cayce, who died in 1945, was considered a great healer and went into trances during which he had visions of past lives and historical eras. Although a Christian, he believed in reincarnation, and Atlantis and ancient Egypt figured heavily in his rereading of history and his prophecies. The Atlantis myth has its origins in one of Plato's dialogues that tells the story of an island that had existed beyond the Straits of Gibraltar nine thousand years earlier, inhabited by the children of the sea god Poseidon, who excelled all others in beauty, wisdom, and virtue. Atlantis was sunk beneath the ocean by Zeus when its people were gradually corrupted by repeated intermarriage with mere mortals and made the mistake of waging war on the Athenians. Cayce believed that the people of Atlantis took refuge in ancient Egypt and buried their most precious documents in a secret chamber underneath the paws of the Sphinx. Cayce claimed to have witnessed all this in his previous incarnation as the high priest Rata. The sleeping prophet predicted that the rediscovery of the Great Hall of Records would bring about the Second Coming of Christ in the year 1998.

In 1971, Lehner, a seeker of twenty-one, hitchhiked from North Dakota to Virginia Beach to reach the headquarters of the Edgar Cayce Foundation and traveled to Egypt with a group of Cayce followers several months later. He vowed on that first trip to return within a year to find the Great Hall of Records that lay buried on the Giza plateau. To aid him in his search, Lehner decided to study archeology and ancient Egyptian at the American University in Cairo. "I spent every free moment I had out at the Sphinx," he said. But Lehner could find no trace of the people of Atlantis and everywhere he looked he found the Cayce theory contradicted in the hard data written in the stones of Giza. "The evidence of the presence of the ancient Egyptians in the construction of these monuments is so overwhelming," he explained.

The final turning point for Lehner was a project carried out in 1977 and 1978 by the Stanford Research Institute (now called SRI) to probe the ground underneath the Sphinx through a technology called electromagnetic resistivity. During the project, which was independent but partially funded by the Edgar Cayce Foundation, researchers placed electrodes in the ground that carried electric current meant to register empty spaces in the rock. They also drilled in several places where they picked up signs of cavities in the rock. "When we did the drilling, we saw nothing but anomalies in the rock—channels of groundwater and eroded rock formation that looked like Swiss cheese," Lehner said. "I started having major doubts about the idea of there being major architectural structures there."

In order to prepare the ground for the resistivity study, Lehner was in charge of some seventy men who did a thorough cleaning of the Sphinx ditch and floor as well as in the nearby temples. Lehner and his Egyptian colleague Zahi Hawass carefully examined all the debris they found. Lying flat and sticking their arms into the ground, they even picked out the debris in a fissure that runs along the floor behind the Sphinx's rump. "Zahi and I found fragments of tools, Old Kingdom pottery, hammer stones made of diorite which were used during the Old Kingdom to smooth away limestone—stuff that was obviously left by the people who had built the Sphinx," Lehner said.

Lehner got over his disappointment at not finding the Great Hall of Records and gradually forged a career as an archeologist. "The ideas I came with from Cayce didn't really stack up with bedrock reality, but bedrock reality became very exciting," he said. "It was the excitement you get from the direct rapport with the data, with the thing itself." He married an Egyptian woman and became fluent in Arabic. At the same time, he continued with ancient Egyptian and set about learning German and French in order to master the vast scholarly literature on ancient Egypt.

In 1979 he became field director of the Sphinx Mapping Project, and in 1984 he began surveying and mapping the entire Giza plateau.

"So much of Egyptology had grown up out of philology and art history, the study of texts and objects, which meant that a site like Giza still yielded an enormous amount of information by one's just looking at what was there without digging at all—the geology, the stratigraphy, tool marks in stone," he said. "It was very exciting for me to read the stories that the stones were telling and I found out that there were a lot of stories that hadn't been told."

The Pyramids were such a big job that people actually lived on them as they were working. They ate and drank, cooked meals, and even defecated on them. Lehner lived in similar intimacy with the monuments for several years. He has slept inside the Great Pyramid, explored its remotest air shafts. He has copied down the graffiti of its builders and studied their careful chisel marks. He has scooped out the refuse, extracting carbonized traces of food, pottery shards, and even feces lodged in the mortar between the stones. Because we are used to seeing these cultural icons in photographs, we tend to think of them as unchanging monolithic objects. There are cracks inside the Sphinx that are large enough for a man to enter and, in fact, Lehner had himself lowered down face first on a rope to explore one of these fissures, in which he found valuable archeological material. He even discovered a passageway inside the Sphinx that had been known to previous excavators but had been lost for several decades. There, he came upon a shoe belonging to a French digger who had worked at the site in 1927. This kind of intimate knowledge of monuments has given Lehner a very particular perspective. "The Sphinx is not a thing; it is a monument undergoing constant change," Lehner said. "Water moves through it, all kinds of organisms and animals live inside it. There are coyotes living on top of the Pyramids." Understanding the Egyptian monuments as "living" things may help us understand and accept that they are, in fact, dying.

Lehner's first marriage eventually broke up, and after fourteen years in Egypt he returned to the United States in 1986 to pursue a Ph.D. in Egyptology at Yale. Not surprisingly, he did his dissertation on the Sphinx. Although the focus of enormous popular interest, the monument had received relatively little scholarly and scientific attention.

In his years as a permanent fixture on the Giza plateau, Lehner watched the New Age fascination with the Sphinx and the Pyramids grow even as his own interests changed. Lehner met the actress and mystic Shirley MacLaine, who spent the night meditating inside the Great Pyramid. She said she believed that the Giza complex was built in 70,000 B.C.—never mind that Neanderthal man was just then coming into his prime—and that there was a giant crystal pyramid buried underneath the Great Pyramid. As MacLaine and Lehner stood at the base of the Pyramid, he pointed out that the ground beneath them was solid bedrock and that it was therefore impossible for there to be another pyramid underneath it. "Mark, it's all a matter of perspective," she replied. "I've been in the acting business a long time and if there's one thing I've learned it's that it's all a matter of perspective."

While the New Age controversies around the Sphinx have their comic side, they also have their disturbing elements. Making aggressive use of pseudoscience and the Internet, the New Agers are changing the way Egyptian monuments are seen by hundreds of thousands of visiting tourists. As the rich historical context and the subtle details of the archeological record fade and crumble, leaving the bare outlines of great monuments, it becomes easier to rewrite history and impose our own fantasies on them.

One source of consolation may be that many of the absurd ideas about ancient Egypt are not entirely the invention of our own silly and fatuous contemporary culture. Every U.S. dollar bill carries, along with a portrait of George Washington, the image of a pyramid with an eye at the top, symbol of the Freemasons. For some two hundred years, scores of authors (known within Egyptology as "pyramidiots") have devised fanciful numerological interpretations of the Pyramids, based on inaccurate measurements of monuments whose dimensions have been significantly reduced by looting and quarrying of stone. In the nineteenth century, these interpretations generally had a Christian twist, arguing that the Jews of the Old Testament built the Great Pyramid in anticipation of the ultimate truth of the gospel of Christ.

In the early nineteenth century, Joseph Smith, founder of the Mormon religion, claimed that his Book of Abraham was a translation of an ancient papyrus he found stashed inside a pair of Egyptian mummies he purchased. When scholars figured out how to decipher hieroglyphs, it turned out that Smith's "translation" bore no relation to the actual text but was purely the product of his inspired imagination.

One problem, which invites wild speculation, is that the Sphinx cannot be dated with mathematical accuracy. Only organic material—such as bones or wooden implements—can be carbon-dated, and the Sphinx is made of solid stone. When geologist Robert Schoch hypothesized a much earlier date for the Sphinx, it was based on the rounded, highly eroded weathering patterns primarily found on the right flank of the Sphinx and on the wall next to it. This, Schoch says, has the look of stone that has been eroded by water rather than by wind. And since the Sahara desert area dried up sometime between 6000 and 5000 B.C., the Sphinx, he concludes, must have been carved before that.

As Schoch himself acknowledges, dating rocks simply on the basis of weathering patterns is an extremely problematic and imperfect science. The geological literature on the dating of rock by weathering patterns is full of caveats that Schoch appears to have ignored, and dozens of other geologists who have spent much more time studying the Giza plateau disagree with Schoch, insisting that there are many processes of erosion that can account for the weathering patterns that Schoch is focusing on. But perhaps the most troubling part of Schoch's work is his inability to provide historical data to back up his hypothesis. Unlike the New Age mystics who believe in the Atlantis theory, Schoch realizes that in order to be taken seriously in the scientific community, the dating of a statue cannot be based on the "look" of its surface. There had to have been real human beings and an organized civilization in the vicinity in order to carve a 240-foot-long, 66-foot-high sculpture out of limestone. Schoch acknowledges that no evidence of any such people or civilization exists in Egypt in the period when he dates the Sphinx (the sixth to eighth millennium B.C.). In fact, there is no evidence of massive stone-carved temples or colossal statuary anywhere in the world before Egypt in the third millennium B.C.

That the total lack of historical evidence invalidates Schoch's date was obvious even to John Anthony West. But, ironically, West has used the lack of evidence to push his own, even more improbable Atlantis theory. "If the Sphinx was as recent as 7000 to 5000 B.C.," he writes, "I think that we probably would have other Egyptian evidence of the civilization that carved it." Since there is no such evidence for Schoch's date, West reasons that the Sphinx must be several thousand years older still. "The missing other evidence is, perhaps, buried deeper than anyone has looked and/or in places no one has yet explored," he writes. The logic of this is truly breathtaking: the date of 7000–5000 B.C. cannot be accepted, because there is no evidence of high culture in Egypt, so West proposes a date for which there is even less evidence, at least 10,500 B.C. or earlier—an era in which there is no sign of large-scale organized societies anywhere on the planet. Yet West was able to produce his film, which NBC aired without providing a forum for rebuttal. Welcome to the Alice in Wonderland world of Atlantis.

When I phoned Schoch in his office in Boston, he tried to disassociate himself as much as possible from West and the Atlanteans. He admitted that his dating had been "hijacked" by West and the writers Hancock and Bauval, who arbitrarily pushed it back by several thousand years. "I don't see any geological basis for their claims. The interpretations that have been made have not been to my taste." If the Sphinx had been carved several thousand years earlier and exposed to torrential rains, he said, "there would be virtually nothing left of it." Despite these feelings, Schoch has traveled to Egypt with West, appeared in his film, and coauthored an article with him, eroding his own credibility more severely than time has eroded the surface of the Sphinx. While privately disowning the Atlantis theory, he has sat back and allowed his work to provide a thin veneer of scientific plausibility to crackpot ideas that totally distort history.

By portraying Egyptian civilization as a "legacy" from a previous, superior culture transmitting a secret code, the New Agers have reduced the ancient Egyptians to the role of caretakers and dupes, blindly copying the symbols of these great monuments generation after generation without understanding their true significance. "We would be surprised if the owners of many of the coffins and tomb walls onto which they were copied had even the faintest inkling that specific astronomical observations and directions were being duplicated at their expense," Hancock and Bauval write. Thus most of Egyptian civilization as the Egyptians themselves understood it is reduced to meaningless mumbo-jumbo filler in which to hide the secret message.

As Lehner and I looked closely at the surface of the Sphinx, it suddenly became obvious what it originally was: a massive wall of limestone rock. Its enormous bulk was carved directly out of the side of the vast limestone quarry that served to build the Pyramids. Because the Sphinx is so large, you can see clearly that it is composed of three highly distinct geological layers. Its head, carved into the likeness of a pharaoh, is made of the highest-quality and hardest stone, which is why it is the best-preserved part of the statue. The lower portions of the Sphinx's lion body are made of much softer stone, some of which is so fragile you can scrape it right off, which Lehner pointed out by taking his fingernails to the enclosure wall just opposite the Sphinx. Embedded in the Sphinx and the quarry wall you can still see fossils of spiral-shaped shellfish and oysters, as well as patches of pocked and spongy-looking rock that are impressions left by sea coral, memories in stone from the time the entire area was underwater. "All this was a coral reef at the bottom of the sea," Lehner said, plucking fossils out of the soft yellow limestone. During the Eocene age, the waters receded, revealing the Giza plateau as we see it now. The stone of the Sphinx is about fifty million years old—a date that makes ancient Egypt seem like an extremely recent event and the fierce debates over the Sphinx's age a matter of only relative importance.

The fossils embedded in the rock provide, however, important evidence placing the Sphinx in the time of the pharaoh Khafre, builder of the second pyramid. The Sphinx is located next to two temples, the Sphinx's Temple and Khafre's Valley Temple. By matching the fossils embedded in the stones, which act almost like fingerprints, Lehner and the German geologist Thomas Aigner were able to determine that the people who carved the Sphinx out of its shelf of limestone ingeniously used the surrounding stone to build the temples. In fact, the stones taken from the top of the quarry, around the Sphinx's head and chest, were used to build Khafre's Valley Temple—suggesting it was probably built first—while the stones taken from lower down in the ditch were used for the Sphinx's Temple. This would indicate strongly that Khafre's Valley Temple was built before the Sphinx was completed and that the two temples and the colossus were part of the same architectural program at Giza during Khafte's reign.

Lehner's partner in much of his work at Giza has been the Egyptian archeologist Zahi Hawass, who is in charge of the site at Giza as well as of the nearby sites of Saqqara and Dashour, which contain many pyramids and tombs immediately preceding and succeeding the Giza complex. In the cautious world of the antiquities bureaucracy, Hawass stands out as an outspoken, charismatic, and highly energetic figure.

When Lehner mentioned Hawass's name to the guards at the gates of Giza, they seemed to snap to attention and there was a flurry of activity, with several repeating the words "Dr. Zahi, Dr. Zahi" in tones of great respect. They greeted Lehner enthusiastically as "Mr. Mark," but Hawass was always referred to as "Dr. Zahi." They directed us to his office in a low-lying sand-colored bunker tucked behind a sand dune near the Great Pyramid.

A burly, powerfully built man of forty-nine with close-cropped hair and a supremely confident, commanding manner, Hawass looked more like an army general than an academic. With a handsome, broad, copper-colored face, severe black eyebrows, dark eyes, and a strong, hawklike nose, he bore a strong resemblance to Egyptian president Mubarak (himself a former air force general), whose photograph hung on the wall directly behind him. On the side walls, there were photographs of Hawass with Hillary and Chelsea Clinton on a visit to the Pyramids. A graduate of Cairo University, with a Ph.D. from the University of Pennsylvania, Hawass has navigated successfully both in the turbid waters of Egyptian cultural politics and in American academic circles. He has friends in high places and coauthored a book on ancient Egyptian women with President Mubarak's wife. At times when Egypt has needed to promote its tourist trade, it has sent Hawass to head a delegation that barnstormed the United States speaking to audiences about ancient Egypt. One lecture I heard him give in New York alternated information about important new discoveries with crowd-pleasing humorous asides. At one point, he showed a slide of himself and Princess Diana and suggested wryly that the photograph might explain the failure of Britain's royal marriage. In recent years, Hawass has been invited to lecture each summer for a month at UCLA, and he enjoys hobnobbing with Hollywood celebrities.

But his jet-setting has not prevented him from conducting serious archeological work. When I first met Hawass in 1996, his assistants recently had found a small pyramid near the Great Pyramid that had been buried under rubble, and their discovery of a major workmen's settlement and cemetery at Giza has contributed enormously to our understanding of the lives of the men who built the Pyramids. Hawass insisted that he is the first in Egypt to adopt the principle of "site management" at Giza, restoring a measure of control at a site that had been overrun by tourists. A few years ago, he removed a road that threaded between the two biggest pyramids and past the Sphinx and that was heavily traveled by huge tourist buses belching exhaust and shaking the ground underneath the Sphinx. In doing so, he uncovered the mortuary temple next to Khufu's pyramid. He demolished a stage erected fifty yards in front of the Sphinx that had served for performances of *Swan Lake* and concerts by everyone from Frank Sinatra to the Grateful Dead. He erected a gate and began charging tickets for admission to the Giza site not only to raise revenue but to keep numbers manageable.

Despite its providing him the opportunity for high-profile friendships, Hawass has an extremely difficult job. He oversees monuments that receive too much attention from tourists and treasure seekers and many that are severely neglected. He is in charge of the controversial restoration of the Sphinx—which has already cost the job of two directors of antiquities—and must try to protect hundreds of other, less famous and equally vulnerable monuments. He must reconcile the often conflicting interests of tourists, local residents, foreign archeologists, and conservators while maintaining support from the government and the antiquities organization. He must oversee and approve the work of numerous foreign excavations, conduct his own archeological digs, try to make money for his monuments from tourism and protect them at the same time. He has a regular pitched battle with the camel drivers at Giza. They want to have free run of the site to be able to offer rides to tourists visiting the Pyramids; Hawass wants them to operate out of a nearby stable so that the animals do not leave their dung all over the site and add to the general wear and tear on the monuments. So far the camel drivers seem to have prevailed since they and their animals were everywhere when I visited Giza. "They are always writing against me to the government," Hawass said of the camel drivers.

The forces that Hawass is fighting against are considerable. "People think that the Pyramids and the Giza plateau are in the desert, but they are not anymore. They are practically in downtown Cairo," he said. Not only does he have to worry about the continued encroachment of the nearby "villages," but there are also rock quarries operating near Giza whose dynamite blasts can be felt at the Sphinx. During the Nasser regime, the government concentrated most of Egyptian heavy industry around Cairo as a showcase of modernization. Many factories were placed to the north of Cairo, perfectly positioned to catch the strong breezes coming down from the Mediterranean, carrying industrial pollution to the city and on to the Pyramid area. This shortsighted policy also drew people from the countryside to the capital, leading to massive overcrowding and traffic and more pollution. Limestone is particularly vulnerable to corrosive gases such as carbon monoxide and carbon dioxide.

At Saqqara, the Step Pyramid of King Dzoser, the grandfather of the Great Pyramid, is developing cracks that neither Hawass nor anyone he has consulted can explain. There are still no Plexiglas barriers keeping the public away from the tombs and you can see in many of them that the inscriptions and wall paintings that are within human touch are infinitely more faded than the areas that are beyond reach.

Although Hawass oversees what may be the world's most durable monuments, even they present serious conservation problems. "We have

an Arab expression that says, 'Man fears time, but time fears pyramids,'"
Hawass explained. "We found out that wasn't true. Even the Pyramids
need to be protected."

He shut the Great Pyramid for a year because of the deteriorating
condition of the inner chambers, where the breath and sweat of tourists
were aggravating the problem of salt crystallization. "The Pyramids
began to be killed. I use the word *killed* because this is really true," he
said. "Anyone who enters gives about twenty grams of water to the monument and that water becomes salt on the interior of the tomb or
pyramid. The thickness of salt [in the Great Pyramid] became five
centimeters and the humidity became 95 percent. I had to make a decision, with the permission of the antiquities service, to close down the
Pyramid for one year."

Hawass enlisted the German Archeological Institute in Cairo to
help with the conservation work, making use of highly innovative new
technology. The Germans hired an engineer to build a robot that could
move up the narrow corridors, some of which are only about ten inches
wide. On the one hand, the technology was a success: it has allowed
Hawass to install a ventilation system in the pyramid and reopen it to
visitors. But the German technician with the robot, Rudolph Gantenbrink, got it into his head to play amateur archeologist and joined forces
with the New Agers. At the end of a long stone shaft, he discovered a
copper handle. Because it was impossible to see down the shaft, his
robot had been working with a video camera that allowed Gantenbrink
to see what he was doing during the cleaning and ventilation work.
But unbeknownst to the German Archeological Institute, Gantenbrink
released his video to the press and announced the discovery of a secret
door that might hold the answer to the mysteries of ancient Egypt or,
perhaps, Atlantean civilization. The institute and the Egyptians were
irritated by Gantenbrink's publicity seeking as well as by his speculation
about a discovery that had not been adequately studied. His requests to
conduct further explorations of the Pyramids have been rejected.

"We cannot permit expeditions by private individuals or amateurs,"
Hawass said. "Our law permits only scholars and institutions. When

Gantenbrink came here he was a member of an expedition. Then he went everywhere in the world, announcing this discovery without telling anyone in the German Institute. And he sold a film he made of his work, all over the world, without taking our permission. We are supporting science that is useful to archeology. These people use science for their own benefit, to make publicity and make money. People come to the Pyramids and they get crazy."

Egyptian pyramids and tombs are full of false doors and hidden chambers since they were designed to confuse intruders, so there is no reason to expect that this copper handle—whether or not it opens a door—will lead us to anything otherworldly. But the fact that the Egyptians would not let Gantenbrink continue with his work has led New Agers to suspect that there is a cover-up and that the copper handle may be the Stargate they have been looking for.

When I visited in 1996, the New Agers were in a state of fibrillation, bombarding Hawass with requests to drill and probe underneath and around the Sphinx, believing that the final revelation, predicted by Edgar Cayce for 1998, was close at hand. And the authors of *The Message of the Sphinx* have excited these messianic hopes. "If we read the message . . . right," they conclude, "then there is something of momentous importance there, waiting to be found—by seismic surveys, by drilling and excavation. . . . [I]t could be the ultimate prize." The year 1998 came and went, without the recovery of Atlantis's Great Hall of Records or the Second Coming.

"What do you think the reaction of the American government would be if we put in a request to excavate underneath the Statue of Liberty on the theory that the ancient Egyptians discovered America?" Hawass said with exasperation. "I have wasted an enormous amount of time in the last six months listening to these people's hallucinations. We are here to protect the Sphinx from hallucinations. The world will judge me if I let those hallucinators do that."

On his desk, Hawass had a thick stack of printouts from the Internet attacking him. John Anthony West, in his latest book, compared Hawass and the traditional Egyptologists to the makers of Agent Orange, who have denied that the poison gas they produced may have affected the health of soldiers fighting in Vietnam. The New Agers even started a letter-writing campaign to get him fired. How any of this will intersect with the power politics in Cairo is anyone's guess. He showed me a fax of a letter that West evidently sent out to his supporters addressed "Dear Investors." "These people are trying to make money from the Sphinx," Hawass said heatedly. "The Sphinx is not for sale!"

Hawass was already removed from his job for a year when he opposed work by a Japanese expedition that he considered unnecessary and potentially damaging to the site. "I don't care if I lose my job, I have to speak the truth," he said. "My job is to protect the monuments." Hawass said he suffered a heart attack four years earlier because of the stress of the endless wrangling.

The mischief created by all this became evident in the days I spent out at Giza with Lehner. "They've found a piece of metal that is unlike any metal known on earth," I overheard a British tourist explaining to her companion as we were all standing in front of the Sphinx. "And there are secret chambers buried underneath, but they are keeping them hidden."

As we walked around the site, Lehner's New Age past kept sticking to him like a piece of stale gum to the bottom of his shoe. As we walked down the causeway of Khafre's pyramid toward the Sphinx, we were stopped by two Italian tourists, father and son, who were under the sway of *The Message of the Sphinx*. "You are Graham Hancock," the father said. "We saw the video." Evidently, the man had seen Lehner rebutting Hancock's theory and confused the two.

"One of his critics," Lehner replied.

A long debate ensued, in which Lehner patiently refuted Hancock and Bauval point by point. Eventually, the father gave up trying to argue, and simply said, "But you know, there is something mysterious. When I first came here two years ago, I didn't know anything. I am a salesman, but I said, 'There is something mysterious here when you go in the gallery of the Grand Pyramid.'"

"That's exactly what the pharaoh wanted people to think," Lehner responded. "They didn't want people to think it was a human monument. But if you look at anything closely you see there is a human hand behind it. Let me ask you: Why is it so important for people like you to believe that it was not these human beings here in Egypt who made them but people who were lost? Why is that idea so attractive? Do you know the movie *The Wizard of Oz*? Do you remember the end, when they want the answers from the big and powerful wizard, but then the dog takes the curtain and it's just a little man? People want mystery."

We had a similar experience when we went into the Tree of Life Bazaar in the village square just opposite the Sphinx. The shop, which sells exotic Egyptian perfumes, is filled with photographs and cards from American New Agers, including Shirley MacLaine herself. Lehner is an old friend of the family that runs the shop. The father, Mohammed Fayed, an old man with a flowing white beard and an Egyptian galabiya, worked at the Sphinx as a teenager during the 1920s when the French were excavating. It was he who had told Lehner which stone to move in order to find the secret passage in the rump of the Sphinx. As we were talking, Mohammed's son, Ahmed, walked in. Ahmed has found a second career leading "metaphysical tours" of Egypt. Indeed, he was working as the Egyptian representative of the Edgar Cayce Foundation, the group that first brought Lehner to Egypt—so that now, ironically, the Egyptian and the American stand on opposite sides of the great Sphinx debate.

Ahmed seemed eager to make peace between Lehner and the Atlanteans. "People ask me, 'Why is Mark Lehner against us?' I say, 'Because he has to be.'"

"Why?" Lehner asked.

"Because he can't be part of the scientific community and support the Atlantis theory," Ahmed replied.

"That's the wrong answer," said Lehner, getting a little heated up. "If the evidence indicated that there was a Hall of Records underneath the Sphinx I would still be looking for it. Let me ask you a question. If there was Atlantis and all these people in 10,000 B.C., where are their books? Where is their pottery? Where are their bodies? Where are their tombs? Where are their boats? Where are their hieroglyphs? Show me just one thing. One thing. Why is that not a big problem for people who believe in Atlantis? Why does this not bother them?"

"I know, it's good to argue, to have a scientific argument," Ahmed said, trying to smooth Lehner's ruffled feathers.

"No, but Ahmed, we can't move away from it," Lehner said. "We have thousands of tombs, thousands of hieroglyphs. If I climb the Pyramid with you, I can show you pottery in the mortar between the stones. We have carbon-dated it. What more do we need? You work with these people. You lecture to them. Why do people need to believe in myths? Why can't they believe in Khufu and Khafre? It's a great civilization. The boat of Khufu is as beautiful and sophisticated as anything produced by ancient civilizations. The statues of Menkaure [builder of the Third Pyramid] and Khafre are as beautiful as anything produced by any civilization of any age. Why are they not good enough? Why do people need them to be by somebody else?"

"People like change, they like to believe in fantasy," Ahmed, the metaphysical guide, said.

"So you don't believe in the Atlantis myth?" Lehner asked.

"I need evidence and there is no evidence," he replied. "So what can I say? But these people, that's what they want to hear. I really do not believe in Atlantis, I just want you to know that. To be honest with you, this is part of my job. If I don't say these things, they will go away. They say the city of Enoch is underneath the Sphinx. It's dangerous, because it's not based on any facts. Their object is to get Zahi fired. With all this trashy stuff on the market—*The Message of the Sphinx*—it is your duty to defend something you love. It makes a lot of people who are naïve turn against you."

"So?" Lehner said. "I bet the people who read Hancock and Bauval won't read an opposing point of view. The thing that worries me about them is that with the Internet and all the cable channels there's now a chance of this point of view reproducing itself more rapidly than the truth and critical thinking. If we don't have a proper understanding of our past and we go careening into the future, I think it's important to understand what contribution the people of Khufu and Khafre made to the history of the world."

We ran into Ahmed the next day over in the parking lot of a nearby hotel, standing next to the enormous air-conditioned red bus he uses for his metaphysical tours. He was wearing a beaded necklace with a round, pitted silver object at the end of it that looked like something you would use to steep tea leaves in. "It's an amulet this group I am taking around wears," Ahmed explained. "Everyone in the group has to wear it for protection before they can enter the Great Pyramid. We are about to go in and do three hours meditating and chanting in the King's Chamber." New Age groups pay extra money to be alone in the Pyramids off-hours when they are normally closed.

As we stood there talking, one of Ahmed's group came up to the entrance of the bus. She was a heavyset young woman from North Carolina wearing slacks, jogging shoes, and teased hair. Except for the amulet, she would have blended into the crowd at any American shopping mall. She appeared to be in her midtwenties and had a round, pleasant, doughy face that seemed unformed by either age or experience.

"Where did you get your amulet?" Lehner asked.

"Judy made them herself and consecrated them in temple," she said, as if everyone on every continent knew Judy.

"What does your tour of Egypt consist of?" I asked.

"Well, our group, we're working on the body," she said. "So it starts with the feet in Abu Simbel [one of the southernmost points in Egypt] and then we go up the body in Luxor—you know, all the shockers."

"What are shockers?" I asked.

"It's *chakras*, a Hindu word," Lehner, the veteran New Ager explained. "They are the vital organs of the body. The feet, the groin, the heart . . ."

"Now we're at the top of Egypt, the Great Pyramid, working on the head," the woman from North Carolina explained. "It's all about awakening cellular memory in the different parts of your body. Like there's this other group that takes people into the King's Chamber of the Pyramid and they lay each person in the sarcophagus and tell them their 'real name,' and it awakens their cellular memory."

"What is cellular memory?" I asked.

"Well, I'm not too good on all that scientific stuff," she said. "You should talk to Pamela, she's the one who can explain all of that in real scientific terms, what it triggers scientifically as far as chemically affecting the body."

After the woman got on the bus, Lehner asked Ahmed how much the group was paying to use the Pyramid after hours. "Two thousand Egyptian pounds [about seven hundred dollars] for the first twenty people," Ahmed said. Although Zahi Hawass does not agree in principle with people visiting tombs, it is impossible to pass up that kind of money. Every person entering the Pyramid that evening will be paying one hundred Egyptian pounds, thirty-three dollars—the same as the monthly salary of a young archeologist working for the Supreme Council of Antiquities. Hawass uses the extra money to increase the salaries of his employees, tripling and quadrupling the pay of his senior aides.

As we left, Ahmed told us about a member of one of his latest tours who wanted to contribute $100,000 to excavations toward the search for Atlantis. "This man has $50 million," Ahmed said. "He paid the way for eighteen people."

After years of battling with the New Agers, Hawass appears to have decided that if you can't beat them, you might as well join them. Although he has not abandoned his earlier views, Hawass and the proponents of Atlantis appear together at public debates. For better or worse, the mystical theories about ancient Egypt draw crowds and prosperous foreign tourists.

In fact, most of the advanced technology brought to Giza during the last thirty years has been used either for high-profile treasure hunting or the New Age search for lost civilizations. In the 1960s, the Nobel Prize winner Louis Alvarez from the University of California at Berkeley measured cosmic rays to look for hidden chambers in the Great Pyramid—and found nothing. The French conducted a similar search with radar with the same result. In 1987, *National Geographic* financed a project to poke a camera into an ancient boat pit next to the Great Pyramid, producing a splashy TV video but little of real scientific value. Last year, a Frenchman was allowed to work inside the Great Pyramid to do a pollution study, but Hawass found out he was drilling into the pyramid walls looking for the mummy of Khufu.

"All these people, they are working for their glory only, glory by advertising their discoveries, and they are not involved in the conservation," Hawass said. "Tell me one individual foreigner or an individual Egyptian with a proposal [to conserve] a whole site. We do not even have an archeological map of Egypt. We do not need more excavations; we need to preserve what we have. I took a photograph of the scene in the Temple of Edfu five years ago, and I took the same scene a year ago. This scene has lost 30 percent in four years. Every day and every week we are losing information. We have only one hundred years and these monuments will be gone if nothing is done. We should cover all the monuments of Egypt again with sand and leave it to another generation that is smarter and sincere and not hungry for fame."

Many of the Sphinx's problems, like those of most other ancient Egyptian monuments, stem from the renewed attention it has received in the past two hundred years. The Sphinx was buried up to its neck in sand when Napoleon invaded Egypt in 1798 and Europe "rediscovered" ancient Egypt. Although the Sphinx and the Pyramids were already well known at the time, virtually all other major Egyptian monuments had been lost for about two thousand years. European knowledge of ancient Egypt had remained frozen at the time of the Greek historian Herodotus, who visited Egypt in the fifth century B.C. and whose book was still the standard travel guide into the nineteenth century, when a new wave of visitors began producing a series of their own books.

Foreign explorers and adventurers competed in a mad scramble to dig up ancient treasures and drag them home, filling the museums and collections of England, France, Italy, Germany, and the United States. But the rape of the Nile, as it has been called, also revolutionized our understanding of ancient Egypt. Knowledge of the ancient Egyptian language had been lost for at least fifteen hundred years. Along with hauling away obelisks, Napoleon's troops dug up the Rosetta Stone, which allowed Jean-François Champollion eventually to decipher the structure of the hieroglyphs, unlocking three thousand years of Egyptian texts and inscriptions.

In the 1840s, French explorers finally freed the Sphinx from the sand. For two thousand years, its condition had been effectively frozen in the desert and with its uncovering, it was as if time began to tick again. The process of deterioration that had evidently plagued the monument in ancient times resumed.

"In Physics, we have the Heisenberg uncertainty principle, which says that we change what we observe," Lehner said. "Something similar happens in archeology: 'You study it, you kill it.'" There is a poignant moment in Federico Fellini's film *Roma* in which workmen uncover brilliantly colored ancient Roman wall paintings while building the city subway, but as they stand there admiring them, the paintings fade and vanish before their eyes from the sudden exposure to the air and light. Something similar, albeit at a much slower rate, is happening to the monuments of Egypt, especially in the delicate painted tombs of the Valleys of the Kings and Queens in Luxor.

Although the Egyptian pharaohs built their pyramids and tombs with the idea that no one should penetrate them, the focus of both modern Western scholarship and mass tourism is on precisely these closed, private spaces. "The absurdity of this struck me one day here at Giza when it was particularly crowded," Lehner said. "It seemed so strange that all of these hot and sweaty people were forcing themselves to crawl up the steep and narrow three-foot-high corridor leading up to the King's Chamber in the Great Pyramid—a place that was built never to be entered again."

The Egyptians constructed the Pyramids to last forever, relying on hard stone, a simple, rugged design, and incredibly massive size. "A geologist in the 1950s did a study that indicated that, at its current rate of deterioration, the Great Pyramid would last another hundred thousand years, by which time it would have crumbled into sand," said Lehner. "I was once flying over Manhattan with my architect friend John Jerde and I asked him how long the skyscrapers would last and he said he had no idea. The pharaohs came about as close to achieving immortality in stone as anyone is likely to."

The Sphinx's life expectancy is much less than that of the Pyramids, mainly because of its smaller size and the nature of its stone. According to Frank Preusser, a conservator who studied the Sphinx for the Getty, the soft middle portion of the Sphinx's body is losing about ten to fifteen inches per century. Eventually, the deterioration will begin to undermine the stability of the Sphinx's head. Although the process may be accelerated by modern developments such as smog and water spillage from the nearby village, the Getty's research concluded that the Sphinx's main enemy is simple dew condensation: each morning, dew collects on the surface and brings out the salt left in the limestone from its millions of years at the bottom of the sea.

As Thutmosis's restoration of the Sphinx in 1401 B.C. makes clear, this problem goes back to antiquity. To protect the Sphinx from the wind, Thutmosis built an enclosure wall around the Sphinx quarry and encased the paws and the bottom third of the monument in blocks of hard, high-quality limestone. These large, elegantly cut blocks are still visible in many places along much of the lower portion of the statue, although they have been supplemented by repairs from the Greco-Roman period, a major French restoration of 1926, and more work done during the 1980s. A large portion of what we have known as the Sphinx is actually a patchwork of restorations at different points in history. The various phases of reconstruction pose an interesting question: What is the Sphinx? Is it only the original statue carved out of its mother rock in the Old Kingdom? Which of the additions made between 1401 B.C. and the twentieth century should be considered part of the original monument? Contrary to our sense of technological progress, the better restorations are the older ones. The stones from thirty-four hundred years ago are still in excellent shape, so well cut that they lie atop one another without needing any mortar between them. The Greco-Roman stones are smaller and a little darker but generally in good condition. The French engineers who worked on the Sphinx in the 1920s filled cracks and holes with liberal amounts of cement, the salt from which has begun to corrode the monument. But the absolute worst work is the restoration work done between 1981 and 1987. Eager to show that they were addressing the problems of the Sphinx, the Egyptians rapidly began building a coat of stone armor around its body without having tested the effect of what they were doing. This restoration made the back left flank and back paws of the Sphinx look like the cinder block façade of a Cairo apartment building. Since cement has a high salt content, the restoration accelerated the process of crystallization. The Sphinx body continued flaking and the new stone armor began to crack, crumble, and fall off. "It's as if the Sphinx were shedding a layer of unwanted skin," Lehner said as we walked around the left flank of the Sphinx, where the clunky wall of 1980s restoration work was collapsing in on itself.

When a huge chunk of the Sphinx's left shoulder fell off in 1988, the Egyptians definitively abandoned the old restoration work and began a new campaign, directed largely by Zahi Hawass. In 1996, Hawass's workmen were busy removing the last parts of the disastrous modern restoration and embarking on a new one. The Egyptians have elected to pursue a conservation strategy that is very much like that of King Thutmosis IV—"but with science!" Hawass hastens to add. Like the New Kingdom pharaoh, Hawass has constructed a sheath of limestone casing around the front and back paws and the soft lower portions of the lion body. The strategy is not unlike the reconstruction that took place between 1979 and 1987, but done with much greater care. Limestone has been chosen to match that of the ancient stones on the Sphinx. Hawass has scrupulously avoided the use of cement. The stones are cut so that they can be laid in place without mortar, although some mortar is plastered on the Sphinx's body to keep the stones secure. The limestone casing has been based precisely on the photogrammetric measurements that Lehner made in the late 1970s and early 1980s, so that the new layer looks as much like the older ones as possible. All ancient stones that are in good condition are being left, with new stones only replacing the shoddy modern restorations and some vulnerable open spaces on the Sphinx. "What we are doing will make the Sphinx live for a thousand years!" Hawass told me with pharaonic rhetorical sweep.

The preservation work has met with qualified praise among foreign archeologists and conservators. "The work is being done carefully, and, above all, it is reversible," said Rainer Stadelmann, director of the German Archeological Institute and a leading expert on the Giza complex. There is no way around the fact that, with the restoration complete, the bottom third of the Sphinx is covered in a casement of brand-new limestone and much of the monument is out of view—perhaps forever. "Problems arise when archeologists endeavor to reconstruct based on their notions of what the monument looked like, and that is often based on misinterpretation," said Neville Agnew of the Getty Conservation Institute. "You really are creating a fake and not an original object. You are looking at an object that has been restored and not conserved."

"Well, I console myself with the notion that Zahi is following in the tradition of the ancient Egyptians and Thutmosis IV," Lehner said diplomatically.

The conservation of the past is also a peculiarly modern preoccupation, born out of a vain hope that we can freeze time and the vain notion that what we are trying to freeze is the past. "In antiquity the Sphinx was painted in bright, comic-book colors," said Lehner. "It was not the solemn, beige ruin we have today." What we are trying to freeze is actually the present, which offers a highly distorted, fragmentary version of the past.

But the fact that our view of the past has been severely altered by what happens to survive does not, in Lehner's view, mean that conservation is a futile or useless business. "There will never be more of the original monument than there is today," he said. Along with the Heisenberg uncertainty principle, the history of the Sphinx restoration would seem to illustrate another important principle of modern physics: the second law of thermodynamics, which establishes that some energy is inevitably lost whenever it is consumed, no matter how efficient the engine. Entropy and decay are fundamental laws and nothing can be kept exactly as it is or returned to its former state. And yet our vision of the "past" is heavily conditioned and distorted by what monuments happen to have survived the ravages of time. The Great Pyramid is the last of the Seven

Wonders of the Ancient World still standing. No doubt the Hanging Gardens of Babylon, the Colossus of Rhodes, and the Lighthouse of Alexandria would exert similar fascination and perhaps even their own New Age cults if they were still around. So many great monuments of ancient Egypt survive in part because of historical accidents: the dry climate of the desert and the Egyptians' use of hard stone. As the Egyptian archeologist Faiza Haykal told me, "We have so much less of the other great civilizations of the ancient Near East because they built a great deal in mud-brick as they had much less available stone." The Egyptians had huge quarries of stone in almost every direction but almost no wood. They had to import cedarwood all the way from Lebanon. The Phoenicians used the abundant wood of Lebanon to become great sailors who explored and colonized much of the Mediterranean, but next to nothing remains of their boats or their monuments.

Similarly, the soft human tissue of ancient Egyptian society has fallen away and crumbled, leaving only its most massive structures. Trying to recover this lost social context—the world of the Pyramid and Sphinx builders—has become the focus of Lehner's work in recent years. It has taken Lehner full circle back to the big questions that brought him to Egypt in the first place. "I came here on a quest and in many ways I am still on it, namely: Why are we here? What is it all about? How do these great monuments fit into the three-thousand-year trajectory of Egyptian civilization? How do they fit into the whole human career?" he said.

Herodotus wrote that it took some hundred thousand souls to build the Great Pyramid; his account conjures up images of an army of slaves laboring under the lash of the pharaoh. But from Lehner's work and other recent excavations, a very different image of life at Giza in the Old Kingdom is emerging. For several years, Lehner has been excavating an ancient bakery he discovered about two hundred yards southeast, in front of and to the right of the Sphinx. The bakery is next to a brewery and a fish-processing plant. Zahi Hawass, in turn, is excavating the workmen's settlement and graveyard. In its first generations, archeology was mainly concerned with finding statues and treasures, uncovering the tombs of princes and pharaohs; the latest generation of archeologists pays much more attention to context and to the structures of everyday life, and the recent work at Giza is beginning to tell us more about the ordinary people who built the Sphinx and the Pyramids.

"My interest has gone beyond the site itself, to the dynamics of the society that produced the pyramids," Lehner said as we walked over the land where his bakery is buried, now covered with protective sand and decorated with camel dung. "I am becoming more and more convinced that ancient Egyptian society was a series of households within households, in an embedded pattern. Rather than having a large Wonder Bread factory, they did things with a kind of single-loaf method, replicating it many, many times." He went on, "Complexity theory in physics tells us how you can create global orders out of local rules, that you can create the complexity of the human body out of DNA or the computer out of simple on-and-off electrical signals. And something similar may have happened in ancient Egypt in which a complex, large-scale society evolved out of the simple household structure. The word *pharaoh* in ancient Egyptian means 'the greatest household.' It seems counterintuitive at first, but in many ways it is more logical that the modern state did not just spring full-blown from the head of Zeus but evolved gradually from the kind of patriarchal society that you find throughout the ancient Near East."

Scholars now believe that the bulk of the work on the Pyramids was done by a group of six to seven thousand highly trained craftsmen who received both payment and prestige for their efforts and that the heavy lifting was done by a group of twenty to thirty thousand laborers who were not slaves but farmers who worked during the summer months when the fields were flooded and could not be cultivated. When an American engineering company was putting in the sewer system for the village near the Sphinx, archeologists working alongside them found what looked like a city that may have covered an area of about nine hundred acres. Rather than living in a large, military-style barracks, the workmen of Giza appear to have lived in small, ordinary mud-brick houses. And these individuals appear to have enjoyed the same rights of individual burial as the priests and members of the royal household buried around the Pyramids. One of the tombs that Hawass found is dedicated to "the overseer of the side of the pyramid." The Egyptians appear to have worked in small, discrete units, each with responsibility for a small part of the whole.

Many of the workmen's tombs that Hawass's men have uncovered resemble the much grander burial places of the nobles but in miniature. "There are little beehivelike domes that look like pyramids, little rectangular tombs, little mastabas, and little false doors as in a doll's house," Lehner explained. "They're a lot like the things you find in the tombs at Giza but they are on a small scale and they are made in mud-brick rather than stone. A lot of Egyptologists use the word *state*, as if the pharaoh and his administration were on one side and the people on the other. We always thought that all we had was 'royal court culture' and that this was different from the popular culture of ancient Egypt. But what we are finding increasingly is that they are all part of the same culture."

Traditional Egyptology, and not just New Age cultists, has suffered, according to Lehner, from seeing Egyptian monuments in isolation, as merely the products of an all-powerful pharaoh. "The great Wizard of Oz is not only all the wacko ideas about a lost civilization and outer-space people, even for many Egyptologists and scholars; it's the notion of the barracks, a huge conscripted workforce, slaves," he told me. Lehner has begun to see the monuments less as the whim of an absolute ruler than as manifestations of the collective will of a new urban society. "The 'little man behind the curtain,'" he said, extending his Wizard of Oz metaphor to explain the reality behind the fantasy, "is the idea that these sublime structures were raised with a household mode of production."

What is gradually emerging is that Giza was not just a religious center but a city of large proportions. "If there were twenty thousand or thirty thousand people working there, it would have been a supercity for the third millennium B.C.," Lehner explained. As he uncovers new things, he is plugging information into a large computer database, which he and his colleagues at the University of Chicago's Oriental Institute are using to create a digitized map not just of the Sphinx but of the entire Giza plateau. Eventually, they hope to produce a computer reconstruction like the one Lehner did with the architect Tom Jaggers, showing the whole of ancient Giza as it may have looked forty-five hundred years ago.

But much of the ancient city Lehner described is no longer visible to the eye. Since the sewer at Nazlet-el-Saman was finished, the workmen's settlement has been asphalted over. The Valley Temple of Khufu, also found during the sewer project, is now covered by the road divider of the main street. "See, right in front of where that fat man is walking was a row of houses," Lehner pointed out. "Underneath that carriage is a house, and where that road is there was a causeway." A Muslim cemetery, which has grown as rapidly as the town itself, covers most of the area where archeological digs conducted at the beginning of the century had revealed a series of streets and houses where the priests who tended the cult of the Pyramids lived. "It is kind of a strange irony that an ancient city of the living is now totally covered by the modern city of the dead," he said.

Other sites that were excavated but left unprotected have deteriorated beyond recognition. The Valley Temple of the Third Pyramid, which was built hastily after the pharaoh's death in mud-brick has eroded, as have dozens of houses of the pyramid city that were not eaten up by the Muslim graveyard. "We have photographs from the 1930s that show walls as high as two meters," Lehner said as we stood on what looks like barren ground. "Now all that is left of them are mud-brick stains on the desert sand." It was simply not the practice of archeologists to rebury and conserve a site after they had extracted what they were looking for. "The excavation of these sites began when my grandfather was a young man and a lot of them are already gone," Lehner said. "Without these petrified remains of the soft tissue of society, these monuments look mysterious. If you don't see the mud-brick houses and tombs, any great monument like the Great Pyramid looks like it was built by space people or a vast military organization. If you don't see the context, you don't see it as a human monument. That's the importance of finding bakeries and houses." Ironically, the pharaohs may have actually achieved what they

hoped for. "The ancient Egyptians didn't want them to be human monuments," Lehner said. "They covered them with casements, stones that
were smoothed. They wanted to create something ethereal and cosmic.
But behind the casement their work was much sloppier, and you can see
the living hand."

2

The Culture of the Copy and the Disappearance of China's Past

WHEN MICHELE CORDARO, the director of Italy's Central Conservation Institute, went to visit the famous army of terra-cotta warriors in Lintong, outside Xi'an, he was dumbstruck by what followed: his Chinese colleagues took him straight from the ancient site to a factory where they were churning out modern replicas of the emperor's tomb soldiers. "They proudly pointed to the copies as if to say, 'See, we can still do it!'" Cordaro said of that first trip to China in 1995. It would be like Italian art authorities taking a foreign visitor to a manufacturing plant outside Florence where they made plaster replicas of Michelangelo's *David*. But the Chinese copies were carefully produced, with the government's permission, from molds made from the original statues and speckled with small imperfections and flecks of mud as if they had been recently dug out of the ground. "The vast majority of the warriors that have gone touring around the West are fakes," Cordaro said. "We call them fakes, but the Chinese have a different sense of the value of original and copy."

This differing view of copies has caused some moments of friction between Chinese and Western art historians when it has come to organizing exhibitions. "I know of cases where, at the insistence of museum directors, the Chinese have sent over, let's say, five originals and twenty-five copies," Cordaro said. "And almost no one can tell which are which." A few years ago the Smithsonian Institution in Washington was forced to cancel a show it had planned on ancient Chinese bells when it discovered that the Chinese were planning on sending copies and not originals. Similarly, Cordaro saw a major exhibition touring Europe of Tang dynasty (A.D. 618–907) mural paintings that he felt certain were reproductions—a suspicion confirmed when Cordaro visited the Xi'an art museum. There he saw some of the originals—evidently too fragile to travel—down in the storeroom, while modern reproductions were exhibited in the display cases, without any labels to indicate that they were copies.

For Cordaro, encountering this culture of the copy was of more than academic interest: he had come to Xi'an, at the behest of the Chinese government, in order to set up a modern laboratory and school of art conservation. Cordaro began to realize what he and his Italian colleagues were confronting in China was a radically different set of attitudes not only toward what is an original artwork and what is a copy but also toward the past, toward art conservation, toward monuments, toward cherished Western ideas of what is ancient and what is new.

"The Chinese, like the Japanese and some other Asian nations, have a tradition of conserving by copying, or rebuilding," Cordaro said. Conserving by rebuilding made considerable sense in China, where, until recently, virtually everything—palaces, temples, and houses—was built of wood. Paradoxically, in architecture, working in perishable materials could potentially offer a superior conservation strategy: rotting wooden parts could simply be replaced as needed so that, just as our bodies replace their old cells with new ones while we remain "ourselves," the buildings would be constantly regenerated, remaining forever new and forever ancient. The epitome of this seemingly Zen approach to conservation is the Ise Shrine in Japan, a Shinto temple originally built in the seventh century A.D. that is ritually destroyed and rebuilt every twenty years. The Japanese think of it as being thirteen hundred years old yet no single piece of it is more than two decades old.

This concept is so alien to Western art historians that UNESCO, after much fierce debate, excluded the Ise Shrine and many other famous Japanese monuments from its list of World Heritage Sites on the grounds that they were not ancient or authentic.

These conflicting attitudes toward monuments are related to profound cultural differences. China and Japan have traditionally had a cyclical view of time. Dynasties would rise and fall, be replaced by new ones, but, like the Forbidden City, reemerging from its latest fire, remain fundamentally the same: each ruling group held the "mandate of heaven." In the imperial era, the Chinese counted the years by dynasty, so that time would begin again with each new one. The upheavals of dynastic change masked a world of remarkable continuity: China has spoken and written the same language for about thirty-five hundred years and kept the customs and social structures of its imperial system in place for more than two thousand years. (Archeologists have found dumplings in ancient tombs that are virtually identical to those eaten by the Chinese today.) In a world that was both eternal and ever-changing, rebuilding monuments made perfect sense.

Every sinologist or person who has had significant dealings with Chinese art has run into this curious cultural difference. "The Chinese language has two different words for copy," Ken DeWoskin, a professor of Chinese studies at the University of Michigan, explained. "*Fang Zhipin* is closer to what we would call a reproduction—a knockoff you would buy in a museum store—while *Fu Zhipin* is a very high quality copy, something worthy of study or putting in a museum." DeWoskin helped arrange the ancient bell show for the Smithsonian to which the Chinese sent *Fu Zhipin*. When the American curators refused to consider exhibiting the carefully made copies, the Chinese were offended.

Copying has traditionally been a major part of artistic training in China—seen as a sign of reverence rather than of lack of originality. Indeed, the most celebrated Chinese artist of the twentieth century, Chang Dai-chien, sometimes called "the Picasso of China," was also a world-famous forger who made and sold thousands of paintings attributed to ancient Chinese masters while enjoying widespread acclaim for the work he signed with his own name. Indeed, in 1956 the French staged two major Chang exhibitions in Paris, one at the Musée d'Art Moderne of his own work, the other at the Musée Cernuschi of his well-known Great Wind Hall collection, a vast selection of scrolls that he managed to pass off as masterpieces of ancient Chinese art. Many of Chang's copies—which include carefully crafted signatures and seals—ended up in major collections around the world. When these works were revealed as forgeries, Chang was scorned by Westerners as a fraud, but he obviously regarded his ancient copies in a very different light. In fact, Chang had little in common with a typical Western forger: he had a solid market for his own signed work and so he did not copy simply for money. Copying was an act of reverence as well as a central expression of his art. Chang felt that by fooling connoisseurs and museum curators he was both showing his profound understanding of ancient masterpieces as well as demonstrating his bravura as an artist. Moreover, many of his "ancient" paintings were not strictly copies but re-creations of paintings described in Chinese literature that no longer existed. He was, in a sense, conserving and inventing the past at the same time. Indeed, because most Chinese painting was done on paper, the work of many great artists has come down through the ages through copies.

The West, by contrast, has always strived for permanence in fresco technique, oil painting, and, above all, building in stone. From the pyramid age in Egypt, Western potentates entertained the grand conceit of creating monuments of stone that would last forever. The Chinese considered this a vain illusion since nothing material, of course, lasts forever. Unlike that of the Chinese, our history has been one of often radical discontinuity, of successive civilizations and eras: the Egyptians, the Persians, the Greeks, the Romans, the Christians. Rather than faithfully copy its predecessors, each new group sought to impose its own language, culture, religion, and architectural style, since the monuments of the past were the fruit of a civilization that was now inaccessible and often incomprehensible. Perhaps because of this layering of civilizations, the West adopted a linear view of time—in the Jewish, Christian, and Islamic calendars, which started from a fixed point in time. In a world where one is always moving away from a date set in antiquity, with its layered history made up of extinct civilizations, dead languages, and stone monuments, the idea of the ruin seems entirely natural. In the Chinese context, the idea of the ruin made little sense. Destroying and rebuilding ex novo fit China's cyclical yet seemingly unchanging world.

Up until about a hundred years ago, one could argue that the Chinese strategy of conservation was far more successful. While Western ancient architecture crumbled into ruins, to be replaced by successive styles, the basic forms of Chinese architecture remained remarkably unaltered for over two thousand years—even if none of the actual buildings remained.

"This system of conserving by copying or rebuilding works well as long as you keep the artisan traditions intact," Cordaro explained to me. "The problem is those traditions have broken down in China, as they have in many countries. Now they are replacing wood with concrete and cement." Once the continuity of Chinese imperial civilization was broken, knowledge of traditional pigments, resins, and textiles, of painting, wood carving, and building techniques quickly began to disappear. After the Republican Revolution of 1911, China began to rely increasingly on Western industrial building techniques. With this technological shift, the millennial tradition of conserving by rebuilding fell apart. Wooden buildings were torn down and replaced with brick or cement. The trend was further accelerated after the Communist Revolution of 1949, whose leaders considered much of imperial art as the useless baggage of a feudal society, to be discarded or suppressed. Traditional artistic and artisan techniques that had been handed down from master to apprentice for generations were lost.

In Beijing alone during the Cultural Revolution of the late 1960s, Red Guards destroyed some 4,922 out of 6,843 officially designated sites of historical and cultural interest, burning temples, hacking statues, and destroying imperial tombs. At a certain point, they set out for the Forbidden City itself but here Chinese premier Zhou Enlai drew the line at Mao's madness, placing a goodly number of Red Army troops outside the old imperial palace.

But the Cultural Revolution was able to wreak so much havoc in part because there was already relatively little to destroy, and much that is now being bulldozed is not particularly old. Even the supposedly ancient monuments—the Forbidden City, for example—are hardly ancient as we in the West understand the term. Built in the fifteenth century, the imperial palace has been wholly or partially destroyed in six major fires, most recently in 1923. Quite aside from the fires, the palace has been rebuilt and repainted countless times. The paint now used is shiny new (much of it a bright industrial red that you might use to paint a fire truck) and the detail work surprisingly crude, nothing like the extraordinarily delicate traditional Chinese painting one can see in museums. Similarly, the Summer Palace, the imperial residence outside Beijing, was entirely destroyed and rebuilt in the twentieth century. Its buildings look more like the Disneyland re-creations or the decor of a fancy restaurant in New York's Chinatown than whatever they may have been during the Ming or Qing dynasty.

Interestingly, the shift to Western industrial techniques that came with the Revolution of 1911 was accompanied by the adoption of the Christian calendar. With the end of the cyclical imperial worldview—and the shift from handcrafts to industrial technique—the culture of the copy broke down. It seems almost as if once the Western linear clock began to tick, the imperial, cyclical world began to disintegrate and fall into ruins, incapable of being rebuilt. Chinese archeology began in the 1920s, under Western influence, as if the ancient dynastic past were not really past as long as the imperial system remained in place; with a new republican system of government, it could be examined with a degree of scientific detachment.

Just in the last several years, the Chinese have woken up to the fact that, unable to count on their traditional knowledge of arts and crafts, they will be left with precious little of their physical past if they don't also adopt Western strategies for conservation. While craftsmen of previous generations might have known instinctively the proper pigment or resin to create a certain effect, now ancient paints and glues must be studied under microscopes and with X-ray machines.

It was fairly natural for the Chinese to turn for help to Italy—another ancient civilization, with perhaps the greatest concentration of antiquities in the world and a five-hundred-year tradition of digging them up and trying to preserve them. Cordaro's institute in Rome enjoys a world reputation and was hired by the Getty Conservation Institute to conserve the famous Egyptian tomb of Queen Nefertari. In 1995, the Chinese and the Italians signed an agreement to set up the Xi'an Center for the Conservation and Restoration of Cultural Relics, with the Italians providing more than $2 million in high-tech equipment and a staff of instructors and the Chinese providing offices, personnel, and twenty-three students to learn a Western approach to art conservation. Xi'an seemed a good place for a conservation center, having been the capital of ancient China on and off for nearly a thousand years, from the time of the first emperor in 221 B.C. until the collapse of the Tang dynasty in A.D. 907.

When Cordaro returned in April 1998 to teach a course in Xi'an, check on the progress of the first class of students, and inspect some Chinese monuments in need of conservation, I decided to accompany him.

Driving in from the Xi'an airport, we passed through the lush green valley of the Wei River, the kind of fertile farmland that made this part of northern China one of the principal concentrations of early Chinese civilization. Rising from the plain were enormous grassy man-made mounds, some several hundred feet long and thirty or forty feet high—each one an unexcavated imperial tomb. Here, as in Rome, it is difficult to put a shovel to the ground without striking something ancient. Just on the other side of the city, in 1953, Chinese archeologists discovered a large Neolithic village from about 4500 B.C., one of the most important prehistoric sites in China. And in 1974, a peasant digging a well uncovered fragments from the tomb containing the vast terra-cotta army of China's first emperor, Qin Shihuangdi, who unified the country and standardized its written language before his death in 221 B.C. Exploratory digging at one of the burial mounds near the airport has revealed another army of warriors, vast in number but only about two and a half feet high, while the warriors of the first emperor are some-what larger than life-size. The other dozen mounds have not been explored and may well yield their own armies of terra-cotta sculptures.

The grassy mounds of the imperial tombs create the impression that the extraordinary fullness of China's past is pressing through the earth's surface into the present. But these largely hidden riches of China's past stand out in stark contrast with the wasteland aboveground. As we approached the modern city of Xi'an, the jarring hulk of a huge coal-burning electricity plant appeared above the tombs and spewed black smoke out its massive, squat concrete smokestacks. The air in Xi'an, as in most other major Chinese cities, is horribly polluted, heavy with the sweet burned odor of coal dust. The weather always seems to be overcast, the sky a lead-colored roof close overhead.

Again, like most other major Chinese cities, Xi'an looks like a mas-sive construction site. The skyline is crisscrossed with tall cranes and the concrete shells of new high-rise buildings, while wrecking balls raze what is left of the city's old one-story courtyard houses. What Communism left untouched, capitalism is now taking aim at. With the Chinese econ-omy growing at nearly 10 percent a year—five times faster than that of most Western countries—the creative destruction of capitalism is oper-ating in China as if it were in fast-forward, with shifts of construction and demolition crews often working straight through the night. In China, the market economy moves like a tornado, taking everything in its wake. It seems an ironic fulfillment of Mao's own iconoclastic dic-tum: "Destroy first, and construction will look after itself."

Although it once rivaled Rome and Constantinople in beauty and importance, there is virtually nothing ancient left in Xi'an. There is a famous Drum Tower, a bell tower, a Taoist temple, two pagodas, and an old mosque for Xi'an's small Muslim community—but all these build-ings have been heavily restored and repainted, many rather crudely, in recent decades. The only authentically old pieces of architecture are the medieval city walls, which date from the fifteenth century, after the Ming dynasty had moved the capital to Beijing, reducing Xi'an to the role of provincial capital. But when we arrived, the majestic brick fortification walls were festooned with bright electric lights, strung along the sawtooth crenellations of the watchtowers, and illuminated at night with a purple-filtered spotlight—giving the city a kind of disco feel.

Cordaro, although he had been to Xi'an two years earlier for the selection of the first class of students, was taken aback by the gaudy spectacle; it was as if the Italians had decided to deck the Coliseum with electric lights. But when we entered the medieval gate into the old city, the decoration of the outer walls seemed sober and restrained: we were greeted by a riot of blinking neon signs, flashing advertisements for everything from computers and televisions to Coca-Cola and Kentucky Fried Chicken. Entire buildings were bathed in red, green, and purple lights, with massive billboards lining their sides and roofs. The center of Xi'an looks like Broadway and 42nd Street in New York; but the flashing electronic billboards in New York are restricted to a few blocks around Times Square, while in Xi'an they run the length of the principal streets.

But when you see the city during the daytime, you realize that it actually looks better lit up at night: almost all new buildings in Xi'an, as in the rest of China, are simply reinforced concrete boxes covered with the same industrial white tile—the kind of cold, easy-to-clean institutional tile you might find in a gas station rest room. "Swimming pool architecture," the Italians at the conservation center call it. Many of the modern buildings have been fitted with upturned Chinese eaves that sit atop the buildings like ill-fitting wigs or guilty afterthoughts on the architect's part. It turns out that the roofs are a legal fig leaf that allows developers to satisfy a requirement for building traditional architecture.

In the two years since Cordaro's previous visit, the city had changed significantly, with buildings going up and coming down with astonishing rapidity. Most Chinese, many of whom have known famine and extraordinary hardships in their own lifetimes, are surprisingly unsentimental about these changes. As we drove through Xi'an and remarked on a bulldozer lining up to demolish another one-story building, one of the Chinese employees of the conservation center said, "These old buildings are no good. They need to widen this road for the cars. Come back in six months, it will look much better." In Xi'an, as elsewhere, the government is planning on demolishing all but a tiny portion of its remaining courtyard houses in the next few years to make room for high-rise apartments, badly needed in a country of 1.2 billion people. Each city will preserve a few old neighborhoods for tourists.

"As a Sicilian, I think I understand something of the neglect of Chinese monuments," said Cordaro, a tall, overweight man with an unruly head of woolly gray hair who was fifty-three when we traveled together in 1998. (He died just two years later of cancer.) In his dark corduroys, checked tweed jacket, sweater vest, and horn-rimmed glasses, Cordaro had a refined professorial look, despite his bearish figure. While a student of art history at the University of Palermo, Cordaro attended the lectures of Cesare Brandi, the founder of the Central Conservation Institute, which Cordaro later directed. Living in the exquisite decadence of Palermo, with its fading former mosques, abandoned Norman palaces, and collapsing Baroque churches, Cordaro naturally developed an interest in conservation. "In both Sicily and China, you have great artistic traditions that, however, were sponsored by autocratic societies that were remote from the lives of ordinary people," he said. But this analogy goes only a short way toward explaining what we were and were not seeing: however dilapidated, Palermo is a cornucopia of historic monuments compared with Xi'an or Beijing.

Imagine France without its châteaus, Gothic cathedrals, or elegant boulevards; Italy without Roman ruins, walled hill towns, medieval towers, Renaissance palaces, or Baroque churches; New England without its brick colonials and wood farmhouses; New York without its brownstones; or Virginia without Thomas Jefferson's architecture, and you begin to get an eerie feeling of contemporary China—where the intangible sense of its rich, glorious, and often tragic history is thick in the air but nowhere visible.

The Xi'an conservation center is located in back of the recently constructed Provincial Art Museum, a couple of miles from the downtown center. The building is a typical example of the new Chinese architecture, a set of concrete boxes with the ubiquitous industrial white tile—with a curving roof and upturned eaves. But virtually everything in the building is made of cement, as are the crudely cast lions that stand guard at the building's main entrance, which in traditional Chinese palaces are often made of bronze.

The center has two floors laid out along a long, thin corridor that travels the back of the museum complex. On the upper floor there is the main classroom, a small library with texts in Chinese, Italian, and English, a computer room, a few offices, and a laboratory and storeroom for art objects in various states of conservation. On the lower floor are the scientific laboratories where technicians are trained in the use of X-ray equipment and electron microscopes and the chemical analysis of art objects. In the morning, the twenty-three Chinese students attend courses in subjects such as the conservation of bronze or ceramics and the treatment of wood surfaces or painted murals. The afternoons are dedicated to laboratory work. Most of the students sit in white coats on stools, hunched over ancient objects: a woman with something that looks like a dentist's drill removes dirt and encrustation from the interior of a cracked bronze vessel; another works on a terra-cotta figure whose little head sits alone on the table detached from its body. The technicians are downstairs X-raying the hidden stress lines of a vase, analyzing the lead content of a bronze, or trying to figure out the molecular makeup of a particular resin. There is a rotating faculty of about seven or eight Italian instructors, who generally come for several weeks or a few months at a time.

"We have an interdisciplinary approach to conservation," Cordaro said, explaining that the work of archeology, art history, conservation, and scientific analysis are all combined. Often one needs to know where an object was found and how it was used to understand its current condition. In recent decades, since the Chinese discovered "scientific conservation," they have tended to view archeology as something apart, sending objects out for conservation the way a doctor might send off a blood sample for analysis.

This can have negative consequences for the work of art, as has been the case with the terra-cotta warriors at Lintong. The entire army of statues, each of them individually sculpted, was originally painted in bright colors, but as the Chinese have dug them out of the ground, the paint has come off and stuck to the earth. The problem arises about the moment the statues are exposed to the air. In the ground, Cordaro said, the statue and the earth surrounding it are exposed to a high degree of humidity; once you begin to remove the earth, the statue, since it is more compact, dries off more quickly than the earth around it, causing the paint to detach from the statue and adhere to the moisture in the ground. The problem has to be dealt with during the excavation itself.

"It's a problem that could be solved, but a very difficult and expensive one," Cordaro explained. "One would have to create a hermetically sealed environment at the excavation site, so that you could minimize the change in relative humidity when you dug up the statues." The Chinese understand the problem, but do not have the resources and expertise to deal with it themselves. At the same time, they have adamantly rejected any offers of help. Part of the initial understanding in creating the joint conservation center was for the Italians to participate in the excavation and conservation of the terra-cotta warriors, but here—as in other areas—the Italians have encountered resistance. "The Chinese will never let any Westerners work at Lintong," Cordaro said with sadness.

Ancient monuments are fraught with political significance and issues of national pride in China. When the terra-cotta warriors were discovered in 1974, the find was immediately put to use in the overheated politics of Mao's Cultural Revolution. "Mao said that the past must serve the present," explained Roberto Ciarla, an Italian archeologist who has been the on-site director of the Xi'an conservation school. The only member of the Italian contingent who speaks fluent Chinese, Ciarla first came to study in China the year of the terra-cotta army's discovery. "At that moment, which was toward the end of Mao's life and the end of the Cultural Revolution, there was a campaign being conducted by the Gang of Four against Lin Biao [a former Chinese prime minister who had died under mysterious circumstances]. The discovery of the terra-cotta warriors was used explicitly in this struggle against Lin Biao and against the neo-Confucianism of the party bureaucracy. Mao Zedong was compared openly to the first Chinese emperor, Qin Shihuangdi, who was reevaluated as a great unifier of the nation." The rehabilitation of a figure once reviled as a violent despot was valuable to the Cultural Revolution. Not only had the first emperor built a tomb with thousands of terra-cotta warriors, he had also apparently buried alive hundreds of Confucian scholars and made an auto-da-fé of their books. Instead of being an anomaly in China, the Cultural Revolution was only the latest in a long tradition of wiping the slate of history clean. Although the Cultural Revolution is by now regarded almost universally as a disaster, the tomb of the first emperor is still an important symbol of national unity—and ceding control of its excavation or conservation would be a blow to national pride.

In some sense, the Italian-Chinese experiment in art conservation is a microcosm of China's larger dilemma: the Chinese authorities are happy to have Italian equipment, money, and expertise but are anxious to maintain political control over the project. As with economic reform in general, the Italians found cooperation and enthusiasm among top-level officials at the national and regional level but pockets of intense resistance among local officials fearful of losing power. When the Italians and Chinese met to choose the first class of students, the Chinese were stunned by the Italians' insistence that the entrance examinations be graded anonymously so as to avoid personal favoritism. The Italians won that battle but have no idea whether the pool of applicants itself was predetermined by personal and party considerations. "We discovered that a member of the admissions committee had a relative among the applicants," Cordaro said.

Having chosen the students, the Italians found that local museum officials balked at handing over art objects in need of conservation—despite clear orders from top officials in Beijing and in Xanshi Province, in which Xi'an is located. The Italians began to realize that many of the local officials in Xi'an wanted to use the center primarily as a means of acquiring control of the expensive high-tech laboratories when the initial three-year agreement lapsed in 1998. Indeed, the Italians' contract was not renewed, meaning that they had to abandon Xi'an, leaving all their equipment behind.

Despite all this, Cordaro considered the experiment a decided success. "They didn't want to give us the objects to work on, but in the end they did," he said. "We are leaving Xi'an, but it looks as if we may be able to participate in the creation of a national conservation center in Beijing. They keep the equipment, but we also leave behind this class of students who have now acquired a whole new method of working. We have planted a seed. If we could do this for another two or three groups of students, we could really make a difference. And you can see the results, which are superb."

All the restored objects were laid out on display when a leading Italian politician came through on a state visit during our two-week stay in Xi'an. Zhou dynasty bronzes with beautifully crafted handles in animal shapes, Neolithic ceramic pots with elegant geometric designs, menacing-looking deities that once stood guard over a royal tomb, an extraordinary bronze "tree of life" sculpture with a fluttering of delicate bronze leaves, two miniature terra-cotta warriors—one, entirely covered in mud, that had not yet been restored, the other almost perfectly intact, its colors nearly as bright as they were the day they were painted. In two years, the center had managed to conserve the contents of an excellent small museum.

The Italians found that they had to break the Chinese students of certain deeply ingrained habits of thought. "They want to remake the object," said Paola Donati, a conservator from Rome with a specialization in ancient bronzes. "When presented with a bronze vessel in fragments, they will say, 'Well, why don't we just solder it back together?' And this still happens after a year and a half." The approach of the Central Conservation Institute—widely shared in most Western conservation labs—is based on three principles: any conservation work must be "recognizable," "reversible," and "compatible." Thus, a Western conservator would piece together the fragments of a bronze vase with a removable glue that would leave faintly visible cracks so that the viewer could distinguish the workmanship of the original craftsman from that of the conservator. Any material used to reconstruct missing parts must be compatible with the original, neither damaging it physically nor creating a strident contrast aesthetically. Soldering, the method most

Chinese conservators prefer, is both irreversible and generally unrecognizable. In some instances, they remove the patina that forms on the metal surface with time—in order to make the piece appear "as good as new." "This is the only country where I have ever encountered this desire to remake the object," said Donati, who has also worked with conservators in Turkey and Greece, where the tendency is not to do much conservation work at all.

While we were in Xi'an, Cordaro taught a course on the theory of conservation, with a special emphasis on copying and rebuilding monuments and works of art. Cordaro showed slides of numerous famous Greek and Roman statues—the *Winged Victory*, the *Venus de Milo*, the *Laocoön*, the *Apollo Belvedere*, among others—a veritable parade of mutilated figures, missing arms, missing legs, chopped-off noses. To Chinese students with no background in Western art history and no tradition of the ruin or the fragment (let alone of the nude), this pageant of mostly naked, handicapped statues appeared strange. To stretch their minds, Cordaro showed them various incarnations of the *Apollo Belvedere*, an extraordinary ancient sculpture of the god that sits in the Belvedere Court at the Vatican. The first photograph showed the statue more or less as it would have appeared after it was dug up in Rome during the 1500s, missing its right arm. Then he showed a picture of the statue after the Vatican commissioned the sixteenth-century sculptor Montorsoli to "complete" it by replacing its lost arm. Then he showed the statue as it appears today, again without the arm. "In the 1920s, the Vatican conservators decided to remove the new right arm," he explained. In the third photograph, one could clearly see the hole in the marble where the substitute arm had been attached, making Apollo look a bit like an amputee without his prosthesis. "So, what is the best way to treat this statue? Should they have left the new arm or removed it?"

The students tend to be rather timid and reluctant to speak up. Finally, one young woman, with short bangs and a lively manner, answered cautiously, trying to hedge her bets: "The statue with the arms looks better, but from the point of conservation, the statue without the arm is correct." She clearly liked the reconstructed *Apollo* better than its mutilated version but understood that the Italians were dead set against remaking artworks. Wrong, Cordaro insisted. "You cannot apply the same rule to all circumstances; you must judge case by case," he said. "In this case, the sixteenth-century arm—itself a very fine piece of work by a first-rate sculptor—is part of the history of the statue. Removing it, we are removing important information. Moreover, removing the sixteenth-century arm, we are not in fact returning the statue to its earlier state. Notice that they had to saw off the arm clean to fit on the new one, and in removing it we are leaving the statue with a visible hole in the marble where an iron pole held the new arm in place. It may have been wrong for the people in the sixteenth century to add an arm, but it was probably also a mistake for the people in the 1920s to remove it."

Between the Chinese respect for authority and Communist discipline, the Italian professors had to push the students to learn to think for themselves. "They are very Confucian: their respect for the teacher is absolute," said Roberto Ciarla, who has spent more time in Xi'an than any of the other Italian instructors. "They almost never ask questions."

"They desperately want a set of fixed rules that they can apply across the board in all circumstances," Donati said. "So sometimes they will come to you confused and ask, 'You say to do such and such and Professor so-and-so says something different. How can this be?'" Indeed, the one moment all the students began scribbling notes madly was when Cordaro announced the three rules of conservation: recognizability, reversibility, and compatibility. But by showing so many examples of different kinds of conservation, Cordaro was trying to demonstrate the complexity of applying these principles. "You must decide everything on a case-by-case basis," he said, "using your experience, taste, and judgment."

As Cordaro's lecture made clear, the instinct to rebuild and copy was alive in the West several centuries ago. Great sculptors such as Gianlorenzo Bernini used their talents to repair the ancient works that were being unearthed during the Renaissance. However, unlike the Chinese, Bernini did not try hard to hide his conservation work: in adding a sword to a famous Roman statue of Mars, Bernini was clearly attempting to outdo the bravura of the ancient sculptor (an effort many consider successful). "The past was alive for Bernini," Cordaro said. Western sculptors continued repairing ancient sculptures until the Italian artist Antonio Canova refused to remake the missing parts of the Elgin Marbles, the famous sculpted frieze taken from the Parthenon in Athens to the British Museum at the beginning of the nineteenth century. Somewhere between Bernini's seventeenth century and Canova's time, the past appears to have become truly past. It was no longer considered appropriate to alter the masterpieces of other eras. "In the eighteenth century you have the birth of art history—the historicizing and periodization," Cordaro said. In the 1730s, the Italians rediscovered Pompeii and began the first systematic excavation of an ancient city, a major event in the founding of modern archeology. In Bernini's time, the Italians were still using the Colosseum as a marble quarry, dismantling its walls to use for new construction; by the eighteenth century, they actually began preserving ancient sites. In that spirit, modern tourism was born, as young European gentlemen from Laurence Sterne and James Boswell to Johann Wolfgang Goethe saw the Grand Tour—surveying the antiquities of Italy and Greece—as a fundamental part of their educations. With this new antiquarian interest, a different aesthetic grew up, an appreciation of the fragment and the ruin. Johann Winckelmann, considered the father of modern art history, developed the idea of "imaginary conservation," that is, using remaining fragments to reimagine the original work of art. It gave rise to the romantic cult of the "ruin," in which English landscape architects would preserve abandoned structures that would have been dismantled or rebuilt in an earlier age or even create fake ruins in order to cultivate the feeling of ancientness, a pleasant melancholy sense of decay and the passage of time. Thus, as the West took its first steps toward the Industrial Revolution, the past receded behind glass cases into the museum or was cordoned off behind the ropes of an archeological site.

It was hard to say what if anything Cordaro's lecture meant to the Chinese students. He delivered it in Italian, but the Chinese interpreter appeared to have a highly uncertain grasp of Italian—she kept asking what the word *reversible* meant—so that between conveying Cordaro's thoughts to the students and conveying theirs back in Italian to him, the opportunities for lost meaning were many. None of the interpreters we encountered, either Chinese-Italian or Chinese-English, was truly fluent in both languages, meaning that it was difficult to stray from basic factual and conceptual conversations. China's opening to the West is still so recent that only a tiny minority of Chinese have traveled abroad, so that their foreign language skills are extremely limited. Add cultural barriers to linguistic ones and the potential for misunderstanding is great. One morning at the hotel where Cordaro and I stayed in Xi'an, we asked for orange juice without ice (in order to avoid drinking the local water); the waitress returned a few minutes later with piping hot orange juice, served as if it were tea. And for several days afterward, we were brought hot orange juice. We did not have the heart to explain what we had meant, and if we had tried, our explanation might have produced an even more bizarre result. The Chinese want very much to please their Western guests, but many of our customs make little sense to them. Thus, many of the attempts at Westernization put one in mind of someone who has memorized the words to a song but has the tune all wrong. One day at lunch we ordered sandwiches, which arrived sprinkled with dried corn flakes. Evidently, the kitchen had been told that Westerners like corn flakes and so we were served them as if they were potato chips.

All this created the feeling that we were at several removes from the Chinese. During the two weeks at Xi'an, however, I did have occasion to talk with many of the students. They were a mix of men and women, generally in their late twenties. Almost all of them were married and were employees of a Chinese state museum or archeological dig. Many of them had made considerable sacrifices to attend the school, living away from their families, sleeping five or six to a room in a university dormitory. But having entered into a market economy, into a world of both greater opportunity and greater uncertainty, they were eager for the professional advantage offered by the conservation program.

All of them, like virtually everyone else in China, wore Western dress; many of them carried pagers, a craze among young Chinese as

among young Americans. What do young Chinese care about? I asked
one girl as she worked cleaning a bronze vessel. "They like karaoke, going
dancing, and going to films," she said. She had just cried her way through
Titanic, the hit movie of the year in China. They all acknowledged that one
of the big topics of conversation among young people was *"fa cai"* (pronounced *fa tsai*), meaning: making money. While the rapidity of change
is disconcerting to some Westerners, for most younger Chinese, it cannot come fast enough. "Xi'an is changing, but it needs to change more
quickly," she said. "Xi'an is still quite poor compared with parts of
southern China."

"In Europe everything is already built," said another student,
Cheng Yan. "When I was there, there were new buildings under construction. In Europe the cultural environment is better than in China.
In China, more energy is spent in developing the country. My mother
says our life is better than before and we can do whatever we want. Xi'an
is better than before. Every day people have new things. Especially in
Shanghai, where everything is new."

What about preserving the past? What does that mean to him and his
peers? "The Chinese have about five thousand years of history. They are
very proud," he said. "Young people in China pay more attention to
today's life. I think the next step is that China will develop something
about the spirit."

Although working in the field of art conservation, virtually all the
students seemed, perhaps understandably, concerned more with making
money, building a career, and having fun than with what some have
called the "uglification" of China's urban landscape. "The Cultural Revolution not only destroyed our monuments, it destroyed people's feeling for them," said a sensitive young architect we met on the trip—one of
the very few Chinese who appeared to have thought about the problem.
"It killed off the sense of beauty."

While the young people were refreshingly open and candid—products
of a much freer, post-Mao culture—considerable diffidence and rigidity
was evident in people over forty, especially those who worked for the state
bureaucracy. When I asked to speak with archeologists or museum cura-

tors in Xi'an about the problems of art conservators, the Chinese-Italian interpreter became panicky. "Please don't. These are very delicate political questions here," he said. "You can't understand. In other provinces or in Beijing, no problem. The people are very open; they will answer all your questions. Here in Xi'an, big problem. Wait until we go to Luoyang."

Not wanting to create more trouble for the Italian-Chinese collaboration in Xi'an, I agreed to wait to speak to officials in the adjoining Henan Province when we made a weekend trip to the city of Luoyang—another former Chinese capital, about 250 miles to the east of Xi'an. Luoyang, whose history dates back to about 2100 B.C., had originally competed with and lost out to Xi'an as a possible seat of the Italian-Chinese conservation center. Now that it appeared as if the Italians were going to be packing their bags and leaving Xi'an, the cultural authorities of Luoyang perceived an opportunity to get much-needed help from the Italians for their monuments. Luoyang is the location of the Longmen Caves, one of the most important sites of Buddhist art in the world. The director of the caves was the leader of the Luoyang delegation; he was accompanied by his chief archeologist.

Rather than having us take the train, which would have taken less time, the Luoyang officials insisted on coming to pick us up by car and driving us back the same eight-hour route the following day. It was not clear if this was an example of extreme Chinese courtesy or a kind of holiday from their normal work routine in which they could commandeer banquets on the state expense account and be chauffeured around in big black cars marked VIP with tinted windows. Certainly, the objective of the trip was not to provide an opportunity to discuss the problems of Luoyang's artistic patrimony. Cordaro and I were put in one car, while the Chinese and our interpreter drove off in the other. After a few hours, we reconvened at lunch—an opportunity, I had hoped, to finally question some Chinese archeologists about their work.

We were an art conservator, a journalist, two archeologists, an interpreter, a Chinese student, and two drivers merely having a roadside lunch, but the meal, like every other meal we had on our trip, was

treated as a formal banquet, with highly elaborate protocol and a carefully choreographed seating arrangement. Although the table was
round, there was invariably a place of honor, marked by a glass with a
napkin folded into the form of a dragon—symbol of the emperor. The
rest of us lowly mortals would have to settle for napkins in the form of
lotus flowers. The most important Chinese official present would
invariably sit at this little "dragon throne." Each new plate brought to
the table would be placed in front of the ranking Chinese official—the
fish pointing toward him. He would be expected to touch the food first
or offer it to someone else. Generally Cordaro would be seated to his
left, and the second most important member of the Chinese delegation
to his right. I would be seated next to Cordaro and our interpreter
would be seated next to the second most important Chinese official.
The other Chinese would fill out the rest of the table in descending
order of rank. All of this Mandarin ceremony in our meetings and banquets made it clear that while the past in China may be invisible it is certainly not dead. (Rather than eliminating the old imperial bureaucracy,
which assigned each civil servant a specific grade, Mao's China expanded
and universalized the system so that, since everyone was a government
employee, everyone in society was assigned a rank between one and
thirty, which determined everything from the kind of apartment one
lived in to the kind of train seat one could sit in.)

After we were seated and food had been brought, I asked our interpreter if I might ask some questions. He shot me a dirty look. "Not
now," he said. "Later, later." I looked at Cordaro. "I think for them it
is impolite to mix business and pleasure," he explained. "And this is
pleasure—or is supposed to be. Perhaps this evening, after they've had a
lot to drink, or tomorrow when we go to see the Buddhist grottoes."

The director of the Longmen Caves, a small but vital-looking man
in his late fifties or early sixties, was famous for his love of making toasts
and his ability to drink people under the table. And every five minutes,
he would stand up and lift his glass of Chinese schnapps, saying, "Gam-
bei!"—the Chinese equivalent of "Cheers"—in a spirited fashion, as if he
were challenging someone to a duel. The person to whom he addressed

the toast would have to rise and drain his glass. Apart from the continual toasts, the Chinese did not address a word to either Cordaro or me, talking animatedly among themselves.

The strange ritual of the banquet was repeated every lunch and dinner for three days running. With each banquet, we would be introduced to another local official from Luoyang, a notch or two up the political pecking order, who would then host the next banquet, occupying the position at table with the dragon napkin, serving the greatest delicacies, and leading the toasts. With each meal, the number and quality of the plates would increase. The table would expand, so that the "emperor" of the previous banquet would slide over a seat or two, sitting among the lotus flowers.

Eventually, I was able to ask a few questions about China's attitudes toward its antiquities. Invariably, I received extremely banal, standard replies: "China's rich and glorious past is extremely important to us and must be safeguarded." "The development of the country must proceed together with the protection of our cultural heritage." "The government has enacted strong laws to make sure this occurs." One seemingly innocuous question on my part appeared, however, to cause some consternation: "Is China's sudden attention to protecting its antiquities related in some way to its process of modernization? In other words, do you think it is particularly important, in this moment when China has opened itself to the West, that it act in order to protect its own cultural identity?" At each banquet, the presiding Chinese official suggested that this question would be better answered by someone of greater wisdom and experience than himself.

Finally, I was passed off to the mayor of Luoyang, who would be hosting the final banquet and who had agreed to meet with us first. We met in one of the principal hotels of the city in a sitting room filled with arm chairs. The seating was once again arranged down to the last person. Cordaro and I were placed strategically on either side of an empty arm chair, designated for the mayor. The preparation, anxious protocol, and arm chairs reminded me of photographs of Nixon's visit to China, with the president and Kissinger seated in arm chairs in the company of Mao and Zhou Enlai. Our interpreter was distraught when he heard that I did not have business cards with me to exchange with the mayor and his deputies, an unvarying ritual in each new encounter in China. I raced upstairs to my hotel room to get them, to the universal relief of the assembled company. I was told to have my questions ready because we would have only about twenty minutes with the mayor, who was a very busy man.

When he finally arrived, however, rather than soliciting questions, the mayor insisted on making a welcoming speech. I had hoped this would be a brief formality. But to my horror, the speech went on and on, with the usual platitudes about the antiquity and beauty of Luoyang, the importance of international cooperation and friendship. I sat there clutching a piece of paper with my questions scribbled on it, feeling a growing sense of the occasion's comic absurdity: this modest interview in a provincial Chinese city being conducted as if it were the Nixon-Mao summit. Equally acutely, I felt the absurdity of my own desperate desire to wrench some profound insight about the nature of China through an interview. I realized that I was not going to get an answer to my questions—and perhaps there was none. Indeed, when I finally asked them, I was handed a copy of a speech the mayor had given, the English title of which renders its flavor and content: "Protect and Develop the Famous City of Luoyang and Bring It to a More Splendid Future."

As we sat through another banquet, with the mayor occupying the dragon throne and making toasts, Cordaro offered me the consolation of a similar experience from his first trip to China. He had found himself at a state banquet in Beijing seated next to a prominent Chinese historian whom he hoped to question about China's culture and history. The man stopped him short with a cryptic story: A European journalist arrived in China with the intention of staying a month in order to write a book. When the time elapsed, he decided to stay for another month and write an article. At the end of the second month, he decided to stay for a third and ended up writing nothing. "And so I decided not to try to understand too much about China, just to try to understand a small piece of it—the world of conservation," Cordaro said.

In fact, infinitely more instructive was our visit to the monuments of Luoyang. The morning after our arrival, we were taken to examine the Longmen Caves. An entire cliff side about a kilometer long and rising up about one hundred feet along the banks of the Yellow River has been sculpted with 2,345 caves with an estimated hundred thousand images of the Buddha. From a distance, the complex of grottoes and niches in the honey-colored limestone looks like a beehive of rock. Carved between A.D. 483 and about 1000, the Buddhas range in size from only a few inches to one that is about the size of a ten-story building. The quality of the sculptures—the work of countless hands over five hundred years— is varied. But the best work is some of the finest sculpture in the world. Ironically, the largest sculptural complex, the Fengxianshi cave, a massive group of eleven gigantic statues, with a Buddha more than fifty feet tall, is among the most delicately carved and expressive of all. Like an immovable center, the Buddha sits in the middle, his eyes downcast in serene contemplation; his beautifully delineated features and the harmony of his proportions make him seem both remarkably human and otherworldly. Other figures on the sides of the group—a Heavenly King nimbly crushing a demon with an elegant swagger and a muscular thirty-foot Vajra warding off evil with an angry expression and eyes that seem to shoot lightning—introduce a note of animation and earthly passion that balances the unmoving equilibrium of the Buddha. Cordaro had seen pictures of the grottoes, but they had not prepared him for the scale and beauty of the site. "This is truly a work of world importance and it must be protected," he said.

There was a steady rain that day, which proved lucky in terms of understanding the grottoes' conservation problems. Water was everywhere, inside and outside the caves, running along the walls and the statues. The builders of the caves had cleverly dug drainage tunnels into the hillside to relieve flooding, but many of the tunnels had not worked for centuries. Because Luoyang was transformed into a major industrial city after the Communist Revolution, the water that eats away at the statues' surfaces contains acid rain. Many of the figures were originally painted, and dabs of red pigment stick tenaciously to the statues amid rivulets of water. "The amazing thing is not how much has been lost but the fact that there is any paint left at all," said Cordaro, whose large, somewhat awkward-seeming body suddenly became alert as he clambered around the caves studying details. Some of the grottoes have a coating that the craftsmen of the Tang dynasty (A.D. 618-907) applied to prevent wind and water erosion. But no one knows any longer what the coating consists of. The chemists at the conservation center in Xi'an are studying samples under their microscopes, hoping to unravel this mystery, which could be crucial to giving the grottoes another thousand years of life.

Before intervening, Cordaro said, it would be necessary to conduct a geological survey of the whole cliff area to understand more about its structure and makeup. The Chinese inserted a protective layer at the top of the cliff, but that only served to redirect the water so that it entered the caves from the sides and not from above. Because the sculptures have held up remarkably well under large amounts of water, trying to dry out the entire cliff might actually be risky. "We need to understand what its effect would be," Cordaro explained.

Hundreds of the statues are missing their heads, either because of intentional defacement during periods when the Chinese tried to suppress Buddhism as a foreign importation or through the systematic depredation of Western colonialists at the beginning of the century. The director of the grottoes pointed to various niches and said, "This is in the Louvre in Paris, that one is in the Metropolitan Museum, this other one is in a museum in Tokyo. . . . "

In one grotto, we saw a Buddha that had been recarved early in the twentieth century, so that it no longer held its hand up in a gesture of blessing and now sported a typical Taoist hair style. The restoration work was carried out under the direction of the last empress dowager, who favored Taoism over Buddhism. "What would you, as a conservator, do?" Cordaro asked a student from the Xi'an conservation center who had accompanied us on the trip. "Would you restore the sculpture to a Buddhist work or leave the twentieth-century invention that transformed it into a Taoist monument?" Sensing a trick question, the student stalled.

"This is a very complex question," the student said. "I need much time to consider it."

Since Luoyang has many great original artworks, it is beginning to see the value in protecting them, if for no other reason than to promote tourism. Already, about one million people a year come to see the Longmen Buddhist grottoes, making it the third most popular tourist site after the Forbidden City in Beijing and the terra-cotta army in Xi'an. Given that Luoyang's massive factories, built during the Stalin period in the 1950s, are now laying off more and more workers as they strive to compete in the new market economy, the officials of Luoyang see tourism as a way of creating a service economy to replace the dying manufacturing base.

But the Chinese art authorities are just becoming accustomed to Western museum culture. In the local museum, copies and original pieces are intermingled without any indication. And when we were there, the authorities of Luoyang were busy preparing a series of copies of some of the more famous sculptures in a hard plastic that looks almost like bronze. They were destined for a show in Japan. Because the Japanese have their own culture of the copy, they are often perfectly open to exhibiting well-made replicas.

The day after our arrival in Luoyang, our hosts took us to see the Luoyang Museum of the Tombs, the place in which the city has decided to display many of its most important recent archeological discoveries. The Museum of the Tombs is located near a number of archeological sites that date back more than two thousand years. Having painstakingly dismantled some twenty ancient tombs, they reassembled them in the museum. But in doing so, they made a rather unusual choice. Instead of placing them in a temperature- and humidity-controlled environment aboveground, they rebuilt the tombs underground, lining them up in a row along a dank basement corridor to re-create the atmosphere of an actual tomb complex. A potentially suggestive form of display, perhaps, but a disaster from a conservation point of view. The whole point of removing them from their original underground site was to protect them from excessive humidity, but by taking them apart and placing them underground, the museum has actually aggravated the problem dramatically. The tombs are small, generally about ten or fifteen feet long by six feet wide; as a result, they fill up with humidity like saunas, the frescoed walls literally dripping with water. Under these conditions, allowing visitors into the tombs is particularly bad for them: opening and closing the doors to the tombs constantly changes the relative humidity, making the frescoed surfaces expand and contract. One could see flakes of paint curling from the ceiling, about to fall. Moreover, since the tombs have no artificial lighting, one visits the frescoes with candles, glimpsing works of considerable beauty: ancient emperors riding chariots, a parade of chimerical animals, astronomical paintings of stars and constellations, copulating dragons, fierce tomb guardians warding off evil, portraits of a husband and wife, a painting of a woman peering out from behind a trompe l'oeil window. Seeing these fading figures of a vanished world by flickering candlelight is extremely poignant but the smoke and heat are bad for the fresco surfaces.

From photographs, one could tell that the color of the paint had already faded dramatically in the five years the museum has been open. The presence of visitors—the opening and shutting of the doors, the humidity of human breath, and the candles—has aggravated an already bad situation. The response has been to close most of the tombs to the public—entirely defeating the original purpose of the museum. Even closed, their condition underground gets steadily worse. The museum made another disastrous decision by building a large cement piazza right above the tombs. "Cement as a material doesn't 'breathe,'" Cordaro explained, "so the humid air is trapped underground.

"The problems begin for tombs when you expose them to the air," Cordaro said. "When they are closed, they are humid but the relative humidity is constant. Then you open and close them. At this point, my advice would be to just leave them open."

Throughout the visit, Cordaro kept shaking his head in disbelief, with a mixture of amusement and horror. "To dismantle underground tombs and re-create them underground. This is the quintessence of China: they have created a copy out of something real, a fake underground tomb out of a real one! If they wanted to reassemble the tombs, they could have at least placed them aboveground."

The Chinese archeologist who excavated most of the tombs recognized the gravity of the situation, acknowledging that although he had the pieces of another tomb already disassembled in boxes. After seeing the deterioration of the other tombs, he hesitated to rebuild it underground. Cordaro asked if we could see some of the fragments of the disassembled tomb. "I will show them to you if you promise not to be angry with me," the archeologist said humorously. Museum workmen hauled several large wooden cases from out of a storeroom and opened them with a crowbar. Inside were hundreds of small pieces of delicately painted frescoes in brilliantly preserved reds, blacks, and whites. "They're perfect," Cordaro said, noting the astonishing contrast with the badly faded colors of the reassembled tombs. The original color on the other tombs had been just as strong, meaning that the tombs placed underground had lost about half their paint in less than ten years. "Leave them here for now and don't rebuild any more tombs underground," Cordaro advised. "That is the strangest museum I've ever seen," he said as we left.

The following morning, our Luoyang hosts took us to see what was perhaps an even more extraordinary site: a wooden Qing dynasty house completed in 1733 that had, miraculously, never been restored or rebuilt. A walled compound with four pavilions spaced across three internal courtyards, the building complex had been a merchants' guild hall during the imperial era. The house was dilapidated, the wood infested with termites, but its ornamentation was almost perfectly intact and infinitely more elaborate and beautiful than any of the remade ancient buildings we had seen. The thatch work of the eaves was not just an architectural detail but genuine sculpture in wood, like the flying buttresses of a Gothic cathedral; the finials were fashioned into the form of writhing serpents or roaring dragons; the latticework was carved like lace into the form of peonies and birds. The wood beams on the ceilings were painted in astonishing vermilions, lapis lazulis, and gold-leaf colors—more brilliant and yet more subtle than anything in the Forbidden City. There was a remarkable glazed terra-cotta emblem of a dragon and a phoenix—

simultaneously a painting and a sculpture—on a level with the ceramic sculptural work of the Della Robbia brothers in Renaissance Florence.

Since the 1949 revolution, the building had become the No. 7 Middle School, the main reception hall used for Ping-Pong and the central courtyard as a recreation yard, with rusting basketball rims at either end. The school had been closed a few years earlier and plants were growing up out of the tiles of the rooftops. Yet this rare, happy instance of benign neglect had been the building's salvation.

After seeing all the crude modern reconstructions of ancient buildings, we suddenly had the sensation of finally looking at the real thing. "How many houses are there like this in China?" Cordaro asked. "Very, very few," our hosts replied. "You have a unique historical document here," Cordaro said. The excitement of discovery was tempered by the realization of how much has been lost in China: if a merchants' guild hall in a provincial city was this elaborate and beautiful, what must the more important buildings—like the Forbidden City or the Summer Palace—have been before they were restored and repainted?

"As a conservation job, this is so easy as to be banal," Cordaro said. "The structure is in almost perfectly preserved condition. You need to do as little as possible to protect what's already here. Get rid of the termites, plug the leaks in the roof, and apply a consolidant to the wood to keep it from disintegrating any further. Above all, we have to prevent them from 'restoring' it." The Luoyang cultural authorities who have now taken charge of the building handed us a fact sheet about it that included some alarming suggestions for its restoration: "The major components of the halls have been seriously damaged. It is suggested that all the wooden components outspreading in the open be replaced with new ones. . . . Restore all colored drawing."

"I would love to do this, but I just don't know if they would allow an Italian team to actually be in charge," Cordaro said, looking around the courtyard.

As China tries increasingly to attract Western tourists to its cities and as its museums deal with their colleagues overseas, it is having to grapple, inevitably, with Western notions of authenticity, originality, and conservation. When we visited one provincial museum, I noticed a series of "bronze" pieces that looked distinctly like copies. The director of the museum readily explained that the original pieces were on loan overseas. When asked why he had not sent the copies for the show, the curator smiled and said that the curators had been very strict about wanting the originals.

The ramifications of moving from a culture of copying to a culture that prizes originality are anything but trivial. Recognizing the importance of the original hand of the artist involves accepting a Western individualistic culture that is against the grain of Chinese tradition. Indeed, the struggles of Cordaro—Western missionary of conservation—against copying and remaking are very much related to the problem Western businesses have getting the Chinese to stop pirating computer software, music CDs, and movie videos and pay copyright fees. "The Chinese do not have a particular sense of individual ownership of cultural monuments or of intellectual property," said Ken DeWoskin of the University of Michigan. "The great books of Chinese literature, *The Romance of the Three Kingdoms* or *The Dream of the Red Chamber*, have been rewritten many times. There are different versions by different authors; some might have a happy ending, others not. This is true of Chinese monuments, as well. The things you see—the Great Wall, the Forbidden City, and the tomb of the terra-cotta army in Xi'an—are monuments of collective labor, monuments to the Chinese ability to organize massive amounts of labor, rather than expressions of individual genius like Michelangelo's Sistine Chapel or Leonardo's *Last Supper*." Teaching Western art preservation—teaching respect for the original object and individual expression—is not a culturally neutral act. It involves a set of subtle assumptions about the nature of the past, individual expression, and individual rights.

The current Chinese leadership seems to believe that it can pursue a market economy without giving up political power and accepting the whole package of capitalist democracy. But as other nations who have tried to create an Asian economic and political model have found, it is very difficult to order à la carte from the menu of capitalism; it seems to come with a fixed menu and a fixed price. Countries like Indonesia and Malaysia were proud of having combined economic growth with authoritarian rule; but after their economies went into crisis in the late 1990s, lending organizations like the International Monetary Fund forced them to open up their economies, and they are under increasing pressure to allow greater political freedom. Could it be that Western notions of art conservation, landmark protection, and copyright law might be a Trojan horse that could open the citadel of human rights?

As we drove out of Luoyang, we passed through a sudden long stretch of uncultivated verdant fields. As in Xi'an, there are vast unexcavated parts of its ancient past, tombs of emperors and Chinese nobility. To its credit, the city of Luoyang has prevented any building near the archeological area, so the fields stretch for miles of brilliant green, with scores of grassy mounds, each probably a tomb, like a vast bumper crop of antiquities waiting to be harvested. "The cities are lost," said Cordaro, noting the monotonous drab squalor of modern Luoyang— indistinguishable from every other Chinese town we visited. But the richness of China's past, just underneath the belly of the soil, may mean that what we see today may not be what we see tomorrow. Chinese archeology is still in its infancy, about where Egyptology was in the middle of the nineteenth century, with many major discoveries ahead. Trying to create a portrait of China now is like photographing a bullet train in motion: whatever one describes will almost certainly be different in five or ten years. Already, the Soviet-style buildings of the 1950s and 1960s are dilapidated ruins, some abandoned, others ripe for the bulldozer. So, too, will the cement white-tiled boxes going up all around them be in twenty or thirty years—to be replaced, perhaps, with something better when China has more money and the luxury of better taste. What has gone will not return, but large segments of China's buried past—even entire terra-cotta cities and imperial courts—may yet emerge from underground.

3

Looting History

FROM THE HILL town of Aidone, about half a mile above sea level, you can see much of eastern Sicily. In the distance, almost at the sea, the snow-capped peak of Mount Etna dominates the landscape, its volcanic crater smoking and flaring. Stretching out beneath it are almost a hundred miles of rich, fertile farmland that drew a growing stream of Greek settlers from the sixth century B.C. onward until, about three hundred years later, the Romans conquered the area, making it the granary of their expanding realm. Burned brown in the summer, the valley is a lush green in wintertime and explodes into a riot of flowers during the spring. The dramatic beauty of its landscape inspired the Greek myth of the creation of the seasons: in these fields, by the lake of Pergusa, beautiful young Persephone was picking flowers when Pluto, god of the underworld, snatched her up and carried her off to the land of the dead. Persephone's mother, Demeter (Ceres to the Romans), grieved so prodigiously that the landscape withered into barrenness. After the intercession of Zeus, Persephone was allowed to spend half the year with her mother, while passing the winter in the underworld. Thus, with the return of Persephone each spring, Demeter, goddess of grain and plenty, would bring the world back to life.

Now, nearly three thousand years later, with Sicily's agriculture in severe decline, the area is the scene of a very different kind of harvest. "You see those holes," Giuseppe Mascara said proudly, pointing to the landscape of ancient settlements, pockmarked as a honeycomb. "I made them all." Coming from Mascara, a small, weather-beaten seventy-year-old with a scar across the bridge of his nose, this claim was more than an empty boast. Unofficially known as the chief of the local *tombaroli* (tomb robbers), he has been in and out of jail for nearly forty years for illegally digging up and trafficking in archeological objects and has some major finds to his credit. In 1968, when the American archeologist Malcolm Bell was a young graduate student, he brought his wife on their honeymoon to the site at Morgantina, the ancient Greek city that lies just below the modern town of Aidone. Suddenly, Bell noticed that somebody had cleared away a piece of hillside, uncovering what looked like the entrance of a tomb. In a state of both excitement and apprehension, Bell and his wife returned with the *carabinieri* and found Mascara and two other men standing in the open door of a tomb filled with about 250 Greek vases and artifacts. The other two fled, but Mascara didn't move. "He could easily have escaped but it was as if he were awestruck by what he had found," Bell explained. "He had discovered what is still the largest tomb at Morgantina. It took us the rest of the summer to excavate it."

The contents of what is informally known as the "Mascara tomb"—including a beautiful terra-cotta statue of a Siren—are in the little museum of Aidone, but catching a *tombarolo* in the act is rare and thousands of objects from Morgantina have found their way into the black market of antiquities.

The great fortune of Morgantina, as compared with other major Greek cities in Sicily, is to have been largely abandoned during the first century A.D. and left almost completely undisturbed for about nineteen hundred years. Many other ancient cities became the sites of more modern towns, so that their monuments were dismantled and built over and their buried treasures dug up years ago. The inhabitants of this area retreated from the valley and built a fortified town during the Middle Ages atop the cone-shaped hill that became the modern town of

Aidone, overlooking the ancient site. Scholars knew of the existence of Morgantina from literary sources but had no idea exactly where it was until Princeton University began systematic excavations in 1955. The area was mostly open fields with a sprinkling of farmhouses. From the fields gradually emerged the ancient Greek agora, or main square, ringed by a grand trapezoidal stairway and containing shops, the foundations of temples and houses with mosaic floors, as well as an elegant limestone theater that was used for dramatic performances and as the political heart of the city. Morgantina, with its entire city plan virtually intact, sits surrounded by olive groves, cyprus trees, and rolling green fields as far as the eye can see, giving one a feeling of a rural Greek city that has been only recently abandoned by its inhabitants.

Morgantina was the last Greek city in Sicily to hold out against the Romans in the third century B.C. Preparing for the arrival of the Roman army, the inhabitants buried all their treasures, sacred objects, and money. Diggers have found entire hoards of Greek coins buried below the floor of an ancient house. This almost virgin archeological site was a boon for both archeologists and *tombaroli*.

In the 1950s, Aidone was a place of such poverty that during the winter, when there was no agricultural work available, the men would pass entire months in bed in order to consume as few calories as possible. And yet, a few began to make an overnight fortune through clandestine digging. Everyone in Aidone remembers the dramatic rise and fall of a *tombarolo* called Mangialepri (Rabbit Eater). One day a farmer came to Mangialepri with an ancient Greek coin he had found by chance. The *tombarolo* told him it was nothing special but asked to see where the man had found it. Mangialepri and his son returned at night and apparently found a vast quantity of rare ancient coins. Not long afterward, he built for himself one of the grandest houses in Aidone. At the end of his life, however, Mangialepri, grown rich and arrogant, was literally beaten to death with sticks by a crowd of old women from the town for having insulted a group of children.

The rise and fall of Mangialepri demonstrates—along with the violent and elemental nature of life in central Sicily—the ephemeral gains of looting. Most of the objects and profits have left the area, and Aidone remains poor, having lost a third of its population to emigration in the last twenty years. With the official unemployment rate at 35 percent, the draw of "night digging" remains overwhelming.

Walking through the main square of Aidone, a town of about six thousand, I passed two ordinary workingmen having an animated conversation of which I overheard the phrase *reperti archeologici* (archeological objects). Antiquities are to this part of Sicily what oil is to the Texas panhandle. Along with being a great economic resource, the presence of the past at Morgantina and other ancient sites in eastern Sicily appears to have gotten into people's bloodstream. Most families, even poor ones, have a few small ancient vases, pot shards, or coins in their homes. Virtually everyone in the area fancies himself an amateur archeologist or historian. A clerk in the town hall of Aidone has written two histories of ancient Morgantina, one of them two hundred pages long, the other three pages, as well as a two-page epic poem in doggerel. "Sicily is full of eccentrics," Bell said. Giuseppe Mascara insists that, at a certain point, it was a genuine love of archeology and not a desire for lucre that kept him digging for treasure, despite numerous arrests and the frustrations of having some of his biggest scores confiscated by police. "It's a passion. It's stronger than I am," he said, while claiming that he is now retired from the business. "My eyes are no good anymore," he added, by way of explanation. Still, his house is filled with books about ancient history, and especially about ancient coins. He, too, is working on a history of ancient Morgantina: he showed me a typed manuscript of about twenty pages.

Thirty-one years after catching Mascara in the act of opening "his" tomb, Bell and Mascara were both still here, but they avoided each other. Mascara is still bitter over the incident in 1968 when Bell prevented him from making off with one of his biggest hauls. Bell, for his part, does not want to be associated with a *tombarolo*, for fear that it would compromise his position as director of the site's legal excavation. Indeed, it would be difficult to find two people less obviously alike. Bell, is a small, slight man in his midfifties with a gray beard and wire-rim

glasses, a classical scholar from an old, distinguished family from Savan-
nah, Georgia, who has taught archeology at the University of Virginia
for the past twenty-eight years. He is a man honest to the point of rigidity, working in a world with a highly elastic sense of legality. With an
ascetic spirit more Spartan than Athenian, Bell insists on sleeping in the
heatless headquarters of the excavation house up in Aidone, which,
because of the altitude, is freezing cold in winter.

And yet both Bell and Mascara share an intense interest in Morgantina. Bell has a grudging admiration for the old tomb robber. "He has a
good eye," Bell said. In the age before the metal detector, *tombaroli* like
Mascara needed to understand something about the layout of the
ancient city in order to suss out likely digging spots.

In a small town where everyone knows everyone else, they are intensely aware of each other and curious to know what the other knows.
The *tombaroli* watch the archeologists for hints of interesting places to dig
and, in turn, they sometimes pass on informal useful information about
clandestine digging. When someone in the area makes a major find,
word travels quickly. The person who discovers an object may show it to
other *tombaroli* out of pride or to better understand what it is and what it's
worth.

Recently, the Italian government began using the combined work of
the *tombarolo* and the archeologists to recover a handful of major pieces
believed to have come from Morgantina that now sit in museums and
collections in the United States.

If Bell and Mascara are at opposite poles of the archeology of Morgantina, Vincenzo Cammarata evidently built one of the greatest collections of ancient art in Sicily by moving between their two different
worlds.

Little was known about Cammarata—outside of Sicily and the rar-
efied subculture of antiquities—until the morning of December 6,1998,
when about fifteen police officers from Catania conducted a raid of his
home in Enna, the provincial capital of the area, about twenty miles
from Aidone. According to news accounts, the police were so stunned

by the quantity of artifacts in the house—cases of Greek vases, marble statues, terra-cotta figurines, theatrical masks, Roman sarcophagi, ancient arms, tools and coins numbering in the tens of thousands—that Cammarata was able to escape on his motorbike and eluded arrest until he turned himself in the following day.

They also raided his eighteenth-century country villa about ten miles from Morgantina, overlooking the other great archeological treasure of the area, the Roman imperial villa at Piazza Armerina, with its acres of perfectly preserved mosaic floors. As if in imitation of his ancient Roman neighbors, Cammarata has attached an alley of Roman-style columns to his home. He even has a collection of medieval instruments of torture, which he keeps in a thirteenth-century castle he purchased several years ago.

Cammarata is a man for whom the lure of antiquity is simply overpowering. "I am not a Sicilian. I am an ancient Greek. I have Greek blood in my veins!" he told friends when explaining his passion for Greek antiquities. Fifty at the time of his arrest, he appears to be a combination of a genuinely knowledgeable and highly cultivated scholar, a classic Sicilian eccentric, and a swashbuckling adventurer. He led people to believe he was a baron, even though his family did not in fact have a noble title.

"He is the closest thing I have met to a Medici prince on the hoof," said Ross Holloway, a professor of ancient history at Brown University. The two saw each other during the 1970s and 1980s at international numismatics conferences. "When I knew him more than ten years ago, he had a very dramatic, aristocratic appearance—tall, slender, handsome, with aquiline features and raven-black hair. He was a very sporty fellow and had been on the Italian water polo team," he added. "There is an entire shadow world of numismatics," said Holloway. "Alongside the academics, there is the world of dealers and collectors." Cammarata was a strange hybrid figure: at numismatics conferences, other scholars would refer to pieces in museums; Cammarata would illustrate his points by taking precious ancient coins out of his briefcase. He was widely rumored to sell as well as buy ancient coins, which everyone in numismatics knows is against Italian law. He was also arrested once in Switzerland for selling false ancient coins. (He was released after returning the buyer's money.) "Cammarata sort of supported the rumors that were going around about him," Holloway recalled. "He tried hard to give you the impression that he knew more than he could tell, that he had not only knowledge but power." Living in eastern Sicily in the middle of one of the richest archeological zones, Cammarata wanted people to believe that he had his finger on all the major clandestine finds.

Cammarata has been charged with being the head of an antiquities smuggling ring that included two Sicilian university professors, the owner of a major auction house, and two well-known businessmen—all of them prominent collectors. "From our investigations we have discovered the existence of a genuine criminal organization dedicated to the recovery and trafficking of archeological objects, in which unsuspectable members of the 'good' society of Catania and Enna are a part," prosecutors wrote in a court document justifying the arrests. Snippets of wiretapped conversations quoted in court papers show that some of the defendants were well acquainted with the tombaroli of Aidone and hovered over the site of Morgantina like flies around a honey pot.

After years of only sporadic efforts to halt the looting of archeological sites, Italian authorities have decided to target collectors and not just tombaroli, on the theory that only by stopping the demand for artifacts can they reduce the supply. Moreover, Cammarata—alone among the defendants—is charged with maintaining ties not just with tombaroli but with full-fledged gangsters. "The novelty of this investigation is the clear presence of the Mafia in the trafficking of antiquities," said Luigi Lombardo, the investigating magistrate in the case. The worldwide trade in illicit antiquities is estimated to be worth between $2 billion and $6 billion a year—third in size after drugs and arms among the world's black markets. Single pieces from Sicily have sold for millions of dollars. "This was too large a business to go unnoticed and unexploited by Cosa Nostra," Lombardo said. "The Mafia has realized that here in Sicily our greatest resource is our rich history and archeological past."

Shortly after the arrests, questions emerged: how had a private individual in a country where it is illegal to buy or sell antiquities that were dug up after 1909 (the year of Italy's first antiquities law) been able to assemble such a collection? Although the police in Catania may have been surprised by the extent of the collection, many others were not. Cammarata had shown his collection to scholars, foreign dignitaries, judges, prosecutors, and members of parliament. And parts of his collection had been displayed in three separate exhibitions in Sicily in recent years. Moreover, Cammarata had taken steps to register his collection with local antiquities officials and was making plans to create a museum.

Cammarata has insisted that his collection is legitimate, and some of it no doubt is. It is perfectly legal to buy antiquities from older Italian collections that were assembled before the 1909 law. And Cammarata is known for buying up old Sicilian collections to keep them from being dispersed. Since most private collections are not registered with the government (as is required) it will be extremely difficult for prosecutors to tell which pieces were acquired legitimately and which may have come from other sources. But given that Cammarata has no stable profession, prosecutors suspect that he must have been selling pieces in order to afford his own prodigious collecting habits.

They hope that as the key figure in the case and the only defendant who was allegedly on close terms with everyone—*tombaroli*, scholars, collectors, international dealers, and mafiosi—Cammarata can illuminate the darker corners of the international antiquities trade. And Cammarata, after his arrest, hinted that he has much to tell, saying he was in "possession of a dossier about all these things that will make Italy tremble." But despite months in prison, he has refused to cooperate with prosecutors—an attitude he has continued to maintain as he awaits trial.

Potentially, at least, the case could make people in the United States nervous as well. Italian authorities maintain that Sicilian *tombaroli* dug up and sold several major ancient masterpieces that now sit in the glass cases of major museums or in the living rooms of important American collectors. A little of what Cammarata knows has trickled out over the years.

Nearly twenty years ago, long before he was under investigation, Cammarata could not help bragging to Ross Holloway: "You Americans at Morgantina didn't find everything." He told Holloway that he had seen a Greek female head that was as beautiful as the sculptures from the

Parthenon in Athens, as well as two rather extraordinary archaic heads with matching hands and feet.

"Cammarata said he had seen them at an antiquarian's shop in Gela—of course, we all know what that means," said Holloway.

Looting at Morgantina escalated dramatically in the 1970s when portable metal detectors became widely available and it had reached a fever pitch by the time Bell became director of the site in 1980. Since the official excavations generally occur in summer, the rest of the year the archeologists must rely on local personnel, who are undermanned, underpaid, and subject to the pressures of living in a community in which antiquities are big business. The archeological area at Morgantina is nearly two hundred acres and in the 1970s and 1980s there was no nighttime security detail. Beyond the boundaries of the official site of the ancient city are at least another four hundred acres of important archeological territory, including the ancient cemeteries—most in private hands, all entirely unsupervised.

Shortly after his arrival, Bell heard persistent rumors about an exceptional find the *tombaroli* had made a couple of years earlier: two life-sized heads of marble, with corresponding hands and feet but no bodies. In certain Greek colonies, such as Sicily, that had a short supply of fine marble, artists would create or import what are known as "acrolithic" statues whose visible parts—head, feet, and hands—were made of stone, while the rest was made of wood or terra-cotta and clothed in drapery. Moreover, the heads had a highly singular look that impressed itself on the people who saw them: the faces were almost triangular, with almond-shaped eyes hollowed out in the stone and strange, enigmatic smiles—typical of certain archaic Greek sculptures from the late sixth and early fifth centuries B.C.

On the basis of the rumors, the Italian government conducted an excavation where the find had supposedly occurred. The archeologists uncovered obvious signs of recent looting, the remains of what appeared to be a sanctuary to Persephone and Demeter, and fragments in terracotta from a large-scale sculptural group, but no heads, hands, or feet. In 1980, the London art dealer Robin Symes bought two acrolithic sculptures in Switzerland that perfectly matched the description of those seen at Morgantina a year earlier, and sold them to New York diamond merchant Maurice Templesman.

When Bell returned to dig in the summer of 1981, he heard more distressing rumors, this time about *"un servizio di argento,"* a silver service. The following year, the Metropolitan Museum in New York bought the first of two installments of a fifteen-piece Greek silver treasure for $2.7 million, which its curators describe as "some of the finest Hellenistic silver known from Magna Graecia." The silver treasure, which includes a small receptacle for the burning of incense, was clearly used for religious purposes, although since it contains bowls and ladles it is easy to see how the *tombaroli* of Aidone might have referred to it as "a silver service." The Metropolitan's silver is full of Sicilian visual motifs: one of its most extraordinary pieces is a delicately worked sculptural relief of Scylla, the girl who was turned into a horrible sea monster and took her revenge by attacking sailors off the eastern coast of Sicily. The Met catalog entry about the treasure is vague about its origins. It says that the hoard "was presumably found together a generation ago" and that it was produced either in "Taranto or in Eastern Sicily" in the second half of the third century B.C.

The Metropolitan put the silver on display in 1984 in a niche off its main lobby. Bell did not know about it until he visited the museum in 1987. He immediately suspected that this was the same silver service he had been hearing about at Morgantina. People there had remarked in particular on seeing two silver horns, which may have originally been attached to a leather helmet. The Met silver also contains two silver horns. "They were the key because they are so unusual," Bell said.

At the same time, Bell passed on the descriptions of the acrolithic sculptures to friends in the field and heard from a colleague that pieces that fit his descriptions were being offered to the Getty Museum.

Bell brought all the information he had gathered on the silver and the acroliths to the attention of a prosecutor in Enna, Silvio Raffiotta, who would become Bell's valued ally and close friend in the attempt to curb looting. Raffiotta grew up in Aidone and his parents have a farmhouse right on the archeological site of Morgantina. Partly under Bell's influence, he caught the archeological bug and he, too, set about writing a history of Morgantina (which was actually published). While beginning to develop a case for the return of the silver and the acroliths, Raffiotta also opened a massive investigation of some fifty *tombaroli*, at whose center was Giuseppe Mascara.

As Bell began to reestablish control over the site, he became the target of acts of vandalism: the window of his car was broken, the air was let out of his tires, an ancient vase on the site was smashed, and columns were knocked over. There were signs that the vandalism was an inside job, the work perhaps of people who were in cahoots with the *tombaroli* and were trying to send Bell a warning to back off. Suspicion fell on one particular administrator of the site who seemed to rule Morgantina like a feudal lord or rural Mafia boss, demanding that the custodians bring him fresh ricotta cheese from their sheep as a kind of baronial tribute. When the administrator was transferred, the vandalism stopped and the looting appeared to diminish significantly.

After Mascara was arrested in early 1988, he began to tell Raffiotta about some of the more important antiquities he had seen dug up at Morgantina, in the hope of receiving a lighter sentence. He described both the acroliths and the Metropolitan silver in considerable detail.

In the summer of 1988, the Getty unveiled the Templesman sculptures together with an extraordinary statue of a Greek goddess thought to represent Aphrodite or Nike, for which the Getty had paid the fabulous sum of $28 million. The sudden appearance of such important and unusual pieces from twenty-five hundred years ago created an immediate sensation—and scandal. Thomas Hoving, the former director of the Metropolitan Museum, who was then the editor of *Connoisseur* magazine, published an exposé maintaining that all the statues had been dug up illegally at Morgantina. Hoving, who had excavated at Morgantina as a graduate student in the 1950s, maintained close ties with the area. As director of the Met, he hired men from Aidone as museum security guards and these contacts have kept him abreast of the news from the clandestine grapevine in Sicily.

Amid the brouhaha that followed the news coverage, the Templesman acroliths suddenly disappeared from the Getty gallery. The museum would reveal only that the sculptures had been returned to their owner, an anonymous private collector who was later identified as Templesman (best known as the last companion of Jacqueline Kennedy Onassis). Many scholars have criticized the Getty for removing the pieces from display without allowing researchers to study them. The sculptures have not been seen in public since. The only images of the sculptures are a few snapshots taken during the short span they were on display at the Getty.

The Italian government, acting on Raffiotta's investigation, asked Templesman to return the acroliths and made a similar request to the Metropolitan for the silver. Templesman has consistently refused to discuss the matter and, until recently, offered only a brief statement through a public relations firm: "In 1980, Mr. Templesman purchased these acroliths from Robin Symes. He bought the sculptures from a reputable dealer and he is pretty convinced that they were acquired legitimately." The Metropolitan also refused to return the silver, insisting that it could not trust a convicted *tombarolo* like Mascara, who might be willing to tell prosecutors whatever they wanted to hear in order to stay out of jail. The Met had published an article with photographs about the treasure in a museum bulletin of 1984 and therefore Mascara could simply have described objects he had seen in photographs. But Raffiotta insists that he never showed Mascara any photographs of the objects. Moreover, Mascara accurately described the Templesman acroliths before they had ever been displayed publicly.

The museum maintains that it has no reason to doubt the word of the dealer who sold it the silver, who said he bought it in Switzerland from a family of Lebanese antique dealers who claim to have owned it for more than twenty years. However, the dealer, Robert Hecht, is hardly a man beyond all suspicion. He was expelled from both Italy and Turkey and declared persona non grata for allegedly smuggling antiquities. He is also the dealer who sold the Metropolitan one of its most famous and notorious antiquities, the Euphronios krater, which also supposedly came from a Lebanese art dealer. Thomas Hoving, who bought the krater for the

Metropolitan in 1971, now believes that it was looted from an Etruscan tomb. "It's like a sitcom rerun," Hoving commented, in response to the Met's embroilment in another controversy over another antiquity from Hecht with a shadowy Lebanese-Swiss provenance.

For a long time, the Metropolitan would not allow Malcolm Bell a closer examination of the treasure—a courtesy commonly extended by museums to scholars. Bell hoped to study inscriptions on the bottom of some of the pieces, in the hope that a peculiarity of the Greek dialect or script, for example, might help pin down where the objects came from.

One person who lent a hand to Raffiotta's investigation of the acroliths was Vincenzo Cammarata. The two are old friends. They both studied at the University of Catania and are part of a small cultural and intellectual elite in the province of Enna; both are also intensely interested in Sicily's ancient past. Cammarata acknowledged under oath what he had told Ross Holloway years earlier: that he had seen the statues while they were still in Italy. This time, however, he admitted that a *tombarolo* had brought them to his country villa and offered them to him for sale. Although Cammarata said he turned down the offer, the episode might have tipped prosecutors off to the fact that he was in the business. But Raffiotta said that Cammarata's name never came up in any of the wiretaps in the Mascara case.

Cammarata's own collecting came under scrutiny quite by accident in 1994 when investigators in the town of Termini Immerese, near Palermo, began to investigate the disappearance of some forty objects from their local museum. It turned out that the museum's director, Silvana Verga, had been selling them, and in the course of searching her apartment, police came upon photographs of a beautifully sculpted fourth-century Greek libation bowl, or phiale. The piece appeared to be highly singular: hammered into a pattern of acorns and beechnuts, it is more than twenty inches in diameter and more than two pounds of 24-karat gold. In the middle of the bowl is a large gold knob, representing the *omphalos*, or mythic navel of the world. A symbol of the earth's abundance, libation bowls were used frequently in Greek temples, but there is only one other golden phiale known to have survived antiquity. Somewhat lighter and made of an inferior grade of gold, it sits in the collection of the Metropolitan Museum.

Under questioning, Verga explained that she had seen the phiale at Cammarata's house. She said that he was interested in selling the piece and wanted to find an American buyer because he didn't think he could get more than 140 million lire (about $90,000) for it in Italy.

Cammarata claimed that he had acquired the bowl in about 1980 from another Sicilian collector, who said that it had been found by chance during the laying of electrical lines in the town of Caltavuturo, an ancient Greek settlement east of Palermo. Cammarata said he had doubts about its authenticity but traded about 30 million lire ($20,000) in other artifacts for it. (Cammarata had no record of the sale, however, and the other dealer is conveniently dead.)

Cammarata admitted selling the phiale to Michael Steinhardt, a well-known New York hedge fund manager, through a Swiss-based art dealer named William Veres. The Italian prosecutors asked for help from federal prosecutors in New York, who then documented exactly how the golden bowl was imported into the United States.

Veres had approached New York dealer Robert Haber, who had sold Steinhardt between twenty and thirty pieces of ancient art for a total of about $4 million to $6 million in the late 1980s and early 1990s. Steinhardt was interested and so, in November 1991, Haber traveled to Sicily to inspect the piece together with Veres. And on December 4, Steinhardt contracted to buy the bowl for about $1.2 million. Steinhardt claims that he knew little about the origins of the piece, except that its seller was "a Sicilian coin merchant." (Even a novice, however, knows that Italy has strict laws against the exporting of antiquities.)

Later that month, Haber flew to Switzerland and returned to New York with the bowl in his luggage. In January 1995, Steinhardt sent it for authentication to the Metropolitan Museum, of which he is a major benefactor. Gold sculpture, because it contains no organic material and cannot be carbon-tested, is difficult to date, but the Met judged the piece to be authentic. At that point, Steinhardt made the final payment on his $1.2 million purchase and began to display the piece on a grand piano in his living room, where it sat until it was seized by U.S. Customs in 1995.

Steinhardt has insisted that he is merely an "innocent buyer" who relied on a reputable dealer, but there is much that suggests that both he and Haber understood they were acting in violation of Italian antiquities laws. "To acquire the Phiale, Haber took great effort to ensure that the Phiale was not exported directly from Italy," wrote New York federal judge Barbara Jones. The vast majority of pieces reaching the U.S. market pass through Switzerland, which serves as a laundry for looted or stolen art. Swiss law automatically grants legal title to a work of art if its present owner can demonstrate that it has been on Swiss soil for at least five years. Thus, after spending the requisite time cooling off in a Swiss warehouse or bank vault (or after the backdating of paperwork), a piece can be sold in London or New York as coming "from a private collection in Europe."

Even though Haber had inspected the phiale in Sicily, he arranged to pick it up in Lugano, a Swiss town located just across the Italian border. As Judge Jones noted, Haber chose to fly in and out of Zurich, driving three hours back and forth across the Swiss Alps, rather than to and from Milan, which is a mere forty miles away from Lugano.

There is also evidence that Haber and Veres went to some lengths to create a phony Swiss provenance for the piece, which the Customs forms describe as coming from a private collection in Lausanne and having a value of $250,000—false statements that allowed Customs to seize the bowl. The contract included a curious clause stating that "a letter is to be written by Dr. Manganaro that he saw the object 15 years ago in Switz.," whereas Haber knew perfectly well the piece had been in Sicily just a month earlier. The clause referred to Professor Giacomo Manganaro, professor of ancient history and numismatics at the University of Catania, a former teacher and a close personal friend of Vincenzo Cammarata (he was Cammarata's best man). Although Manganaro denies he ever agreed to write any such letter, Haber and Veres evidently hoped that they could use Manganaro's academic reputation to help create a false provenance for the golden bowl.

Manganaro, who was seventy at the time of his arrest in 1998, was charged with being part of the antiquities smuggling ring. Cammarata and his long association suggests a symbiotic relationship: Cammarata gave Manganaro access to his vast collection of previously unknown coins and artifacts, allowing Manganaro to publish the first monographs on the rarest and most important pieces. The articles served as a feather in Manganaro's scholarly cap as well as lending value and professorial weight to the pieces. Prosecutors suspect that Cammarata may have ingratiated himself with Manganaro by letting him know about the availability of ancient artifacts that he knew the professor might like to buy.

Manganaro's professional prestige played a critical role in Cammarata's selling of the golden phiale. Although Cammarata now claims he thought the piece was a modern fake, in 1988 Manganaro published an article in a French scholarly journal presenting the phiale as an authentic Greek masterpiece from the fourth century B.C. Perhaps the strongest element of proof was that an ancient Greek inscription on the bowl could be fully understood only in the light of research into the ancient Doric dialect used in the area of Caltavuturo that was published after 1980. Therefore, Manganaro reasoned, it would have been impossible for even the most ingenious forger to have produced such an inscription during the 1970s when the first surfaced. The article declaring the authenticity of the phiale by one of the most respected experts on ancient Greek epigraphy dramatically increased the value of the piece. And it appears that Cammarata began to try to sell the piece only after Manganaro's article was published.

In 2000, the United States returned the phiale to Italy, establishing a precedent that could go a long way toward changing the legal landscape of art collecting. The United States, which in 1972 ratified a UNESCO treaty designed to prevent antiquities smuggling, has been increasingly sympathetic to foreign claims that regard all illegally exported cultural property as "stolen."

"In one fell swoop, it has taken a large step toward criminalizing the antiquities field," said Ashton Hawkins, former general counsel and vice president of the Metropolitan Museum.

Breaking ranks with other museums, the Getty—long reviled as the worst offender in the purchasing of undocumented antiquities—has joined forces with the archeologists in backing Italy in the Steinhardt case. If the American antiquities market has been governed by a "don't ask, don't tell," mind-set, the Getty now insists it is time for major museums and collectors to give up once and for all the purchase of antiquities without a clear and convincing history. In that spirit, Marion True, the museum's chief curator of antiquities, recently returned three major pieces to Italy after Italian authorities presented what the Getty felt was convincing proof that they had, in fact, been either stolen directly from Italian collections or looted from an Italian archeological site. The U.S. government has decided to accept this much more restrictive attitude. In early 2001, it signed a treaty with Italy stipulating that any antiquity entering the country has to have a clear provenance.

Cammarata, meanwhile, is in criminal court for exporting the golden bowl from Italy, even as he is facing a second, much more serious set of charges in the broader investigation of the alleged smuggling ring. This second case broke open in 1997 in the course of an investigation of the mafia in Caltanisetta, the province adjoining that of Enna. To the surprise of prosecutors, some of the mafiosi arrested in the case turned out to be *tombaroli* from the area around Enna and Aidone. Testifying as a witness for the state, one of them told prosecutors: "All the archeological pieces coming from the digs would be shown to Baron Cammarata, so that he could say whether he was interested in buying them or not."

Prosecutors placed taps on the telephones of Cammarata, Manganaro, and three other prominent Sicilian collectors. From the small amount of evidence that has so far been made public, there is little independent confirmation of contact with known mafiosi. The wiretapped conversations quoted in the prosecutors' request to keep the defendants in prison read more like the minutes of a coin collectors' club than the workings of a criminal organization. "The charge of racketeering is ridiculous," said Enrico Trantino, the lawyer for a Sicilian businessman who was found with a large collection of undocumented ancient coins. "I think it was used to justify a spectacular arrest that landed on the front page of the papers. The charge of buying illegal antiquities will be harder to defend. My client is a collector of ancient coins. Collecting is like a drug; it is stronger than he is."

Most of the defendants were found to be in possession of thousands of ancient coins and artifacts. Two defendants were found with metal detectors in their homes, and wiretaps reveal contact with *tombaroli* and trips to Aidone to see newly looted coins from Morgantina. Surveillance also showed that Cammarata, Manganaro, and another professor at the University of Catania met with "a trafficker in archeological materials who operates in Great Britain, yet to be identified, who was supposed to provide them with false receipts in order to lend 'apparent justification' of their receiving ancient artifacts from Cammarata."

One of the defendants, Gianfranco Casolari, who runs an auction house, is accused of producing false sales documents in order to give looted pieces a clean provenance. Although he lives in Rimini, in central Italy, his auction house is in the republic of San Marino, a tiny independent state inside Italian national territory that acts as a kind of tiny Switzerland within Italy.

After the arrest of Cammarata and his fellow collectors, prosecutors in Catania began to consider whether collusion among public officials had allowed him to avoid scrutiny in the past. Charges have been brought against Silvio Raffiotta, the chief prosecutor of Enna and the man who led the investigations into the Templesman acroliths and the Metropolitan silver.

The case against Raffiotta adds a bizarre Pirandellian twist to the story, offering two completely contradictory versions of reality. On the one hand, a Mafia witness claims to have participated in a meeting with both Cammarata and Raffiotta in which they were discussing the sale of antiquities. If that is true, then the chief legal defender of antiquities in Sicily would be the occult head of a smuggling ring. On the other hand, many, in particular Bell, find the accusations against Raffiotta absurd and incredible. "Silvio Raffiotta has done more than any other person to protect archeological sites in Sicily," he said.

Raffiotta himself insists he is probably being paid back for protecting archeological sites: recently he blocked the completion of a $60 million dam that would have flooded an ancient Roman site. "The least they can do is brand me as a *tombarolo*," he said.

Charges were brought against Raffiotta in 1999 and the case was still pending in late 2001. In the cauldron of provincial Sicilian life—where everyone is either lifelong friends or mortal enemies—the prosecutor could very well be the victim of a complex machination. "Nothing would surprise me," said a prosecutor working in another part of Sicily. "When I came here my boss, the chief prosecutor, was accused of collusion with the Mafia and he was convicted."

As the Cammarata investigation proceeds, there are signs that the local underworld may be sending disturbing messages to the authorities. Shortly after Cammarata's arrest, someone broke into the Roman imperial villa at Piazza Armerina (adjacent to Cammarata's country estate) and threw paint onto the mosaics for the fourth time in recent months. So far, the culprits have used removable paint, as if their intent were to show that they, and not the government, control the area and that they can violate the elaborate security system of the villa and destroy the mosaics at will. Some disgruntled custodians were initially suspected, but after the fourth attack, investigators began to doubt that a few isolated men could penetrate the well-guarded villa without the existence of a larger conspiracy, one involving the so-called *Mafia dei reperti*, the Mafia of the archeological objects.

Energized, perhaps, by their success with the golden bowl and in their negotiations with the Getty Museum, the Italian government asked Malcolm Bell to conduct an excavation at Morgantina in an area where police informants indicated that the Metropolitan silver treasure had been found. Bell had already had his suspicions about this area. In the summer of 1982, he had seen a big, burly man working a bulldozer there; the land was in private hands at the time, but right next to the archeological area and therefore subject to restrictions. "They are not supposed to use any earthmoving equipment there," Bell explained. "I asked him what he was doing and he said, with a smile I didn't like,

'Preparing for the harvest.'" In retrospect, Bell imagines that the man was filling in the holes made by the *tombaroli*.

In fact, when Bell and his students began excavating in 1997 they found the walls of an ancient Greek house showing telltale signs of looting, with the stratigraphic layers turned upside down and mixed together. The house has now been completely cleared, revealing waist-high walls made out of small, uneven pieces of tan-colored limestone; a stone stairway, indicating the presence of a second floor; and packed dirt floors. Bell was impressed by the thoroughness of the *tombaroli*'s digging. They dug all the way down to the floor in all of the rooms, a sign, perhaps, that they had found something extremely important and wanted to be sure not to miss anything. "After digging down to the floor, they obviously passed a metal detector across it," he said as we walked around the ancient house. While most of the floors were left intact, Bell found two good-sized holes where the *tombaroli* had evidently chosen to dig deeper. The Metropolitan Museum silver was bought in two installments, one in 1981, the second in 1982, suggesting that the treasure may also have been buried and discovered in two separate batches.

Near one of the holes, Bell found a modern Italian coin dated 1978. Evidently, a *tombarolo*, as he was crawling around and digging at night, had lost it from his pocket. Clearly, the looting of the site occurred after 1978: the discovery of a "silver service" at Morgantina was supposed to have occurred in 1980 and 1981 and the Met bought its ancient Greek treasure in 1981 and 1982.

Digging deeper, Bell eventually found a small ancient coin that had eluded the *tombaroli*. Minted in Syracuse between 212 and 214 B.C., this second coin provided a *terminus ante quem*, the date after which whatever the *tombaroli* found was buried in the house. It fit perfectly with what is known about the area at the end of third century B.C. At the time, Morgantina was part of the kingdom of Syracuse, one of the great city-states of the Greek world, where Aeschylus produced some of his plays, Plato came to try to create his ideal republic on earth, and the great mathematician and engineer Archimedes was slain in 212 B.C. by a Roman soldier, supposedly as he was absorbed in working out a geometry problem in the dirt. Many refugees from Syracuse fled to Morgantina—the last Greek city to hold out against the Romans—taking their money and all the precious possessions they could carry. Bell believes that the silver treasure—work of the very highest order—was probably produced in Syracuse, which was renowned for its silversmiths. The Metropolitan insists that the silver, although probably Sicilian or southern Italian and made at the end of the third century B.C., could have been made anywhere in the Mediterranean area of Magna Graecia from Turkey to North Africa. Bell claims this is patently untrue. Many of the pieces are decorated with very specific architectural motifs—Doric columns with an Ionic entablature, a highly unusual combination but one used frequently at Syracuse.

At first Bell was surprised to have found a dirt floor rather than an elaborate mosaic pavement in the house where such an important treasure was buried. Grander houses with mosaics can be found in the center of Morgantina, near the agora. But as Bell worked on the excavation, the location began to make increasing sense to him. "If you were hiding a treasure in a house with a mosaic floor, you would have to break open the pavement, leaving obvious signs of digging," he said. By contrast, a treasure hidden in the dirt floor of a dark basement room far from the city center would stand a much better chance of eluding the Roman invaders—as proved to be the case.

The basement level was filled with clay jars, some of them as large as six feet tall, for storing grain, oil, and wine. "The owner of the house was probably a wealthy farmer who used his basement for storing his goods. We also know that he was a pious farmer."

In fact, as Bell sifted through the rubble left in the house by the *tombaroli*, he found a broken set of terra-cotta pieces extremely similar to the silver pieces at the Met, a "service" of cups, bowls, and containers meant to be laid out on an altar and used for pouring wine or burning incense during religious ceremonies. "The pieces are typologically almost identical," Bell said. The terra-cotta pieces contain the same unusual architectural motif as the Met silver. The inexpensive terra-cotta service would have been used by the house's owner for his own household altar, while the silver one was almost certainly used for a shrine. Indeed, one of the pieces at the Metropolitan bears an inscription that says: "sacred to the gods." Moreover, the word "all" has been inserted hastily in a kind of graffito, rendering the inscription: "sacred to all the gods." To that has been added: "for the war."

Presented with the new evidence and responding to the changed climate around the question of cultural property, the Metropolitan reversed course and suddenly, in early 1999, invited Bell to examine the silver treasure. Around the same time, a spokesman for Templesman said that the New York collector was examining new documents sent to him by the Italian government and trying to make a good-faith effort to determine whether he should return the acroliths.

But why should collectors and museums return looted objects like the silver when it was clandestine digging that brought them to light in the first place?

The Italian state does not always take good care of the innumerable antiquities it already owns. Many museums, particularly local ones like that at Aidone, don't have the space or money to display most of their objects; as a result, artifacts are frequently stolen from storerooms or are left for decades in fragments, waiting to be recomposed. Some feel that overly rigid laws are part of the problem. "Restrictive laws have had the perverse effect of encouraging the export of antiquities," said Raffiotta. "Since many Italian collectors are afraid of buying illegal pieces, the best pieces of greatest importance, the ones worthy of being in a museum, all end up going abroad." The freer circulation of objects—allowing either for the sale of highly redundant pieces or for long-term loans that last for decades rather than months—might generate income that could be used to fund more legal excavations, conservation, or security.

"Collectors feel that objects move from place to place," said Shelby White, who together with her husband, Leon Levy, is one of the largest antiquities collectors in America. "Whose objects are these? Is a Greek

vase that is found in Italy Greek or Italian? Turkey is a country whose
boundaries were only created in the nineteenth century. And the modern Turks have no connection to the ancient Greeks or Romans." (A
view many Turks might dispute.)

Museums fear that foreign claims will multiply and empty the shelves
of their galleries, although the Italians say this concern is unfounded.
"We are pragmatists," said General Conforti, the head of the division of
the Italian police in charge of recovering looted and stolen art. "We have
no interest in going way back in time or making a large number of
requests. We know that it would be counterproductive and the United
States would pass new laws to protect its museums. We are interested in a
handful of important pieces that are closely tied to the cultural identity
of a particular place or time."

The Italians hope that the return of the silver treasure and the
Templesman acroliths will make Morgantina a major tourist site and help
revive the town's moribund economy. But the problem is not just about
the ownership of objects. "It doesn't matter that much whether an object
is in the British Museum or in a museum in Italy. The problem is that
when objects are looted and smuggled the context in which they existed
is destroyed," said Maria Antonietta Rizzo, the superintendent of the
Etruscan site of Cerveteri. "To find a single object, entire buildings are
destroyed, stratigraphic layers are turned upside down. The clandestine
excavations are not scientific and they destroy an enormous amount
of data."

Rather than wonder "whose objects are these?" collectors might ask
themselves why private individuals need to possess other cultures' antiquities. The impulse is as old as conquering armies carting away their enemies' national treasures as a way of appropriating their symbolic power.
The Romans, the popes of the Renaissance, Napoleon, and even modern
New Yorkers all erected Egyptian obelisks in order to further their claims
of creating major new centers of culture and power. French kings and
English lords collected ancient statues in their bids to inherit the mantle
of imperial Rome, and American robber barons and millionaires have
followed suit. But the obsession with objects has its cost.

Ripped from their context, smuggled out of the country, their origin camouflaged in order to make them legally salable, antiquities lose much of their meaning and value. It is true that the silver treasure gains much greater visibility in a major museum like the Metropolitan than in a small museum in provincial Sicily, and perhaps Templesman will donate the acroliths to a museum someday. But to justify their acquisition, the current owners must maintain that they do not and cannot determine where the pieces came from, turning them into generic objects produced somewhere in the Mediterranean. They have become mere art objects, beautiful but mute, stripped of their history.

By contrast, when placed back in their context, the acroliths and the silver service are like bookends bracketing the story of Morgantina itself.

The enigmatic smiling acrolithic heads of Persephone and Demeter tell us much about the city's origins. While Greeks settled the towns of the Sicilian coast in the eighth century B.C., they did not push into the interior until nearly two hundred years later, gradually Hellenizing the culture of Sicily's previous wave of settlers, the Siculi. "The acroliths are tremendously important artistic and historical documents of the Hellenization of Morgantina in the sixth century," Bell said. They also show that the worship of Persephone and Demeter was firmly established by the sixth century and was to remain the dominant religious cult in eastern Sicily for the next three hundred years. Since the Met silver also contains a depiction of Demeter, the two sets of objects demonstrate that the cult of Persephone and her mother remained a central feature of life in ancient Morgantina from its beginning to its desperate end.

The silver tells the story of those final days. Bell believes that the silver treasure was taken from a public sanctuary to the gods and buried in the basement floor of the pious farmer. Whoever buried it wanted to leave a message for whoever might dig it up: the treasure was buried because of the war and was for the gods. The phrase "to all the gods" was added as if to warn the finder against making off with the pieces and to emphasize that they were sacred objects that belonged in a shrine.

In light of the current debate over cultural property, the inscription "sacred to all the gods" acquires a particular poignancy and meaning: it seems to be a warning against looting itself. "I realized that these were inscriptions to protect the silver from abuse, intended to be read by someone who found them," Bell said. "There was this extraordinary possibility for listening to an ancient voice that was crying out at a moment of incredible difficulty, similar to what happened in Bosnia or Kosovo. None of this can be understood without the context."

4

The Ganges' Next Life

EVERY DAY, shortly after dawn, Veer Bhadra Mishra, a silver-haired Brahman in a traditional Indian dhoti, or loincloth, walks slowly and stiffly down the long, steep stairway from his temple in the city of Varanasi to the banks of the Ganges, as he has almost every day of the fifty-eight years of his life. All around him, along a seven-kilometer stretch of the river dominated by majestic, crumbling temples, palaces, and ashrams built atop the bank, the pageant of Indian life passes by. Tens of thousands of bathers, at eighty different ghats, or landing areas, plunge into India's holiest river. White-bearded ascetics raise their emaciated arms to salute the sun god; housewives in brightly colored saris toss yellow garlands of marigolds to Mother Ganges; adolescent boys in G-strings do push-ups, flex their muscles, and wash their bodies; naked children splash playfully in the water; and families carry their dead to the "burning ghats" to cremate their loved ones and scatter the ashes on the river.

The tug of these traditions, some of which stretch back three thousand years to the founding of Varanasi (also known as Banaras, an older name), pulls Mishra irresistibly to the river, despite a bad hip broken a few years earlier that makes walking painful. But on this particular day in early 1997, he remained at the water's edge because of a nagging cold and the poor quality of the water, which is filled with raw sewage, human and industrial waste, and the charred remains of dead bodies and animal carcasses. Normally, Mishra tries to perform five full immersions—five is an auspicious number, he explained. But even when he is feeling well he holds his nose as he puts his head in, and he no longer drinks the river water.

"There is a struggle and turmoil inside my heart," Mishra said. "I want to take a holy dip—I need it to live. The day does not begin for me without the holy dip. But at the same time, I know that the condition of the river water is not good. I know what is 'BOD'—'biochemical oxygen demand'—and I know what is 'fecal coliform,'" he continued, referring to some of the scientific indices of water pollution. For Mishra, this struggle of the heart is particularly acute because of his complex double identity: he is the mahant—the head or holy man—of Sankat Mochan Temple, one of the principal temples of Varanasi, as well as a professor of hydraulic engineering at Banaras Hindu University.

As a devout Hindu, Mishra views the Ganges as a goddess—"Maa Ganga," or Mother Ganges, a river that, because of its divine origin, is pure and purifies all those faithful who immerse themselves in her waters. Just as Muslims vow to visit Mecca, it is the dream of all good Hindus to visit Varanasi and bathe in the Ganges at least once in their lives. People from across India keep a little Ganges water in their homes to use as a religious offering or to add to their household cooking. It is said that one drop of Ganges water in a breeze that lands on your cheek hundreds of miles away is enough to cleanse a lifetime of sins. At their deaths, all Hindus seek to have their ashes scattered along the Ganges, and it is considered particularly lucky to die in Varanasi, because your soul will travel straight to heaven.

But as a scientist, Mishra cannot forget what he knows about the condition of the river water. Up in the temple complex behind him, as he sits cross-legged in front of the water saying his prayers, stands a state-of-the-art laboratory where bacteria cultures are being grown in special incubators that measure the level of pathogens at various points along the river. In some places at Varanasi the fecal coliform count has been known to reach the astronomical level of 170 million bacteria per 100 milliliters of water, a terrifying 340,000 times above the acceptable level of 500 bacteria per 100 milliliters. Similar levels are routinely registered at all the major cities along the river, which starts in the Himalayas in Nepal, flows fourteen hundred miles through India and Bangladesh, and empties into the Bay of Bengal at Calcutta.

Some 500 million people in India and Bangladesh—one out of every twelve in the world—now live in the basin of the Ganges and its tributaries. One hundred and fourteen small and large cities dump their sewage directly into its waters, meaning that millions of people are bathing in and drinking their own filth. Not surprisingly, waterborne illnesses—hepatitis, amoebic dysentery, typhoid, and cholera—are common killers, helping to account for the more than two million Indian children who die each year.

What is particularly disturbing about these numbers is that they come not at the beginning but at the end of a ten-year government cleanup project—an effort most people, even in the government, concede has failed. The central government in New Delhi spent about $150 million building Western-style high-technology wastewater plants that were particularly ill suited to Indian conditions. Designed primarily to deal with industrial waste, most of the plants made little or no provision for dealing with human waste, which accounts for 80 percent of India's water pollution. The treatment facilities run on electricity and when power goes out—as happens several times a day in many Indian cities—they stop operating. Similarly, the plants become overwhelmed during the monsoon season and simply shut down for extended periods. Even when they are working, the facilities are so expensive and difficult to operate correctly that they do not function properly. In Varanasi, sewage backs up into people's toilets or forms fetid puddles in their backyards and streets. Not long before I visited, local residents became so enraged that they forced a city water engineer to stand for several hours in a pool of sewage so that he could better acquaint himself with the problem. When I visited in 1997, the government was preparing for the second phase of the Ganges cleanup and Mishra was in high gear, trying to see that the government didn't repeat its mistakes and pushing a new plan to save the river.

The battle to clean the Ganges is about much more than the environmental future of a river. Just as the river is a symbol of India, its cleanup is an emblematic test of India's condition fifty years after independence, and the outcome may answer some of the fundamental questions about the country's future. Will India (and other parts of the third world) master its problems or descend into a nightmarish Malthusian struggle over diminishing natural resources? Will India find creative ways to preserve its rich cultural traditions or will it become homogenized into the new global economy? Will the ancient rituals of India, such as bathing in the Ganges, survive the onslaught of modernity?

Varanasi is one of the oldest continuously occupied cities in the world, its founding contemporary with the dynasties of ancient Egypt or Greece. But while no one sacrifices to the Egyptian sun god Ra or Homer's Zeus anymore, some sixty thousand devotees take the holy dip each day in Varanasi, lighting fires along the shores of the Ganges to Lord Shiva, the god who is believed to have brought the river down to earth from heaven in the tangled locks of his hair. "Please consider them an endangered species, these people who have a living relationship with the river," Mishra said with passion. "Not just birds and plants but those who still have this faith. If birds can be saved, if plants can be saved, let this species of people be saved by granting them holy water."

Mishra, as the mahant of Sankat Mochan Temple, is himself the living link to one of Varanasi's most cherished legacies. He is the spiritual heir of a greatly revered Hindu saint, Tulsi Das, a sixteenth-century figure who wrote one of the most important versions of the *Ramayana*, one of the most important texts of Hinduism. Mahantji—as Mishra is almost universally known in Varanasi (Indians add the suffix *ji* to a name to denote affection and respect)—lives with his family in the house that Tulsi Das himself built overlooking the Ganges above the ghat that now bears his name, Tulsi Ghat. The house contains an ancient copy of the

Ramayana and a pair of wooden sandals that belonged to the saint. Mishra's position as mahant, which has been passed from father to son in his family for many generations, accords him a semidivine status among the disciples of Tulsi Das, and as we spoke about things like bio-gas and biomass, a steady stream of worshipers stopped by to touch his feet—a traditional sign of respect in India. Just down the corridor from the room where we sat is a shrine to the monkey god Hunaman, a beloved figure in the *Ramayana*, and our conversation blended with the tintinnabulation of cymbals that devotees beat together as they chant to the god. Outside the room, real monkeys played in the trees and along the side of the house.

For a man regarded by some worshipers as a god, Mishra wears his status lightly. He is a person of exquisite courtesy and genuine warmth, without a hint of arrogance or self-regard. He has a handsome, tan face with dark brown eyes, an elegant head of silver hair with a shock of black in the center, and a gray mustache. If his lower body is slow and awkward from his bad hip, his face is highly mobile and expressive—as if to underscore the Hindu belief that the body is but an imperfect vessel for the noble spirit. He smiles and laughs a lot, frequently at himself. He jokes about his "throne room," the name his Western friends have teas-ingly given the room where he receives guests. It is in fact a modestly decorated room on the ground floor of his house, with a large wooden platform covered with mattresses where the mahant sits cross-legged or leaning back on a cushion. He dresses almost invariably in a light-blue dhoti—a single swath of cotton that wraps around his body like a toga—and generally goes barefoot. The one exception is when he goes to lec-ture at the university; then he puts on a pair of loafers and a brown Western-style suit, in which he looks somewhat ill at ease.

In 1982, with two other engineers from Banaras Hindu University, Mishra founded the Sankat Mochan Foundation, a private secular orga-nization dedicated to cleaning up the Ganges. The Clean the Ganges campaign has taken Mishra far from the traditional feudal role of mahant and brought him into contact with politicians in New Delhi, American State Department officials, and environmentalists and scientists around the world. From his revered and sheltered life in Varanasi, Mishra has traveled to places like Sydney, New York, and San Francisco in order to explore wastewater technologies, all the while wearing his dhoti, observing strict dietary restrictions, and carrying jars of Ganges water to use in his morning pujas, or prayers. Like India itself at the start of the millennium, Mishra is trying to incorporate what is best from the West so as to preserve the Hindu traditions that he loves.

While now housing a modern environmental foundation, Tulsi Ghat continues much as if it were a medieval village within the city. Devotees troop through at all hours to worship at one of the several pagodalike shrines in the courtyard—some ten or fifteen feet tall, others only two or three feet high. Sanskrit students pass through on their way to the school the temple runs in one of the buildings built into the stairway. In the back of Mishra's house is an arena with a round corrugated tin roof where each morning young men in bikini-style briefs practice *akara*, a traditional form of Hindu wrestling.

The boundaries here (as in much of the rest of India) between public and private, religious and secular are extremely fluid. While the mahant, his extended family (aunt, wife, two children, one daughter-in-law, and two grandchildren), and the foundation offices occupy the four buildings at the top of the bluff, there are dozens of other people living on a temporary or semipermanent basis on the grounds of the complex. A woman in a dirty blue sari has lived for years on a bench in the courtyard tucked behind one of the shrines. Numerous homeless people or passing pilgrims sleep in various abandoned structures that are built into the steps leading down to the ghats. During the day, they can be seen in the courtyard, sometimes performing yoga or brushing their teeth with twigs.

The combination of traditional Indian life with modern environmental activism seems as extraordinary to Mishra and his colleagues as it does to us. "Even in my wildest dreams I would not have thought that something like this would happen in my life," he said with a burst of laughter as we discussed the curious and fortuitous turns his life has taken. (Nothing in Mishra's early life prepared him for a life of science and political engagement.) "My father and my grandfather had the traditional education, which means Sanskrit and wrestling and music. There was no reason to deviate." When his father died suddenly in 1952, the role of mahant was thrust upon the fourteen-year-old Mishra, conditioning his destiny still further. "From that time onward, there would be a distance between me and the other people," he said rather ruefully. "Because of traditional respect, even old people would come and touch my feet to pay respect, so there was no intimate interaction. My life was very protected."

But when he reached the age of seventeen, Mishra made a radical and unprecedented move: he enrolled at Banaras Hindu University, Varanasi's modern university of the arts and sciences. "I don't know why this happened," he said, his voice rising with genuine perplexity. "In my family, I am the first person to go to university." There his path became even more unusual: he started taking science courses. "Why did I study physics, chemistry, and mathematics? I don't know. Why did I become a civil engineer with a specialty in hydraulics? I don't know. I can now see this as a scheme of the gods."

Although there are no other known cases of someone combining the vocation of mahant with that of a civil engineer, Mishra's seems typical of India's uncanny ability to preserve its unique and ancient culture while surviving countless foreign occupations and absorbing new influences, from the Persians, Greeks, and Islamic Mughal conquerors to the departure of the British in 1947. The Indian writer Gita Mehta, in her collection of essays *Snakes and Ladders*, tells a story that sums up this quality of Indian culture very well. There were two men who were considered the holiest in India, one called the Diamond Hard Ascetic and the other called the Field of Experience. The Diamond Hard Ascetic challenged his rival to a duel to prove that he was the holiest of all. He had become so hard through countless austerities, he said, that someone could strike him with a sword of steel. And indeed the sword bounced off him. When he took the sword to the Field of Experience, it simply went through him, at which point the Ascetic had to concede that the other man was holier. The Field of Experience, Mehta writes, is India: seeming to offer no resistance and yet impregnable. Other traditional societies, like

China, Burma, and Saudi Arabia, preserve themselves by steeling themselves against the outside world, but they may be much more vulnerable
as they begin to open up. India is a wide-open society through which
numerous armies have marched, and yet it remains remarkably itself.

Despite having been written off as an economic disaster area in the
past, India has begun to emerge as a force during the last several years.
Since a policy of economic liberalization was adopted in 1991, the
Indian economy has been growing at a rapid clip of 6 percent a year,
enjoying a boom similar to that of China, but it has been doing so while
the country remains the world's largest democracy. Although its problems are colossal in scale, so are its assets. It has more poor people than
any other country in the world, but it also has a sizable well-educated
middle class: more than one hundred million people speak English,
which is more than in Great Britain, Australia, and New Zealand combined. It is not an accident that software developers have turned to India
for highly skilled software engineers. Half a world away, computer companies in Silicon Valley send their work problems to technicians in Ban-
galore, who work on them all day while the people in California sleep.
Bill Gates, king of Microsoft, arrived in Delhi while I was there, and his
arrival was treated with the pomp of Queen Victoria's Diamond Jubilee
during the days of the Raj. There was an enormous billboard on the
route from the Delhi airport saying "Welcome Bill Gates!" and his visit
was front-page news for days. Gates is contemplating a major investment in India. With its huge multilingual population, India is in a
better position than most nations to adapt to the new information
economy.

"These things—satellite television, Internet surfing—are with us
whether we like it or not," said Mishra. "They are means. They can be used
in a beautiful way. It is as if you are riding a lion; you should be strong
enough to tame the lion or it will eat you." In keeping with that spirit, the
Sankat Mochan Foundation is believed to have been the first group in
Varanasi to sign up for an electronic mail and Internet connection.

This extremely open attitude toward the outside, however, has (so
far at least) in no way lessened the country's intense religiosity. To a

remarkable degree, Indians have adapted new technology to their own traditional purposes. When Indian television broadcast a movie version of the *Ramayana*, many Indian families placed their sets up on their household altars and worshiped before them. Some observers might have been scandalized, but these people were not worshiping the television; they were worshiping their gods. (The mahant's youngest son, Vepul, had a tape of the *Ramayana* movie sitting next to his television and VCR.) In Varanasi, on the night celebrating the wedding anniversary of the gods Shiva and Parvati, I saw numerous shrines to Shiva elaborately decorated with flashing electric lights pulsing to the beat of Indi-pop disco music. To Western eyes these shrines, built around an ancient phallic symbol and decked out like the entrances to Las Vegas nightclubs, seemed sacrilegious and surreal, but ordinary Indians were clustered around them in devout worship, as they would have been a generation or a millennium ago.

"I think in India this lion will be tamed!" Mishra said with a delighted laugh when I mentioned the disco shrines to Shiva.

I had first heard about Mishra from an acquaintance of mine, Bailey Green, who is an engineer in Berkeley, California, and has been working on the Ganges project. The Friends of the Ganges, U.S.A.—a group of American environmentalists in San Francisco working closely with the Sankat Mochan Foundation—contacted Green in the attempt to find a solution to Varanasi's water pollution problems. A big, burly man with a bushy black beard and the look of a lumberjack, Green is a former Yale divinity student who became an environmental engineer after seeing too many children die of waterborne diseases while he was doing missionary work in Africa. Green and his former professor at the University of California at Berkeley, William Oswald, have an engineering firm, Oswald & Green, that designs highly ecological wastewater systems.

In 1994, the mahant traveled to northern California and visited the pond systems built by Oswald, the pioneer of a kind of "back to the future" approach to modern urban waste called Advanced Integrated Wastewater Pond Systems, in which sewage is treated in a carefully engineered series of natural algae ponds. In 1996, Earl Kessler, a member of the U.S. State Department Agency for International Development (USAID), made the trip as well. Kessler came away sufficiently impressed that USAID gave a grant to both Oswald & Green and Mishra's Sankat Mochan Foundation to prepare a feasibility study for a waste pond system at Varanasi. In the spring of 1997, Oswald and Green flew to India to complete the study and try to win Indian government support for the plan, and I decided to accompany them on their two-week trip.

"Remember that to many traditional Hindus we Westerners are polluted," Catherine Porter, executive director of Friends of the Ganges, U.S.A, had explained to me on the phone before I left for India. "Mahantji has received some criticism about all these polluted people who hang around the temple and the house. You are not supposed to touch a holy man." Porter described a scene when Mishra arrived at the San Francisco airport and a big, strapping American environmentalist embraced him, picking him up and spinning him in the air. "I thought Mahantji would be apoplectic. Instead he had this big smile on his face," she said. A man of the world, Mishra has decided that the rules of Varanasi do not necessarily apply elsewhere or to everyone. When we arrived, Mishra hugged Bailey Green, who had already spent quite a bit of time at Varanasi, and shook my and William Oswald's hands.

In Professors Mishra and Oswald, the Ganges cleanup project has brought together two very different men who have, nonetheless, arrived at the same solution to the same problem. While Mishra is a deeply spiritual man with a sacred conception of the river, Oswald is a pragmatic scientist with an earthy sense of humor. When told that the Hindus believed that they would go straight to heaven if they died in Varanasi, Oswald replied, "They'll get there a lot faster if they go in that water." At the time Oswald was a gray-haired seventy-seven-year-old with elephant ears, two hearing aids, and an impish smile; he looked a little like the wise, old teacher Yoda in *Star Wars*—but without the mystical vein. His pond systems are not a utopian environmentalist's fantasy. Before the age of mechanized treatment plants, ponds were one of the primary means of taking care of sewage, and they are still used in about seventy-five hundred municipalities around the United States. Waste decomposes naturally in water through the processes of microbial fermentation and photosynthesis; ponds are actually cheaper and clean wastewater more thoroughly than mechanical treatment plants, but they generally require more land. As a result, most major U.S. cities have switched to mechanized plants in recent decades, relegating pond systems to smaller towns and cities.

Oswald, who is an emeritus professor of engineering at Berkeley, has devoted his life to devising pond systems that improve on nature by handling waste in an accelerated fashion. This technology would seem ideally suited to India because it costs less, uses little electricity, involves less high-tech maintenance, and takes advantage of one of India's most abundant resources, the almost unlimited sunlight available for photosynthesis.

It is also a piece of poetic justice that the scientific key to the modern problems of Varanasi—India's most ancient city—could be one of the most ancient and simple life forms: algae. Oswald is to algae what Michael Jordan is to basketball. When we first met in Delhi, he excused himself in advance for not remembering my name: "For every new person's name I learn, I forget the name of an algae," he said. At one point, Oswald, at the request of the United States space program, invented something called an algatron, a system for growing algae in space to provide oxygen for astronauts living at a space station. Although it has been tried out only on mice, Oswald proved, in principle, that you could create a self-sustaining ecosystem using water, sunlight, algae, and animals. In Oswald's view, algae are among the great unsung heroes of the planet. Algae and bacteria have a symbiotic relationship that performs natural miracles in converting toxic or disease-carrying waste into oxygen, new plant life, and valuable protein for other forms of life to feed on. Bacteria grow on and decompose sewage into its constituent components (carbon, nitrogen, hydrogen, etc.); the algae assimilate these nutrients and, as their green biomass grows, produce oxygen through photosynthesis. Algae are the most efficient producers of oxygen on the planet: they produce more than one and a half times their weight in oxygen and are the largest single source of atmospheric oxygen in the air we breathe.

The oxygen that the algae produce keeps the aquatic life of a pond or river alive: fish both feed on algae and breathe the oxygen they produce; aerobic bacteria also use the oxygen to keep the process of decomposition going in a self-sustaining cycle of creation and decay.

Oswald, who grew up on a farm in northern California, did pioneering work on the waste-absorbing properties of algae in the forties and fifties and then set about trying to design pond systems that took advantage of these qualities in a practical, efficient manner. By means of gravity and paddle wheels, Oswald moves water through a linked sequence of ponds, each with its own special environment, meant to encourage different kinds of decomposition and waste treatment. The first series of ponds are dug very deep, to create a dark, sunless environment without oxygen, where anaerobic bacteria decompose the heavier solid wastes. The second set of ponds are shallow so that all the water is exposed to sunlight to encourage photosynthesis, while the third are deep, still ponds, in which the algae settle and can be easily harvested to be fed to pigs or chickens or be left in the water to feed fish, which can then be caught and eaten. In the final phase, the water passes into large reservoirlike ponds for reuse in irrigation.

When Oswald and Green arrived in Varanasi, Mishra and two of his close colleagues at the foundation presented the American engineers with a surveyor's map they had prepared of the area, with carefully traced markings for ground elevation and soil composition. They spread the map out on a table in the guest house overlooking a grassy lawn where a colored tent and a stage festooned with marigolds were decked out for the foundation's annual festival of *druphad mele*—the most ancient form of Indian classical music—which was set to begin later that evening.

As they studied the map, Oswald fretted over the possible hitches in the project, which, if realized, would be the largest of his career. "Are you sure that a dike that is seventy-five meters above sea level will be high enough for the monsoon?" he asked. "This is going to cost a lot of money. Are you prepared for that?" (During the last thirty years, Oswald has seen a lot of ambitious pond projects in the third world evaporate for a host of technical, political, and financial reasons.) But after fifteen years of work, the mahant is anxious to see the Varanasi project succeed and to brush aside all possible complications. "We will find a way to get the money—perhaps donations," he said. "We will show that Dr. Oswald's pond system can work even in India!" he added grandly. "I don't want to be a hero," Oswald replied. "I just want to be right."

The musicians outside began to tune up their instruments, and the conversation about the soil composition of the proposed pond site continued over the drone of sitars. The musicians played from eight in the evening until six-thirty in the morning so that, as we lay under our mosquito nets at night, ancient ragas and the sound of sitars ran through our waking and sleeping thoughts.

The following afternoon, we set off by boat down the Ganges to examine the site where Oswald & Green has proposed a system of thirty-two ponds in a former river channel that lies about ten miles downstream from Varanasi. The pond system may also help develop a nearby island in the river that is largely cut off from the outside world.

There were about twenty of us on a long, flat, beat-up wooden boat with a put-put motor and a canvas sheet stretched across it like an awning to protect against the midday sun. Aside from the mahant and his fellow engineers, most of those aboard were young volunteers from the Varanasi area, devotees of the temple who also donate their time to the Clean the Ganges campaign. (The foundation can afford only two full-time staff members. One of Mishra's household servants often doubles as a laboratory assistant.) Because Tulsi Ghat is at the far north end of Varanasi, the trip took us in slow procession past the entire city. The principal temples and palaces of Varanasi are built along the Ganges above the series of about eighty ghats that stretch about five miles. The ghats rise up dramatically out of the water atop tall stairways, making the Ganges a kind of two-way theater: people on the ghats observe the activity on the river below, while those passing by on boats observe the doings of the people up above.

Although Varanasi is the chief center of Hindu learning and culture, almost every religious practice and region of India is represented among its ghats. There is a ghat for the Dandi Panth ascetics and a ghat leading to a temple full of erotic Nepalese sculptures. There are pagoda-like ghats reminiscent of southern India and fortresslike ghats that recall the warlike Mughul conquerors of the north. Some are old and built of somber earth-colored stone, while others are made of modern concrete and are painted white, yellow, pink, red, and green. There are ghats and shrines for almost every divinity. Saffron-robed pilgrims carrying saffron walking sticks stop at each holy spot: the Charandpaduka Ghat, where the god Vishnu is thought to have left his footprint; the Manikarnika Ghat, where Shiva's bride, Parvati, is supposed to have lost an earring. There is a ghat for the goddess of smallpox and a ghat for the lord of the moon that is supposed to help cure disease.

"The whole of Ganga is holy, but I believe I would not exaggerate if I say she becomes holier in Varanasi," said Mishra. "In India we have many sects and many types of religious practices, languages, and ethnic groups. Ganga is where all these faiths and religious practices come together. In a society with so much diversity, it is very important that there is one such entity that provides a unifying force."

Along with all the different religious practices, equally evident are all the different forms of pollution along the Ganges. There are ghats where herds of water buffalo cool off in the water. At others, dhobis, or washerwomen, rinse out their laundry on the shore as a rainbow of colored saris lie drying on the steps. Hinduism contains many rituals of purification and hygiene, but many people ignore the prohibition against using soap in the Ganges.

The attitudes of ordinary bathers vary from traditional reverence for Maa Ganga to a creeping distrust about the water's purity, according to Avantika Rao, an Indian American undergraduate from Los Angeles on a junior year abroad who had been interviewing women at the Ganges and came along for the river ride. "How many people come from all over, from so far away to see this sacred river? They bathe, make it dirty, and then leave," one woman told Rao, who speaks both Hindi and English. But the women are hesitant to blame the Ganges, distinguishing between the filth in the water and the larger entity that is the river. "What is her fault? People come to wash their sins and she doesn't refuse," one bather said. Another told Rao, "Mahantji and all these people say it is polluted but we don't feel it is. How can we believe she is impure?"

There is much ignorance, Mishra explained, not just among illiterate bathers but also among the priests and leaders of Varanasi. Many people believe that a brick water tower just down from Tulsi Ghat is a treatment plant cleansing the river of sewage when it actually holds polluted water that has been piped in from the river for drinking.

After a few minutes, we slowly passed the first of the "burning" ghats, where the faithful come to cremate their dead. At all hours of the day and night, the funeral pyres burn on the shore, with family members circling the fire and saying prayers. When the firewood has been consumed, the ashes of the dead are consigned to the river to begin their journey from this world to the next. In some cases, the bodies may not be fully consumed, and their remains scatter into the river. There is an average of about forty thousand traditional funerals performed on the banks of the Ganges at Varanasi each year. In addition, about three thousand other dead bodies—those of people too poor to afford a funeral—along with about nine thousand dead cattle are tossed into the river annually. As part of the government's Ganga Action Plan, 28,820 turtles were released at Varanasi, in the hope that they would eat any decomposing body parts. But the government's turtle farm is now empty and there are no turtles in the river. Many suspect that the turtles were poached for food.

One extremely important thing that the government cleanup did accomplish, however, was the building of an electric crematorium at one of the two main burning ghats to cut back on the traditional funerals. The program seems to be working, and the lines are much longer in front of the crematorium than in front of the men selling wood for the pyres. This, in Mishra's view, is an instance of India's adaptability. "The reasons are economic," he explained. "A traditional funeral today will cost not less than fifteen hundred to two thousand rupees; the charge for the electric crematorium is seventy rupees." Unfortunately, the crematorium stops when power goes off in Varanasi, and there is need for a second electric crematorium at the other principal burning ghat.

Still, funeral pyres, water buffaloes, and washerwomen, while striking to the eye and certainly a contributing factor, are not the main pollution problem at Varanasi. An estimated 80 percent of the pollution (a figure similar to that in other large cities on the river) comes from the city's sewage, which flows into the river. If you look closely, even along the bathing ghats, you can see large sewage pipes draining directly into the river, the sewage backed up from the over-loaded treatment plant. The city's sewer system, built by the British in 1917, is strained beyond capacity. As recently as fifty years ago, the population of Varanasi was just over one quarter million; now it is 1.2 million and the pond system Oswald & Green is projecting is for a city that will be home to one and a half million people in just ten or fif-teen years.

As we leave Varanasi, reaching the point where the Varuna River meets the Ganges, the surface of the water is literally bubbling like a cauldron of hot soup on a low flame—raw sewage turning into methane gas. Just a mile or so up the Varuna is a huge pumping station that the Indian government built, which is supposed to transport the city's sewage to a large treatment plant at the town of Dinapur, a few miles far-ther downstream. Able to handle but a fraction of the city's 200 million liters of sewage per day under the best of conditions, the plant pumps the sewage of Varanasi several hundred yards away from the center of the city, only to dump the vast majority of it into the Varuna River, where it then travels right back to the Ganges.

The sewage backup is placing a new strain on the city's octogenarian brick sewer system. "The main trunk sewer is known to be structurally questionable," says a USAID report on Varanasi. "Its collapse could cre-ate a disaster."

A few miles farther downstream on the Ganges, there is a sudden explosion of algae blooms, in such unnatural quantities that for several hundred yards the Ganges takes on the unhealthy appearance of a swamp. It is here that the Indian government placed its big treatment plant, built by a British company. It performs only what in the waste business is called "primary treatment"—the equivalent of going through only the first of Oswald's four ponds—which does about 60 percent of the job. In this case, it appeared to be doing far less than that.

"What you have here is a eutrophic environment," Oswald explained.

"What does that mean?"

"It means something is eating itself," he said. "*Eu* in Greek means 'self' and *troph* means 'eat.'"

In other words, sewage-filled water chock-full of bacteria is stimulating far more algae than the natural resources of the river can absorb. "The algae are just going to pile up and putrefy," Oswald said. And as they decompose, they consume rather than create oxygen, putting a strain on the marine life of the river. This condition shows up when the oxygen level of the water is tested in a laboratory: biochemical oxygen demand, or BOD, is one of the principal measures of water pollution. Where pollution places a high demand on oxygen, there is less for fish and other organisms.

"Besides, it's the wrong kind of algae," Oswald continued. "You have the conditions of botulism: high pH, warm temperature, and no oxygen."

"They have done such blunders," the mahant said. "It is like a theme park of failed technology."

As bad as it looks, however, the Ganges' condition is no worse than that of most major rivers in Europe and better than that of many U.S. rivers before the Clean Water Act of 1972, which helped revive many streams that had become virtually dead. In fact, the water north of Varanasi is still very clean, as it is considerably farther downstream. In keeping with Hindu legend, the Ganges (like all other large rivers) cleans itself naturally through the process of dilution. For the moment, at least, the Ganges' problems are concentrated around its major cities, where sewage is routinely dumped. But it is, of course, precisely in these highly populated areas where most people are at risk.

It is still common practice in Europe for sewage treatment plants to discharge partially cleaned effluent into rivers, but the inhabitants of London and Paris would not dream of bathing in or drinking out of the

Thames or the Seine. The Indian government in Delhi adopted a cleanup strategy using British technology without considering the radically different way that people use the rivers in India. Most European countries are mainly concerned with maintaining reasonable levels of BOD to preserve marine life, but they do not worry much about high levels of fecal coliform, the disease-carrying pathogens that afflict humans. The Indian government has followed this approach and has incomprehensibly failed to equip most of its new plants (including the one in Varanasi) with disinfection units to remove fecal coliform. In other words, the Indian government adopted a European technology that was designed more to protect fish than to protect people.

Some of the same effluent that is pouring into the river from the treatment plant is being given to farmers to irrigate their fields—with disastrous results. The nearby villages have suffered outbreaks of cholera, hepatitis, typhoid, and a variety of nasty skin diseases. The potatoes grown in the area have become so hard that no one will buy them in the marketplace, and people from other villages are reluctant to marry anyone from the affected area.

Although our trip downriver to the island of Dhob was only about ten miles, it took us nearly five hours because the boat kept running aground in shallow water. With each successive stop, more and more members of our party were out in the river pushing the boat, leaving the dwindling number in it hoping with growing anxiety that the craft would come unstuck and resume its journey. The small Western contingent was busy calculating the probability of catching some dread tropical disease if we were forced to take an unanticipated holy dip to reach shore.

While the Ganges is usually a mile or two wide throughout its course, it becomes shallow in the dry months leading up to the summer monsoons. The problem has become worse in recent years as more and more river water has been diverted for irrigation. Throughout our journey, you could see massive pipes sucking water out of the Ganges toward distant fields. Part of the reason for the worship and divinization of the Ganges and other rivers in Hinduism is the relative scarcity of water in India and its precious role in maintaining life. Although India has

20 percent of the world's people, it has only 4 percent of the world's fresh water. With its population approaching one billion and the country scheduled to overtake China in the next twenty years as the world's most populous nation, India's future growth could mean mass starvation. Some 300 million Indians are already listed by the U.S. State Department as "food insecure"—a bad monsoon away from starvation.

Under these circumstances, wars over water—one of the specters that haunt the twenty-first century—have already become a reality in India. India and Bangladesh have come close to breaking off diplomatic relations over the use of Ganges water. And in 1994 the city of Haryana simply diverted a sizable portion of Delhi's water supply, claiming it needed the water for irrigation. The struggle for water can only get worse as India's growing urban population demands Western standards of plumbing. The seventeen five-star hotels of Delhi consume 800,000 liters of water daily, enough for the requirements of 1.3 million slum dwellers.

The need to cut down more and more forests for farmland and firewood could also bring about an ecological disaster in India, one of the world's richest sources of rare plants and animals. To stave off massive losses of species, the U.S. State Department is promoting the creation of quarantine greenhouses to collect some 800,000 germ plasmas of India's vast abundance of plant life and after decades of backing expensive high-tech megadevelopment projects, is now a proponent of "sustainable technology"—projects like Oswald's ponds, which cost less, use little electric energy, and can be maintained with relatively little training by local people.

As I contemplated the prospect of biological Armageddon during our on-again, off-again voyage in the shallow waters of the Ganges, we heard the distant sound of a brass band. There was a large crowd massed on the banks on the island of Dhob; even though it was nearly sunset and the people had been waiting all afternoon, they greeted the arrival of the Sankat Mochan Foundation and their Western guests with triumphal music and wild jubilation.

Dhob is one of the pockets of rural India that have been largely left out of the past fifty years of development: it has no electricity and no year-round bridge to the mainland. About ten miles long and a few miles wide, with a population of forty thousand, Dhob has a curious geographical configuration: it is an island during the rainy season and a tenuous part of the mainland the rest of the year. As the course of the Ganges gradually shifted toward the west, it exposed a former sandbar to the east of the island, which can be crossed during the drier months of the year but still floods during the summer. This wide former river channel is sandy, infertile, and without a proper road. It is here, in this former riverbed known as the Sota, that the Sankat Mochan Foundation would like to put its system of wastewater ponds. The plan also involves laying four roads across the dikes of the ponds to connect Dhob to the mainland—roads that could contain buried cable, providing the electric spark that would unite the people of Dhob with the rest of the world.

Amid cries of "Hail to the gods!" we climbed up the banks of a shore thick with eagerly waiting villagers, who were ready with armfuls of carefully sewn flower wreaths. With wise forethought, the Sankat Mochan Foundation had sent a few cars ahead to the island so that we would not have to attempt returning by boat at night. So we proceeded slowly, stopping at every village cluster for a new celebration. Again and again, there were bands and painted banners and entire canopies of marigolds. At each stop, mothers sent their children forward to touch our feet, lay on wreaths, and say prayers. Soon, the wreaths worn by the mahant, Oswald, and Green had climbed up their chests and reached their mouths. But no sooner were they removed for easier breathing than more arrived. Everywhere, packs of children pressed against the car windows and simply stared.

It was dark before we reached our last stop and the main ceremony, in which we were invited to eat a sticky orange sweet and drink some lemon tea. The mahant and the elected chiefs of the villages read a declaration stating their support for the Oswald pond project. The declaration ended with the fervent wish that this good deed would bring *mukti* and *bhukti*—happiness in this life and salvation in the next.

The wild sense of expectation and hope on the island—the sense that the pond project might serve as deus ex machina to transform people's lives—was both moving and sobering. While there is legitimate worry about the leveling effect of every remote outpost plugging into the world grid, Dhob's desire to be part of the wider world was palpable and over-powering. On a clear night from certain parts of the island, the villagers can see the lights of a distant railroad yard. They stand and watch this bright symbol of the world they yearn to be a part of—a world of lights, power tools, modern appliances, and, of course, television.

"Our moral responsibility is now very great," the mahant said as we packed off for Varanasi amid final cheers.

The next ten days at Tulsi Ghat were filled with feverish activity on various fronts. The foundation members were busy trying to set up high-level seminars to present the American engineers and their plan to local officials and the mayor of Varanasi, to technocrats at the water commission in Lucknow, the state capital, and to a major conference in Delhi with national ministers, politicians, and environmental activists. Oswald and Green were working almost around the clock with their pencils and calculators, drawing up a new set of site-specific engineer-ing plans, with precise figures on the money and land that would be needed to build the pond system. Staff and volunteers of the foundation were scurrying around trying to track down things like the cost of mov-ing a ton of earth in Varanasi. We made a second visit to the proposed pond site to examine it carefully in daylight.

An endless stream of special visitors passed through the throne room: engineers, village chiefs, politicians, local bureaucrats, univer-sity professors, and anyone thought to have the ear of some important decision-making body. In between meetings, the mahant was on his cordless phone lining up support and making sure that people who had promised to attend a particular meeting would actually show up. For the first time, the central government in Delhi said that it was open to oxidation ponds, although it would not make a final decision until later. Meanwhile, the foundation would have to line up political support and funding.

The day after we returned from the island, Mishra received a phone call from a member of the Indian parliament representing Varanasi, who was eager to hear about the trip. The people of Dhob were evidently so fed up with traditional politicians they would no longer receive them. It seemed the mahant had inadvertently tapped into a small political gold mine—a unified packet of approximately twenty-five thousand highly motivated voters.

As a result, the mahant has found himself in the role of power broker, a position with which he feels some discomfort. "We are not political people and it is still not clear to me what we should do with this consensus," he explained as we sat in the throne room overlooking the Ganges. "Before every election, the newspapers in Varanasi print stories saying that Mahantji is going to run for parliament with this group or that group. All the politicians come and say good words, but because I have no ties with any party, they do nothing." And yet, perhaps the only way to realize the pond project is through judiciously applied political pressure. "We have to have a more effective way to influence the politicians and harness the support we have built in the community," he said.

Suddenly, one morning during this period, a band of musicians all dressed in white cotton appeared piping celebratory music on ancient reed instruments. During the night, the wife of Mishra's eldest son had been hustled off to the hospital and had delivered a son, the couple's first male child and therefore, in all likelihood, the future mahant. We Westerners knew nothing—we had never seen the women of the mahant's household—but the surrounding community knew everything with great speed and by morning the musicians appeared as if out of nowhere.

The mahant did not go to the hospital, because he did not want to make his daughter-in-law uncomfortable. She would feel, he explained, an obligation to touch his feet and cover her head in his presence. In their family life, the Mishras remain highly traditional. All three married children have accepted matches arranged by their father. At the same time, all five of his children—three boys and two girls—have followed his example by going to university. Mishra's eldest son is an electrical engineer, the second was pursuing a Ph.D. in computer science at Reading University in England, and the youngest was completing his medical training in Varanasi. The daughters, too, have attended university and one of them, a scholar of classical Indian culture, lives in Delhi with her husband.

"Many things are changing," the mahant reflected. "People are moving from the country to the city. Extended families—three generations living together—are breaking up." What about arranged marriages? I asked. "That, too, is changing. We will change as much as is necessary," he said, bringing to mind the great Sicilian novel *The Leopard* and its famous line: "We must change everything, in order that nothing change." "The mahants and the religious leaders have to face these challenges and see that the entry into our society of these changes is gentle in order to prevent a derailment," Mishra said.

Indeed, the ritual-filled life at Tulsi Ghat moved at the stately pace of the Ganges, while the activity of the Sankat Mochan Foundation hurried to the high-pitched squeal of the fax machine, which was busy sending data to engineers in California and receiving it back. A large man with a Nehru hat and a handlebar mustache sold perfumes made from hand-crushed flowers. A figure black with coal dust, carrying a hammer, smashed pieces of coal into smaller chunks to use as fuel. A snake charmer with a cobra in his basket stopped by, looking to make a few rupees. Sacred cows wandered through, while goats walked into the shrines to eat the flowers that worshipers had left for the gods.

Mishra shuttled between these two worlds, finding time, despite long meetings and conferences, to keep up his religious duties, from his holy dip at dawn to the closing ceremonies at the temple, which sometimes did not end until midnight.

On the eve of our departure from Varanasi—after a long, tension-filled day in which Oswald & Green presented its plan to the mayor of Varanasi—I accompanied the mahant to the temple. Located in what used to be a wooded area where Tulsi Das is said to have found a divine image of Hunaman, the monkey god, the temple has a spacious courtyard full of trees that preserves a little of its original feel as a secluded wood. The devotees, as usual, were clustered around the shrine, chanting and beating cymbals and repeating the words "SitaRamSitaRamSitaRam." Sita and Ram, wife and husband (as well as avatars of the gods), are the principal heroes of the *Ramayana*, and Hindus believe that there is no sound more delightful to the monkey god than the names of his closest friends. The main shrine, which contains an orange monkey statue, lines up on an axis with a second shrine, where there are images of Sita and Ram, so that the three gods can contemplate and enjoy one another's presence. As the closing ceremony began, the worshipers lined up along this perspective, careful not to block the monkey god's view of his friends.

The mahant did not actually officiate at the ceremony. There are several full-time priests who perform the ritual functions at the temple. Mishra presided over the end, standing a bit apart, deep in prayer. Although it was nearly eleven o'clock at this point, his night was not finished: he had a music lesson. After speaking with some of the followers at the temple, he trudged wearily up to a little room where a music master with an old wooden harmonium appeared. For fifteen or twenty minutes, the mahant practiced his scales in a style that sounded almost like jazz scat singing and then he and his instructor sang for the better part of an hour.

Toward the end, they sang an unusually beautiful song with a tone of sadness and longing. It was a love song, Mishra explained, that is both a devotional hymn and a popular romantic favorite in Varanasi. It is sung by Radha, the consort of the god Krishna, who is both a greatly revered divinity and a shameless philanderer, always leaving Radha to seduce shepherdesses with his exquisite flute playing. And yet in her song Radha expresses nothing but desire and affection for her beautiful, promiscuous god. "The forest has become lonely and who will play the flute now?" she sings.

"Every action," Mishra said, explaining the mixture of religious and secular, sacred and profane in the song, "can be done in a worldly spirit or in a spiritual way. In our spiritual practice, we believe that you can experience God through the five senses—and through the great austerities of the ascetic, reduced to just skin and bones. We believe that the first sense to perceive God is that of sound. I have not experienced this— and I am not an ascetic—but I am very sensitive to sound."

At the conclusion of the lesson, he gave each of us a *prasad*—a little woven basket with "holy food" (sweets prepared by people at the temple)— and a string of flowers. It was very late by then, but the mahant appeared greatly refreshed by his music making and the conversation turned, as it often did, to his attempts to blend Hinduism and Western science.

While Mishra realizes that there is much India must borrow from the West, he feels equally strongly that ancient Indian thinking has much to offer. For all its power, Western scientific thinking tends to see nature as a series of known physical and mechanical processes, reducing it to another resource to be used and exploited by man. For Hindus, the natural world is saturated in divinity: Hindus believe that there are some 330 million different gods at work in the cosmos. People regard trees, lakes, animals, mountains, and streams as gods, and even a simple plant seed can be seen as sacred. "The Almighty has appointed various gods to take care of nature so while we are enjoying nature, deriving happiness from it, so we have to take care of it also," Mishra said. For him, as for many other Indians, this deep sense of reverence is not an abstraction. Mishra sleeps in a room overlooking the Ganges so that it is the first thing that he sees each day. "We believe that the first thing that you see in the morning has an effect on your day and you should look at some auspicious thing and say auspicious words at the beginning of each day," he explained. "I get up and the first thing I look at is Gangaji and I say my prayers in order to prepare to take the holy dip."

The mahant is convinced that the traditional reverence for the Ganges can be tapped through an intelligent, "culturally consistent" public education program among the people who use the river. The Western approach, based on fear about the possibility of ecological disaster, he said, will not work. "If you go to people who have a living relationship with Ganga and you say, 'Ganga is polluted, the water is dirty,' they will say, 'Stop saying that. Ganga is not polluted. You are abusing the river.' But if you say, 'Ganga is our mother. Come and see what is being thrown on the body of our mother—sewage and filth. Should we tolerate sewage being smeared on the body of our mother?' you will get a very different reaction, and you can harness that energy."

One of the attractions of the Oswald pond system is that it seems to combine modern science with traditional Hindu ideas. It is an almost entirely "natural" system that relies mainly on the self-cleansing properties of nature. Indeed, there is a curious parallel between Oswald's descriptions of the self-sustaining ecology of a pond system and certain traditional Hindu beliefs about the universe. "All living organisms fit into one of three categories," Oswald had explained to me. "They are either producers, like algae and other plants that create oxygen; consumers, like cows that eat plants or humans who eat plants and cows; or decomposers, such as fungi, which dispose of things when they are dead." Hinduism, in its mythopoeic description of the universe, may have intuited something similar. "There are three gods," Mishra said. "Brahma, the creator; Vishnu, the sustainer; and Shiva, the god who provides us happiness in this world that is decaying every day." When I remarked to Mishra on the analogy, he seemed intrigued. "What did Professor say when you mentioned this?" he asked. "I'll leave that to your literary imagination," Oswald had replied with sardonic humor. "If I go back to California talking about Lord Shiva, they'll put me in a straitjacket."

Mishra, however, sees no necessary contradiction between the mythological and the scientific. "When I say that oxidation ponds should be the solution, I say that also as a scientist," he said. "There is no type of treatment that reduces the level of fecal coliform as effectively. The primary reason is technical, but it is culturally consistent with Hinduism as well." Indeed, the practice of harnessing the metaphors of Hindu mythology to create a new environmental ethos is common in India. Even secular magazines like *India Today* invoke Lord Krishna's love of the forest in talking about the need to protect against the denuding of the Indian landscape. Similarly, the Sankat Mochan Foundation weaves its new message about the Ganges into its other traditional activities. "There will be some Swatcha Ganga [Clean the Ganges] reflected in our music, and there will be some music in our Swatcha Ganga," Mishra said.

"I am very happy that this scientific training and traditional background have synthesized in this manner," he continued. "With all this, a meaning has been given to my religious background and my scientific background. If both these backgrounds were not there, probably I would not have done this. At times, it appears that both are two different areas, but now I feel that they have some interface also. Life is like a stream: one bank is the Vedas [the ancient Sanskrit texts that are the basis of Hindu thought] and the other bank is the contemporary world, which includes science and technology. If both banks are not firm, the water will scatter. If both banks are firm, the river will run its course.

"According to our traditions, there is no knowledge other than the Vedas. This is the claim of the ancient pundits, and science says that everything can be explained by science."

But Mishra believes that neither the claims of science nor those of religion are absolute. "Truth is infinite," he said. "We may realize the nose of the truth; another person may realize the hand of the truth. It is impossible for human beings to realize the truth in totality, so we pursue our efforts and realize one part of it. Physical sciences are one part of the realization, the Vedic wisdom is another."

Mishra is fully aware that his two worlds have no direct relationship with each other. "These two banks do not meet. They are two aspects of the truth. But they have an interesting interface—that interface is this human life. This science and these Vedas are for this planet, for all the living human beings and all the other living beings on this earth. If they don't make us happy, and our living happy, then they are irrelevant and useless."

5

Saving Species in Madagascar

W E HAVE AN emergency," Patricia Wright said at the entrance to Ranomafana National Park, a tropical rain forest preserve in central Madagascar. "A wounded lemur has escaped from the forest and crossed the road," Wright explained as she and several coworkers piled into two four-wheel-drive vehicles and sped to a nearby village where a small black-and-white lemur with a blinded eye and a bleeding wound on its side huddled in the frame of a half-built wooden house. The forest is the home of some twelve species of lemur, the endangered early primates that exist only on this large, remote island in the Indian Ocean.

For the next two hours, as Wright and her crew worked to capture the wounded lemur, using a blow gun, darts, tranquilizers, and a net, a crowd of barefoot villagers in tattered clothes gathered to watch, seemingly amused and puzzled by the extraordinary means deployed to treat a single wounded animal. The scene was a study in the strange contradictions of man and nature, among Westerners, lemurs, and local people in Madagascar.

Along with being a natural wonderland, Madagascar is also one of the poorest countries in the world, and the rural villages near Ranomafana are rife with malaria, dysentery, cholera, typhoid, and even the plague. The doctors for humans in Ranomafana have no cars and travel hours by foot to visit the more distant villages. Indeed, an intense struggle has been taking place on the island in recent years between conservationists seeking to save rare species and their habitats and local farmers looking to clear forests in order to plant crops and feed their families.

At the center of the battle is Patricia Wright, one of the world's leading primatologists, who is described as "a visionary," "an inspiration," and a kind of "Mary Poppins" of conservation by her fans and as "totalitarian," "Machiavellian," and, half-jokingly, "the spawn of the devil" by her critics. But so far only one side of the debate—Wright and the conservation movement—has dominated the public discussion and presented its image of Madagascar to the world.

In 1986, Wright helped discover a new species, the golden bamboo lemur, and located another species, the greater bamboo lemur, which had not been seen in years and was thought to have become extinct. On the strength of these discoveries, Wright was able to convince both the Malagasy and the United States governments to create an enormous national park at Ranomafana, cordoning off a huge 160-square-kilometer swath of rain forest.

The fourth-largest island in the world—a chunk of land the size of Texas that broke off from the African continent some 160 million years ago and drifted 250 miles out into the Indian Ocean—Madagascar remained uninhabited until just two thousand years ago, the last major landmass other than frozen Antarctica to be populated by humans. Its size and isolation made it a fabulous evolutionary laboratory, a parallel universe where nature elaborated very different sorts of creatures. There are no native dogs or cats on Madagascar, so the island developed its own kind of carnivore called the fossa, a sleek, long-bodied mammal that has the snout of a fox, the body of a giant mongoose, and retractable claws that allow it to climb trees like a cat. There is even a weird species of lemur called the aye-aye, which performs the same ecological function as the woodpecker, using a bizarre skeletal middle finger and long, rodentlike teeth to dig termites out of the bark of trees. Eighty percent of Madagascar's plants and animals exist nowhere else on earth, making the island, according to the U.S. State Department Agency for International Development (USAID), "the single-highest major conservation priority in the world."

The park at Ranomafana—one of six large U.S.-financed projects in Madagascar—has been touted as a model of sensitive conservation in the third world. The project was based on the premise that if the government wanted to stop local farmers from clearing more forest, it had to offer them alternative sources of income and economic development. Wright worked closely with the Malagasy government, and half of the park's entrance fees go to the local villages so that they can benefit from the growing ecotourism. And so Ranomafana has been seen as a win-win situation where foreign scientists, the national government, and local villagers were all working in unison to preserve the environment. Wright won a MacArthur grant for her work and was knighted by the Malagasy government, the first foreigner to be so honored. She has become a conservation celebrity—featured on the BBC and on Japanese television—and is one of the main subjects of a recent documentary film, *Me and Isaac Newton*, profiling seven inspirational scientists.

But the view from the ground is very different from the glossy pictures in nature magazines and documentaries. The big conservation projects in Madagascar are highly unpopular among most local people, who see them as simply the latest attempt of foreigners and their own national government to take away their land. In some national parks in Madagascar—though not Ranomafana—angry villagers have slit the throats of lemurs and hung them from trees as acts of protest. In one park set up by the World Wildlife Fund local farmers burned down a quarter of the forest in response to harsh restrictions on land use.

The benefits of ecotourism are thinly spread among a few hundred people living near the parks. Most alternative development schemes have failed to work and the USAID budget for development in Ranomafana has been eliminated. Thus local people have lost access to ancestral lands but have yet to see many of the promised benefits. "We have a proverb," one villager near Ranomafana told me. "'When you slaughter a head of cattle, the owner gets the choicest piece.' We are supposed to be the owners of the forest, but we get none of its fruits."

For many rural Malagasy, the forest is their economic safety net, a resource to be drawn upon when food is scarce: they collect wood for fuel, gather honey, eels, shrimp, and crayfish to eat or sell, and, if they were allowed, they would cut down trees in order to plant crops. In a place where malnutrition is rampant and starvation not uncommon, the restrictions of the park are anything but trivial.

Anthropologists working in Madagascar see the ambitious conservation program as an example of "green imperialism," a case of Western scientists declaring the environment a "global resource" to justify seizing control over other countries' territory. "It's a colonial enterprise," said Maurice Bloch, a French anthropologist who has been a widely respected expert on Madagascar for more than thirty years. "People are under the authority of a biology professor who has been given absolute power over their lives." The whole idea of biodiversity and species, Bloch said, is itself a Western notion of relatively little meaning to people involved in a struggle for basic survival. "The very word *nature* doesn't exist in Malagasy," Bloch said. "It's the imposition of a foreign idea, a fad, on people through a kind of economic and police control."

Pat Wright and the ecologists insist that conservation is far more than a fad. "If we don't protect the forest, the headwaters of the whole country will dry up," she said. According to ecologists, 80 percent of the country's rain forests have already been destroyed and the remaining forest plays a critical role in holding moisture on the eastern escarpment of the country, which feeds the rivers and irrigation systems on which much of the rest of the country depends for its livelihood.

"The problem is that both sides are right," said David Burney, a professor of biology at Fordham University in New York, who has studied extinct species in Madagascar for many years. "It's true that we have tended to overlook the human impact of conservation, but it is also true that if Pat had done nothing there probably wouldn't be much forest left."

*　　*　　*

When we met in 1999, Wright was a slightly overweight fifty-four-year-old woman with shoulder-length brown hair parted to one side and a mouth full of crooked teeth that somehow added up to a winning smile. She wore green Wellington boots, a green rain jacket, and a tan mesh vest full of pockets filled with various things she uses in the rain forest: notebook, flashlight, compass, and binoculars. And although she looks like a physically unprepossessing middle-aged woman, she can move through a forest with considerable speed and purpose when in pursuit of a lemur. She has a way of tilting her head sideways and nodding when she is listening to others that conveys a sense of sincerity and empathy, but to some it is a clever mask that hides a steely determination to eliminate all obstacles in her path.

She has traveled a considerable distance to reach her position of prominence in the rain forests of Madagascar. Although she majored in biology, Wright became a social worker in Brooklyn in the mid-1960s and helped put her first husband through art school. Her career as a primatologist began in 1968 when she and her husband bought a nocturnal owl monkey named Herbie at a pet store for forty dollars. Wright became fascinated observing Herbie and later traveled to South America to find him a mate. The Wrights and the monkeys became parents during the same week and Wright was interested to note that Herby did most of the work raising his infant while she assumed all the child-care duties in her own family. Gradually, Wright became interested in the evolutionary basis of this parenting behavior and decided to study South American night monkeys in the wild—something that had never been done before. Despite having no background as a primatologist, she eventually succeeded in getting a small grant to conduct research as an independent scholar.

In 1976, Wright, her husband, and their three-year-old daughter headed off for the rain forests of Peru, and she spent nights out alone with a flashlight in a forest populated with jaguars, poisonous snakes, and wild boars. Wright's work in South America was very well received and led her to seek a doctorate at the City University of New York; but as she began graduate school, her husband of ten years suddenly left her. Wright soldiered on, raising her daughter, doing fieldwork in Peru, and earning a Ph.D. in 1985.

Wright's focus on monogamy, parenting, and gender roles among primates was met with considerable interest by a new generation of scholars influenced by the feminist movement. In the first part of the century, primatology, like most other academic disciplines, was dominated by men, who tended to look at apes and monkeys in a very male way, making blanket declarations such as: "Competition is peculiar to the male sex." As women began entering the field in large numbers—and women have been particularly prominent in primatology—the field began asking different questions and getting different answers and led Wright, quite naturally, to Madagascar.

In 1966, a female primatologist at Princeton, Alison Jolly, documented the fact that in one major family of primates—lemurs—females were the dominant gender. Lemurs dramatically contradicted the notion that aggression and competition were a male monopoly: female lemurs lead the troop, and if a male lemur even thinks about trying to eat the choice fruit of the tree, he will be chased away until he backs down and makes submissive cries. Lemur research, however, remained on hold through most of the 1970s, as Madagascar embarked on a post-colonial socialist experiment during which Western scientists were largely unwelcome.

Pat Wright arrived at just the right time, in 1984. Within scholarly circles interest in gender issues was keen and Madagascar, on the edge of bankruptcy, had decided to reopen itself to the West. The World Bank and USAID were eager to help Madagascar with its debt but insisted on economic austerity measures and an ambitious Environmental Action Plan. Suddenly, biodiversity—a term coined by scientists in the 1970s—had become, within a decade, an arm of American foreign policy as well as a central tenet of the World Bank. Rarely has an idea spawned in academe had such a swift and dramatic impact. International donors agreed to pour more than $120 million into Madagascar, a country of only fourteen million people, in order to expand Madagascar's protected areas and create a new national park service.

At first, Wright found Madagascar tremendously depressing—a desperately poor country with a devastated natural landscape, reeling from the effects of decolonization. In the early 1970s, after a revolution and a presidential assassination, Madagascar became a socialist dictatorship, taking its economic advice from places like the China of Mao Zedong and the North Korea of Kim Il-Sung. As a result, it saw its per capita income drop by half at the same time as its population doubled. What had been a poor but self-sufficient rural country became, in the space of a generation, one of the poorest nations in the world, with an average income of $230 a year.

The capital, Antananarivo, whose population has mushroomed to over a million in the last twenty years, still has the look of a rural cow town that has been improvised overnight into a city. Just a few hundred yards from the center, there are rice paddies, thatch-roofed huts, and farmers herding cattle. Rice cultivation is part of Madagascar's Asian heritage. Many of the country's first settlers are believed to have come from the Pacific islands near Indonesia, and the Malagasy language is closest to dialects spoken in the highlands of Borneo. But the cattle in the fields—the hump-backed long-horned zebu—came from Africa, where the early colonists are believed to have settled before making the trip across the Mozambique Channel to Madagascar. Thus the people and culture are a fusion of African and Asian influences.

With the countryside unable to sustain Madagascar's bulging population, hundreds of thousands have migrated in recent years to the cities in search of opportunity, often finding none. Bands of hungry children beg aggressively in the streets and it is not uncommon to see grown men lying on the sidewalk, evidently on the brink of starving to death, their thighs almost as thin as their wrists. At the same time, Antananarivo's streets are now congested with four-wheel-drive vehicles—a symbol of Madagascar's conservation boom. The World Bank's "structural adjustment" has done little to alleviate poverty but it has, along with reducing inflation and the budget deficit, succeeded in creating a thin veneer of new rich. Rather than the Mercedes or BMW, the four-wheel-drive Jeep is the vehicle of choice for Madagascar's elite, a reflection of both fashion and the country's miserable disrepair. The French left Madagascar in 1960 with approximately thirty thousand kilometers of good asphalt roads; now about two-thirds of them are so badly pitted with potholes that they are virtually impassable without a Jeep. Rather than fix the roads, Madagascar's parliament voted to give all its members four-wheel-drive vehicles.

Madagascar is nominally a democracy. However, its current president, Didier Ratsiraka, is the same socialist dictator who drove the country into the ground between 1975 and 1991. Unfortunately, after he left office his democratically elected successor proved no better at managing the economy and so Ratsiraka was narrowly voted back into office in 1997. Some have compared the election to "a choice between cholera and the plague." Adapting himself to the times, Ratsiraka ran on an "ecologist-humanist" platform.

Despite its reputation for biodiversity, the landscape of central Madagascar—heading south from Antananarivo to the rain forest of Ranomafana—is surprisingly bleak and monotonous. The road is lined almost exclusively with pines and eucalyptus trees imported by the French colonial administration; beyond them are large empty fields of dull, brownish grass in which no crops grow and no cattle graze. Occasionally, near the rivers, there are rice paddies or, in the distant hills, one can see the orange and black of fields burning where farmers are practicing slash-and-burn agriculture.

It was this vast, barren landscape that Wright first saw when she flew over Madagascar. "It breaks my heart," Wright said during a trip we took through the highlands. "This land has literally been baked," she said, fingering a shelf of hard reddish earth that looks like clay fired in a potter's oven.

The soil of Madagascar is surprisingly infertile, a fact that weighs heavily in the history of both the country's lemurs and its human beings. Farmers cut down the trees and set fire to the underbrush, the ashes of which serve as nutrients to the harsh, infertile soil. The system of slash-

and-burn agriculture works well as long as there is enough land to allow farmers to keep moving around, giving the burned land fifteen or twenty years to grow back. But with increased population, much of the best land has become overfarmed and overgrazed and the soil has become increasingly eroded and poor. As a result, the central highland plateau has become largely barren and in the last century farmers have been pushing farther down the slopes of the eastern escarpment that leads to the lowlands by the coast of the Indian Ocean. The escarpment, which runs north-south almost the thousand-mile length of Madagascar, is the location of the country's largest rain forests, which were once upon a time synonymous in Madagascar with infinite abundance. "There will be no end, like the eastern forest," goes one Malagasy expression.

Now the barren landscape extends almost an eight-hour drive south from Antananarivo, and only when the ground becomes treacherously steep and mountainous does the terrain suddenly come alive. The arid fields and the pine and eucalyptus are suddenly replaced by an explosion of tropical flora. Ravenala, a native plant with huge dark green leaves four or five feet long and a Madagascar relative of the banana, whose long, thin leaves unfold like a giant fan, lines the roadside. The hilltops are covered with closed-canopy forest thick with bamboo, rosewood, guava, mango, and fig trees. The slopes in this part of the escarpment are so steep and wet that they are difficult to burn, let alone farm. As unpromising as it may seem for agriculture, the forest is Madagascar's last frontier, coveted by both farmers and conservationists.

It was here that Wright first came in 1986, on an expedition sponsored by the World Wildlife Fund to try to find the greater bamboo lemur, *Hapalemur simus*, a species that had been sighted only a handful of times in this century and was presumed by many to be extinct. Walking through the forest at Ranomafana, Wright spied stands of giant bamboo towering sixty-five feet in the air. Since the greater bamboo lemur (and two other types of lemur) feed on bamboo, it seemed a natural place to look. After weeks of tramping around the forest in the rain, she and her guides caught a few glimpses of a large lemur eating bamboo. Its size suggested that it might be the greater bamboo lemur, except that it was a golden reddish color while *Hapalemur simus* was supposed to be gray. It then vanished. Subsequently, about twenty miles away, Wright and her team finally located a population of greater bamboo lemurs that fit the classic description of the group. This established firmly that the species was not extinct but raised another question: what was that red-colored lemur Wright had mistaken for *Hapalemur simus* back in the Ranomafana forest?

When they returned to Ranomafana, Wright and her team were presented with a couple of troubling novelties. A logging company was chopping down precious rosewood and mahogany trees. The area, considered a "classified forest" (under rules originally laid down by the French), could be exploited with special permission, and the Malagasy government had granted concessions to eight different logging companies to harvest parts of the Ranomafana forest. In fact, in an ironic contradiction, Madagascar's Ministry of Water and Forests was entirely dependent on logging concessions for its income. "They were knocking down ten trees for every one they were taking," Wright said. "I realized that if we didn't save the forest, I was going to have nothing left to study."

The other new development was that a German primatologist, Bernard Maier, was in the forest observing the red-colored lemur that Wright had previously glimpsed. Maier suspected that the red-colored lemur was not simply a variation of the great bamboo lemur but a whole new species; if he was correct, the discovery was the sort on which academic careers are built. Wright and Maier worked separately tracking the reddish lemur, trying to distinguish it from the other known bamboo lemurs.

Maier and his group were able to capture specimens from the different groups and to take blood samples, and DNA analysis confirmed that the reddish lemur was indeed a separate species. Maier accepted Wright's word that she had seen the red lemur on her first visit to Ranomafana and the two agreed to share credit for discovering the new species—*Hapalemur aureus*, the golden bamboo lemur. Cooperation rather than competition, they agreed, would better serve the cause of creating a park and protecting the lemurs' habitat.

"Pat flew back to the States and began to work on getting funding for the park, and the next thing you knew it was her discovery and her park," said a former park employee who did not want to be identified.

In the scientific paper announcing the new species, Maier and his colleagues get top billing, with Wright's name coming last, but in the popular media, it is her name, and usually her name alone, that appears again and again in association with the golden bamboo lemur and the park of Ranomafana. (Some say the credit should go to the local villagers who had spotted the red-colored lemur well before either of the Western scientists arrived on the scene.) Wright dutifully cites Maier's initial article in her scholarly work but says that the media attention she has attracted was instrumental in rallying support for the creation of a national park.

"She's great at politicking, she charms people, she had people at USAID, ambassadors, and Malagasy government ministers eating out of her hand. She's great at raising a lot of money, getting a lot of attention," said Paul Ferraro, who came to Ranomafana in 1989 while still an undergraduate at Duke University and spent time there over the next several years pursuing graduate work in environmental science. "She put that project on the map and kept it on the map."

In August 1990, USAID gave Wright a grant of $3.237 million for the first phase of the creation of Ranomafana National Park, effectively trumping the bids of the logging companies, whose concessions were set to expire.

Ranomafana now has the look of a moderately prosperous rural African market town. The main street is a short strip of flimsily built wooden shops with corrugated tin roofs selling bananas, spices, soft drinks, and slabs of zebu meat hanging on hooks, attracting flies. Looming in the background, above the fields on either side of the road, is the mountainous rain forest, an intense dark green shrouded in a gossamer mist.

There are still only a sprinkling of cars in the town. Here, as in most of the rest of Madagascar, the vast majority of people walk everywhere they go and the asphalted roads are lined at all hours of the day with a stream of people: small children heading off to school, occasionally breaking into a run as they play tag or race one another; women carrying baskets of laundry on their heads; farmers trudging off to their rice fields, carrying either an axe or a hoe on their shoulders. Some are dressed in traditional Malagasy shawls, others in Western-style clothes; most are barefoot. Shoes in this part of the world are a sign of relative prosperity.

Most of the cars on the road are trucks delivering goods to the town or the four-wheel vans belonging to the park service or to small eco-tourist operations.

"The communities around the park seem very poor, but they were so much poorer before," Wright said as we drove through town in her Toyota Land Cruiser. "People are making money now. They have steady jobs. We employ over a hundred people," she added, pointing out the achievements of the park project. There is a little museum with exhibits on Madagascar's environment, a souvenir shop, a small health clinic, a basketball court in the middle of town, and new buildings for the local elementary school. When Wright first came to Ranomafana only one business in town, the Hotel Thermal, had electricity; now a number of businesses and homes do. "It's just an amazing boom in the area," she said, getting a little carried away. There was still only one phone in Ranomafana—at the post office—but cellular phone service was expected soon. "That will make a world of difference," Wright said. Rather than lay thousands of miles of cables, Madagascar may simply leapfrog straight to cell towers. There are a few modest new hotels—mostly uninsulated wooden bungalows with communal baths and toilets—but they have attracted a certain number of adventurous, outdoorsy tourists, principally from France. "This year, we had thirteen thousand tourists in the park, up from zero when we started in 1991," Wright said in late 1999.

The main entrance to the national park is about five miles outside the town. Visitors buy tickets and souvenirs at a wooden cabin or hire trained local guides who are adept at spotting lemurs and other rare animals and plants. The entrance leads down a path to the forest, across a wooden bridge over the Namorana River. "It's called 'the bridge of gold,' because of the golden bamboo lemur," Wright said. "The reason that there is a park is because of the golden bamboo lemur, and they talk about that, their 'golden treasure.' They connect the forest with their economic growth."

On the other side of the river, there was a maze of marked trails leading through the forest. One of them led to two wooden cabins that have served as Wright's headquarters for the last several years. Nearby were a cluster of tents in the forest where Wright and a community of about thirty people were camped. There was a group of about ten "scientific tourists" from the environmental group Earthwatch, who pay a small fee to study lemurs for two weeks, each assigned to note every move of one particular animal in five-minute increments. There were ten or so undergraduates from the State University of New York at Stony Brook, where Wright teaches, taking a semester abroad. One of the cabins served as a classroom, the other as a kind of mess hall, where everyone took meals of mostly rice and beans at long tables inside and outside the cabin. There were also a few Malagasy students from the University of Antananarivo and a small stream of visiting scientists. Some come to study lemurs, others plants, insects, small mammals, fish, or reptiles.

Although Wright will soon be building a much grander dormitory and laboratory with hot water and many other modern conveniences, for more than ten years she has spent about half her time here, sleeping in a tent, taking cold showers, and eating rice and beans. And yet even so, with running water, electricity, computers, and a full-time cook, the research cabin is luxurious by local standards. Moreover, the park is a place of extraordinary peace and beauty: the sound of the rushing river mingles with the calls of exotic, brightly colored birds. There are no large carnivores or poisonous snakes, making its nature quite gentle and unthreatening. And for a primatologist, the place is pure heaven: outside the research cabin, you can easily see the greater bamboo lemur—once thought to be extinct—gnawing away at a stalk of bamboo, or a *Microcebus* lemur, the world's smallest primate, a tiny, mouse-size creature with the large, curious eyes of a primate.

Although relatively lush, this is not the sort of dense jungle one normally associates with rain forests. Because of the infertility of the soil, it takes a long time for the trees here to grow back. "In South America you needed a machete to get through the forest and if you came back in a few months, it was all grown back," Wright said. "Here, it takes twenty or thirty years for the forest to recover."

The infertility of the land also turns out to be one of the keys to female dominance among lemurs, Wright and other primatologists believe. Because the soil is poor, the crowns of its trees are much smaller and produce much less food. The scarcity in the forest has meant that keeping the lactating female lemur well fed is the species' overwhelming priority. At the same time, the absence of large carnivores has greatly reduced the need for large, brawny males to defend against attackers. In the richer environments of Africa and South America, it is both possible and necessary to feed large male monkeys who can fend off big predators; in Madagascar, they are an unnecessary luxury.

Thus, rather than being divinely ordained, male dominance is the chance product of circumstance and subject to change. "It was very liberating," Wright said of realizing how variable and arbitrary gender roles are. If lemurs are a "relic" species—an earlier kind of primate that died out in other parts of the world—what does lemur behavior tell us about humans? I asked Wright. "Well, one thing it tells you is that in any group someone has to lead," she said.

In Madagascar, Wright herself is a dominant leader. And Wright acknowledges that being female in Madagascar has its advantages in the human world, too. "I think, because of the history of colonialism, a Western man coming in and trying to do this would have been too threatening to the Malagasy," she said.

When Wright arrived at Ranomafana, only two of the twelve lemur species in the forest had been studied closely. Now ten have been. Two of the ten, including the golden bamboo lemur, are known to exist only in this forest. One of the interesting things researchers have discovered about the golden bamboo lemur is that, in order not to compete for food with the two other bamboo lemurs in the forest, it eats a part of the bamboo tree loaded with enough cyanide to kill a horse. Studying how it processes the poison through its digestive tract could yield medically useful information. Already, the rosy periwinkle plant, unique to Madagascar, has proven invaluable for treating certain kinds of childhood leukemia.

And although the park at Ranomafana was set up because of the lemurs, visiting scientists there study a host of other species as well. When I was there, three scientists passed through Wright's research cabin who were studying crayfish. There are, it turns out, six species of crayfish in Madagascar, all of them endemic. Five of them live in the streams of the Ranomafana rain forest. Thus, although the park was designed initially to protect lemurs, it has the added side benefit of preserving crayfish, too. Moreover, the Madagascar crayfish, *Astacoides madagascarensis*, one of the oldest living species, is a potential key to understanding Madagascar's and the planet's early history. Crayfish are at least 265 million years old, older than the dinosaurs and older than the island of Madagascar itself. Madagascar did not break off from Africa and become an island until 160 million years ago and yet, for some reason, Africa is the one continent on earth with no crayfish in its streams and rivers. So, why are there crayfish on Madagascar but none in Africa? DNA analysis, according to Keith Crandall, a zoologist at Brigham Young University in Utah and the leader of the crayfish expedition to Ranomafana, reveals that the Madagascar crayfish are most closely related to those in Australia and New Zealand, as well as those along the coast of Chile in South America.

The *Astacoides madagascarensis* may therefore be a critical piece of evidence in the emerging theory that Australia, South America, and Madagascar at an earlier time, during the Permian and Triassic ages, were all connected to one another through the continent of Antarctica. Madagascar then drifted north, bumped into the coast of Africa, and then later moved out to sea to its present position. This theory of geobiology was suggested by similarities between dinosaur fossils found in Madagascar, Australia, and South America, but crayfish are one of the few live survivors of this migration of continents. By examining the differentiation in the DNA of the different crayfish, scientists can reconstruct the dates of these major geological events, using DNA as a "molecular clock." And so the live tissue of the humble but very ancient crayfish may hold an important secret of our past: the merging and breakup of entire continents hundreds of millions of years ago.

As well as containing important biological data, the Madagascar crayfish are also a mainstay of the local economy. Many local residents make their living catching and selling crayfish and regard the restrictions of the park as a threat to their survival. A study of nineteen villages near Ranomafana showed that nearly a third got about half their income from crayfish and two villages lived almost entirely off them. Crandall found that villagers were having to travel farther and farther into the rain forest to find crayfish, suggesting that they were becoming increasingly scarce. Two of Madagascar's six crayfish species are already endangered and the other four may soon join them on the list. Thus, the ecologists say, if the trade continues unchecked, there will be no more crayfish either for villagers or for scientists and conservation is, therefore, ultimately in the interest of both. Crandall noted, however, that crayfish harvesting has increased significantly in recent years, perhaps unwittingly stimulated by the park project itself: by preventing villagers from using the forest for logging and other forms of economic exploitation, it appears to have made them more dependent on fishing. Moreover, the growing ecotourism trade has created a growing market for the crayfish in local restaurants serving foreigners who come to visit the park. The story of the crayfish is a parable of the catch-22 nature of conservation and development in Madagascar.

While few inside the park doubt its value, to those on the outside looking in, the project appears very different indeed. "For us, the park means death," Norbert Butovao, a farmer and landowner in the village of Ranovao told me.

This may seem a dramatic statement, but in rural Madagascar it is not so far-fetched. Lost access to the forest and several broader national trends—overpopulation, declining soil quality, cuts in social spending—have combined to push some of the poorest rural people in villages closer to the edge. Overcrowded villages full of malnourished people are particularly vulnerable to diseases that suddenly rip through the area. Earlier in the year, eleven people died of bubonic plague in one village in just two days. In another village, seventeen people—nearly 10 percent of the population—died of dysentery in the span of a few months. Both were pilot villages that had received special attention from the park project. Although Wright had been in Ranomafana most of the fall, she had no idea about the two lethal epidemics. In fact, she pointed to the plague-stricken village as we drove by one day, saying, "That's one of our model villages. We built a school there." It was only a few days later, when we visited the offices of the health clinic in the town of Ranomafana, that we learned of the catastrophe. We also learned that Wright's health team had not been paid in six months and had consequently dwindled from nine to three people. Nine years after the creation of the park, they still do not even have a motor scooter for transportation, limiting their ability to visit the more remote villages.

In fairness to Wright, she deserves credit for there being a health team in the first place; USAID did not provide funding for health care. Wright raised the money from the Liz Claiborne Foundation in the United States, but the funding has run out. But Wright's having succeeded in raising money from the National Science Foundation for a new laboratory and research center while failing to get new money for health and other social programs reflects the fact that most of her time and energy is going toward lemur research; the problems of the local Malagasy have receded into the background. It also reflects the fact that charitable donors in the United States are interested more in Madagascar's biodiversity than in its people and Wright, as one of the most prominent spokespersons for Madagascar in the United States, bears some responsibility for this lopsided view. She has worked hard to offer a rosy vision of Ranomafana and downplayed problems that have been evident from the beginning.

"It's all PR," said Janice Harper, an anthropologist at the University of Houston who did her doctoral research in one of the pilot villages in the area near the park. "When I started my work I believed that the project was a good thing, but when I saw the indifference to the consequences of the project on people's lives and livelihoods, I was appalled."

Social scientists insist that Ranomafana and most of the other big conservation projects in Madagascar suffer from a kind of original sin: they were born because of the sudden interest in biodiversity and have generally been led by conservationists. The lack of knowledge about Madagascar's culture and history, they argue, has skewed the priorities of the park. They offer a counterhistory of the project considerably at variance with Wright's vision of Ranomafana as a dream come true. It is a portrait, in the words of Janice Harper, of "a world gone wrong, a system broken by outsiders and insiders."

The village of Ranovao, where Harper lived and worked, is about a six-mile walk from the road that cuts through Ranomafana—along narrow, mostly uphill dirt paths, offering spectacular views of shimmering rice paddies and mist-covered forest.

"The Malagasy language has no word for landscape," observed my guide and interpreter, Solo Raharinjanahary, a professor of ethnolinguistics at the University of Antananarivo. Locked for centuries into a difficult struggle for material survival, the Malagasy tend to have a functional view of nature. "When I show my students snapshots of beautiful landscapes, they don't say, 'How pretty,' they say, 'That's the area where my uncle is from or where such and such event happened,'" said Raharinjanahary. "When they see Westerners photographing a sunset without any people in it, they think, These *vazaha* [foreigners] are crazy." As a passionate student of Malagasy culture and a professor who studied and teaches in French, Raharinjanahary lives between the two worlds: he is in favor of nature preserves and conservation but does not want them imposed unilaterally on local people. "We have to think about future generations, but you have to offer valid alternatives," he said. "You can't just say, 'Don't do slash and burn.' People have to be convinced that it makes sense."

After about two hours of hiking, we spotted the village of Ranovao, a community with about thirty-five small mud-brick houses and about three hundred people. Most of the houses have thatched roofs and are about fifteen feet long and ten feet wide. They generally have packed dirt floors with handmade straw mats laid out on top. In some, the only furniture might be a bed or a low wooden bench placed by the wall so that visitors can lean back against it while sitting on the floor. In the middle, there is generally a little hearth with burning kindling or firewood, the only source of heat in the area, whose mountain air can be cool even in the spring and summer. There are a few somewhat larger houses with corrugated tin roofs and perhaps a table and a couple of chairs. These are the houses of the "rich" of Ranovao. Although there is no running water or electricity in the village, these houses have a few precious items such as a battery-powered radio or a hand-operated sewing machine.

All the people are rail-thin and virtually none have shoes or even a pair of plastic sandals. Many are dressed in torn, dirty rags that look as if they had been worn continuously for fifteen or twenty years. When the park project was begun, the park health team found that 69 percent of the children under the age of ten were underweight, 11 percent so drastically as to be classified as "wasted." This was fairly typical of rural Madagascar, where about half the children were stunted from malnutrition. Malaria was found in about half the children in this area and virtually all of them suffered from parasites or tapeworms.

Unfortunately, the health survey has not been repeated, but sickness appears to be very much present in the village when I was visiting. Most of the children cough repeatedly and many have liquid running from their noses, eyes, or mouths.

A few chickens scurry around between the houses and coffee beans are frequently laid out on the ground to dry. There are wooden granaries—filled with supplies of rice—built on stilts several feet high to keep out rats. The common rat, *Rattus rattus,* is not native to Madagascar but came with European sailors and, as in the Middle Ages, is a carrier of bubonic plague and other diseases. Wright and the conservationists note that the ascendancy of *Rattus rattus* is a practical argument in favor of biodiversity: rats are almost entirely absent from the rain forest, which is dominated by endemic rodents that do not carry disease, while the common rat has increased dramatically in the areas that have been cleared for cultivation, where the human population is concentrated.

Ranovao is a village of an ethnic group called the Tanala, meaning "people of the forest." The Tanala first took refuge in these rain forests in the late eighteenth century to escape slave traders who were selling them off on both the domestic and the international market. The Tanala bury their ancestors in the forest and ask their permission before burning or cultivating a particular piece of land. After the French occupied Madagascar in 1896, they tried to force the Tanala out of the forest and down to the road so that they could tax them and use them on forced labor gangs. Resistance to this policy led to a rebellion in 1947 in which some eighty thousand Malagasy were killed by French forces.

These historical memories are fresh in the minds of all Tanala farmers in and around Ranomafana and make them regard the park project with immediate suspicion. "First we were colonized by the French, now we have been colonized by the park," said Jean-Pierre Tvelo, the mayor of Ranomafana.

One of the cardinal premises of USAID-funded Integrated Conservation and Development Projects is that they should be carried out with the consensus and participation of the local people. If local people don't share the goals of the project, they won't respect its rules and will eventually destroy the forest. Wright often repeats the story of how she and a colleague from Duke University, Patrick Daniels, walked the entire boundaries of the vast park in order to listen to the concerns of the villages located nearby. But Paul Ferraro, who as a Duke undergraduate accompanied Wright on some of those walks, said that much of the consultation was more apparent than real, in part because of Wright's lack of understanding of the Malagasy language. "Pat and Patrick Daniels would ask people's views, but the forestry agent didn't necessarily translate what they said," remarked Ferraro, who was learning Malagasy at the time and eventually became conversant in the language. "The forestry agents have never been involved with community participation. The villagers were simply told what the boundaries would be."

In Ranovao, they remember Wright's arrival well. While unhappy about the restrictions of the park, villagers were excited by some of the promises that Wright made. "She was very good. She asked, 'What do you need?'" said Norbert Butovao, the farmer. The villagers spoke about their need for access to health care, schooling, and improved agricultural methods. "The park people made all kinds of promises, but they didn't keep them," several villagers repeated. "They seduced us."

To win support for the park, Wright and others did indeed promise or appear to promise many things that would prove difficult or impossible to deliver. There are some 160 villages located within a few miles of the boundaries of the national park, but there was funding for development projects in only twenty-six pilot villages, so even under the best of circumstances the project could help only a small fraction of the people in the area.

Since Wright had no background in development, she arranged for teams from North Carolina State University and Cornell to manage the development half of the project. But neither Wright nor the development teams people knew much about the particular problems of Madagascar. The principal thrust of the development efforts in the project were to provide alternatives to slash-and-burn agriculture by promoting things like fish ponds and mini-dams to irrigate rice paddies, which can be farmed again and again each year. But the fish ponds failed, in part because the Western technicians didn't understand that due to the poor quality of Madagascar's soil the fish didn't receive sufficient nutrients in the man-made ponds and failed to grow large enough to eat. Moreover, the villagers were required to buy the minnows to start the farms, meaning that only the wealthier farmers with capital to spare could afford to try them.

Also, by emphasizing rice paddies the project penalized those with hilly land that cannot be irrigated. "They helped the people with irrigated rice fields, who were also the wealthiest people, the most sophisticated in dealing with foreigners, and these people appropriated virtually all the land and resources in the village," said Janice Harper, who lived in Ranovao from 1995 to 1996.

Unwittingly, as Harper discovered, the project stirred up ancient social divisions. The village had a history of slavery and many of the park development projects were taken over by the former slave-owning families. "Within a period of a few years, the social structure of the village changed from one in which all households had access to forest land for subsistence agriculture to one in which the majority of the households worked as agricultural wage laborers for a minority controlling irrigated rice fields," Harper wrote in her dissertation.

Because development in Ranovao did not appear to be working, the park essentially dropped it as one of its pilot villages. In the first three years of the project, Ranovao received monthly visits from the park's health team (along with development assistance), but then the doctors stopped coming. "People perceived this as punishment for not going along with the schemes of the project," said Harper. The women of the village, for example, refused to practice birth control. Between the deteriorating economic position of the village's poorest families and the lack of medical care, people in Ranovao began dying in alarming numbers.

"While I was there, 10 percent of the villagers died," Harper said. "There were about 180 people living there and eighteen died in fourteen months." Shocked and frightened by the situation, Harper began to make a fuss with the park officials and wrote to Patricia Wright in the United States. Lyn Robinson, who was the park technical advisor from 1993 until 1997, wanted to make Harper leave the country. In fact, at a meeting with both Robinson and Wright, Harper was asked to sign a typed statement in which she promised not to discuss her views of the park project with the villagers and not to interview people without park staff present. Harper refused to sign the document and left Madagascar a few months before the planned completion of her research.

Wright was clearly embarrassed when I asked about the episode. "I was away a lot that year," she said. "I only heard about all of this second-hand. Janice, because she was confronted with all these deaths, was extremely hysterical. I can't say I blame her. On the other hand, I had this technical adviser who was extremely hardheaded and not as much in favor of researchers. I was getting these reports of Janice being hysterical in town, drinking too much and getting really out of hand. I had never seen her in that state, so it was difficult for me to understand why Lyn was so adamant about wanting to get Janice out of here. I said, 'Let's wait a minute.' I had approved Janice's project. I had thought it would be useful to have input from cultural anthropologists in the villages. So I called her adviser, who said she was doing good work. He came over to Madagascar. And we had a meeting."

When I mentioned that she had been present at the meeting at which Harper had been presented with a written ultimatum, Wright reacted with alarm. "I didn't write that letter. Lyn Robinson wrote that letter. Does Janice have a copy of that letter?" Later she added, "I realized that I was losing control of the project. [Lyn] was a very controlling individual," Wright said. "And anyone who didn't do exactly what she wanted was fired or thrown out in some way or another. Finally, [Lyn] just had to leave because she became destructive of the goals of the project."

Harper, however, feels that Wright is hiding behind Robinson. "Pat was aware of everything that went on, no matter how much she denies it," said Harper.

In Ranovao, villagers said they signed a petition in support of Harper. "Janice thought that the lives of people were more important than those of beasts," said Mira, a ninety-year-old woman.

While a visit to Ranovao and another pilot village revealed a virtually unanimous dislike of the park project, it also made clear the extreme difficulty of improving the condition of such places. The population when Harper was living in Ranovao in 1995 was about 180. By the end of 1999, it had reached 300—almost guaranteeing that the village will have a harder and harder time feeding itself. Moreover, the villagers have a tradition of burying their dead in the forest upstream of where they take their drinking water—something that might help explain the high rates of disease.

Despite these considerable objective difficulties, it is also true that very little of the money spent in the Ranomafana park project was actually used for the pilot villages. "By my own calculations, less than two percent of the $3.237 million in Phase I went toward 'village projects,'" Joe Peters, who was a part of the North Carolina State University development team that worked in Ranomafana from 1991 to 1993, wrote in a recent article. "A full 18 percent of the total went toward U.S. university 'overhead,' while nearly 37 percent went to expatriate personnel. I know because I was one of them."

From the beginning, the great bulk of the energy and money for the project was concentrated in and around the town of Ranomafana. There are only a few hundred people who benefit directly from the project, working for the park, for the museum, or in the small local hotels and restaurants. Virtually none of the people operating the local hotels are actually from Ranomafana; they were already moderately prosperous businesspeople from the general vicinity. In good part, the project has benefited well-to-do people who had money to invest and were in a position to take advantage of the opportunities of ecotourism. "When I started the park project I decided to go to the five richest businessmen in the area because I felt I needed to get them on board if this was going to work," Wright said. "Maybe that was wrong."

"Most of the money is going to people who don't need help," said Jamie Spencer, a Scotsman who volunteered to work for Wright in 1990 but quit in disgust six months later. Spencer formed his own private charity in Scotland, raising and distributing money for rural development in the province around Ranomafana. "She took the political, easy option," said Spencer. "The quickest way to get things done in a poor country is throwing money at the richest people."

Paul Ferraro, who was there at the same time, agrees with Spencer but thinks he is too harsh on Wright. "It is naïve to think you can ignore the big players," he said. "They can stop your project. They have contacts with the political people." They also have the know-how to get work done quickly and efficiently. Ferraro recalls one project in which Wright tried to use a small local builder, a relative of one of the park guides, to build a school. "It was so badly built that it had to be torn down," he said. "So she ended up dealing with the bigger players. Perhaps she went overboard."

The incident where most people think Wright went overboard was in contracting with a notorious local character to build the Ranomafana museum. Although a former local police chief, he had enriched himself through illegal logging in the rain forest. Wright defended the choice. "This man came to me and said, 'How am I going to make a living?'" she recalled. "I told him I would hire him to build the building where we have our museum. That way he could find a legitimate way of making a living rather than cutting down the forest." However, the man was caught and arrested for illegal logging even after the park project began. Thus it is possible that the handsomely carved wood doors of the museum are actually made of lumber plundered from the rain forest whose protection the museum celebrates.

This relationship, according to Spencer and others, created a terrible example for the local people. "It made them tremendously cynical: here is USAID shooting itself in the foot by working with the most corrupt people," he said. Adding insult to injury, for several years the only wall label in the museum that was in the Malagasy language was the one marking a small wooden cabinet that says: "Who is destroying the forest?" When you open the cabinet, there is a mirror. "Local people were absolutely horrified," said Spencer.

Although Wright touts the fact that half of the entrance fees to the park go to local villages, only about 10 of the 160 villages near the park receive any money—and only for development projects that are considered worthy. "We want to encourage them to do things that are consistent with conservation," said Benjamin Andriamihaja, Wright's Malagasy partner in the park project. This selectivity contributes to the sense among the villages that the park administration plays favorites. Park administrators acknowledge that they are funding projects only in villages near the road in order to encourage people to move away from the forest—subtly reproducing the dynamic of the French colonial administration.

The park is now managed by a Malagasy state agency, but some feel that in Ranomafana Wright used local networks and nepotism to create her own private power base. Virtually all the park guides are from a single village, Ambatolahy, located near the park entrance, and many of them are related. "The guides are excellent and very loyal but they are her little army," Spencer said. He recalled that Wright would encourage graduate students and visiting researchers to leave some of their equipment—fancy foreign-made trekking boots, binoculars, or rain gear—for the guides. "Of course, what graduate student is going to disobey a professor?" Spencer asked. In an extremely poor village in Madagascar, Wright's generosity toward her guides overturned the social structure in their village. One of the village elders, Spencer said, simply left the village and moved several miles away because he had lost all authority. "It was a classic case of giving too much to too few, disrupting the social cohesion of the village. Here were these dudish guys driving around in their four-wheel-drive vehicles, with their boots and sunglasses and Leica binoculars, going into town and getting pissed."

Ironically, Paul Ferraro, who went on to get a Ph.D. in environmental economics at Cornell, found that some of the research guides from Ambatolahy were using the money they earned at the park to hire laborers to do slash-and-burn agriculture. When Ferraro presented a paper detailing his findings on a 1995 trip to Ranomafana, the park management succeeded in having him declared persona non grata and asked him to leave the country.

Ferraro's work focused on the problem of linking conservation and development—the crucial problem at Ranomafana, as at all the USAID's Integrated Conservation and Development Projects. Members of the North Carolina State team say they were told initially that during the first three-year phase of the project, conservation would take precedence over development, while in the second phase, roles would be reversed. But relations began to deteriorate between Wright and the North Carolina development group rather quickly: the development people learned that their share of the budget would be only 29 percent with the rest going to conservation. Moreover, they had different ideas about development in Madagascar. Led by Dennis del Castillo and Joe Peters, they favored what they called a more "participatory" kind of development.

"I think they had a much more realistic idea of community development and community participation and a much more transparent way of working," said Jamie Spencer. The North Carolina team felt that Wright had a paternalistic view of development, making the grand gesture—promising to build a school, a pond, or a dam—rather than slowly and patiently trying to improve the productivity of local agricultural methods. "Pat would completely undermine their work," said Spencer. "She is a good-hearted person, but they were there permanently and she was out there for short periods and would promise all kinds of things and then leave them to deal with the consequences."

When it became apparent that Wright was not prepared to cede control of the project in the second phase, the North Carolina team decided to pull out, agreeing to remain until the end of 1993. "Suddenly all these nasty rumors about the NC State people started swirling around," said one researcher who was there at the time but not a member of either group. The acting governor of the province where Ranomafana is located sent a letter to Patricia Wright complaining that del Castillo and Joe Peters's wife, Dai, were conducting an open affair, an offense to the customs and culture of the Malagasy people. Wright apparently forwarded the letter to USAID in Antananarivo, and within three weeks the heads of the team, Peters and del Castillo, were asked to leave the country. USAID sent an official down to Ranomafana to investigate and concluded, after seeing Dai Peters ride into town on the back of del Castillo's motorcycle wearing a pair of short shorts, that the rumors were true. Others who were at Ranomafana say that there were signs that del Castillo and Dai Peters were having an affair and certainly not an open one. Had it been the case, it would hardly have shocked local Malagasy. Madagascar was until fairly recently a polygamous society and adultery is far from uncommon.

Many Americans working at Ranomafana at the time of the incident claim that the sexual accusations were trumped up in order to get rid of the North Carolina team during the delicate evaluation process that would determine the funding and direction of the second phase of the project. The North Carolina team had stated clearly that they would not remain if Pat Wright were head of the project—forcing the U.S. and Malagasy governments with a clear choice. "This was typical of Madagascar: when you want to get rid of someone you start a rumor campaign against them," said one American scientist who has worked in Madagascar for many years. "It was one of the ugliest and low-down power plays I've ever seen," said a USAID consultant who was involved in monitoring the project.

In 1995, USAID had tentatively decided to take away the overall direction of the program from Wright. Consultants working for USAID felt that Wright was away too much of the time and that she was a poor administrator, sloppy in filing reports and accounting for money, and much better equipped to do scientific research and conservation than to run a complex multimillion-dollar conservation and development project. Wright, however, got a congressman to intervene and had the decision reversed.

"There is a pattern at Ranomafana that anyone who stands up to Pat gets removed from the scene," said one U.S. government official. "But Ranomafana was hardly the only project with problems. Things got so bad between the development and conservation people at Amber Mountain National Park there was a legal divorce. But when all is said and done, I still think that Ranomafana was one of our more successful projects."

The problem goes much deeper than personality conflicts. The bigger issue, according to Jamie Spencer, is the short-term mentality of so much foreign aid. "Every project has to be three years. Why three years?" he said. Foreign technicians come in for a limited time and are under pressure to produce rapid results. Huge amounts of money are suddenly poured into a desperately poor country but for a very short period. Almost inevitably, the money will be spent in a hurried, haphazard fashion and local people will rush to cash in while it lasts.

"Donors are so quick to abandon projects," said Paul Ferraro. "They move on to the next thing. The attitude is, 'We're sending in the cavalry and we're getting results.'" This, Ferraro said, helps account for why the managers of Ranomafana were so terrified of any criticism of the project. "Donors don't respond well to criticism. If you said, 'We screwed up and we'd like to try again,' you would not get any more funds."

USAID has now had its budget slashed by the Senate Foreign Relations Committee, and so while $120 million was available for conservation in Madagascar between 1995 and 1999, only $40 million will be available for the next five years. USAID has essentially abandoned the idea of Integrated Conservation and Development Projects. Pouring large sums of money into the areas affected by the creation of the parks, it concluded, could as easily hurt the environment as help it. In some cases, it found that poor Malagasy from neighboring areas moved into villages near the park in order to benefit from the aid, adding to the pressures on the surrounding forest. In other cases, villagers went out of their way to destroy ecological resources in hopes of receiving assistance. USAID has decided to spread its money more thinly throughout the rain forest area rather than concentrate around the national parks.

Thus, after promising the twenty-seven thousand residents of the park's peripheral zone economic development in return for giving up access to the forest, the United States has, in some sense, reneged on its half of the deal. "I agree with the villagers who feel they have been seduced and abandoned," said Patricia Wright.

Many believe that farmers should simply be compensated for the loss of their land—as property owners are in the United States. Joe Peters now feels that the $6 million spent at Ranomafana from 1991 to 1997 could have been better used to establish an endowment, whose interest alone could have provided compensation—supplied fertilizer for farmers or financed public works projects indefinitely.

Ferraro proposes a somewhat different scheme, which calls for paying farmers for every acre of forest they leave still standing. "It's simpler and fairer," he said. If biodiversity is so important to people in the West, he said, let them pay for it. The idea of compensation is based on the principle that the villagers are the owners of the forest but gives them an economic incentive to preserve it. Presumably, they could then invest their earnings in more intensive agriculture techniques of their own choosing that would allow them to get more productivity out of the land that would remain under cultivation.

*   *   *

It would be unfair, however, to suggest that the millions of dollars spent in Ranomafana have been wasted entirely. The project has helped to create a park infrastructure, to train and equip the new Malagasy park administration, and to build the foundations of a new ecotourism economy that may bring wider and more evenly distributed benefits in the future. The efforts of the last fifteen years have created an environmental consciousness that did not exist before the program. Many of the villagers whom I interviewed clearly understood and appreciated the value of conservation; they simply didn't want to be the only ones to bear its cost.

Wright and the other Westerners, however, have very little notion of the impact—for good or ill—that their presence has had on the place. By mere virtue of the extraordinary economic disparity between the two countries, even lowly graduate students and ill-paid academics have the weight of mighty viceroys here. The entire budget of the township of Ranomafana (including several outlying villages) is fifteen thousand dollars, while Wright's new research center and laboratory will cost one million dollars, making her overwhelmingly the most powerful figure for miles around.

Patricia Wright may have concentrated too much power into her own hands, but she has done valuable work forging strong relationships with Malagasy researchers and scholars. Some fifty students from the University of Antananarivo have come to Ranomafana in the last decade and Wright has gotten graduate school fellowships in the United States for six of them.

At the end of my time in Ranomafana, I traveled with Wright and several others to a site by the Indian Ocean where a Malagasy graduate student of hers from Stony Brook was studying lemurs in a rain forest that had nearly been destroyed by a recent cyclone. Smart, dedicated, and passionate about his work, Jonah Ratsimbazafy is an impressive example of a new generation of Malagasy scientists and conservationists—perhaps the most positive and enduring legacy of the Ranomafana project. Rather than simply repeating by rote the bywords of the conservation movement ("We must preserve the forest for future generations"), Ratsimbazafy was bursting with knowledge about and interest in lemurs, biodiversity, and Madagascar. For him, knowledge of Madagascar's nature has become part of his sense of Malagasy identity. "They teach us hardly anything about our own nature here in Madagascar," he said. "For example, I didn't realize until I went to university that lemurs exist only in Madagascar. We learn more about lions and tigers and monkeys than about our own nature."

For months at a time, he has lived at a campsite near the Manombo rain forest with several local teenage boys whom he has trained as guides. They are helping him do an inventory of a forest whose lemur population has been reduced by a violent cyclone to numbers that place it in danger of extinction. When Wright and her group arrived, the young guides led us through the thick underbrush of the forest to the spots frequented by various species of lemur. They were clearly proud to be able to show off months of work and their obvious knowledge of the forest and its animals. The presence of these local guides, who will remain behind after Ratsimbazafy has finished his Ph.D. research, could be crucial to protecting the area against illegal deforestation—at minimal cost.

Along with visiting the Manombo forest, Wright was following up an intriguing rumor. Villagers in the Manombo area had reported seeing a huge aquatic animal, a creature twelve or fifteen feet long, in a riverbed. There are almost no large animals in modern Madagascar other than crocodiles and so the rumor aroused Wright's interest. There was, hundreds of years ago, a pygmy hippopotamus. Could it be a surviving hippo or some other entirely unknown Malagasy species, a Malagasy Loch Ness monster?

Out in the field, Wright's best qualities come to the fore: her boundless energy and drive, her curiosity about everything, and her appetite for her work. For more than eight hours, she sat good-naturedly in the back of a hot, crowded Land Cruiser as it bumped its way slowly across the miserable roads, forced to stop once because of a flat tire. She shared a room with a female Malagasy graduate student in order to save her program a few dollars. She enjoyed crawling around the underbrush of the Manombo forest looking for lemurs. As I boarded a plane to return to the capital, I could not help admiring Wright, a fifty-four-year-old woman excited to be heading off for a twelve-hour walk into the bush in search of the mysterious and possibly fictitious Madagascar Loch Ness monster. "It's probably nothing," she said, "but if I find it I'll be on the cover of *Science* magazine for sure!"

6

The Man Who Remembers

Back in the early 1970s, when anthropologist Giancarlo Scoditti
began his fieldwork on the remote island of Kitawa, off the coast
of Papua New Guinea, a powerful sorcerer gave him the name by which
he is known there to this day: Toruruwai, meaning "the man who
remembers."

The islanders were struck by the ability of this peculiar outsider—
the second Westerner and the first anthropologist to live on Kitawa—
who was constantly scribbling in his notebook, to recall the tiniest
details of their cultural rituals with extraordinary precision. While the
Kitawans were impressed with the technology of writing, Scoditti, for
his part, marveled at the ingenious strategies of an oral society for successfully transmitting its culture and traditions intact from one generation to the next.

But in the past twenty-five years, Scoditti has seen aspects of that
culture gradually disappear. Some of the islanders in the area now use
motorboats instead of canoes, eat canned food or bags of government
rice, and use Western tools and clothing. Seeing the erosion of traditional customs on neighboring islands, many Kitawans seem to be losing
confidence in their own culture. None of the three villages on the island

has held its traditional dances celebrating the harvest since 1994. No one has carved a ceremonial canoe—the art that originally attracted Scoditti to the region—in nearly a decade. And when Scoditti made a trip to the island in November 1997, he found the last oral poet on the island, whom he had recorded extensively and written about, lying alone and emaciated in his thatched hut, unwilling to transmit his art to his son or other young islanders, whom he considered insufficiently respectful of the traditions.

Now that many of the artists, poets, wise men, and sorcerers whom Scoditti first interviewed and recorded in the 1970s and 1980s either are dead or have turned away in mute protest, some islanders who are curious about their culture turn to Scoditti with questions about the meaning of the words of a poem, the sequence of a dance ritual, or the magical formulae to be pronounced in a particular ceremony.

Oral culture, Scoditti has found, is both tremendously robust and extremely fragile. In comparative isolation, most Pacific Islands successfully maintained their cultures from generation to generation for hundreds, if not thousands, of years. But on impact with other cultures and technologies, they have suddenly become extremely vulnerable. If the chain of knowledge breaks down and one generation fails to transmit what it knows to the next, millennia of accumulated wisdom can unravel in a few decades. "Like all oral cultures, operating in such an aggressive context, Kitawa has no means with which to defend itself," he said.

Thus Giancarlo Scoditti, bespectacled Italian professor at the University of Urbino, has become the repository of an entire culture, a small but rich, vital, and ancient civilization undergoing dramatic and irreversible changes.

Although in his early sixties and totally bald, Scoditti seems much younger; he generally dresses as simply and casually as a graduate student, wearing blue jeans and carrying a backpack. He is thin and agile in his movements, befitting someone who has spent years living the demanding physical life of Kitawa. An extremely shy, introverted man, he tends to eat his words when he speaks. Although he is a person of genuine warmth and unusual courtesy, an air of loneliness hangs about him: after an early marriage that ended many years ago, he has never remarried or put down roots. His reticence and lack of facile urbanity give one the impression that, like Swift's Gulliver, Scoditti feels more at home on his travels than in "civilization."

Although it has a population of only a few million people, the vast constellation of small islands that dot the South Pacific (generally called Melanesia, Micronesia, and Polynesia) is home to about one-sixth of the world's sixty-five hundred languages. Because of the number of islands that have lived long in comparative isolation, the region is to linguistic and cultural diversity what the Galápagos Islands or Madagascar is to biodiversity. And yet it is estimated that approximately half of the world's languages will disappear over the next century under the rapid homogenizing effects of globalization. Each one of these languages represents a culture, almost always an oral culture that dies with little trace.

I first met Scoditti in New York in 1996, when he spent a year as a visiting fellow of the Metropolitan Museum, and then again in 1997 when he returned as a visiting scholar at Columbia University's Italian Academy after another field trip to Kitawa. As I got to know him, I was struck by his predicament and that of Kitawa. What, if any, is the future of the world's thousands of tiny regional cultures under the assault of world modernization? What responsibilities does a scholar who has established a unique relationship to a particular culture have for its preservation? Why do we in the West care so much about documenting in excruciating scholarly detail a culture that may be largely gone when, and if, the area opens up to the outside world and is finally visited by other Westerners? Kitawa seemed to pose a philosophical question similar to that of whether a tree falling in the forest makes a noise if no one is there to hear it.

Writing about a place that I was unable to visit, that no Westerner except Scoditti and one other person has ever lived on presented unusual journalistic problems. As I sat listening with rapt attention to Scoditti's stories of ritual dances, "nights of love," village chieftains, sorcerers, "flying witches," and mythic heroes, the heretical thought occurred to me: What if he's made it all up? Of course, Scoditti has been extremely painstaking in documenting everything he has written about: in films, photographs, and tape recordings, many of which I have since seen and heard. Well-known scholars who have worked on other islands in the area have scrutinized and approved Scoditti's work. His book on Kitawan canoe carvers even includes a full text of his interviews with local artists in Nowau, the Kitawan language, but he is the only person who can read it. Even though I have no doubt that Scoditti is an unusually diligent and honest scholar, it seemed interesting to write about one of the few remaining corners of the world beyond verification, where you cannot telephone to check facts.

After completing a degree in philosophy at the University of Rome, Scoditti went to England to pursue a doctorate at the School for Oriental Studies in London. Sir Edmund Leach, the great Cambridge anthropologist, urged Scoditti to pursue his interest in the aesthetics of elaborately carved and decorated canoe prow boards from the Trobriand Islands, which Scoditti had been studying in museums. "The canoe is to these islands what the Gothic cathedral was to the people of the Middle Ages," Scoditti said: the product of sustained collective effort and devotion as well as the visual expression of the community's worldview.

One of Leach's own teachers, Bronislaw Malinowski, had done groundbreaking work in the area at the beginning of the century, producing the anthropological classic *Argonauts of the Western Pacific*. Each spring and fall, the adult males of the region set sail to other islands to participate in a series of ceremonial exchanges of gifts. Malinowski documented this dense network of ritual exchanges known as the "kula ring," which is the center of much of the cultural, social, and political life of the region. Malinowski was concerned, however, with the social and sexual customs of the region and had virtually no interest in the visual or artistic culture.

Although Malinowski wrote often about Kitawa as the source of many of the most finely crafted canoes in the area and of many of the beliefs and practices of the kula ring, including its central legend, the myth of the flying canoe, he never got to the island. Malinowski met some Kitawans when they passed through during their travels, but none would ever take him to their island. "They would give him an appointment on the beach and then never show up," Scoditti said with amused satisfaction. Malinowski's diaries display an attitude of arrogant disdain for the natives and Scoditti would like to believe that the Kitawans picked up on this and demonstrated characteristic good sense in ditching the Anglo-Polish anthropologist.

To reach Kitawa, Scoditti flew to Sydney, Australia, and from there to Port Moresby, the capital city of New Guinea, the largest island in Papua New Guinea. From there he took a small prop plane to the island of Kiriwina, the site of most of Malinowski's research and—now, as then—of a Catholic mission. Given the lack of interest in Oceania (as the South Pacific islands are sometimes called) in most universities, Scoditti was traveling with money from his parents. He planned to stay between eight and twelve months. After all, the French anthropologist Claude Lévi-Strauss built much of his reputation on the books *Tristes Tropiques* and *The Savage Mind*, written after he had lived less than eight months among the natives of the Amazon rain forest in South America.

Scoditti spent a couple of months on Kiriwina trying to find a boat to Kitawa. Many people with whom he spoke warned him against going to the island. Among the islands to its west, Kitawa is known as home to "flying witches," powerful female sorcerers who supposedly take the form of bats at night and sow disease and misfortune among their chosen victims. As Scoditti was to learn, the people of Kitawa have similar beliefs about the islands to its east. "The east," he said, "is always associated with magic, sorcerers, and witches."

Finally, an Australian official agreed to take him in a beat-up old motorboat with a crew of two or three natives of Kiriwina. It took about six hours to make the twenty-five-kilometer trip through a bad storm, until suddenly Scoditti found himself approaching the island he had imagined for so many years. A relatively small island (eight kilometers long and four and a half kilometers wide), it sits on the water like a somewhat forbidding presence. Although it is a coral reef and is ringed by a thin band of white sand beaches, it rises up steeply and plateaus at some five hundred feet above sea level so that it looks a bit like a volcano that has been cut in half. This small mountain of coral rock is covered with dense jungle vegetation and it appears to be surrounded by mist, adding to its sense of mystery and inaccessibility. "It is a kind of menacing shadow," Scoditti said. The mist is actually smoke produced by farmers burning vines and weeds to keep the yam fields clear.

As the boat approached the western shore of the island, Scoditti could see the thatched hangars built to hold the ceremonial canoes and the prow boards staring out to sea. There were some Kitawan men on the beach and the Australian explained through an interpreter he had brought that Scoditti would be staying on Kitawa for a while; he did not, though, say who Scoditti was or what he would be doing. The man promised Scoditti that he would pass by again in a month or two to see how he was doing—but he never showed up.

The Kitawans on the beach helped unload Scoditti's numerous heavy trunks containing photo and film cameras, batteries, food supplies, research equipment. In total silence, since they had no language in common, Scoditti and this caravan of Kitawans trudged slowly up through the forest toward the village.

"The island rises up gradually on five plateaus, and with each new plateau there was less breeze from the sea and the forest seemed to close in on me," Scoditti said. "I felt a sudden sense of abandonment."

After about a forty-minute walk, they arrived at Kumwageya, one of three villages located on the island's central plateau. The village, which houses only about three hundred people, is composed of orderly rows of huts, all built a bit off the ground on stilts to protect against flooding and animals. Each hut has a thatched roof over its bedroom and a small veranda for cooking, sitting outside, or receiving guests. The villagers gave the stranger a hut, one that had probably been left empty after the death of an elderly member of the community.

Before Scoditti's arrival, the Kitawans had had fairly limited and generally negative contact with Westerners. For a time, an Australian trader, known to other Westerners as the King of Kitawa, took up residence on an uninhabited part of the island but had little to do with the villagers other than occasionally demanding access to local women. The Australians had governed Papua New Guinea for a while, and before independence in 1975 a government official in a motorboat might turn up from time to time. But never having a Westerner living on close terms with them, the villagers were curious about this new arrival and expressed it by touching him. "They touched the soles of my feet, and they still do today," Scoditti said. Walking from childhood on hard coral stone, the Kitawans develop feet as tough as shoe leather and regard Scoditti's tender Western feet as exotic and strange. "They find it extremely funny," he said. Scoditti did not feel threatened by their physical curiosity. "I never felt afraid of them. I was afraid of nature. There were all these strange sounds that I had never heard before. They left me in this hut. I slept very little."

As a highly intellectual and rather impractical young man, Scoditti had asked his advisers every possible methodological question but not one about the day-to-day problems he would encounter living on a remote Pacific island, such as how he would eat, drink, wash, shave, or go to the bathroom without any means of communicating with his hosts. The villagers kindly brought him baked yams—their dietary staple—and fresh water. "They never let me lack for anything," said Scoditti. It was a courtesy Scoditti grew to appreciate greatly since food could be scarce and women and children had to cart heavy vessels of water up from wells near the beach every morning.

After adjusting to the shock of arrival, he found his new surroundings far more rich and fascinating than the world he had read about in Malinowski. "That man had no aesthetic sense. It's as if he was color-blind," Scoditti said. "Reading Malinowski, when he talks of the canoe prow boards or the dances, one sees a world of absolute grayness. I was overwhelmed by the colors and vivacity of everything."

Shortly after his arrival, dances were held in the nearby village of Okabalula. In the hours before the dances, the young people of the village (dancers must be young and graceful) begin to decorate their bodies. They paint their faces black and white. On their heads they place bright yellow feathers which stick straight up in their thick, frizzy hair, forming a kind of crown of light meant to represent the rising sun, as Scoditti would learn with time.

Back in the slick, renovated offices of the Italian Academy at Columbia University in New York, Scoditti and I watched videotapes of the dances he had filmed many years before. The dancers form a spiral, with the tallest and best dancers at the front and the rest gradually descending in size and experience. The spiral resembles a particularly prized shell found in the area, the *Nautilus pompilius,* whose spiral shape unfolds, as Western scientists have discovered, according to the precise mathematical rules of the "golden section." (In other words, each ring of the spiral is proportional to the other circles according to an unvarying mathematical formula.) Although mathematics is extremely rudimentary on Kitawa, Scoditti thinks that some Kitawa may have intuitively understood this relationship between the *Nautilus pompilius* and the golden section. Whatever the case, the Kitawans regard the shell, which appears on Scoditti's beloved prow boards, as a symbol of perfection. The spiral, to Scoditti, is a kind of metaphor for Kitawan culture as a whole: it moves forward and out from its point of origin yet always circles back around it, much as Kitawans "circle back" around their tradition. Theirs is not a static society that simply repeats itself but one that changes gradually, yet always within the framework of tradition. I thought of this as we watched the spiral of dancers open and close like a pulsing, living organism.

The period of dances is accompanied by what Scoditti calls "nights of love," a time of sexual liberty for unmarried young men and women. "At the end of the harvest, as they celebrate the new year, just before the start of the dances, during the evening, they play the drums and the young men and women make love freely," he explained. Although no one told him the meaning of this custom that first summer, it wasn't hard to understand what was happening. "The boys and girls gathered around the fire; they were affectionate with one another," Scoditti said. "They disappeared into the forest and then you heard sounds of pleasure. I couldn't speak the language, but I could still add two and two and get four."

In his book *The Sexual Life of Savages,* Malinowski appears scandalized by the comparative freedom of sexual customs in Melanesia. "He was a devout Catholic and describes them as totally depraved," Scoditti said. "It all seemed perfectly natural to me."

As Scoditti was to understand later, the freedom of the nights of love went hand in hand with considerable restrictions the rest of the year. In a small, highly regulated society where—for reasons of genetic diversity—people are forbidden from marrying anyone inside their own subclan and are not supposed to marry anyone within their own clan, the nights of love provide an element of freedom against the strictures of society. "It's a form of compensation: they try to balance the interests of the clan against the interests of the heart," Scoditti said. People on the island use a series of herbs as birth control. "It seems to work, since the population of the island is quite stable," Scoditti said.

After the initial excitement of discovery wore off, Scoditti began to slip into a severe depression, overwhelmed by a sense of isolation and abandonment. He was surrounded by people but unable to speak with them. They had no idea who he was or why he was there: the only Westerners they had ever seen were missionaries, traders, or Australian government bureaucrats. Scoditti had no means to express his humblest needs—or to tell a subject from a verb—let alone explain the purpose of his voyage. After the late-summer rains, Scoditti caught malaria and sweated through long nights of fever; he was devoured by thousands of tiny insects, and as he scratched his bites, his legs became red, bloated, and immobile. Living on a monotonous diet of yams, he suffered from protein deficiency and became extremely weak. He was convinced he would simply die alone on the island. For a time, he wept from despair every day and contemplated suicide. His Kitawan neighbors noted his distress but, since he could not understand their language, had no way to comfort him.

Scoditti took quinine pills to help with the malaria and a village sorcerer treated his bitten legs with a plaster that brought the swelling down considerably. When he was able, Scoditti spent long days on the beach drawing the ceremonial canoes and prow boards he had come to study.

From this, people on the island began to understand something of his interests. Gradually, after about six months, as he started to pick up the language, he began to form relationships with the master carvers and enter into their world. As they understood the nature of his work, they welcomed him into their society. After this breakthrough, Scoditti's mood turned from depression to joy, all the sweeter and more intense because of the depth of the despair through which he had passed. Suddenly, he was observing close up and in person many of the things that Malinowski had been forced to relate based on secondhand information. He observed the impressive spectacle of the cutting and carving of the ceremonial canoe—an extraordinary example of collective labor and masterful low-technology engineering.

"I will never forget the first time I witnessed the cutting of a canoe. It was perhaps the most moving thing I had ever seen," Scoditti said. The creation of a ceremonial canoe—a boat of sixty or seventy feet in length that can carry forty or fifty men—is an enterprise that involves the entire village. Commissioning a canoe is both extremely prestigious and costly. "There are lots of stories about clans that have been ruined by commissioning a canoe," Scoditti said. "There are a series of poetic formulae that are recited to the spirits of the woods, mischievous little spirits, that say, 'Come down from the tree, because tomorrow I am going to cut it,'" he said. To make a ceremonial canoe more than sixty feet long, one must choose an extremely tall, solid tree, since the main hull is composed of a single dug-out tree trunk. But the biggest challenge is getting the tree from the middle of the forest down to the beach, which is often a few miles away and some 150 meters downhill. Scoditti watched in amazement as the Kitawans created a "road in the air," using vines, ropes, and ramps to lift the tree and direct it through the forest to the beach without its ever touching the ground. "It was an incredible piece of engineering," Scoditti said. "The whole process is highly ritualized, with chants of encouragement."

As he watched the tree move in the air through the forest, suddenly the central myth of the kula ring, the myth of the flying canoe, took on new meaning for Scoditti. In the myth, a hero ancestor insists, improbably, on

carving his canoe in the middle of Kitawa, defying the villagers who wonder how they are going to get the heavy boat to the shore. But when the
work is done, the hero ancestor invites everyone to get into the canoe and,
with the use of powerful magic, sends them flying from the village to the
ocean and then past all the other canoes in the water. "Malinowski
repeated it from secondhand sources," Scoditti said. But in the light of his
own experience on Kitawa, the most fantastic elements of the myth of the
flying canoe appeared to have their origin in a quite literal description of
the extraordinary feat of getting the canoe across the mountainous terrain
at the island's center and down to the beach.

The canoe is then hollowed out and carved on the beach, while the
prow boards are commissioned from master carvers, who enjoy a position of special prestige on the island. They are spared the duty of working in the fields and are plied with yams and fresh fish to keep them
happy.

The undisputed master carver of Kumwageya, the village where
Scoditti lived, was an old man named Towitara. "He was tall and thin,
almost six feet, and, like other old people, he never wore anything other
than a white loincloth, rain or shine, even in the colder months like
January and February," he said. Kitawans do not count years, but
Scoditti guesses that Towitara must have been in his eighties. Nonetheless, he had a steady hand and carved with great strength and precision.
Although he was not chief of the village, he was clearly a person of
importance.

In the evenings, Towitara would step out of his hut and speak to the
village about the problems in the community. As Scoditti understood
more of the language, he understood that these were jeremiads meant
to keep the community in line. "He would say things like, 'This person
has been neglecting his duties in the fields. The hut of one of the older
people is falling apart and should be rebuilt,'" Scoditti said. Towitara
walked with a dignified bearing, hands behind his back, reminding
Scoditti of a Cambridge economist with whom he had been friendly in
England.

The art of the carver is a carefully guarded secret on Kitawa. It requires a secret initiation, strict dietary rules, and many years of hard training. Families court the master carver with gifts and food in hopes that he will take one of their sons on as an apprentice. But Towitara seemed to understand immediately the importance of imparting his knowledge to Scoditti in order to preserve it for posterity. Under cover of darkness, Towitara would visit Scoditti in his hut and they would talk well into the night. The intelligence Scoditti found in Towitara was similar to that he experienced in one of his mentors in England, the art historian Sir Ernst Gombrich. "In both Towitara and Gombrich I felt I touched real wisdom," Scoditti said.

Towitara explained the symbolism of the canoe prow boards and the meaning of many Kitawan rituals in ways—unusual for Kitawa—that were comprehensible to Scoditti's Western way of thinking. "They have very definite ideas about why something is beautiful or ugly, well made or poorly made, and why. I found it extremely interesting to understand the aesthetic principles that made an object more or less beautiful," Scoditti said.

Although the older Kitawans themselves had not been directly exposed to writing, they quickly understood its potential. Some children on the island had studied at a missionary school. "They understood that I was able to record and control a great deal of information," Scoditti said. "They immediately saw the fascination of writing as a powerful device of memory." The Kitawans wanted to be sure that Scoditti would publish his research in English, even though no one on Kitawa could speak or read it. "We don't know English, but our grandchildren might," they said.

Scoditti was impressed by the infinite strategies Kitawan society has for preserving its traditions. "There is an incredibly complex system of control: one clan is responsible for the dance, another for the self-decoration of the body, a third for the music, and so on," he said. In a kind of system of checks and balances, each clan carefully watches and scrutinizes the other, commenting on whether a particular dance or song is well executed. The transmission of important myths or stories is not left to chance: they are considered the "property" and responsibility of specific individuals, who pass them on to their heirs. "When someone tells you that a story is 'true,' they are careful about its genealogy. They mean that that person is the true 'owner' of the story, therefore it is authentic," Scoditti said.

Even an instance of cannibalism that Scoditti observed was, in fact, a memory device. When the beloved son of an older man died suddenly and prematurely, the family removed the young man's head and boiled it in a pot. The father drank the soup made from the head and then the family placed the skull inside their hut. "They kept the skull in the hut for a year and the father would take it out from time to time and hold the skull in his hands, a little like Hamlet with the skull of Yorick," Scoditti explained. "The skull was a reminder of the dead son, like a photo album would be for us. I could not hide a sense of physical revulsion. But my friends reproached me and explained the meaning of the custom to me. And so I went to the man and discussed it with him." (All acts of cannibalism were banned by the government of Papua New Guinea in 1975.)

After nearly a year on the island and having solidified his friendship with Towitara, Scoditti was included in the kula ring, meaning that he would finally have the opportunity to leave the island. The men decorated their canoes, bathed their bodies in sweet-smelling oils, and set sail in an atmosphere of festive joy, smoking tobacco, chewing betel nuts, and singing songs meant to ensure an auspicious journey. "I was euphoric," Scoditti said. Through these ceremonial voyages, the inhabitants of the Trobriands relive the experience of their ancestors, the intrepid explorers who settled these remote islands. "There is a great sense of adventure and of confronting the challenge of nature," said Scoditti. "It is a trial you must overcome, showing that you know how to read the stars and recognize the currents." The trips are a test of skill and endurance, covering considerable distances and sometimes requiring the sailors to stay awake in the crowded narrow canoe for two days and nights as it passes through rough seas and dangerous storms that can prove fatal.

Some of the islands in the region were almost certainly colonized by force, and a residue of the early conquering spirit comes through in the kula trips. When the men arrive at another island, they wash themselves and put unguent from a sea pine on their bodies and head to the village. "Everyone gets in line and the first one in line blows a large conch shell, which takes a lot of lung power. When you arrive in the village, you make noise and a little disturbance. You might throw stones against a hut. I've often seen them destroy a hut. The village knows: 'They've arrived for the kula!'" In this controlled bit of mischief the aggressive impulses of the region's warring past have been ritualized and channeled into the friendly exchange of gifts.

The kula ceremony is a truly ingenious social institution that has fascinated anthropologists for several decades. Each man in the kula has a number of partners with whom he exchanges gifts. The gifts are either arm bracelets made by breaking off the tops of conelike white shells (the *conus millepunctatus*), which are greatly prized ornamental objects in the entire area of Papua New Guinea, or necklaces made from the red *spondylus* shell. The exchange of gifts is highly formalized so that when they travel east in early spring, the Kitawans give away the red-shelled necklaces and receive white-shelled arm bracelets. When they travel west in the fall, they are expected to give away the arm bracelets they received earlier in the year and receive necklaces they will distribute on their next voyage east. Thus, over the course of a year (at least in theory) all the men would have traveled the entire circuit and the gifts would have all changed hands.

Although kula partners are expected to reciprocate, there is an element of sport and competition to the exchange. Thus, the boats race to arrive first on a particular island. The total number of gifts in circulation is fixed, but the way they are distributed is discretionary. Each individual partner may choose to give the finest and largest number of gifts to other partners traveling the circuit. "It's partly a game or a competition. A person receives more gifts if he is a good talker, if he is eloquent and able to tell stories," Scoditti said.

As a neophyte, Scoditti had to be "introduced" into the kula. Towitara gave him two of his partners, Scoditti said. While the average islander might have just a few partners, Towitara, a man of long life and much prestige, had many. On one of his first ceremonial canoe trips, Scoditti found himself back on Kiriwina, the island from which he had set off for Kitawa. He even saw the Australian official who had taken him by boat to Kitawa but then failed to return and check on him. The man did not apologize for his conduct but offered Scoditti a bed in his home, assuming he would prefer staying in a Western-style house to sleeping out on the beach with the Kitawans. "I told him I would rather stay with my friends," Scoditti said with a heat that showed that he was still angry at having been casually abandoned in a situation in which he could well have died. Yet once he had survived that deep personal crisis, he had no particular desire to return to the West. As someone who had, up to that point, been something of a restless, eternal student, batting around universities in Italy and England, Scoditti finally felt at age thirty-five that he had found his place in life.

As Scoditti began to participate fully in Kitawan life, he took a wife. Scoditti had noticed an attractive young woman named Kabata and eventually got up his courage to speak of his interest to a friend. The marriage was arranged through her maternal uncle. Marriage is a relatively low-key affair in Melanesia and in this case, once it was agreed upon, Kabata simply moved into his hut. And within a few months, they had conceived a child. The match was treated as perfectly ordinary by most Kitawans, with one notable exception. "Towitara had a lot to say about it," Scoditti said.

Towitara saw that it was unrealistic for Scoditti to imagine living full-time and forever on Kitawa. Moreover, he was concerned that Scoditti not lose sight of his initial objective—making a permanent record of Kitawan culture. "He explained to me that my duty was to return and to try to conserve with documentation this culture that is gradually unraveling," Scoditti said. "Towitara saw all this, although at the time the signs were not particularly evident."

Thus, after nearly two years, Scoditti decided in late 1974 to return to Europe and complete his doctorate. Shortly before leaving, he had a series of intense conversations with Towitara, in which the old man imparted the contents of the initiation ceremony to him.

Scoditti translated part of the formulae as follows:

my mind, enveloped, creates images
lost in dreams will create images
images for our companions
you are transformed into me,
you are transformed into me, Towitara.

Towitara had not transmitted these poetic formulae to his favorite pupil, Togaruwa, because the young artist had disobeyed the ascetic dietary rules of the master carver. "They believe that if you eat the tail of the fish your carving hand will shake like the tail of the fish and if you eat the boar's intestines your symbols will be confused like the boar's intestines," Scoditti explained.

"My departure was a kind of epic scene," he said. "There was practically the entire island there. Lots of women crying. I was crying. Towitara was crying. In the water up to his chest, he gave the last push to the canoe. 'Come back, and don't forget the island,' he said. We set off in three canoes, about sixty men with all these trunks."

When he finally returned to Italy, his family was surprised to see him, convinced that he was lost or dead or that he had simply decided not to return.

"My mother used to say, half jokingly, 'They're probably eating him piece by piece,'" Scoditti's older sister, Maria Teresa, told me. Although she worked for many years as an accountant, Maria Teresa shares her brother's taste for faraway, exotic places and has traveled through much of Africa and Asia. Their love of distant travel and foreign cultures began in their childhood home in Anzio, a small seaside town south of Rome, where the family lived for many years. Scoditti was born in 1939, but when he was just a few years old, his father, Americo Scoditti, an artillery officer in the Italian army, was captured by the British army in North Africa and sent to a prisoner-of-war camp in India. There he converted to Hinduism under the influence of an Indian who worked in the camp. Americo Scoditti was so taken with his new religion that, rather than return after the war to his wife and children, he disappeared into the Himalayas on a spiritual quest. A year or two later, he resumed his previous life as artillery officer, husband, and father. He remained a Hindu, however, and Giancarlo Scoditti grew up in a household filled with strange volumes in English on India and Hinduism and where, on Thursday evenings, his father held what Scoditti believes were séances. His father's Indian experience cast a spell over his childhood. In this family context, Scoditti's decision to set off for Papua New Guinea in 1973 seemed quite natural.

Indeed, his father seemed puzzled and almost disappointed when Scoditti returned to Italy nearly two years later. "Why did you come back?" he asked. Although he was glad to know his son was still alive, he may have been thinking with a moment of regret about his own decision to abandon his spiritual quest in the Himalayas for family life in Italy.

Scoditti began work on his dissertation on the aesthetics of Kitawan prow board carvers, making frequent trips back to the island for further research. As expected, Towitara was dead when he returned two years later, but Scoditti followed his advice and continued working with the gradually dwindling core of master carvers. He recorded all of their interviews, conducted an extensive linguistic analysis of the Nowau language, and even created a dictionary. Scoditti spent years on this project, finally publishing *Kitawa: A Linguistic and Aesthetic Analysis of Visual Art in Melanesia.* In a foreword to the book, Ernst Gombrich compared Scoditti's carefully recorded dialogues with Kitawan artists to a famous seventeenth-century diary in which the Frenchman Paul Fréart de Chantelou took down his conversations with the famous Italian sculptor and architect Gianlorenzo Bernini. "If we have reason to be grateful to the French art-lover . . . how much more must we and posterity be beholden to Giancarlo Scoditti who spared no effort and shrank from no hardship to seek out and preserve the thoughts and practices of the craftsmen who produced the beautiful prows of canoes for their tribe in the remotest islands of the South Seas," Gombrich wrote.

After he finished his work on the canoe carvers of Kitawa, Scoditti did not abandon the island, for reasons that were personal as well as professional. When he returned for his second long stay, in 1976, he met his son, who had been born after his departure in late 1974. At a certain point—Scoditti is reticent about furnishing details on highly personal matters—Kabata had found another husband on a nearby island. There are no prohibitions against divorce and remarriage in Melanesia. Since Scoditti had clearly chosen to base his life in Italy and not in Kitawa, he accepted Kabata's decision as perfectly natural. For similar reasons, he decided not to take up with other women on Kitawa lest he use the island as a place of sexual tourism, as so many Westerners in the Pacific islands have. At the same time, the amount of time and energy he devoted to Kitawa made it difficult to maintain a long-term relationship back in Europe. Although Kabata moved away, their son remained on the island to be raised by his mother's family, giving Scoditti another reason to return regularly to Kitawa.

In the mid-1980s, he began working on a book on the oral poetry of the island. He recorded extensively the most renowned poet of Kitawa, Ipaiya. As in virtually all other oral societies, poetry is an extremely important part of life in Kitawa; it marks and accompanies almost all significant rituals and events. Already when working on the prow board carvers, Scoditti had begun to record songs and incantations that surround the various moments in the cutting, carving, and sailing of the ceremonial canoes. Homer's *Iliad,* along with its poetic beauty, is an encyclopedia of early Greek civilization, full of practical advice about proper conduct in relation to gods, friends, family, strangers, or enemies in battle. Similarly, the poetry of Kitawa reinforces, and gives meaning to, the norms and rituals of Kitawan culture:

> *I shall set sail against the waves in the festive canoe*
> *raising the pole high I shall thrust it into the sea*
> *as I stand there the village in the west will appear,*
> *a light wind will stretch the sail,*
> *there is the magic mountain: come toward me,*
> *surround me, fight if you desire me,*
> *and, like a breath, flow to the distant transformed island*
> *I am water, I am shell, I yield myself to this seduction.*

Much of the poetry of the kula voyages has an ecstatic, almost erotic quality, as in this passage, in which the singer invokes the presence of the mythic hero while sailing into a tempest at sea:

Sky darkening with the gathering storm
dark sky surround me, break me open
hurl your red lightning against me.

As an outsider and a total novelty, Scoditti began to enjoy a privileged position in Kitawan society. Since many of the most important people on the island had understood that Scoditti was recording what would be known about their society, they were keen to have their own point of view represented. He even persuaded the sorcerers and witches of the island to reveal to him the magic spells they normally only repeat silently, under their breath. Some of them insisted on doing so in secret. "I moved around a lot at night," Scoditti recalled. "The night is sort of reserved for the witches and sorcerers. It has a kind of political and diplomatic function. The sorcerers defend their village against the activity of the others. I was a kind of passe-partout who could go anywhere. When you move around at night you can smell the highly perfumed wild basil that the sorcerers put on their bodies."

As he recorded the Kitawans, they got to hear their own voices played back on magnetic tape for the first time. "They had a great time and wanted to hear it again and again," Scoditti said. "I would have to say no, because the batteries were being used up, and they complained. When one of my technological devices fails to work, they find it extremely funny. They have a very curious and ironic attitude toward Western technology."

With each successive trip, Scoditti began to assemble an impressive collection of objects from the area, and the Pigorini Museum in Rome, Italy's national museum of ethnography, became interested in his work. For Scoditti, the collaboration with the Pigorini is a cautionary tale of what can go wrong in collecting art from Oceania. The director of the museum persuaded Scoditti to bring back an entire ceremonial canoe with carved and painted prow boards. The museum was willing to pay for the objects, but Scoditti explained that people on Kitawa would not sell a canoe. He would have to persuade the islanders to give him the canoe and he would, in turn, donate it to the museum. Scoditti was delighted when he was able to obtain the canoe for which Towitara had carved his final prow board. Indeed, the canoe, about sixty feet in length with a red hull and delicately carved prow boards at front and back, today has pride of place in the lobby of the Pigorini.

But the canoe almost never made it to Rome. Scoditti had brought it to the provincial capital of Alatan, leaving it to Italian officials to arrange for its transfer to Rome. After more than a year, he was informed by the head of the museum that the canoe had arrived in Italian customs. They went to fetch it, but when they unwrapped the boat, Scoditti was mortified. It was not his canoe, he said. "The director of the museum said to me: 'Well, so what? It's still a canoe. One canoe is as good as another.' I was furious. This canoe was much less beautiful and much smaller and it did not have Towitara's prow board." Besides, the whole point of his gift was to provide a canoe whose entire creation and context were thoroughly documented. Scoditti had interviewed its principal creators about what they understood themselves to be doing. The notion that one canoe was as good as another represented the kind of arrogant disregard for Oceanic art that Scoditti had been fighting throughout his career.

Eventually, he got wind that Towitara's canoe had wound up in a museum in Osaka, Japan. Apparently, a curator from the museum saw the canoe in Alatan, decided he liked it better than anything he could buy, and simply took it, replacing it with an inferior canoe. Scoditti persuaded an Italian friend who was going to Japan to go to Osaka and photograph the canoe. Armed with this photographic evidence, Scoditti pressured the Italian officials to seek the canoe's return. "I told them if they didn't, I was going to take it all to the press and create a nice scandal!" he said. Finally, the Italian officials were able to persuade the Japanese museum to return Scoditti's canoe. Although it is prominently displayed at the Pigorini, Scoditti regrets donating the canoe to the Italian museum. "It is exposed to drafts and is badly in need of conservation," he said. And yet, sitting there in the hallway of this Fascist-era building on the outskirts of Rome, the canoe has given a small measure of immortality to the old carver, Towitara, as he evidently wished. Words of a song he sang are placed next to the canoe:

I'll sail tomorrow in my festive canoe. . . .
my name, Towitara, will be the roar of thunder!

Although the Pigorini has offered to buy Scoditti's collection, he has rejected the idea. Because of his concern that the art objects not be separated from the ethnographic material, he has had trouble trying to give the collection away. A number of museums in the United States want the art but are not prepared to take on the financial responsibility of housing and curating twenty-five years of tape recordings, film, photographs, and field notes, which Scoditti regards as of paramount importance. While there is a boom in non-Western art at many museums, the art of Oceania is something of a poor cousin, in part because it lacks the local constituency that African, South American, and Asian art has lobbying for it in this country. "The Peabody Museum at Harvard would like the collection, but they told me I have to find a sponsor who will fund it. So I am supposed to give the art and then find the money to maintain it," he said.

In order to see the collection, I visited Scoditti in his home in a small suburban town in the Alban Hills outside Rome. (For reasons of security, Scoditti asked me not to give the name.) He lives in a five-room flat in an unremarkable middle-class apartment complex. But as soon as you enter the front door it loses any resemblance to its immediate surroundings. The apartment is jammed to the gills with orderly clutter; Scoditti's two main preoccupations—books and the art of Papua New Guinea—war for space, covering every available surface in room after room. Many of the walls of the apartment are occupied by floor-to-ceiling bookshelves; in fact, even the front door is actually a bookcase that opens like the trick library door in old Hollywood detective films.

On the remaining walls and on top of some of the bookshelves are a small museum's worth of objects of various sizes. In both his study and his living room there are enormous masks between four and six feet tall, long, thin abstractions of the human face from the Sepik region of Papua New Guinea that were made to stand guard over storehouses of yams. From Kitawa, there are small wooden sculptures and finely carved ebony mortars and pestles used to grind betel nuts. On top of a revolving bookcase there is an extraordinary wooden bowl, some three feet across and carved from a single piece of wood, meant to hold food at special feasts. On top of other revolving bookcases there are Plexiglas cases with tiny wooden models of ceremonial canoes from Kitawa. Master carvers and their apprentices often make miniature wooden models before carving an actual canoe. On the walls of the study there are sections of canoe prow boards and drawings of prow boards by a local artist. In one of the bedrooms of the apartment there is a little wooden basin in the shape of a canoe that is used to wash newborn babies. Real canoes are sometimes used as coffins for especially prestigious members of the community. On Kitawa, people are born into canoes and are buried in them when they die.

The shades in the apartment were drawn, in part to keep out the summer heat, in part to protect the objects from light. We looked at slides of the island and listened to tapes of songs and poems in the semidarkness, with the large, somewhat menacing Sepik masks watching over us as they once watched over the yams somewhere in Papua New Guinea. We discussed the future of Kitawa and of his own work there.

Although the island has remained relatively unchanged, outside influences have begun to make themselves felt in curious indirect ways. As the Kitawans travel to other islands, they see a rapid increase in Western goods. "They are attracted to plastic—which I despise—in an almost morbid fashion because it is strong and lasts," Scoditti said with an air of regret. Kitawan objects made of wood, wood fiber, or leaves are beautiful but more fragile. "It is the dream of every Kitawan woman to own an aluminum pot. They are crazy about Western shoes, even though they make their feet hurt terribly."

These would be harmless enough passions, except that trading in these goods puts a tremendous strain on the traditional Kitawan economy. The islanders begin to trade more and more of their food surplus for manufactured goods, meaning that there is less food for the older members of the community who can no longer work. The effects were evident on Scoditti's most recent trip to Kitawa, in November 1997. When he went to visit Ipaiya, the oral poet, Scoditti found the old man lying alone in his hut, blind, emaciated, and bitter. "I am waiting for death. I hope someone poisons me," Ipaiya told him. "I want you to sing," Scoditti replied, hoping to check whether there were many variations when the poet performed his songs. "My voice is weak and ugly. I've sung all I could. Leave me." Ipaiya's son, Scoditti said, does not give him enough food. "And he avenges himself by not giving the son his poetic formulae."

In a traditional oral culture, the elderly play a particularly important role, having stored up the greatest wealth of direct experience and traditional knowledge. But as younger people become more interested in acquiring things outside the island, this currency is devalued. There is a severe generational crisis on the island. Some young people are no longer willing to spend the effort carving canoes or working long hours in the fields cultivating yams. In fact, some have even begun to steal—an unusual and alarming sign of social breakdown.

In this gradual erosion of local culture, the government and Christian missionaries have had a certain part. In 1975, Papua New Guinea became an independent nation, but within the British Commonwealth; as a result, Christianity is its principal religion and English its first language. At the moment, an estimated 52 percent of the population is Christian and about the same percentage is literate. In this part of the world, reading and writing are virtually synonymous with the death of traditional culture since they are almost invariably introduced in the form of Bible study. The Catholic Church, in Scoditti's experience, is more respectful of local customs, but the evangelical Protestant missionaries are very aggressive and quite ruthless in trying to discourage such traditional practices as dancing or the kula exchange. In some cases, they use the lure of Western medicine to encourage conversion. "There is a lot of implicit blackmail," Scoditti explained. "'You come to school, I'll give you quinine,' Or: 'You want quinine, but you didn't come to church on Sunday.' They know that the sorcerers recite magic spells for the ceremonial exchange and so they prohibit it. They try to inculcate the fact that it is an extremely grave sin to recite magic words."

Theoretically, Papua New Guinea is a Western-style democracy, but its system is entirely antithetical to traditional island life. Each of Kitawa's three small villages has its own assembly. Voting for candidates they have never seen on a national or provincial level makes no sense to Kitawans and ignores their own traditional system of governance.

Although the vast majority of Kitawans still adhere to their traditions, a sense of malaise appears to be eating away at the culture. "No one has commissioned a new canoe in several years," Scoditti said. "No new carvers have been initiated." In Kumwageya, the village where Scoditti lived during his first stay on Kitawa, there have been no dances since 1974. In the other two villages, there has been no dancing in the last few years. "These are things that I am afraid I will never see again," he said. "In 1993, the last time, they failed to execute certain steps. Dance is an art that is learned by imitation. If the first dancer doesn't execute something, the others won't learn it. You can lose the art pretty quickly."

There is a small primary school on Kitawa where English is taught, and some children leave the island to continue their education, but most come back within a few years. "Very few get to high school," Scoditti said. "They manage to pick up certain Western values and desires but are unable to realize them. They return to the island but they aren't able to fish and sail and aren't able to cultivate yams. They become a dead weight on the society. Some begin to steal." There is a small but growing group of disaffected young people who, under the influence of a young man who studied at a Christian mission on another island, have refused to participate in the village assemblies or in the traditional dances. Much to Scoditti's personal chagrin, his own son is among these rebels without a cause.

"For a time, our relationship was really nice," Scoditti said. "He used to come every evening to my hut. He was ironic and affectionate. But on my last few trips I had the impression he didn't really want to see me. And on this most recent trip he didn't even come to say hello to me."

In the minds of younger people on the island, Toruruwai, "the man who remembers," has become a pillar of traditional Kitawan society. In fact, the younger people, who were not around when he first arrived on the island in 1973, actually believe that Scoditti is a Kitawan, although he dresses and acts like a Westerner. Years ago, his friends on the island used to kid Scoditti by saying that he was the son of a Kitawan woman and an Italian sailor who stopped on the island during World War II. The sailor took his Kitawan bride back to Rome but then sent her son back to Kitawa to learn its language and culture. What started as a joke has now passed in many younger people's minds for historical fact.

Over the quarter century that Scoditti has been going to Kitawa, many of his older friends have died. Others are now old or infirm. Life expectancy on Kitawa is lower than in Europe and men in their fifties or sixties are considered old. They start to talk about death—their own and Scoditti's. What are we going to do, they ask him, if you die when you are not on the island? "They are terrified of the idea of not being on the island when they die," he explained. It deprives a person of proper burial. In fact, Scoditti intends to be buried on the island.

In the Kitawan worldview, the passage from life to death is gradual and not absolute. "When the soul of the dead person departs, he travels by sea and stops at the first rock and is moved because he can still hear the voices of his loved ones crying," Scoditti said. "At the second rock, he can still see the smoke rising from the yam fields where they are burning weeds. And on the third rock, he grabs a little piece of algae and heads toward the island of the dead."

In the past twenty-five years, it seems that traditional Kitawan culture has been suffering a similar destiny, becoming fainter, like the voices from the village as the soul departs. "I feel that a phase has ended both for me and for them," Scoditti said.

Other anthropologists question his view that the culture of the kula ring is disappearing. "I disagree with the whole premise that cultures 'die' or 'disappear.' They simply change," says Nancy Munn, a scholar at the University of Chicago who worked on Gawa, another island that is part of the kula circuit. "There is a certain romanticism about Scoditti's work, a notion of these societies as existing in a kind of static, noble savage condition. These are trading societies that have always been in contact with other people. These societies have always changed." Munn admits that the current changes they are undergoing may be more rapid and radical than at other times. "They may abandon certain cultural practices but they remain vital societies," she said.

But for Scoditti, the loss of practices such as canoe making, celebratory dances, and oral poetry represents a fundamental break with traditions that evolved slowly over hundreds, if not thousands, of years. Change may have been a constant in the life of the Trobriand Islands, he said, but in the past change was much more gradual. Contemporary Hawaii is an extremely vital society, but it bears little resemblance to the place that Captain Cook first encountered in 1778.

Along with noting disturbing signs of decline, Scoditti may have made an important archeological discovery on his last trip to Kitawa. When farmers were clearing a field that had not been under cultivation recently, they uncovered a series of megaliths organized in an oval formation at some point in the past. The megaliths correspond to a story in one of the foundation myths still told on Kitawa: that the original ancestors of the island emerged from the ground and that when they died they buried themselves under a formation of rocks that seem to resemble the megaliths uncovered last year. Scoditti did some digging in the area and found what appear to be human bones and has taken them back to Rome for carbon-dating. The islands of Melanesia are believed to have been settled some twenty thousand years ago. If the bones Scoditti discovered prove to be that old, it would mean that Kitawa successfully transmitted a genuine historical event from generation to generation for twenty thousand years—transforming it into myth along the way.

Thus, as some of the art forms he came to study disappear, Scoditti has begun to turn from the anthropological study of Kitawa's present to the archeological study of its remote past. His arrival on the island in 1973 was providential, and yet the very act of someone's preserving the culture in writing was also a presage of the culture's eventual demise, as if this remote culture began to fade when we opened it to our own curious gaze.

7

War of Words: Oral Poetry, Writing, and Tape Cassettes in Somalia

O N T H E S T R E E T S of Hargeysa, the capital of the self-proclaimed Republic of Somaliland, the northern part of what used to be called Somalia, there are audio- and videotape shops on nearly every corner. Tapes of Somali oral poetry sell alongside videos of the latest Hollywood movies of Sylvester Stallone and Jean-Claude Van Damme. Poetry is routinely broadcast on the radio and beamed in by satellite TV from neighboring Djibouti. And one of the hottest new cassettes on the Somali market when I arrived in the summer of 2000 was the wedding video of one of the country's leading poets, Mohammed Ibrahim Warsame, known universally among Somalis by his nickname, Hadrawi. Even the immigration officials who questioned me on my arrival brightened when I mentioned his name and they proceeded to tell me in detail about the poet's recent marriage.

That the wedding video of a poet—showing a traditional Somali ceremony with guests seated on straw mats, drinking camel's milk and eating dates, but filled, like most other wedding videos, with random footage of cars arriving and crowds milling around—should have commercial appeal is a perfect expression of Somalia in the new millennium, a strange hybrid of ancient nomadic culture and modern technology.

The last things most people recall about Somalia are the images of United States marines being dragged through the streets of Mogadishu and the withdrawal of United Nations troops in 1993. But while Somalia no longer has a seat at the U.N., it has continued to be a part of the world of international media. There is no internationally recognized government, but there are five different phone companies competing ferociously for business and a cellular phone system that offers the lowest rates in Africa. Satellite dishes sit perched atop many of the homes and shops, where people watch European soccer and CNN. Indeed, in the absence of formal structures, with about a million Somali refugees scattered around the globe—from Stockholm and London to Toronto and Minneapolis—the Somalis have formed a kind of virtual nation, knitted together by a strange combination of electronic signals and traditional kinship relationships.

But all of these media are audiovisual. Somalia is still a largely oral society, most of its population made up of non-literate nomads. There are no publishing houses and the one real newspaper sells only two thousand copies a day. Indeed, there is remarkably little writing to be seen by way of billboards and advertisements. Instead of written signs, many shops have elaborately painted storefronts illustrating the goods and services they offer, clearly meant for a public that is largely illiterate. An ad for a cellular phone company consists of a picture of a camel with a transmitting tower on its back, symbolic of Somalia's strange new hybrid culture. A sizable fraction of the city's population of 250,000 live in makeshift huts in squatters' camps, but most of the squatters have tape recorders and radios. "If they had to choose between a tape recorder and a sack of rice, they'd take the tape recorder," one Somali told me.

The Somali language was not written down until the 1970s, and poetry—as in ancient Greece at the time of Homer—is one of the principal forms of mass communication as well as of entertainment. And in an oral society—even a postmodern oral society—the poet is king. In 1972, the dictator Mohammed Siad Barre chose the Latin alphabet as the official script for the Somali language and tried to use writing as a means of imposing the control of the state on the new Somali nation. But the inexpensive tape recorder arrived at about the same time and was, in many ways, better suited to transmitting Somalia's oral culture. Opposition to the Barre regime took the form of oral poetry dictated onto cassettes. Although Barre tried arresting Hadrawi and other poets, the cassettes continued to circulate. Indeed, many Somalis believe that the beginning of the end of the Barre regime was a "poetic duel," a chain of poems started by Hadrawi and another prominent Somali poet in 1979 that turned into a national debate about the government. When almost all the poems ended up criticizing the government and Barre proved powerless to stop the underground cassette traffic, it was clear that the government had lost its popular mandate.

A visit to Somalia seems like a trip to a post-Gutenberg galaxy, to use Marshall McLuhan's phrase. In the early 1960s, McLuhan wrote with surprising clairvoyance of the "fragmenting" effects of electronic media and the coming of the "global village." New, decentralized interactive media, he prophesied, would allow people to communicate globally while remaining grouped in small clusters. Borderless electronic media would erode the power of the traditional nation-state and end the hegemony of the printed word (what he called the "Gutenberg galaxy"), bringing about the return of a largely oral culture. McLuhan's global village, in many ways, anticipated the Internet, but it also describes contemporary Somalia.

The recent introduction of writing into an oral society, and the added presence of electronic media, raises a host of fundamental questions. Is writing still a necessary precondition for creating a modern society? Or is it possible to leapfrog the five-thousand-year history of writing and move directly from preindustrial to postindustrial media? Will new media ultimately preserve or destroy Somalia's traditional culture? Or will writing and electronic media mingle in new and unexpected ways that allow Somalia both to retain aspects of its oral culture and to participate in the global economy?

After a few days in Hargeysa, I traveled with an interpreter to see Hadrawi at his family home in Burao, a medium-sized city about two hundred kilometers to the east. We drove across the northern plain of

Somalia, located on the Horn of Africa, that part of the continent's eastern coast that reaches up toward the Red Sea and sits just across from Yemen and the Arabian Peninsula. When we arrived, he was standing in front of the nomad hut he had built for his wedding several days earlier. He is a distinguished-looking man of fifty-seven with pensive dark brown eyes, a head of closely cropped gray-black hair, muttonchop sideburns, and a mustache with a light, stubbly beard. His skin is a reddish dark brown, but his straight nose and other features seem more Arab than African, reflecting the long-standing contacts between Somalia and the Middle East. He wore a brightly colored *shaal,* the wrap Somali men traditionally wear around their waist, together with a Western shirt. His dress, like so much else in Somalia today, is a hybrid of indigenous and foreign elements.

The wedding hut was a large, igloo-shaped structure, a rounded, domelike tent about ten feet high and fifteen or twenty feet in diameter, built with a frame of slender, flexible tree branches covered with animal skins and mats of straw artfully woven into elaborate geometric patterns. It stood somewhat incongruously inside the walled courtyard of a modern green concrete house. The nomad hut, however, was part of Hadrawi's current poetic strategy. "The purpose of the wedding for me was to show the Somali people that their forefathers left something for them, even if they don't follow that example—that they should not live in a vacuum and lose their identity," Hadrawi said.

Poets in Somalia enjoy a status that combines the role of prophet, intellectual, and rock star. Traditionally, Somali poets were believed to possess the gift of prophecy and many Somalis whom I met—those in the West as well as those living in Somalia—insisted that "things that Hadrawi wrote twenty years ago came true exactly." Hadrawi says that all he did was describe what seemed obvious at the time: that the corruption and repression of the Barre dictatorship would eventually bring about its downfall. Many of his poems—like those of several other leading Somali poets—are put to music and performed by popular singers, so that among Somalis he is as famous as a pop musician. Thus, when he decided to take a third wife (Somalia is a Muslim country and Islam allows men to take up to four wives), the wedding was an event of national importance. Thousands followed the wedding procession, the president of the newly constituted Somaliland sent ten thousand dollars to help defray costs (which Hadrawi insisted he would give away to worthwhile social causes), and several cassette shops in Somalia sent cameramen to film the event.

Somalis have begun to imitate their relatives in Europe and North America, whose wedding videos they frequently see. So by allowing his wedding to be filmed, Hadrawi was trying to send a countermessage encouraging them to resist the pressures of Westernization and return to tradition. "It will be seen in Toronto, Minneapolis, Norway—wherever there are Somalis!" he said with a certain amused pride. Hadrawi is not unaware of the contradictions of his situation, but in a technological world, Hadrawi feels he has no choice but to fight fire with fire.

Along with the ten thousand dollars, Somaliland's president, Mohammed Ibrahim Egal, sent a large number of security forces to the wedding. "There were rumors that it was not a wedding but a camouflage for a big political meeting and so there were a lot of security people present," Hadrawi explained with a laugh. "Poets in Somalia are not just admired, they are feared," said my interpreter, Saeed, "because if a poet writes a negative poem about you, people may repeat it for the rest of your days."

Inside the hut, we sat on straw mats and goat skins and the women who created the hut showed us how they outfitted it with traditional hand-carved plates, bowls, and implements. Demonstrating how they would use a wooden jug to make butter from camel's milk, they started singing as they moved back and forth as if churning butter.

"Somalia is a nation of poetry. Even children of a few years old who herd sheep have songs they have created themselves," Hadrawi said. "If you are tending a herd or making handicrafts, poetry becomes your companion. If you ask for something, it is traditional to ask with poetry. People cannot do their jobs without poetry. At a certain point, poetry became a necessity, like food. It became the only thing that could move society."

In traditional Somali society, every clan had its own poet and the poet played a key role in both making war and making peace. "If the American presidential election had taken place in Somalia, Bush and Gore would be poets or they would have had poets on their staff. The campaign would have been conducted in verse," says John Johnson, an expert on Somali poetry who teaches at Indiana University in Bloomington, which has what may be the largest collection of Somali poetry in the world—almost all on tape.

Hadrawi explained that he grew up in a hut like this one, living the nomadic life, raising goats and camels. Then, at the age of ten, he was sent to stay with an uncle who lived in Yemen so that he might get a formal education. He learned Arabic fluently and some English and was thus exposed to writing, albeit in foreign languages. Educated Somalis who had been exposed to writing were experimenting at the time with different systems for writing down their language. Hadrawi used the Latin script to transcribe his work (as did some others), but since there was no agreement on standard spelling, each Somali writer was making up his own private orthography, which only he could understand without difficulty. Nonetheless, Hadrawi was among the first generation of Somali poets to compose poetry in written rather than oral form— something he said he regretted.

"I would love not to write my poems with pen and paper but to recite it all by heart," he said. "Poetry was a repository of all knowledge. It was our dictionary, our encyclopedia. It told you everything you needed to live. In the past, there was actually a competition over how much knowledge a person could carry in him. In earlier times, if someone had had to refer to a book to recite a poem, people would have laughed at him. Our traditional poets used to recite poems without buying any notebooks. They used to recite hundreds of poems from their minds. Here," he said, touching his head. "The more dependent you become on pen and paper or on other technology, the more you lose your values."

Listening to him, I thought of one of Plato's dialogues in which Socrates argues that writing is a device not of memory but of forgetfulness.

"I agree with Socrates!" Hadrawi said happily when I mentioned it. In many ways, modern Somalia is struggling with the same issues that ancient Greece faced in the fourth century B.C.—the transition between oral and written society, between a clan society and a modern state governed by written law. But despite the prominence of poets in Somalia today, Hadrawi is pessimistic about the future, which he sees as increasingly dominated by Western media and technology. "My poetry is the expression of a world that is coming to an end," he said matter-of-factly.

The introduction of the written Somali language can be traced to a particular time and place. On the evening of October 20, 1972—the third anniversary of the coup d'état that brought Mohammed Siad Barre and his socialist Supreme Revolutionary Council to power—most of the inhabitants of the city of Mogadishu were out in the streets lined up along the parade route. Suddenly, a helicopter appeared overhead, swooped down above the crowd, and began to drop thousands of brightly colored leaflets as if in a heavenly dispensation. People picked up the pamphlets and puzzled over them. They were not in a language that anyone in the crowd recognized: they were not in Arabic or Italian or English. "They began to fight with their tongues to read the new writing," the government English-language newspaper later reported. But gradually some people in the crowd began to realize, "This is Somali!"

At the same time, since only a small percentage of the crowd could read, the written message was accompanied by broadcasts of poetic songs on Radio Mogadishu proclaiming the new script in the homely metaphors of nomadic verse:

> In the history of the world, our Language was taking no part;
> But the sunrise appeared uncovering our Language from darkness;
> The fence was cleared, so the livestock could graze.
> Give me your pen, the words I write for you.
> It is not a Foreign Language; the tongue does not slip,
> Like milk, it can be swallowed smoothly.

Somalia, a semiarid land with few natural resources, was spared colonization until late in the nineteenth century, when the Italians established themselves in the south and the British set up a colonial base in
the north. The colonial administrations used their respective tongues as
the languages of government, but because the colonization of Somalia
was late and rather superficial, probably less than 10 percent of the population learned how to read and write English and Italian. When Somalia gained its independence in 1960, the two former colonies agreed to
merge, forming a single Somali nation, with its capital in the south at
Mogadishu. Since the new Somali state was trying to combine the old
Italian and English administrations, the lack of a common language
quickly became a major problem. All official documents had to be in
both languages. The civil servants in the north tended to know English,
while those in the south knew Italian, and very few knew both, creating a
bureaucratic nightmare. Moreover, since few Somalis knew any foreign
language, writing constituted a barrier that excluded the vast majority
of citizens from access to government. The government agreed that it
needed to create a script for the Somali language, but deciding which
script to use became a paralyzing political issue.

Some pushed for the Arabic script, which some Somalis learn while
attending Koranic schools as children. But Arabic, which does not have
vowel symbols, is not well-suited to the Somali language, which has
twenty-two different vowel sounds, more vowels than consonants. The
Latin alphabet appeared a more practical solution: its five vowels could
be used in different combinations to approximate the intonations of
Somali speech. Moreover, educated Somalis who had studied English or
Italian already knew Latin letters and the government could continue
using its store of European typewriters. But the alphabet faced stiff
political opposition. The Muslim sheiks coined a clever slogan, "Laatiin,
Laa Diin," playing on the similarity between *Latin* and the Somali word
for "godless." Somali nationalists also regarded the Latin script as a
residue of the country's colonial domination. At one point, when the
government put up a few street signs in Somali with the Latin alphabet, a
riot ensued. Some nationalists insisted that to be truly independent,

Somalia must have its own indigenous alphabet, and several Somali intellectuals created their own sets of symbols, which they proposed as alternative scripts. One contender even went to the trouble and expense of having several typewriters custom made to show that his script could be adapted to modern technology. (This script had a problem, too: some characters were composed from right to left, others from left to right, making rapid cursive writing difficult.) Soon there were twenty-three candidates competing to become the national script. But many of the indigenous scripts ran afoul of clan politics: any Somali script came to be associated with the clan of its inventor and was therefore regarded with suspicion by the other clans, which then backed the alphabetic systems generated by their own clansmen. Faced with this babel of scripts and a set of thorny political problems, the early independent governments chose the path of least resistance: doing nothing.

The paralysis in solving the language problem was emblematic of the failure of the first postindependence governments, which were characterized by inefficiency, corruption, and interclan squabbling. The discord paved the way for Siad Barre, who took power in a bloodless coup in 1969, promising order, progress, socialism, and an end to the clan system. He was met with ululation and wild joy in the streets. "I welcomed the revolution like everyone else," Hadrawi said. "We were nationalists."

In fact, far from repudiating writing, Hadrawi had been writing in Somali well before the introduction of an official script. And after returning from his studies in Yemen in 1967, he wrote and performed a couple of poetic plays that helped establish his reputation as a poet. He was invited to teach at the National Teachers Education College, near Mogadishu, one of the new national universities that had sprung up with independence. "Because it was clear that he was a great poet, we insisted on having him at the college as a teacher," said Said Sallah, a Somali poet who lives in Minneapolis, a city with a significant Somali refugee community. Sallah was amazed to hear that Hadrawi was now against written language, since they collaborated together on a play called *Knowledge and Understanding*, produced in 1972, that openly called

for the written Somali script, just months before the launch of the government's literacy campaign.

But the way writing was introduced soured Hadrawi on the idea.
"There was no substance to it," he said. "[Barre] should have translated world knowledge into Somali. Instead, he only used the script
for political propaganda." Emulating Mao's China and Castro's
Cuba, Barre sent all high school and university students out to the
countryside for a year to teach the nomads in the bush how to read
and write about the feats of the revolution. He kept all publishing
under strict government control and even made it difficult for an
individual to own a typewriter. The principal newspaper, the *October
Star,* printed a picture of Barre on its cover every day and was written
in the hagiographic style of the average socialist dictatorship. With
little of interest to read, many gradually reverted to illiteracy. Hadrawi
went to work for the government's information office but became
increasingly disillusioned.

Barre also tried to get an iron grip on poetry. "Siad Barre was one of
the most sensitive people to the dangers of poetry," Hadrawi said. "He
had a strategic plan to use poetry instead of fighting against it. He tried
to control all the poets and everything else in the area of literature. All
the Somalia media, Radio Mogadishu, Radio Hargeysa, were focusing
on the propaganda of the regime."

This kind of one-way broadcast communication ran against the
grain of Somali culture. "People were not accustomed to a 'dictation
culture,'" Hadrawi said, using the phrase "dictation culture" in English.
Somali nomads live a life of considerable freedom and autonomy and
their culture is surprisingly egalitarian. They move around in relatively
small encampments of several families who customarily make decisions
collectively. "The man who dictates separates himself from others," says
a famous Somali proverb. "Even the sultan needs to be taught," says
another.

The old oral tradition now found a new ally: the cassette player.
"Since Siad Barre had taken over the radio, the medium of cassettes
became stronger," Hadrawi said. "People felt they had lost something

when their literature was taken away from them, so that's when the underground literature started." Inexpensive tape recorders became a staple of Somali life in the early 1970s, when Somalis working overseas brought them back in large numbers and gave them to their families so that, in the absence of writing, families could exchange oral "letters." Thus Somalis, already used to making their own tapes, would copy or rerecord poetry cassettes and circulate them.

Somalis began using the tape recorder to transmit dissent in poetic form. Somalis have a long tradition of conducting what are called "poetic duels" or "poetic chains" as a form of public debate. One poet will write a poem on a given theme, using a particular alliterative scheme—Somali poetry is based on the alliteration of a letter or sound in a poem rather than rhyming—and other poets will then answer, addressing the same theme and using the same alliteration. The chain has a competitive element, like a poetry slam, with the poets vying with one another to come up with unusual words or clever neologisms to vary the alliteration while remaining on point. At the same time, the poetic duel is conducted in metaphorical language that allows society to deal with thorny problems without provoking irrevocable conflict. "Allegory cools down speech," an old Somali proverb goes. The poetic duel became a perfect means for dealing with government censorship because the standard tropes of Somali poetry—a bitter drought or a cleansing storm—might either have a subversive meaning or just be about the vicissitudes of nomad life. "People need entertainment," Hadrawi said. "Somalis like to sit around and listen in the afternoon as they chew *qat* [a green-leafed plant that is a mild stimulant]. So everybody would listen to the tapes and then they would compare interpretations the next morning."

Hadrawi became one of the most popular poets in this informal cassette market because of his political independence. "I was one of the few people who refused to change the nature of my poetry to praise Siad Barre," he said. Hadrawi had already attracted the suspicions of the government through the play *Knowledge and Understanding*, which toured Somalia. Several of the poetic songs, written by Hadrawi and put to music by one of Somali's leading singers, had become popular favorites. One of them, entitled "Saxarla" (pronounced "Saharla"), sparked a poetic duel that is known as the "Sin-ley" poems, meaning "S-chain" in Somali, because of the "s" sound in "Saxarla." Although "Saxarla" is a love song, the character in the play named Saxarla is a blind woman thought to represent the newly independent Somalia groping around in the dark, and the tone of impatient longing seemed to suggest a hidden political meaning. As a result, the Sin-ley chain of poems evolved into a political debate, albeit masked in allusive poetic language.

To some the song's desire to rescue Saxarla appeared to be a desire to free Somalia from dictatorship; to others it was a call to liberate the Somali-speaking territories in Kenya, Ethiopia, and Djibouti. "There were so many interpretations," said Said Sallah. Poems on cassette began pouring in from different parts of Somalia and from Somalis in other countries. Some used strange symbolism like five little sheep or five lamps to represent the different regions of Somalia. And there were poems about a famous spear that served for a cryptic discussion of the government's military might. All these were topics that were impossible to discuss openly. "In Somalia, poetry is not an intellectual exercise, as in the Western world. It is the life of the people," said Sallah, who contributed two of the approximately forty poems in the chain. Indeed, poetry is so much a part of Sallah's life that he named his eldest daughter Saxarla in honor of Hadrawi's song. And even though he and his family live in the United States, all of Sallah's children and grandchildren have names beginning with the letter S, following the alliterative scheme of the Sin-ley poetic chain. "We are the S-family," he said with a laugh when I interviewed him on the phone.

"The Sin-ley [chain] was very important because it was the first time that people really questioned the identity of Somalia," said Ali Jimale Ahmed, who was in Somalia at the time, left during the civil war of the 1980s, and now teaches comparative literature at the City University of New York in Queens.

"People were changing my poems and making them political," Hadrawi said. Listeners either inferred political meaning in the poems or actually changed the words and rerecorded them. "People were starved for reality and they wanted a chance to talk about social issues and so they read them into the poems. They created their own folk form. People decided to have their own free literature and that's when the revolution started."

Siad Barre paid close attention to the phenomenon and is said to have amassed a formidable collection of tapes. In 1973, he called Hadrawi to the presidential palace. "Ask me whatever you want, any job you want, as long as you don't write poems that are against us," he said, according to Hadrawi, who responded by writing his most overtly political poetry yet. He wrote a poetic play called *The She-Camel* describing the slaughter for a feast that is enjoyed only by a few while the multitude watch from a distance—an apparent reference to the growing corruption and cronyism of the Barre government. The central poem seemed to allude to an upcoming struggle:

> *With the news of a slaughtered she-camel*
> *Everybody hurried to the scene.*
> *The fun will be to see the others*
> *Who saw the smoke from the high peaks*
> *And will come rushing down the slopes and the ridges.*
> *Laughter is a crime.*
> *The hero gave his neck.*
> *In the shed there was a snake.*

The poem also contained a clear response to Siad Barre's attempt to buy Hadrawi off: "I will not eat the demeaning scraps from your table."

"It was obvious he was talking about Siad Barre," said Professor Ahmed at CUNY. "It is a beautiful poem aesthetically."

The play was performed before the censorship board, attended by the vice president and two ministers of the government. "The play dealt openly with social problems like prostitution and lack of education," problems that were not supposed to exist in Barre's socialist paradise, said Said Sallah, who helped produce it. The censors demanded numerous changes, but Hadrawi refused. The play was never performed publicly, and Hadrawi was arrested and sent to live under house arrest in solitary confinement about 350 miles from Mogadishu. But the poem *The She-Camel* was put to music and circulated widely on tape while Hadrawi was in confinement.

Hadrawi wrote no political poetry while under house arrest, but when he was released in 1978 he found a political situation he could no longer ignore. The previous year, Barre had started a war with Ethiopia in order to annex the Ogaden region, which is inhabited by many ethnic Somalis. But by 1978, the Ethiopians had mounted a major counterattack, sending hundreds of thousands of ethnic Somalis across the border into Somalia and marking the beginning of a twenty-year refugee crisis. Not only did the war create a humanitarian disaster, it stirred up latent ethnic tensions within Somalia, which Barre consciously exploited. Since most of the Somalis in the Ogaden belonged to Barre's clan, the Darod, many Somalis viewed the invasion as an effort to increase the strength of his own clan. Moreover, he tried to solve the refugee crisis by promising his displaced clansmen land that was already occupied by others. Thus, after declaring that he had eliminated the clan system, Siad Barre was favoring his own clan over others. It became clear that Barre had no desire to resolve the plight of the refugees: their numbers deliberately inflated by Barre to increase foreign aid, they became a cash cow for him and his circle, which was increasingly composed of men from his own subclan and immediate family. Since his adversary, Ethiopia, received aid from the Soviet Union, Barre began to play Cold War politics to win massive amounts of military and foreign aid from the United States and Europe. The father of Somali socialism had turned overnight into the bulwark against Communism in Africa. Within a few short years, he had revealed that all his grandest proclamations were a sham, amounting to little more than an increasingly rapacious and brutal grab for power and wealth.

"People were absolutely miserable," Hadrawi said, describing the atmosphere after his release.

Not long after returning to Mogadishu, Hadrawi was roused from bed at 5:00 a.m. by agents of Siad Barre and told to come right away to the president's palace. Barre, a chronic insomniac who chain-smoked Benson & Hedges cigarettes much of the night, was in the habit of waking up whomever he wanted to see. "He told me to bring various men of literature with me and he tried to convert us to his ideas," Hadrawi said.

The poets listened and politely but firmly declined. "We couldn't swallow it. People wanted deeds and not demagoguery," Hadrawi said. In one poem from this period, he answered Siad Barre's request for support with a direct slap in the face:

How can I say something good about you?
Where shall I start?
You are not brave enough.
You are not kind enough.
You are not wise enough.
You are a dust storm
and a summer drought.
You are an empty wind
and a bad harvest.
You are made of a bad clay.

And then in December 1979, Hadrawi and one of the poets who attended the meeting, Mohamed Hashi Dhamac (known by his nick-name, Gaariye), decided to launch a poetic duel that would directly confront the regime. "We said to each other: 'History will not forgive us if we don't respond.' That was the beginning of the end. From that day on, we made war on the regime."

The duel was composed of poems beginning with the letter *D*, and they became known as the De-ley (or D-chain) poems. And if the Sin-ley poems were ambiguous in their meaning, now the poets directly took on the new reality of Somalia, reeling from its refugee crisis and swimming in stolen foreign aid money.

In his poem "Debatiel," Hadrawi wrote:

Where does all this money come from?
It doesn't come from people's work.
Who has paid for
All these colorfully decorated houses?
Where do these Japanese cars come from
When most people have nothing?
They do not come from the sky.
These people are flaunting their wealth instead of hiding their shame.
Don't they know that they will have to stand for their crimes?
That there will be a day of reckoning?

The poems began to circulate on cassette. "People would listen to them, then copy them and distribute them," Hadrawi said. The poems stirred up the latent, unvocalized dissent that was underneath the surface of Somali life. Some sixty different poets joined in the chain, contributing a total of about 120 poems.

Given the traditional role of poets in Somali society, everyone in the country understood the gravity of the challenge. One poet responded by sounding a note of worried caution:

All things that were hidden
Are now unveiled
Gone are the days of genteel language
Lo, the poets have formed two antagonistic camps.

The regime tried to step in and ban the poems, but people continued taping and recording them just the same. "We were expecting to be imprisoned every night, but nothing happened," Hadrawi said. The reason, he explained, was that Barre understood that his position had become dangerously weak. "If he had had the support of the people, he could have smashed us in a minute as he did in 1973. Instead, the poetry shook the foundation of the state."

"The tapes were everywhere. You could find them in Italy, England, Sweden, Egypt," said Professor Johnson, who began collecting the De-ley tapes when he was doing research in Somalia during the 1980s. "Poetry represents social debate in Somalia. The poems were flying back and forth. You'd have to duck to miss one." Johnson tracked down tapes of most of the De-ley poems and assembled for Indiana University what is probably the largest collection of Somali poetry—almost all on cassette— bribing a government censor in order to smuggle them out of the country. "It was called 'the socialist handshake' back then," Johnson said. "That fellow is probably still drinking the tea I bought him."

The view that the De-ley chain was a crucial turning point in Somali life is shared by many nonpoets as well. "The poetry was more important to us than guns and cannons," said Abdulrahman Yousseff (known as Bobe), a freedom fighter for the Somali National Movement (SNM). "These songs opened up discussion for people. They were becoming educated and informed. They would sit around listening to the songs and talk. People generally didn't listen to these songs alone. They listened with other people and they had to screen the people whom they were listening with and so these were the basis of political groupings. So Siad Barre was not wrong to be afraid of the poets."

In January 1981—about thirteen months after the beginning of the De-ley poetic chain—the SNM, one of the first and largest groups of armed resistance against the regime, was formed, operating from a base in Ethiopia. The movement was composed heavily of people from northern Somalia, where sentiment against the Barre regime was particularly high. Hadrawi and his fellow poet Gaariye remained in Mogadishu until May 1, 1982, when, taking advantage of the national holiday for May Day, the international workers' day, they slipped out of the city, were driven north to Hargeysa, and then were spirited across the border into Ethiopia by Jeep in the middle of the night. "That same afternoon, there was an announcement on the independent radio of the movement that we had joined the opposition," Hadrawi recalled. "I said: 'Hargeysa, awaken!' And the armed poetry started."

The support of some of Somalia's leading poets lent prestige and respectability to the armed resistance and the SNM radio frequently broadcast their poetry from a station in Addis Ababa, the capital of Ethiopia. When Siad Barre made peace with Ethiopia in 1988 in order to convince Ethiopia to expel the Somali resistance groups, the SNM used a mobile radio transmitter that moved around strapped to the back of a camel. In 1988, the SNM captured Hargeysa, prompting a ferocious response by the Barre government. The Somali air force bombed the city and razed much of it to the ground, killing an estimated fifty thousand people.

In 1991, Siad Barre fell from power and the country was carved up into several pieces, each controlled by warlords associated with different Somali clans. Some scholars have theorized that the lack of a solid written tradition, especially of written law—an objective standard of norms applying equally to all sectors of society—has forced many African countries to fall back onto their ethnic and clan affiliations and that this, in turn, has contributed to the ethnic massacres in places like Somalia, Rwanda, Liberia, and Uganda. Radio broadcasts urging one group to kill another are thought by many to have played a key role in the genocidal killings in Rwanda. (In this, African warlords followed the lead of Hitler and Mussolini, who first used radio for mass propaganda.) Is there something inherent about the emotional appeal of oral discourse (the immediacy of radio and television) that makes it particularly well suited to whipping up the crowd? And is there, by contrast, something about the quiet detachment of the printed word, a critical distance in the act of silent reading, that acts as a brake to our most violent passions? Indeed, the collapse of the nation-state in Somalia, taken over by bands of illiterate teenagers with Kalashnikov rifles and Sony Walkmen, could be a grim McLuhanesque fable of postmodern neo-orality run amok, reminiscent of Stanley Kubrick's *A Clockwork Orange.* But the experience of the mini-state of Somaliland offers a more intriguing, complex, and reassuring picture.

With virtually no international aid, northern Somalia has rebuilt itself from the ground up with remarkable speed. Hargeysa, which was a semideserted pile of rubble with only a few thousand residents in 1991, is now a bustling city of 250,000. Houses are being built, businesses are opening, and almost all of it is happening with minimal government involvement. Somali refugees living in the West are returning or sending money to their relatives to invest and rebuild. "The Somalis are making a kind of spontaneous experiment in Reaganomics," said Mohamed Said Mohamed, who, although the minister of finance, is known throughout Hargeysa by the nickname Gees. Schools are reopening with a mix of private and public money. There is a functioning bus service run by a private company. A courier service delivers mail. People are using private doctors and clinics, and a beautiful new maternity hospital—built entirely with private donations—is going up in a part of Hargeysa that never had a hospital in the years when Somalia was one of the world's largest per capita recipients of foreign aid. "We want a central government, but a central government that is not very powerful," Gees said. "We are just a referee for law and order." New technology has helped to make this possible. It used to take a large central government to offer something like telephone service; now it is made available by a series of private companies. There is no central bank but a network of wire-transfer and courier companies that move money in and out of the country with relative ease.

Gees, a former professor of physics who studied at Eastern Michigan University, is a large man with big tortoiseshell glasses and a warm, affable manner. When I saw him in his somewhat ramshackle offices at the Ministry of Finance he was dressed in a brown Western-style polyester leisure suit, but when I visited him that afternoon at home, he was dressed in a long white caftan and sandals and was smoking tobacco from a water pipe as he listened to Somali music on a tape recorder. He invited the interpreter and me into his *mefrish,* a receiving room lined with cushions on the floor where Somalis congregate in the afternoons and drink tea and chew *qat.* "It's only a mild stimulant. It's not like cocaine," he said, by way of explanation as he began to chew on a few green leaves.

"The government accounts for only 5 percent of the GDP," Gees explained. Half of this goes toward paying unemployed former militia fighters who overthrew the government of Siad Barre. The traditional postcolonial African government was modeled after the Western nation-state, a centralized government with a strong leader at the head of a big government, but this model proved an unmitigated disaster in Somalia as elsewhere, leading to massive corruption and murderous dictatorship. There is something appealing about the small-scale state in Somaliland. "I walk to and from the office, and anyone can come up and talk to me," the minister said.

Gees and others admit that Somaliland needs international recognition and governmental involvement to accomplish certain basic goals: building and repairing roads, setting up a banking and credit card system, and creating a postal system that serves the entire country. But the forced experiment in self-reliance—and the disastrous history of foreign aid in recent Somali history—indicates that Somaliland, a weak state in a market society, could provide a potential model for the rest of Africa as it tries to find a way out of decades of repression and economic stagnation. Like many other African societies, Somalia has been much more decentralized by tradition than industrialized nation-states, and adopting a form of government that is more consistent with its culture may produce happier results than applying a Western model. "We are a clan society and it is better to admit it and try to use the positive aspects of clanism than to pretend that it doesn't exist," said Gees. "We are more practical. We tried to develop a system that would be suitable to our type of society, which is a clan society, and yet have a society in which every individual is equal under the law." Somaliland has set up a parliament of clan elders, who have been instrumental in bringing peace to northern Somalia and in maintaining order. It is adopting a new constitution that requires that each candidate for parliament win at least 20 percent of the vote in all six regions of Somaliland to be elected. This stipulation is meant to prevent any single clan from ruling at the expense of other groups. "We found the draft of the Nigerian law on the Internet," Gees explained.

But, I asked, doesn't a clan system make the government vulnerable to patronage and corruption in which jobs and resources are distributed based on clan affiliation rather than merit? "Yes, this is a problem,"

Gees replied. And, as if on cue, several men entered the *mefrish* at that moment. "These are my clansmen. I cannot refuse them hospitality," he said with a laugh as he motioned to them to sit. "And so, this is why it is important that our government remain small: there is less patronage for the government to distribute and fight over."

New technology may also help to make Somaliland's new government more accountable than previous ones. Somaliland's president, Mohammed Ibrahim Egal, has a fax machine in his office that jams with angry messages whenever he makes an unpopular move. He has tried changing the number several times, but because the phone companies are private and not public, the new number always leaks out and Somalis within the country and around the world continue to bombard the president with their opinions. Government critics maintain that Egal, who was prime minister of united Somalia during the 1960s and was subsequently jailed for graft, is still a corrupt authoritarian ruler of the old school. He has, on occasion, had journalists of the independent Somali newspaper *Jamhuriya* jailed when the paper attacked him, but the jailings have been brief and have become increasingly infrequent. Many believe that the fax machine in his office—which he has started to mention humorously and almost affectionately in public speeches—has had the effect of reining him in. "Gradually, I think the government has come to realize that having an independent source of information is actually to their advantage," said Yusuf Abdi Gabobe, editor of the *Republican,* the English-language weekly version of *Jamhuriya.*

Although literacy was greatly retarded by nearly twenty years of civil war, it is slowly making a comeback. Schools are teaching both Somali and English, and *Jamhuriya* has a small but loyal readership. Although it prints only two thousand copies a day, Gabobe insists that its circulation is limited more by lack of paper stock than by lack of popular demand. Despite crude graphics and only eight pages of text, the newspaper nonetheless contains frank coverage of Somaliland's issues and problems, including unvarnished articles about nepotism and corruption in the government. On a continent where most countries have a servile and muzzled press, Somaliland is a small, encouraging exception.

While the popular culture remains oral, Somali's educated elite is gradually rebuilding itself, greatly reinforced by the tens or even hundreds of thousands of Somali refugees who took advantage of the displacement of the long civil war to attend university, get advanced degrees, or start businesses overseas. The town of Buruma, on its own initiative, has built a university and already has a library of seventy-five thousand books, almost all in English, sent by Somalis living in the diaspora. This wave of partly Westernized Somalis—like Gees and others—has injected new blood and new influences into Somali society. It is difficult to meet a Somali who does not have close relatives who have lived or now live in the West.

Hadrawi is one of the many refugees who have moved back recently to Somaliland after spending time in London and Norway while Somalia was embroiled in civil war and interclan violence. He was granted a hero's welcome, and his return was seen as a major recognition of the legitimacy of the self-proclaimed Republic of Somaliland. Although he is treated as a de facto poet laureate, Hadrawi's feelings about the country he has helped to create are decidedly ambivalent.

"The people of Somaliland love Somaliland: what is small and good is better than what is big and doesn't work," he said, comparing the new, small Republic of Somaliland with the old, unified Somalia. "Much good has been accomplished, usually despite the government. The government is supposed to represent the nomads, but it is the government of technology, people in three-piece suits living off the taxes of the nomad people."

The same technology that helped make him famous and that he continues to use—the tape recorder and the video—are now the conduit for foreign cultural influences that he sees as undermining Somali society. "We are slaves of technology," he said. Somalia is increasingly part of the global consumer economy, but the problem, according to Hadrawi, is that it absorbs much more from the outside than it transmits. "Everything that you see in Somalia costs money—these glasses, these plates—and advertising creates a thirst for more and more. Every day, I buy so many things that come from Britain and America, but nothing that I make is sold in Britain or America. It is good to have an exchange, but there is exchange only if I am in a position to offer something. Today we are under one global concept and it is not good for mankind. When there is diversity—the diversity is what makes life beautiful. Uniformity in taste is totally useless."

While oral culture has been given new life by technology, he sees the changes as like the bright light at twilight, a harbinger of the end and not the beginning of something new. "Poetry is alive, but the conditions of life that it expresses are at an end," he said. "We've lost a lot of our skills and our knowledge and our culture because of this modern civilization."

He was aware that he is part of Somalia's most cosmopolitan and technologically savvy generation of poets. He railed against writing yet he went to great pains to have a book of his verse published in Norway. He lambasted technology but used it to record his poetry and allowed his wedding to be videoed and encouraged its distribution. "I use video but I have my misgivings," he said. "It has a role in the present world. It is a reality that exists, although it has its negative aspects. But I have recently written a poem of over eight hundred lines about how technology is undermining our civilization." And he proudly pulled out a photocopy of a new set of poems, with elaborate computer-generated graphics. "It is all pure gold," he said. In his new anti-technology mood, he has even written a poem against Darwinian evolution. He insists that he envies his purely oral poetic predecessors, who relied entirely on their memories but whose work—since very little of it was recorded or copied down—has faded into the mists of legend.

While it would be easy to dismiss Hadrawi's stance as romantic, Luddite nostalgia, he is registering an epochal change in Somali life: the disappearance of the world in which he grew up, a highly distinct, pastoral nomadic life that developed over centuries in considerable isolation. What Hadrawi finds so appealing about this world is that its poets kept not just their poetry in their heads but an entire cosmos. And that a truly oral world is one in which poetry reigns supreme: "People knew their life by heart, they knew how to answer their needs and expectations," he said. "They knew the names of all the plants and trees and what their properties were. Man felt at home in his environment. A great deal of knowledge that has been slowly accumulated for hundreds and hundreds of years is now coming to an end. It is knowledge that has been molded slowly and carefully."

Yet what Hadrawi may not fully recognize is that he is very much a product of the hybrid culture that is growing up in Somalia, a defender of tradition and an agent of many of the changes he deplores. The traditional Somali poets tended to be closely tied to their clans and limited in their range. Hadrawi's universalism—even his critique of globalization and technology—is the critique of an educated man who has read and traveled. He is a man with one foot in the old oral world and one in the new world of writing and the tape recorder.

"This is a transitional period when our society is moving from the past to another kind of history. Roles are changing and the role of poetry is changing," said Rasheed Ahmed, a good friend of Hadrawi's who was a socialist newspaper editor during the early Barre years and is now the head of Somaliland's War Crimes Commission, which is investigating human rights violations during the civil war. A man with light brown skin and green eyes, he has the scholarly air and graying beard of an Islamic mullah but offered a remarkably lucid and worldly analysis of Somalia's dilemma in excellent English. "Life is more complicated now and poetry is no longer enough. The Somali nomad is integrated into the global economy, trading livestock to the Middle East and buying products from abroad. The Somali nomads used to make their own clothes, but now the camel man is wearing jeans. But he is still a pastoralist and his education and his skills are still the same. The world of technology is imposing itself on our world—you find it in every corner of our life. But the Somali nomad does not produce technology; he is a consumer of the products of the Western world. And it makes for an imbalance in our life. Poetry is important. It's a necessity for the Somali mind. But poetry can't tell people everything they need to know about the world. Poetry can give you feeling, but it cannot solve your problems. Poetry does not speak the language of facts and figures, and to solve our problems we need analysis, research, planning. Hadrawi raises some important questions. But the answer is not to isolate ourselves and go back in time. Even if we wanted to, it would be impossible. Development cannot be stopped. We have to use technology. We have to reconcile with technology and to impress our own personality, Somali culture, and national characteristics, on it."

8

Living with a Dead Language

A MAN IN a blue polyester jumpsuit surrounded by a small crowd stands at the edge of the Palatine Hill in Rome overlooking the ancient Circus Maximus at sunset. To the tune of a Gregorian chant, he sings a hymn to Apollo by the poet Horace in clear, fluent Latin.

This is not a pagan rite of a group of modern sun worshipers. It is a typical day in the life of Father Reginald Foster, a Carmelite monk from Milwaukee, Wisconsin. For the last twenty-five years, Foster has served as Latin secretary to three different popes and today he is senior Latinist to Pope John Paul II.

For Father Foster, Latin is anything but a dead tongue. A man of phenomenal energy, he wakes up well before dawn to say Latin Mass and to start preparing and correcting the hundreds of Latin homework sheets he assigns each week. At about 8:30 he goes to the Vatican to perhaps the only job in the world where he can write and speak Latin in the course of ordinary business. Along with translating the Vatican's public proclamations into the official language of the church, Father Foster is a kind of full-time Latin missionary who gives free lessons to anyone who is willing to study. After working in the Vatican all morning, he teaches until evening, and on his day off he takes his pupils to visit Roman sites where they read Latin texts in their original context. In the summers, Foster offers intensive free courses for Latin teachers from around the world, to whom he imparts his innovative approach to the language in the hope that they will spread the gospel when they return home. A one-man Audubon Society for the Latin language, he is determined to save it from extinction.

Living in Rome I kept hearing stories about Foster's singular relationship with Latin. I met people who had sung Latin songs with him to the cows of Castel Gandolfo, site of the emperor Domitian's villa and now the pope's summer residence. A friend described her surprise at tramping through the ruins of Ostia Antica and suddenly hearing someone telling ribald jokes in Latin. It was Foster, of course, showing his class the two-thousand-year-old graffiti on the bathroom walls of the old Roman port city.

Although he is one of the world's finest Latinists, Foster insists on teaching Latin at all levels, including the most elementary, so that he can make new converts. I decided in 1991 to take his introductory course to see for myself.

Since 1977, Foster has taught at the Pontifical Gregorian University, the center of Jesuit learning in downtown Rome. The building's exterior, bristling with papal tiaras and coats of arms, has the imposing air of a fortress. Huge studded metal doors lead to an equally prepossessing two-story atrium presided over by a life-size statue of Jesus.

The introductory course, with more than seventy students, is filled largely with novice priests and nuns wearing the cassocks and habits of various orders, from somber black to bright blue. Most of the seminarians—in keeping with the change in the Catholic clergy—are from Africa and Asia, where Catholic traditions are now hardiest. Their names—echoing those of popes, saints, and martyrs—recall the bygone era of the Vatican's mighty temporal power: Ignatius, Innocent, Clement, Hyacinth, Linus, Titus, Bernardino, Vincent.

But beyond the setting and composition of the class, resemblances between other classes at the Gregorian and Foster's "First Experience" (as he calls his introductory course) quickly break down. Outsiders—as long as they are seriously committed—are welcome to take the course, for free. Foster is impatient with traditional Church pomp and formality. "We'll call each other by our first names, freedom and joy and all that," he says with a twist of self-irony. Instead of his monk's habit, Foster always wears his metal-blue polyester suit: blue pants, a matching wind-breaker, a wash-and-wear blue shirt, and heavy black work shoes. He does not wear a clerical collar. The outfit combines a blue-collar work ethic with the spartan simplicity of the monastic ideal without calling attention to him as a "holy man." He looks as if he might sooner check your carburetor or fix your boiler than reveal the mysteries of Ovid or Saint Augustine.

Foster is a fit-looking man of fifty-four, with a round, ruddy, bald-ing head and frameless wire-rim glasses. The thin wreath of hair that runs above his ears looks a little like a medieval tonsure. His spectacles, his wide, open face, and his friendly smile give him a mild-mannered, unworldly appearance—an impression dispelled almost as soon as Foster opens his mouth. His deep, sandpapery voice projects loudly through the class; it starts out at a low growl but rises suddenly when he is trying to make a point—which is most of the time—to a thundering sonic boom or a high-pitched screech. Foster delivers his introductory class barking like a drill sergeant breaking in a bunch of raw recruits to the rigors of marine boot camp.

"You don't have to be all that intelligent, but Latin takes a little bit of toughness," he growls. "I hope you are all here voluntarily. I don't like the idea that some of you have been pushed into this classroom by some REQUIREMENT." A word he pronounces with the utmost scorn and distaste. "Because if that's the case I'd like to push you RIGHT BACK OUT. . . . If you have to take Latin and don't want to, there is a list here and you can just put your name on it and leave. And I will give you a passing grade for the year. I'm interested in teaching Latin to people who want to learn. . . . So, if you DON'T like me or you DON'T like Latin, then you can leave and that will be that. Got it? If you want to learn Latin, we'll learn Latin.

"If you are registered, I don't care. You can sit here for five years and not be registered. I don't know how much they're charging downstairs—I think it's too much."

There is nothing pleading or apologetic about Foster's presentation of Latin. Many teachers treat Latin grammar as if it were bad-tasting medicine that will eventually prove beneficial—a few dull years of memorizing conjugations and declensions that have to be put up with before one slogs through Caesar's *Gallic War*. Foster does not concede an inch, firmly convinced that from the very first class the study of Latin should be a revelation of the greatest urgency and importance.

"Why do you want to study Latin? THE QUESTION IS, WHY DON'T PEOPLE WANT TO STUDY LATIN?" he asks the class in a rhetorical shout, pacing back and forth in front of the blackboard. "If you don't know Latin, you know nothing! I had my first experience of Latin forty years ago and I have not been bored by Latin for ten minutes in these forty years. Latin is one of the greatest things that ever happened in human history!"

When Foster begins to shift into high gear, he picks up in speed and volume, like a high-performance car moving into overdrive. "If you don't know Latin, you're sitting out there on the sidelines—don't worry, most of the world is out there with you. But if you want to see what's going on in this whole stream of two thousand years' worth of gorgeous literature, then you need Latin."

Foster distributes a ten-page handout, a sampling of Latin literature from the comic playwright Terence (185–159 B.C.) to a papal decree of 1990. This is the closest we will get to a textbook all year. "I am going to put real Latin in front of you. We are studying what Latin is on PLANET EARTH," he booms. "One of the things I don't like about these textbooks they give you is you fool around with these phony little made-up sentences. We are going to deal with real sentences from the first day."

After this brief introduction, Foster rolls up his sleeves and starts to explain his teaching method. "There will be no grammar books, no textbooks. . . . you are going to have me, whether you like it or not. That's the system. Every student is going to get a good Latin dictionary."

Along with coming to class on Mondays and Fridays, students are required to do homework sheets that Foster invents twice a week.

"You work this thing all by yourself," he says. "The idea is that you teach yourself. This sheet is due a week from now—there won't be class on Friday because there's some kind of nonsense over at St. Peter's Basilica." He is referring to the anniversary of the canonization of Saint Birgitta, a Swedish nun of the fourteenth century.

The reason Latin is generally boring, Foster says, is that it is taught all wrong. The grammar is presented as an enormous and complex abstract system of bizarre and arcane rules divorced from its actual context inside a real and living language.

"People are not told what Latin is all about," Foster says. "They are just told to memorize all the forms, the conjugations and declensions. Latin has nothing to do with memorization. Every bum and prostitute in ancient Rome spoke Latin and they didn't learn it by memorization. GOT IT?"

"Got it?"—generally pronounced in a raspy growl—is a constant refrain in the Reginald Foster experience.

Foster tries to get students to stop thinking in English and to enter the Latin mind-set by immediately stressing some of the difficulties and peculiarities of the language.

"The hardest thing for people who have grown up speaking English or one of the Romance languages is to grasp the fact that Latin does not depend on word order," Foster explains. "That is the thing that drives people crazy. In English you more or less have your subject, you more or less have your verb, and you more or less have your object. If I say, 'Jane sends Jim to me' and then change the order of the words—'Jim sends Jane to me' or 'Me to Jim sends Jane'—the whole meaning changes.

"The meaning of a Latin sentence does not come from the word order but from the word endings. It means that if I write, *'Marcum Joanna mittit,'* I can have them in any order and it will mean the same thing: Jane sends Mark. I pick this up from the endings, the 'um' indicates object, the 'a' indicates subject. By changing the ending I am changing the function. But I can make it *'mittit Marcum Joanna'* and there's no change in meaning. That's what the whole thing in Latin is all about: AN INFINITY OF POSSIBILITIES. Infinite combinations and the word order is FREE—FREE!!" he shouts, emphasizing "free" like a discounter announcing an unbeatable sale.

As he promised, Foster plunged us, from the very first day, right into real Latin texts—Cicero, Petronius, and the Latin Vulgate Bible—which meant that learning grammar was never separated from the enormous aesthetic pleasure of the language itself. Thus, once we had finished identifying the subject, the object, and the verb, we found ourselves staring at sentences of extraordinary beauty.

To illustrate his point about word order, Foster had us look at a letter Cicero wrote on June 13, 44 B.C., to his closest friend, Atticus. Because so many of Cicero's letters survive and because they are written in such a fresh and direct fashion, they capture his daily life in all its particularity as if in suspended animation, the way the volcanic ash and lava of Vesuvius preserved Pompeii and Herculaneum. Reading them is like accidentally overhearing a conversation from two thousand years ago.

"L. Antonio male sit, si quidem Buthrotiis molestus est!" the letter begins, meaning: "Let Lucius Antonius be hanged if he's going to be obnoxious to the Buthrotians!" *"Molestus*—like molest, annoying or obnoxious," Foster says. Cicero is commiserating with Atticus over a real estate deal in northern Greece (Buthrotum) that has gone sour. He moves on to his own nagging financial problems—a constant of his correspondence—then turns to the heart of the matter, the burning political situation following the death of Julius Caesar.

"REGINAM ODI!" says Foster in a stately, dramatic voice. "*'Regina'* is the word for 'queen,' *'odere'* is the verb 'to hate,'" he says. "Like odious. Got it? DON'T SAY THE QUEEN HATES! THE QUEEN DOESN'T HATE ANYONE!"

Foster screams at full volume. "It says: 'I hate the queen!' Notice, the object comes first, the verb last. *'Regina'* becomes *'reginam'* when it's used as an object.

"'The queen' is Cleopatra. Oooohhh," he croons. "Julius Caesar had been in Egypt and had spent about nine months playing around with Cleopatra. If you've been in Trastevere [a neighborhood in downtown Rome just across the Tiber River] you may have seen there is an area called the Horti Caesaris, the road of the Gardens of Caesar. Caesar brought her back to Rome and had her living in his gardens over in Trastevere. When I come home tonight, I will pass right by the gardens Cicero is talking about here. So when Cicero writes this letter, this queen is floating around Rome and Cicero says, 'I hate the queen!' She was right down the street in Trastevere. She was thrown out of Rome after Caesar's assassination.

"Cicero hates the queen. See what Latin's all about?" By now, his voice has dropped to a stage whisper and the class is in rapt silence.

"'*Superbiam autem ipsius reginae.*' Once again Cicero is starting his sentence with the object. '*Superbiam*' means 'haughtiness.' The haughtiness of the queen herself '*cum esset,*' when she was, '*trans Tiberim,*' across the Tiber, '*in hortis,*' in Caesar's gardens, '*commemorare sine magno dolore,*' remember without great pain, '*non possum*'—finally we have the verb—I cannot, I am not able."

He then reads the whole sentence: "The haughtiness of the queen herself when she was living in Caesar's gardens across the Tiber I cannot recall without great pain in my heart!"

Foster becomes so excited he exclaims, "IT'S OUT OF THIS WORLD! LATIN IS SIMPLY THE GREATEST THING THAT EVER HAPPENED! DON'T LET YOURSELF GO BECAUSE YOU MIGHT JUST FALL IN LOVE WITH IT!"

For Reginald Foster (or Reginaldus as he is sometimes known), Latin was love at first sight. He can still remember vividly his first Latin class in 1953 at St. Francis Minor Seminary in Milwaukee, when he was thirteen. "I saw right away how clever it was," he said. "I liked the way you could play around with this and say so much just with the little endings and switch things around. It was like a little puzzle. . . . It seemed kind of mysterious and clever. . . . I decided this Latin thing was going to be my endeavor, my contribution."

Except for one year in Milwaukee, Foster has spent nearly forty years living in the Carmelite monastery attached to the church of San Pancrazio on Rome's Janiculum Hill. The monastery is simple, spare, and modern, with linoleum floors and plastic furniture, like an elementary school or a budget motel. But the monastery's pleasant tree-lined grounds occupy some of Rome's finest real estate, sharing the same view as the splendid seventeenth-century Villa Doria Pamphili, suburban retreat of the family of Pope Innocent X.

Foster is exactly where he wants to be, doing exactly what he always hoped to do. "By the time I was fifteen years old I wanted to be three things in life: the first thing, as a little kid I wanted to be a priest. The second thing is I wanted to be a Latin teacher. The third thing is I wanted to be a member of a religious community, rather than a diocesan priest. And so by the time I was fifteen I knew I wanted to be these three things and since then I have never had a moment's doubt about any of them. . . . No wandering around until I was thirty figuring out what I wanted to become."

Foster wanted to be a priest from as far back as anyone in the family can remember. At the age of six, according to his mother, Margaret Foster, young Reggie tore up old sheets to use as vestments and—instead of playing cops and robbers—he would pretend to be a priest and perform Mass. Mildly embarrassed by this maternal revelation, Father Foster explained: "A lot of kids did that in those days. . . . It wasn't quite as strange a thing as it might seem today."

This early religious and scholarly vocation seems to have been entirely Reggie's idea. His family was Catholic but without particular emphasis. Foster's father and grandfather were both plumbers and his mother was a homemaker. Reggie was a straight-A student and valedictorian of his eighth-grade class in parochial school. His brother, Tom, still runs the family plumbing business and his sister, Susan, is a housewife and mother.

Mrs. Foster seemed more surprised than anyone at having produced a scholarly monk for a son. "I always say, I think they got the babies mixed up at the hospital. He can't belong to us. He's not like any of us!"

she recounted. But her own words belie her thought: you can hear—in her Milwaukee twang, her feisty conversational style, and her mix of piety and irreverent humor—echoes of her son Reginald.

Foster's interest in language was stimulated by the severe German nuns who taught him in parochial school. "The sisters were very into this grammar thing," Foster said. "They taught us English grammar until it came out of our ears. We had to have it perfect. I liked that very much."

Aside from school and church, young Reggie had a series of solitary interests that he pursued with quiet but total dedication. From books he took out of the library, he taught himself to play the organ and to swim.

When Foster graduated from grade school, he decided to enter St. Francis Minor Seminary, a Catholic high school for students who intended to become priests. The arrival of adolescence coincided with a quantum leap in his already intense religiosity. "When I was twelve, thirteen I got really turned on by religion, most of which I've abandoned now," he said, laughing. "I went through a period they call 'scrupulosity'—this is a famous syndrome that psychologists have studied. It's a time in your life when people become especially religious, and puberty is one of them. I was almost out of my mind: I was committing mortal sins every other minute. It was terrible. I couldn't laugh. I couldn't even look at a woman because it was a sin. I thought everything was a sin. I started reading *The Lives of the Saints*, about the penances they did and so on. . . . I was driving everyone crazy with my religious fanaticism, candles, all that. It wasn't my parents who were pushing this on me. They thought I was a little crazy. . . . This is natural when you're twelve years old. You grow out of it. In the midst of it, I decided to join the priesthood."

Some people were concerned that Reggie took things too seriously. One day a woman in the neighborhood saw him standing alone in front of a statue of the Madonna in the parish church with tears streaming down his face. The woman telephoned Margaret Foster to tell her what she had seen. "I thought it was ridiculous. I wasn't that upset," said Mrs. Foster, not long before her death in 1992. But she did talk to their priest, who told her simply: "They go through a stage like that."

In the throes of this personal crisis, during the summer between his freshman and sophomore years of high school, Foster decided he wanted to be a monk, living apart from the world. "I wanted to belong to a religious community. The Carmelites were a perfect middle ground for me. I didn't want to be a complete hermit like a Cistercian. But on the other hand, I didn't want a place like a train station or a boarding-house. Our order really has the best of both. There's perfect silence here, there's prayer together but a lot of solitude and study. . . . I like being able to turn it on and off. When I am outside I am very much on; when I come home I'm a complete hermit."

As the idea to join the Carmelites crystallized, so did Foster's consuming passion for Latin. Even though his first-year Latin course was taught according to the old method of memorization, he was totally absorbed by it; he took the textbooks home during his summer vacation, learned them backward and forward, and returned to school ready for advanced Latin. "That whole training in English grammar I had had with the nuns, of analyzing things linguistically, switched over and blossomed in Latin," he said.

In the fall of 1955, at age fifteen, Foster left Milwaukee for the Monadnock Mountains of New Hampshire, where the Carmelites had their training seminary. Waiting for him when he got off the overnight train from Chicago to Worcester, Massachusetts, was a young Carmelite monk named Conrad Fliess, who immediately struck up an animated conversation in Latin. For Foster, it was a revelation: suddenly this mysterious ancient language that he had studied in silence leapt off the page and came to life. The two rattled on in Latin all the way back to New Hampshire in the seminary van. "He was all wild for Latin," Foster said. "We had Latin plays and had to write Latin compositions every week. He saw right away that I already knew Latin very well and so he tutored me. We were great friends and remained so until the end of his life. . . . Meeting this man changed my whole deal, my whole approach to Latin."

The move to the Carmelite seminary proved providential in many ways. "That's what really got me going," Foster said. "I would have been like most people had I stayed [in Milwaukee]. I found the Carmelites and

I love them very much." Living in a sympathetic religious community also helped him get past his painful period of scrupulosity. "I saw other young people like me who didn't have this problem. And there were some priests who talked with me and helped me. It just disappeared. . . . It's almost like having glasses—you just see things in a certain light, which was that of sin. . . . If I took a toothpick off the table I was stealing from my parents. . . . I just started seeing things differently."

Foster spent three years studying with Fliess in New Hampshire. In addition to receiving the standard religious training, he learned German and ancient Greek and, of course, took intensive Latin. He officially joined the Carmelite order in Boston in 1959 and then went on to do an advanced degree in philosophy at a Carmelite monastery near Milwaukee, where he was reunited with Father Fliess.

In 1962, Foster began theology training in Rome. Arriving at the center of the Roman world was the culmination of all his years of passionate study. "The day after I came to Rome I went to the Roman Forum and I saw all this stuff that I had read about as a kid and studied—the place Cicero gave his orations. I just lost my mind. . . . Here was this whole living language which I had come to love in the United States. . . . To come here and to imagine—as I still like to do—people walking around the Forum speaking Latin . . . to read Cicero's orations out loud and hear the same words bouncing off the walls that bounced off the walls in Caesar's presence in September of 46 B.C. It's just too much!"

Foster's insistence on Latin as a living language may seem eccentric to some—like Don Quixote setting off in medieval armor to revive the age of chivalry in seventeenth-century Spain. But it is easy to forget how much more prevalent Latin was only forty years ago, when Foster received his religious training. Not only was the Mass said in Latin, all of Foster's classes—theology, philosophy, canon law, archeology, and church history—were taught in Latin. All priests were required to take seven or eight years of Latin and everyone in the Catholic Church, from San Francisco to Sydney, had some degree of proficiency in Latin. International Vatican meetings were conducted in Latin. Popes, cardinals, and bishops corresponded and sometimes conversed in it. The current pope, Karol Wojtyla, wrote his doctoral dissertation in Latin when he was a student in Rome. The pope's Latin, Foster said, "is a little on the spaghetti side, but totally functional." "Spaghetti" or "macaroni" Latin is Foster's term for highly Italianized Latin.

"All priests knew Latin," he says. "It was hard in those days. If you said, 'I want to be a great Latinist,' you were competing with everybody in the class and in every class around the world. I see some of my old col-leagues, we still converse in Latin. It was totally normal. Now it seems like some divine gift. Anyone who knows some Latin is a man with one eye in the land of the blind."

The great decline of Latin began in the sixties as a result of the Sec-ond Vatican Council (1962–65), which attempted to radically modern-ize the Catholic Church. Although all the meetings of Vatican II were conducted in Latin and the council took no steps to eliminate it, Latin became one of its unintended victims. "In all the upheaval—which I think was very salutary—Latin got clipped. . . . It was inevitable. . . . Latin was identified with the old system. . . . Latin tyranny. . . . Any-way, they threw all the old statues on the junk pile, and Latin went on the junk pile with the statues."

Aside from the junking of Latin, Foster was delighted with the reform of the Church. "It was just sensible and rational," he said. "We're just treated like adults now, that's all. Under the old system, we were treated like *bambini* in the name of obedience. . . . In 1962, you couldn't go out the front door without permission and there was silence at meals. You got to go out once a week for a walk. At ten o'clock all the lights had to be out. You couldn't stay up reading. Lord help us, you couldn't have any money. . . . If you needed two hundred lire [about 15 cents], you had to go to your superior. It was a reign of ter-ror. . . . But in those days it wasn't a horror story, because we knew nothing else. Now, it's a totally different world. We're much more responsible. . . . I have certain tasks, I take care of my work, and that's it. . . . The rest they don't even ask about. . . . They can't put that toothpaste back in the tube. Some people would like to, but it's not going to work."

The demolition of the Church's millennial Latin legacy was equally swift. Foster was spared the painful moment of transition. Called back to Milwaukee in the spring of 1967, he returned to his monastery in Rome a year later and found a different world. All the public notices and signs in the monastery that had been written in Latin were now in Italian. Latin had been removed as the teaching language and all classes were in broken Italian. "That whole system was demolished, taken down, burned up, and melted, and that was it," Foster said.

Rather than link Latin to the reactionary elements in the Church, Foster identifies it with the tradition of Christian humanism—the Renaissance scholars and churchmen who passionately studied the texts of the ancient world: Saint Thomas More, Erasmus of Rotterdam, Pope Leo X, Pope Pius II, Pico della Mirandola. For Foster, the humanists represent the most enlightened and tolerant tradition within the Church; they are the forebears of the more open-minded ecumenical spirit of the modern Church.

Politically, Foster is decidedly in the liberal wing of the Church, critical of the Church's rigid dogmatism on many moral issues, such as birth control. "Erasmus says in a dispute with a Protestant theologian: 'We are getting our theology from wells that are not clean on all sides,'" Foster explained. "He said we have to get back to the writings of the gospels. Not crazy theological stuff. The Gospels don't say anything about condoms or abortion."

As Foster was finishing his graduate studies, an elderly cardinal who had been Latinist to three popes asked him (in Latin), So what are you going to do with all this Latin? *"Deus providebit"*—"God will provide"— Foster answered. As fate would have it, Foster would be called on to fill the cardinal's old job. In 1969, when one of the pope's two principal Latinists, Amleto Tondini, who held the ancient title of Secretary for Briefs to Princes, died of a heart attack, Foster, at the age of thirty-two was selected to take his place. Foster had been chosen by the other Latin luminary of the Vatican, Carlo Egger, Secretary of Latin Letters to Pope Paul VI, who had been enormously impressed by Foster when he had him as a student at the Pontificium Institutum Altioris Latinitatis (the Pontifical Institute of Higher Latin Studies).

The office of Latin secretary has a long and distinguished history, stretching back to Saint Jerome, who was secretary to Pope Damasus (366–84). Jerome left his enduring mark by translating the Bible into the famous Latin Vulgate, which served as the Bible of the Western world from the fourth century A.D. until the Protestant Reformation, when there was a proliferation of new vernacular translations. In the Catholic world, Jerome's Vulgate continued until recently to be the principal Bible. Because of the absolute centrality of Latin within the Church, the Latin secretary was traditionally one of the pope's closest advisers and generally lived in the pope's apartments at the Vatican palace.

On Foster's arrival at the Vatican, the august but archaic title Secretariat for Briefs to Princes was replaced by the more modern-sounding Latin Language Department of the First Section of the Vatican Secretariat of State—which is where Foster works to this day. Foster's job involves composing the pope's official correspondence—letters to bishops and archbishops—as well as translating Vatican communiqués, ceremonial speeches, decrees, and encyclicals.

Through much of the 1970s, Egger and Foster handled the entire volume of work by themselves—a job now handled by a department of seven people. "And the workload has nosedived," Foster said. "When I think of the good old days when we were writing letters all over the world!" Even fifteen or twenty years ago, the Vatican could effectively use Latin as its principal tool of communication and expect that prelates around the world would understand it. Increasingly, Latin is being reduced to a merely ceremonial or decorative function—like the colorful uniforms worn by the pope's Swiss Guards or the elegant calligraphy that adorns official Vatican invitations. There is some talk about eliminating the calligraphy department as an unnecessary extravagance, and Foster is worried that one day in the not-too-distant future the same will happen to the Latin department. "There is no illusion about Latin taking off. It's not," Foster said. "It's definitely going down." At a recent synod of European bishops, Pope John Paul II chose to give his final address in Latin, but, said Foster, most people didn't have any idea what he was saying. For the moment, anyway, the Vatican Secretariat of State remains an oasis of Latin activity. Foster and his colleagues communicate exclusively in

Latin. A Franciscan monk poked his head into Foster's office when I was visiting, and they chatted briefly in rapid, colloquial Latin. The one phrase I picked up was *"medicum dentium"* ("doctor of the teeth")—the Franciscan was on his way to the dentist.

Foster's own office is as spare as can be, three plants and virtually no decorations on the wall. He has had an ongoing feud with one of his bosses, who kept trying to get Foster to put up a crucifix and a photograph of the pope—standard issue in most Vatican offices. During one tussle, Foster told him: "If you bring those things in here I will sell them at Porta Portese!" (the local flea market). Finally, the Church hierarchy prevailed and installed the photograph and the crucifix, with the image of the pontiff placed, curiously, above that of the Redeemer. Foster prefers the extreme simplicity of the early Christians to the pomp and bureaucracy of the modern Church. Passing by a nicely (but not luxuriously) furnished Vatican conference room, he pointed. "That's where all that collection money is going!" he says, laughing a mischievous, boyish laugh.

Nonetheless, he is rather indulgent of the extravagances of the Renaissance popes who built the Vatican palace—especially if they were great patrons of Latin. He made sure to point out the wonderful little bathroom that Raphael frescoed in Pompeian style for Cardinal Bernardo Bibbiena, humanist adviser to Pope Leo X. Not only does the room show Raphael's fascination with the newly discovered wall paintings of ancient Rome, it is a typical expression of its patrons, the learned Cardinal Bibbiena and Leo X, who himself cultivated a fine Latin prose style.

Despite his pessimism about the fate of Latin within the Church, Foster continues to fight the good fight, composing new Latin prose, convinced that Latin's marvelous flexibility and concision continue to make it a living, breathing language even in this *aetas informaticae disciplinae,* or age of the computer.

"The problems are not things, like photocopiers or computers," said Foster, "but all the jargon going around. There are so many concepts that the Romans didn't really have. Power sharing. The 'realization of the organization of work.' To 'SCUD' something. 'They acclimatized themselves.' *'Se accommodaverunt locis et temporibus'*—'They adapted themselves to places and times'—which is much nicer. It's much more concrete."

From the moment he arrived at the Vatican over thirty years ago, Foster must have seemed a singular presence. He drove to and from work on a little Ciao motorbike. At the time, he was seriously over-weight, weighing nearly 250 pounds, and as he sped along in his monk's cassock he must have looked like a circus bear riding a motorcycle.

But it was only after 1974, when he started teaching, that Foster came into his own, creating his own persona and life mission. He started taking off his cassock because it was getting covered with chalk in the classroom. Then when he was at home one August he found his trademark blue jumpsuit sitting on a rack at J. C. Penney. It seemed to speak to him, answering all his needs. "I need something very durable. I want to do my own laundry—the nuns used to do our laundry, which I never liked. I want something perma-press, neat and trim. And this is the kind of thing that workers in America wear, the gas station attendant or the electrician. It keeps its shape and color for about a year and a half. Twenty dollars for clothes every year and a half is not bad. . . . They have my name and measurements at Penney's. . . . I am for sim-plicity—I have two blue shirts and that's it. I don't have any hair, so I don't have to worry about it. You save all kinds of time and money by having nothing to choose." The last time he wore his Carmelite habit was when he came home to visit his mother in Milwaukee. Proud of hav-ing a monk for a son, she wanted to see him in his traditional garb. So on the flight between Detroit and Milwaukee, he did a quick change in the bathroom and emerged, like Superman from a phone booth, in his Carmelite cassock.

In order to stay within the measurements of his jumpsuit, Foster has to wage a daily battle against fat. "I have to watch my diet something ter-rible," he says. As a result, soon after Foster gave up his habit, he also gave up his place in the monastery dining room. As Foster began to con-centrate more and more on teaching, he developed his own separate life. He wakes up at 3:58 in the morning so he can listen to Voice of America on his shortwave radio at 4:00. Up before anyone else in the house, he sings Mass in Latin by himself in the chapel at 4:30. He is in his room at 5:30, ready to start work. He works on Latin until about 8:30, when he leaves the monastery and walks down from the Janiculum Hill to his job at the Vatican. He walks from there to the Gregorian, where he teaches all afternoon. He usually gets home at about 8:00 p.m. and prepares or corrects Latin homework until about 11:00, when he goes to bed. "I sleep about five hours, which is enough," he says. "Life is short. I don't want to spend my life sleeping."

Foster's schedule became more and more rigorous as he kept expanding and developing his teaching program. He started teaching informally, borrowing various classrooms around town from 1974 to 1977, when the Gregorian invited him to teach a course. Gradually, at his own initiative, he has built up his current curriculum of five "Latin experiences." There are four levels of Latin language instruction and one class—the "Second Experience"—of conversational Latin. In 1985, he started his summer course, and he has gradually increased his repertoire of Latin literary tours.

The heart of Foster's mission is in the classroom, where he is trying to turn Latin instruction on its head. Since it is considered a dead tongue, Latin is virtually never spoken in traditional classrooms and often not even read aloud. Latin literature has been defined narrowly as the literature of ancient Rome, ending at about A.D. 300—despite the fact that for at least another fourteen hundred years dozens of the greatest minds of Western thought—Saint Augustine, Saint Thomas Aquinas, Erasmus, Saint Thomas More, Descartes, Spinoza, Galileo, Newton, and Leibniz (to name only a few)—wrote part or all of their work in Latin. (Many important Latin dictionaries do not even list words and meanings that entered the language after the second or third century A.D.)

Students spend years repeating verb forms—*amo, amas, amat, amamus, amatis, amant*—as if they were a series of magical incantations. The nouns are taught in declensions, listed almost invariably in tables following a standard format, and in the same order, because it's easier (at least initially) to remember things in a singsong sequence, just as we teach children to repeat the alphabet. Many teachers specialize (even at the university level) in mnemonic tricks to help students keep the conjugation and declension tables straight. At the highly regarded summer Latin program at City University of New York, students are taught rhyming ditties like "In conjugation number three, the sign of the future is long 'e.' In conjugation number four, the 'e' of the future appears once more." These mnemonic games can even be fun, like learning to recite Lewis Carroll's nonsense poem, "Jabberwocky," but the knowledge is divorced from understanding.

Foster, instead, explains the inner logic of the language from which the grammar naturally flows. Latin, unlike English or any of the Romance languages, is an inflected language, meaning that the endings of the words change as their function changes. The role of a noun in the sentence (whether something is a subject or an object) and much of the connective tissue between words (*to, of, from, by,* etc.) are encoded in the endings. If you understand the function a word has in a sentence, then you will understand quite naturally—and without undue memorization—what ending it should take.

Not only does Foster not require his students to memorize forms, he actively prevents it. To get around memorizing declension tables, he teaches one case at a time. For the first three months of class, Foster hammered away at the idea of the subject and object (we never heard the words *nominative case* and *accusative case*). The point is to understand the function of the word in a sentence and to see how a word changes when it goes from being a subject to being an object. The form is therefore always connected to its function. Not only is it more interesting to learn grammar this way, it is more effective. If you understand the way the grammar works, what you learn sticks with you. When you learn grammar mnemonically, as soon as you stop repeating the singsong jingles you forget them, which is why most people can't go beyond the first line of "Jabberwocky" and remember only *"Amo, amas, amat . . ."* from their years of Latin training.

To avoid rote learning, Foster never teaches verbs in the usual "I, you, he/she/it, we, you, they" sequence. Instead of asking a student to repeat an entire verb tense, he breaks up the pattern and changes the verbs, asking: "He sings?" (*cantat*), "They praise?" (*laudant*), "We ask?" (*rogamus*), so that the form is never separate from its meaning and the student has to think about each response rather than rely on the automatisms of his or her reptile brain. Endings, he explains, are not an arbitrary set of sounds but ways of expressing ideas. The Romans express the third-person singular with a *t*, as in *cantat*. In the plural it becomes *nt* (*cantant, sunt:* "they sing," "they are"). The Romans say "we" through the ending *mus* (*rogamus*). "I" is expressed as either *o* (*amo, rogo, laudo*) or *i* (*amavi:* "I loved") or *m* (*amabam:* "I was loving"). "You" singular is expressed with an *s*, while "you" plural becomes *tis* (*es, estis:* "you are"; *ambulas, ambulatis:* "you walk"). Once you understand—and hear—these endings as another way of expressing "I," "you," "he," you can add new tenses easily without memorizing entire verb tables.

The intuition at the core of Foster's method is to treat Latin as a language. Grammar is always reinforced by immediate contact with Latin literature so that it is seen in context and learned inductively. "The students have to let Latin grow on them," he said. "What do we do with other languages? We go to Italian class; meanwhile we see billboards, we see television, we see the newspaper, we overhear people on the bus. You start picking it up. . . . This is naturally learning a language." Foster believes that students should not only read Latin from different periods and styles but hear the language, speak, and write it. And while the "First Experience" is taught almost exclusively in English, he reads and has students read passages aloud in Latin. With each level he gradually introduces more and more spoken Latin. He will begin a "Third Experience" class by describing something he saw recently—a pickpocketing on the bus—or by asking a student to describe the weather. By the "Fifth Experience" most of the class is rattling on in Latin. Foster recognizes that Latin is never going to be a widely spoken language, but it has to be taught as a language, not as a brittle, dried parchment in a glass case. What Foster advocates seems so simple and logical as to appear completely obvious and yet it runs counter to the way the language has been taught for more than a century.

Just how unusual Foster's oral Latin method is became obvious when two experienced Latin teachers tagged along on Foster's literary tour of the Roman Forum; they were agog when he suddenly broke into fluent, colloquial Latin describing Cicero's problems with his no-good son. *"Pater eius cupiebat ut haberetur par educatis omnibus aliis adulescentibus. Ah, quia senatores divites omnes mittebant filios suos ad studiorum universitatem Atheniensem—Harvard, Princeton—got it?"* ("His father wanted him to have the same education as all the other kids. All the rich senators were sending their sons to study at the university in Athens.") "In years of graduate school and twenty-one years of teaching I had never heard anyone speak Latin," observed Margaret Brucia, who has a Ph.D. in classics and is head of the Foreign Language Department at Port Jefferson High School on Long Island.

"The incredible thing is that he can speak fluently in just about any Latin style and pronunciation from any period," said Bernard Frischer, chairman of the classics department at UCLA. Frischer, too, in all his years of training and teaching, had never heard spoken Latin before meeting Foster. "I was skeptical because, like many classicists, I had heard that the Church Latin priests speak was of a very poor quality." Frischer decided to make a video of one of Foster's Latin tours. "I asked him to speak in classical style and he was using an extremely complex Ciceronian style, with sentences that were a paragraph long with several dependent clauses and corresponding nouns, adjectives, and verbs miles apart from each other. At the time, I was wondering whether he was making any mistakes, but when we transcribed the tape and analyzed his sentences, everything lined up perfectly."

Frischer became convinced that the traditional approach to Latin he learned just doesn't work. "When I came to Italy for the first time in the 1970s after finishing my Ph.D., I was living in an Italian family and after six weeks I spoke and read Italian better than I did Latin, which I had studied for more than ten years and of which I was a professor," he said.

The fatal mistake of most Latin textbooks and teachers is to try to make Latin seem as much like English as possible; they use invented

Latin sentences that follow English word order or, if they use real Latin, they doctor it to make it conform to English syntax. Even the greatest and most complex authors write straightforward sentences that can be read immediately and used as examples of basic grammatical construction. Thus, as we were learning subjects and objects, verbs or relative pronouns, Foster had us hunting down examples in passages from Terence, Cicero, Ovid, the Vulgate Bible, the natural history of Saint Hildegard, or a papal proclamation from 1990.

Already in the second class, Foster shows us a passage from the *Satyricon*, the great comic, surrealistic novel of Petronius Arbiter, whose refinement was such that he was made "arbiter" of taste at the wildly decadent court of the emperor Nero. Later, Nero, in his paranoia, forced Petronius to commit suicide.

Foster set the scene. "The narrator is sitting by himself at this banquet and he is trying to figure out why there is a wild boar running around the *triclinium* (dining room) with a hat on its head. He is wearing the type of hat reserved for slaves who have been freed. Crazy stuff. The narrator screws up his courage to ask the person next to him what this wild boar is doing running around the banquet with a freedom hat on. The guy looks at him and says, 'Any slave could tell you that. *Non enim aenigma est, sed res aperta.*' '*Aenigma*'—meaning just what you'd expect—is the subject, so the sentence is: 'It is not an enigma, *sed res aperta,* but an open thing.'"

Then one of the participants at the banquet stands up and says, "*Dies nihil est*" ("Daytime is nothing"). "*Dum versas te.*" "*Dum*" means "while"; the verb is "*versare,*" "to turn." So the sentence is: "While you turn over [in bed], *nox fit,* night falls." "This guy sleeps all day and eats and drinks all night," says Foster. "'*Itaque nihil est melius, quam de cubiculo recta in triclinium ire. Nihil est melius quam'?*" Foster calls on someone—although there are about seventy students in his "First Experience," by the second or third week he knows everyone by name. "Nothing is better than," comes the answer. "Than what? Where's the verb? At the end of the sentence—'*ire,*' 'to go.' 'Nothing is better than to go *de cubiculo recta in triclinium,* from the bedroom directly into the dining room.' . . . This is how they lived under Nero—don't be scandalized, friends." Translating, he says, "'It's cold when I get up, but *tamen calda potio vestiarius est,* nevertheless a hot drink is like a set of clothes.' It's not Saint Augustine. *'Matus sum,* I am soaked,' " Foster explains. "*'Vinus mihi in cerebrum abiit.'* The subject is clearly *'vinus,* wine'; the verb, once again, is at the end of the sentence—*'abiit,* vanished, gone,' *'mihi in cerebrum,* into my brain.' Cerebrum, cerebral—got it? 'I am completely soaked, the wine has gone up into my brain.' This is Latin, friends, of 1,930 years ago. They were doing mostly the same things we do. They had the same virtues and vices."

In the middle of all this wild banqueting and crazy speechifying a voice of realism speaks up: *"Narratis quod nec ad caelum nec ad terram pertinet, cum interim nemo curat, quid annona mordet."* "What is *'narratis'* going to be?" Foster asks. "'You'—plural—'narrate *quod,* that which.' What's the verb that goes with *'quod'*?" he yells with urgency. "*'Pertinet'*—pertains—'that which pertains' *nec ad caelum nec ad terram,* neither to heaven nor to earth.' 'You people are talking about that which pertains neither to heaven nor to earth, *cum interim,* when in the interim, *nemo curat,* no one cares *quid annona mordet.'* *Annona* is the price of bread or the cost of living. 'How the cost of living bites, *mordet.'* Mordant, got it? See, in the midst of all this banqueting, the cost of living is biting."

Translating for a moment, he says: "'For a year now, I can't find a mouthful of bread and the drought keeps on.' Then look at this phrase: *'Aediles cum pistoribus COLLUDANT. Aediles'*—'judges,' plural, subject—*'colludant'*—third-person plural—'are colluding *cum pistoribus,* with the bakers.' So the judges are in collusion with the bakers and they are getting all the bread during the drought. *'Serva me, servabo.* You take care of me, I'll take care of you.' It's like the Mafia, see? That's how they talked in the streets of Rome."

Reading this ironic satire of corruption under Nero, we began to get an idea of why the emperor might have forced Petronius to commit suicide.

Accustomed as we were to thinking of Latin as something remote and stuffy—oaths to gods and goddesses, centurions crossing the river and edifying tales of "pious Aeneas"—it was almost a shock to discover such earthy colloquial language. *"Annona mordet,* the cost of living bites." *"Serva me, servabo,* You take care of me, I'll take care of you." But what takes ten words to say in English, Petronius says beautifully in just three. "THAT'S what Latin is all about!" Foster says.

Part of what enables Foster to get away without textbooks and forms are his extremely rigorous and ingenious homework sheets, known as the *"ludi domestici"* (literally "home games" or, more loosely, "games to be played at home"). The *ludi* are deftly constructed engines of thought that force students to master the grammatical problems they are dealing with in class while working through important passages of literature. Each sheet introduces the students to a new author with passages plucked from Foster's seemingly inexhaustible storehouse of Latin literature: the comic playwright Plautus, Saint Thomas Aquinas, the Stoic philosopher Seneca, the poet Horace, the Church Father Petrus Chrysologus, the etymologist Saint Isidore of Seville, the English Renaissance medical doctor Thomas Linacre. Aside from their aesthetic merit, the passages are chosen to illustrate a particular grammatical construction: the genitive case, reflexive verbs, the passive voice, the comparative.

Foster will often start out by giving a passage, but before asking for the translation, he will make students answer a series of questions that force them to pick apart the grammar of the sentences: If a certain word is a noun, what is its role in the sentence? What is the verb? What tense is the verb? What noun must such-and-such adjective modify? Why? Write the same sentence, changing it from singular to plural.

By the time you've answered the questions, you've decoded the whole passage and the translation generally comes quite easily.

The *ludi,* written in Foster's inimitable style, are both hyperbolic and humorous. They are composed on a typewriter that has no lowercase lettering, only TWO KINDS OF UPPERCASE—the perfect typographic equivalent of Foster's voice, which has only two volumes, Loud! and LOUDER. The *ludi* are also marked with FREQUENT UNDERLINING AND EXCLAMATION POINTS! so that reading a *ludus* is like hearing Foster.

A couple of *ludi* give an idea of Foster's singular style:

> ROME'S GREATEST AND ONLY REAL PHILOSOPHER, THE
> SUPER-STOIC LUCIUS ANNAEUS SENECA (4 ANTE–65 POST
> CHR.), HAS SOME SENTENCES FROM HIS FAMOUS "MORAL LET-
> TERS" WHICH YOU CAN AND MUST UNDERSTAND AFTER TWO
> DAYS OF LATIN.

Ludus number 30 began with the following paean to his hero Saint Augustine:

> THE GREAT MATURITY WHICH YOU HAVE NOW OBTAINED IN
> LATIN STUDIES WILL FINALLY ALLOW YOU TO UNDERSTAND
> THE SPECTACULAR LANGUAGE AND APPRECIATE THE HEAVENLY
> CONTENT OF THE VARIOUS WRITINGS OF THE DEEPEST MIND IN
> THE WHOLE WESTERN WORLD, AURELIUS AUGUSTINUS (354–430
> POST CHR.).

Although each *ludus* fits on a single page, Foster usually creates a dense forest of about a thousand words, with several different passages and scores of questions. Although the exercises are fun—combining the pleasures of reading a good book and doing a crossword puzzle—it can take the better part of a day to finish a *ludus*. Each one functions like a chapter in a textbook.

Many students like the *ludi* so much that they collect and keep them for years. Former students in various parts of the world still send Foster old *ludi* to correct.

Although Foster has been teaching at the Gregorian for twenty-five years, he continues to write new *ludi* for each of his courses every year. Once, when I asked him to give me the next homework sheet a few days in advance because I was going to have to miss a class, he said, "I don't have the sheet for Friday. I haven't made it up yet." In other words, as often as he has taught basic Latin he is still inventing it afresh, trying to react to the needs and progress of each new group of students. So, along with correcting about 240 sheets a week, he has to invent eight different *ludi* for his four basic classes, hunting for new passages and thinking up new questions for each of them. This is why he gets up at 3:58.

As word of mouth about Foster's courses has spread, the numbers have grown, increasing his workload. But Foster dismisses the possibility of allowing an experienced assistant to help him correct homework. "I wouldn't allow that. It would be shirking my responsibilities," he says. "I believe the teacher has to work harder than the students."

Foster's eagerness to teach Latin is such that he finds it almost impossible to turn down a serious student. He conducts a kind of correspondence course with a convict in a federal prison in California who wrote to him for help in learning Latin. "He asked me where he could find certain books, without mentioning he was in prison," Foster says. "So I wrote back saying they would be in the nearest library. He explained that he would not be able to get there until about the year 2010—I don't know what he did!—so I sent him some books."

But for all the hard work, Foster is committed to the notion that learning Latin must be fun or it shouldn't be done at all. His classes are always punctuated by extravagant utterances, shouts, howls, whistles, dramatic renditions, comic mimicry—even singing. In part the theatrics allow him to express his lively and imaginative personality, in part they are a calculated device to keep his students paying attention.

Foster has been known to teach his students insults from the plays of Plautus such as *vervex* ("muttonhead"), *vomitus* ("a puke"), *caudex* ("a block of wood, a blockhead") and enjoys shocking his classes of young seminarians at the Gregorian by making irreverent comments about the Vatican or showing them mildly racy passages of Latin literature. For example, he picked a passage from *De animalibus* ("About Animals"), a natural history written by the German nun Saint Hildegard (1098–1179), for its use of the comparative (*"Asinus est plus calidus quam frigidus"*: "The ass is hotter than he is cold") and for its highly amusing observations on sexuality (*"Fere caecus de superfluitate naturae, quam in libidine habet"*: "When [the ass] is in heat [*in libidine*] he is nearly blind [*fere caecus*] from excess of lust [*superfluitate naturae*—literally, 'superfluity of nature']"). "'The sexiness of the jackass makes it practically blind,'" Foster explains. "This was her objective study of nature as seen from her convent window! . . . Don't worry about the philosophy," he reassures the seminarians. "Even Saint Thomas Aquinas said some silly things."

It is part of Foster's conception of Latin instruction that it should include all things from the ridiculous to the sublime, like life itself. During the annual class trip to Ostia Antica, we read everything from Cicero and Virgil to the graffiti in the so-called House of the Seven Sages, a bathroom in an ancient Roman apartment complex. Poking fun at the self-importance of philosophers, the frescoes here represent Greek sages offering bathroom humor in the form of philosophical maxims. *"Bene caca et declina medicos"* ("Shit well and avoid doctors"), says one philosopher in clearly legible Latin. *"Mulcine sedes?"* ("Mulcinus, are you still sitting there?") says another. *"Propero!"* ("I'm hurrying!"), comes the reply. "This is Latin from seventeen hundred years ago!" Foster says. Changing key, we go from the bathroom to the building where Saint Monica, mother of Saint Augustine, is thought to have died. There we read a long, moving account of his mother's death from Augustine's *Confessions*.

Foster is not only trying to shock and amuse his students by introducing them to Petronius or to Saint Hildegard's reflections on the mating habits of jackasses and bears. They are part of his vision of Latin and the Church.

"For me Latin is liberating and the humanists were broad-minded," Foster said. "I gave the 'Fifth Experience' some epigrams by Saint Thomas More. Some of these epigrams are very risqué—not obscene but crude and very funny. He said: 'Look at that woman riding the horse. Not sidesaddle, got it? 'If she can get her legs around a horse, she can get her legs around any man.' This is Saint Thomas More! Humanists. Real neat stuff. Brilliant. Wonderful! . . . This idea that Latin is like a lead blanket. It's not. It's liberating."

Foster then started laughing as he remembers a description More gives of a man getting seasick over the side of a boat. "More writes: 'You are very charitable, you have this mutual relationship with the sea. You just ate some fish from the sea and now you're giving back to the sea what you ate.' They weren't afraid of those things. Now it's so phony and prudish. What we're missing is this happiness, this healthiness that Christian humanism would bring. We can't even joke about ourselves, about life, bodily functions. . . . They weren't afraid of *amorini* [naked cupids] or of nude statues. . . . There's a certain kind of hypocritical conservatism. We can't talk about this or we can't talk about that." While some might regard the celebration of nudity and sexuality in authors like Catullus, Petronius, and Ovid antithetical to the celibate priesthood, Foster disagrees. Celibacy, he said, "is a choice and a way of life. A lot of people do it for different reasons. . . . I can still appreciate that stuff. Let's live!"

Foster has come a long way from the years when he stood weeping in front of statues of the Virgin. "In the beginning the Catholic Church was this gorgeous monolith, an unchangeable institution, and Latin was just one of the glories of the Church, like St. Peter's Basilica. . . . That all kind of collapsed because they found out that the Church was changeable. And now my vision of Latin and the Church is, I would hope, much more mature and more rational. I need to know why she says what she says, and what the sources are, where the categories are coming from. This is all from Latin. . . . Saint Bernard paraphrases Virgil. And Augustine is quoting Horace. Saint Thomas quotes Cicero in his famous *Summa theologica* 196 times. . . . This is a whole continuity here that's very nice for me to see. . . . Now, of course, [the Vatican] wouldn't quote Cicero. Out of the question—it would be seen as pagan or something. . . . The humanists took what was good and solid in the pagans."

In his years at the Gregorian, Foster has watched his own program flourish while the general condition of Latin deteriorates. Originally, his course was supposed to be a kind of finishing school for those students who needed to round off their Latin education. But as more and more students were arriving with little or no Latin training, he began offering an introductory course. Although Latin is no longer a required course, students are expected to have a working knowledge of the language and must take a proficiency exam when they enter.

"Supposedly, we have 3,500 students at the Gregorian and only 120 need Latin and the others are fine," he said. "The Latin situation at the Gregorian is a disaster. You have these professors quoting Latin passages to the students and they might as well be quoting Chinese." Confirmation of his gloomy assessment came in 1992 when the university stopped teaching canon law in Latin—the last course to hold out against the change. "They can't find teachers who can express themselves with any grace and ease in Latin," he said. "They were making up baby sentences in their head when they wanted to spew out all kinds of golden wisdom on Church law.

"Thirty-seven years [after the end of Vatican II] there is a whole generation that knows very little," he said. "It's like stopping music training, piano training throughout the U.S. for a generation. And a couple of generations later it will be totally dead. I think that is totally tragic."

If Latin is dying in the Catholic Church, there are hopeful signs outside it. After a period of swift and steady decline in the United States, Latin study is enjoying something of a revival.

In the 1930s, more than half of American high school students took Latin as part of their standard curriculum. The numbers remained fairly high until the early 1960s, with some 702,000 students still taking Latin in public high schools alone—while hundreds of thousands of others studied the language in private schools. But in the decade that followed, Latin enrollment in public schools collapsed, dropping to a mere 150,000 by 1976.

Latin appeared on the point of extinction. "Somehow, a subject that had been considered for more than a century a staple in the general education of very large numbers of American high school students . . . was suddenly considered irrelevant," wrote Sally Davis, who teaches Latin at Wakefield High School in Arlington, Virginia. "The crash was the result of the craziness of the sixties," says Davis. "Relevance was the catchword of the day and Latin wasn't relevant."

Since its nadir in the mid-1970s, however, Latin has made a modest comeback. Davis estimates that Latin enrollment is now at about 190,000 in public high schools, with a similar number in private schools. Latin remains the third most popular language in American public schools after Spanish and French.

With the decline of basic reading and writing skills, many schools turned back to Latin. Statistics show that students who take Latin consistently do better on their SATs than students who don't. Moreover, Latin courses have been used effectively in recent years to improve language and logic skills among students in poorer inner-city schools, said Richard Gascoyne of the New York State Department of Education, which sponsors a number of such projects.

"There are plenty of good reasons," said Davis. "About 70 percent of the words in the English dictionary come from Latin. Once you learn about 150 Latin roots, that will give you a command of maybe a few thousand words. And it is the basis for all the Romance languages."

Latin has also had some success in selling itself to both sides of today's education debate. It appeals to those who argue for greater "cultural literacy," since the Latin language and Roman civilization are so central to the Western tradition. At the same time, Latin can respond effectively to the concerns of both multiculturalists and Afrocentrists. Rome was a supremely multicultural society, encompassing peoples across North Africa, Asia Minor, and the Middle East as well as most of Europe, who became not only citizens of the Roman Empire but often its leaders as well. There were even African Roman emperors, such as Septimius Severus and his son Caracalla, while the great Roman playwright Terence was a freed African slave. His Roman name was Publius Terentius Afer, *"Afer"* meaning "African."

In the attempt to defend and revive Latin, American teachers have tried to find new ways to teach it, exploring alternatives to the rote memorization of grammar. There is much more emphasis on Roman civilization, on etymology and word building, and on learning grammar by induction from reading rather than by the study of form. In New York State, Richard Gascoyne is trying to introduce more spoken Latin in classes. In some ways, Foster is in the mainstream of this change. Indeed, a number of influential Latin reformers have come to Rome to study in his summer program.

Bernard Frischer of UCLA would like to revolutionize Latin teaching by introducing a new curriculum based directly on Foster's oral method. He is hoping to get funding for a project that would, in essence, clone Foster. The idea would be to bring a sizable number of Latin professors to Rome to become fluent in Latin and develop a series of textbooks and videocassettes to apply his method nationwide.

In the tight-knit fraternity of American Latin teachers, Foster's summer course has become legendary. "For anyone who loves Latin, it's like heaven," said Davis. "Finally someone who loves the language, who truly knows the language, knows how to teach it, and who loves to teach it with unbounded enthusiasm and energy that never stops. . . . This was like finding the place I've been looking for my whole life. . . . College professors are almost only interested in the literature. There are many people who spend twenty or thirty years in the classics who do not really know the language well."

But Foster remains a one-man institution, with no ties to any of the various philological and pedagogical associations promoting Latin studies. He is harshly critical of the American academic establishment and is not sure whether some of the current reforms aren't as bad as what they are trying to replace. This conflict came to a head when Foster was invited to give the final address at a conference in 1992 at the American Academy in Rome sponsored by members of the College Board and teachers preparing the high school Advanced Placement examination.

During the afternoon, Foster sat with increasing impatience through a long, soporific session in which teachers and testers discussed the weighting and grading of exam questions, problems with the multiple-choice section, and methods of preparing students. When a teacher from Atlanta explained how he photocopied exercises out of a certain textbook because he didn't have time to make up his own, Foster made a groaning noise like someone whose appendix had suddenly burst.

By the time Foster approached the podium, his normally ruddy complexion was redder than usual. "Most of what I'm going to say is not going to please you, but that's all right. . . . Latin, for me, is a completely different thing than what I've heard since four o'clock. Teaching Latin as preparation for an exam has no place in my concept at all. . . . I'm troubled by this business of using Latin for remedial purposes. . . . Latin was not devised to help people with English. It's like the people who play the piano to help them with their arthritis. You don't study Mozart because of arthritis and you don't study Latin because your school is a disaster! AFTER WHAT I'VE HEARD TODAY, I'M SURPRISED THAT ANYONE IS TAKING LATIN!" Foster said with the fury of Christ tossing the money changers out of the temple.

"The AP thing sounds like the typical American quick fix—some way to hurry things up, and push them through so that they come out . . . with a degree and not much education."

Along with criticizing the old-fashioned textbooks that rely on memorization, Foster railed against the new ones that rely on little Latin stories about a typical Roman family. "I saw this Oxford [University Press] textbook—this is absolute madness," he said. "After two volumes, the students are still reading sentences made up by the authors, not by real Latin authors. So that after two years the students have not moved one inch. . . . They've learned all about this melon-headed family from Pompeii but they've never seen real Latin. The word order of the sentences is the same, the verb is in the same place. . . . Why don't we start with some easy stuff right from the beginning: *'Multum te amamus,'* 'We love you very much,' Cicero writes to Atticus. Why not start with that the first day? 'No, we don't do Cicero until the fourth year.' Who says? . . . You can take two or three lines from Cicero's letters that may be very easy and are just out of this world."

When, in the third or fourth year, students finally get down to reading real Latin, Foster went on, they tend almost exclusively to read poetry—Virgil, Horace, and Catullus. "What is this obsession with poetry? Why don't we get into some of these prose people? Poets are gorgeous and wonderful, but if you were to be shown nothing but poetry in French or Italian it would be very hard to get to the language. I don't think the Romans on the street talked in verse.

"It seems that with Latin we refuse to do what we do in other areas of life," Foster said. "With other languages you hear and see the thing right away, but teachers refuse to do it in Latin. . . . When you teach swimming, you put them in the water. . . . But what we do with Latin is we keep them on the sidelines and tell them, 'You see, this is what water's about,' instead of getting in there and doing it. Or, 'Let's talk about the theory of the piano,' and you just sit there for three years and look at the piano instead of pounding out a few tunes. But have them play a few sonatas that are so gorgeous they're knocked off their feet and then they'll pass any examination.

"Someone said, 'I don't have time to do this.' I shouldn't have time to do this either, but if I don't I'll get out of it and not teach. We've got to decide what we want to do. Either we're going to teach or we're going to do something else. I love Latin too much to treat it that way."

When Foster finished his jeremiad, the crowd appeared somewhat stunned. "I've been waiting for years to meet Reginald Foster. He's a little different than I expected," said Barbara Weiden-Boyd, professor of classics at Bowdoin College and a member of the group that prepares the AP Latin exam. Her husband, Mike Boyd, summed up the general mood. "I came expecting to meet Mr. Chips and I got the Terminator."

Despite his lack of diplomatic skills, Foster has attracted a growing number of dedicated students, from Australia and Ghana to South Dakota and San Diego. "He has a loyal fan club around the world. It becomes a central part of who they are," said Bernard Frischer.

His summer course—meant primarily for teachers and other advanced Latinists—gets larger every year. What started as an informal gathering of five people in 1985 has grown to over forty students—more than Foster would like. He refuses to charge for the course and has a hard time saying no. Several people return to do the course for a second or third time, which—given the grueling schedule—says a lot. The intense group experience has fostered numerous romances and more than a couple of marriages. Two recent students told Foster that they would not get married unless he came to Maine to officiate at their wedding.

The summer course is practically a Latin marathon. After working at his usual morning job at the Vatican, Foster teaches from two until six, then holds optional classes *sub arboribus* ("under the trees") in the garden at his monastery from seven to nine, in which students read, drink wine, and talk in Latin until the sun goes down. "And after that he would tutor whoever needed it," said Sally Davis, who studied with Foster during the summer of 1987 and again in 1992. Along with the time in the classroom, the course includes the usual two *ludi* a week. This goes on six days a week and the seventh day, far from being a day of rest, is taken up with one of his Latin literary tours. Some of them, like the trips to Pompeii and Herculaneum, to Cicero's birthplace at Arpinum, to Horace's Sabine farm, and to Thomas Aquinas's birth and death places are all-day affairs lasting anywhere from twelve to sixteen hours.

Paul Gwynne, a historian of Renaissance Latin literature, stumbled onto Foster's course in 1991 and was so impressed he dropped everything to stay in Rome so he could take all five of Foster's levels simultaneously. "He is not just the best Latin teacher I've ever seen, he's simply the best teacher I've ever seen," said Gwynne, who had the opportunity to study with some excellent teachers while getting a Ph.D. in classical studies at the prestigious Warburg Institute in London. "It's a Renaissance historian's dream come true," he said. "Studying Latin with the pope's apostolic secretary, for whom the language is alive, using the city of Rome as a classroom. . . . It changed my whole outlook on life, really."

"Historical texts are presented as living things," said Gwynne. "I loathe Thomas Aquinas, and medieval scholasticism, but the Thomas Aquinas tour was one of the most delightful days of my entire existence. Climbing up that mountain into that ruined castle, reading about the birth of Thomas Aquinas, then singing some of his songs. You're not just given a text of one of his hymns, you're out there singing it. . . . Then you clamber down the hill to Fossanova, sit in the room where he died, and read a moving account of his death. And not only that but have his exposition on the Lord's Prayer. Suddenly this whole world of medieval scholasticism comes to life. That's something that a lot of medieval historians don't do and can't do. Then you go and get drunk in a pizzeria. What could be nicer than that?"

All the elements of Foster's method come together in his Latin literary tours: each of the senses is engaged as you hear, read, speak, and sing Latin while seeing the sights and smelling the smells that Cicero, Horace, Plautus, or Augustine saw and smelled. The Roman world from its highest to its most frivolous literary expressions comes off the page and takes shape around you as the ruined monuments of antiquity momentarily assume their former life.

Seeing Rome with Reginald Foster is somewhat like hearing music for the first time. The city is threaded with a vast web of Latin inscriptions. They line the cornices of buildings, the bases of statues and monuments, the tops of fountains and gates. The biographies of tens of thousands of dead souls are carved onto tombs and sarcofagi. They provide a running commentary on all you see, although virtually all of Rome's 3 million inhabitants walk by them without noticing them. To see Rome without having access to this Latin subtext is like going to the opera without a libretto—you can love the music, the singing, and the spectacle but you miss a lot of the drama.

For Foster the air buzzes with meaning and the words of Cicero, Tacitus, Martial, and Livy tug at his ear. The intersection where Via Cavour and Via dei Fori Imperiali meet is the place where the emperor Augustus placed a series of busts from the Republican era to remind people of the old Roman virtues. Outside the Colosseum where pushcarts now sell soft drinks and postcards stood a massive statue of Nero, which was decapitated after the emperor killed himself. A bare plot of ground in the Forum is the spot where Cicero gave his famous Catalline oration; on that pile of rubble the emperor Caligula built himself a temple and declared himself a god; here, along a crowded sidewalk, shopkeepers from before the time of Christ had their stores and hawked their wares to potential customers on their way to the Capitol.

There are, of course, many other classicists who know ancient Rome, but very few have Foster's incredibly broad range. Foster is steeped not only in the classical authors but in medieval Latin and the doctors of the Church; he can recount the glories and vices of the Renaissance popes and recite the inscriptions on all the Egyptian obelisks erected by Sixtus V. He is as interested in the Latin on Mussolini's Fascist monuments as he is in the dedications on the buildings commissioned by the emperors Augustus and Hadrian.

More than just a walking encyclopedia of Latin literature, Foster also has an active imagination and a theatrical talent for conjuring up the past. When we were walking across the Palatine Hill—the green residential area in ancient Rome that overlooks the Roman Forum—Foster took us down to the cryptoporticus beneath an imperial villa where Caligula is believed to have been assassinated. As we stood looking at the elaborate stuccowork in this underground passageway, Foster read the scene from Suetonius and, when he came to the denouement, shouted "REPETE! REPETE!" ("Again! Again!") and could not help himself from making a stabbing motion with his arm at a spot on the ground where the hated emperor might have lain. Foster's dramatic skills are such that BBC Radio broadcast large segments of his annual Ides of March tour in commemoration of the death of Caesar.

At the beginning of each tour, Foster hands out a leaflet with as many as fifteen dense pages of text, all of it relating to the places to be seen that day. He will often provide seven or eight different authors' descriptions of the same site or event, plucking out lines of poetry, long-vanished inscriptions, even a passage from an eighteenth-century Latin encyclopedia, to create a multilayered richness that corresponds to the palimpsest of Rome itself. For example, on the tour of the Colosseum and the Palatine Hill, he gave us 101 passages from twenty-four different Latin authors—in addition to writings scratched onto the walls of the slave quarters now buried underneath the Palatine, which he read aloud in passing. For the Ides of March walk, Foster chose not only Plutarch's famous account of Caesar's assassination—which Shakespeare used for his play—but also a page of the correspondence between Caesar and Cicero at the time of the civil war (49 B.C.) that installed Caesar as the first Roman emperor. The letters describe the terrible psychological predicament of Cicero: Caesar is advancing rapidly from the north, Pompey is in the south, in retreat, and Cicero is in the middle at his villa near Formia, trying to decide what to do. He knows Caesar will win but, in the end, backs Pompey, because he is sure Caesar will destroy the Republic. Meanwhile, Caesar is trying to woo Cicero to add prestige to his cause, and the correspondence between the two of them in the summer of 49 B.C. is a complex game of cat and mouse and elegant word-play. "Look at what Cicero says to Atticus in the next letter," Foster says to the crowd of thirty or so standing around dodging cars in the streets of Rome. "Cicero notices that in Caesar's letters asking for support, he uses the word *'ops,'* which, if you notice, friends, means 'help' in the singular but in the plural often means 'resources, money.' So Cicero, who was a very clever man, says: *'Quibus iam "opes" meas, non ut superioribus litteris "opem" exspectat.'* 'In which letter he is asking for my resources, not, as in the previous letter, for my help,' says Foster, translating literally. Then Foster offers his own free translation: "So Cicero says: 'Now what does he want? My bank account!'" The tour ends in front of Caesar's statue just outside the Forum, with Foster leading the group in a Latin song to Caesar sung to the tune of "My Darling Clementine."

Despite the fact that the radio program was forty-five minutes long and about Latin, listeners were so enthusiastic that the BBC immediately rebroadcast it. A few months later, when Foster was leading a group through Ostia Antica, a British tourist recognized Foster's unmistakable loud, raspy voice. "You must be Father Foster!" the man said, speaking with great animation about the broadcast and repeating entire lines from it. "'Casca, you bum!'" he said, imitating Foster's invective against one of Caesar's assassins.

Foster pokes fun at himself and even at his favorite Latin authors. He enjoys the absurdity as well as the glories of the Roman world, which the Romans, with their well-developed sense of irony, never failed to notice. Visiting the site of Cicero's house on the Palatine Hill, we read a serious account of its destruction by Cicero's political enemies along with a humorous letter Cicero wrote about hearing his next-door neighbor snoring: *"Haec ego scribebam Marcellus candidatus ita stertebat ut ego vici-*

nus audirem" ("As I was writing this, Marcellus the candidate was really snoring so that I, his neighbor, could hear").

The same day, as we were passing the house of Augustus Caesar, Foster read from a passage in Suetonius listing the emperor's many virtues, then mentioning that he wore *"calciamentis altiusculis"*—literally, "higher shoes" or "elevator shoes." It is typical of both Suetonius and Foster not to miss such a small telling detail, which quite literally brings his subject down to human size.

Even places I thought I knew reasonably well, like the Capitoline Hill, took on a totally different meaning during our walks—starting with the origin of its name. When the Romans were digging a temple to Jove on the other side of the hill, they found a human head that, according to legend, was perfectly intact. The Romans took this to be an excellent augury and made the hill the center of the city, calling it the Capitoline, after the Latin word for "head," *"caput."* On the other side of the hill was the temple to Juno, Jove's nagging wife. "The first mint in Rome was right here in front of the temple," Foster said. The goddess, known as Juno Moneta (Juno the Warner), was supposed to watch over the mint and warn against fake or impure coins. As a result, the first Roman coins were stamped *"moneta"* ("warns"), which is the word for coin in Italian and the origin of the English word *money.*

To keep things from getting too solemn, halfway through many of his walks Foster will break out and pass around a huge bottle of inexpensive jug wine, adding an element of celebration to the occasion. Because he does not take himself too seriously, he does not mind when curious bystanders—intrigued by a monk in a blue polyester suit declaiming in Latin—suddenly interject themselves into one of his outings. Foster enjoys the give-and-take and absorbs it into the experience. When we were standing in the neighborhood that once held the theater of Pompey, a local resident who fancied himself a knowledgeable cicerone came over to explain about the assassination of Caesar. Instead of dismissing the man, Foster invited him to tell us what he knew. "They stabbed Caesar twenty-three times," the man said in Italian. Foster then pointed to our reading sheet and found the passage in Plutarch saying that Caesar had indeed been stabbed twenty-three times. "Even today, in Rome," the man said, "twenty-three is a lucky number." Plutarch's reference to the number of wounds on Caesar's body may explain why many Romans today pencil "23" onto their lottery cards.

In the same vein, Paul Gwynne recalled a moment on a trip to Horace's Sabine farm in the countryside in Latium outside Rome. The group had clambered through the weeds and brambles to find the remains of Horace's house and a Roman fountain, the Fons Bandusiae, to which Horace dedicated one of his most beautiful poems. The group read the Latin poem and talked about it, then read Virgil on Horace with various commentaries, ancient and modern. But then the local custodian charged with looking after Horace's estate wanted to join the group and recite the poem in Italian. "This guy was five foot nothing, as tall as he was wide, with a dark complexion—glowing with life. . . . It was wonderful, because we had just read a description of Horace, which said he was about five foot nothing and as tall as he was wide, with a dark complexion. And so you've got this guy—who obviously enjoys life in the country—who recites this poem of Horace about the fountain which we're all standing in front of. It was almost as if the country gods had come down and said, 'Here we are.'"

These uncanny moments happen a lot when you spend time with Foster: for someone for whom Latin is a living language, time seems to bend; past becomes present and present past, and the long banished *genii loci* appear to return.

Such moments are especially precious because they are probably unrepeatable. Even as he reached his sixties, Foster shows no signs of wanting to leave behind a legacy. He has many intensely enthusiastic students but no disciples. Since he doesn't believe in textbooks, he has never written one. He was supposed to write a textbook using the letters of Cicero to teach Latin as his Ph.D. thesis, but he still hasn't gotten around to it. "I don't have the time," Foster said. "Maybe when I get too old to keep on teaching." But most of his students believe that he will never do that and that when he goes it will be in midsentence, hammering away at a passage of Cicero or Augustine.

"If he couldn't teach at the Gregorian he'd be out on the street teaching, and none of the students would mind and if it rained they'd bring an umbrella," said Gwynne. "How many people do you know who can inspire that?"

As the end of the school year approached, someone in the class suggested that Foster at least publish a collection of his homework assignments, the *ludi,* in book form. "You see these?" he said, picking up a batch of homework sheets. "You know what will happen to these in a few weeks? I'll burn them all." He destroys his elaborately constructed work sheets so that he has to reinvent his courses every year, making each one new and unique.

9

The Return of the
Vanished Library

I N A CROWDED, poor, and badly dilapidated Egyptian city, a large construction site billboard boldly announced in both English and Arabic: THE REVIVAL OF THE ANCIENT LIBRARY OF ALEXANDRIA. Cars whizzed noisily by on a nearby road that fronts the Mediterranean, seemingly indifferent to the mammoth building taking shape beside them.

Its vast architecture is in keeping with its ambitious claim. A huge glass roof the length of a football field but in the shape of a disk tilts up at an angle, rising from below the ground about a hundred feet in the air. It is meant to look like the sun at dawn emerging from the sea. At the same time, the surface of the roof, made of hundreds of different-colored tinted panes, resembles a massive computer circuit chip. On the back of the building, workers were finishing up an enormous curved wall encased in granite on which are inscribed letters of all the scripts and alphabets of the world's languages, symbolizing the vast universalist aims of the new project. After all, the ancient library of Alexandria had tried to collect all the books in the known world—a mad, noble, and ultimately impossible enterprise.

For seven centuries—from the time of Alexander the Great, who founded the city in 332 B.C., until well into the fourth century of the

Christian era—Alexandria was the intellectual capital of the Western world, a vast cosmopolitan capital, the crossroads of different cultures, races, and religions.

After Alexander's death in 323 B.C., his empire was divided up among his Macedonian generals, and Egypt passed to Ptolemy Soter. Ptolemy and his descendants were eager to legitimate their reign with intellectual prestige. They created the Great Library, known as the Mouseion, the Temple of the Muses, which collected great scholars as well as great books. Ptolemy Soter invited the great mathematician Euclid to Alexandria and his famous *Elements of Geometry* was dedicated to the ruler.

The Ptolemies were insatiable in the pursuit of books. They issued a decree requiring every ship that passed through the thriving port of Alexandria to hand over any manuscript or scroll on board in order that it might be copied. The Alexandrians then returned the copy and kept the original. They tricked the Athenians into giving them a complete set of the Greek tragedies and paid a fortune for what they believed was the library of the philosopher Aristotle.

The Ptolemies also called upon the sovereigns and rulers of the world to send them all books worthy of inclusion and summoned seventy-two Hebrew scholars to translate the Jewish Torah, creating the famous ancient Greek Bible known as the Septuagint. They gathered Buddhist texts from India and a work on Zoroaster said to have been composed of two million lines. They succeeded in amassing about 500,000 scrolls.

The scholars at the Mouseion mapped and measured the earth and the stars and produced the greatest work of ancient astronomy, the *Almagest* of Claudius Ptolemy. They virtually invented modern scholarship, creating the definitive text of Homer's *Iliad* and *Odyssey*. And in the common era, Alexandria produced the Christian philosopher Plotinus, the Gnostic gospels, and the work of the Jewish thinker Philo. But in circumstances that remain mysterious, the vast majority of the Great Library's texts were destroyed, surviving only in fragments, copies, or quotations in later texts.

In the world of scholarship, the destruction of the ancient library of Alexandria is the ultimate romantic topos, a kind of paradise lost. "One ghostly image haunts all of us charged with preserving the creative heritage of humanity: the specter of the great, lost library of Alexandria," said James Billington, the United States librarian of Congress, in a 1993 speech. This image captured the imagination of UNESCO, which gave its support to the revival of the library. Designed to house up to eight million books, the new library planned to become the eighth largest in the world. But as the project neared completion, romance began to give way to reality and questions emerged: What does it mean to "revive" an ancient library whose exact location and contents are unknown? Can a collection that starts with about 250,000 books—far fewer than in the library of an average small four-year college in the United States—hope to live up to its grand ambitions? Does it make sense to build a huge library with stacks for eight million books at a moment when so much information is moving from printed to digital form? In the age of the Internet, does it even make sense to conceive of a universal library in terms of glass, steel, and concrete?

Moreover, for Egypt, a relatively poor country riven by ideological and religious divisions, the project poses numerous difficulties. The Egyptian government is spending hundreds of millions of dollars on a new library in Alexandria when its only major library, the National Library in Cairo, is in total shambles and when it is stepping up its censorship and banning of books and newspapers.

The library, so rich in symbolic meaning, is the sum of the contradictions, tensions, and hopes of Egyptian society today. The decision to build a major international library in Alexandria, by the sea, facing north toward Europe, is part of a larger effort to open Egypt up to foreign investment, satellite television, the Internet, and cellular phones. At the same time, the government of Hosni Mubarak is going to increasing lengths to placate Islamic fundamentalists and to protect Egypt's military regime's hold on power.

"It's a bit of a paradox that the government is building a library while it is banning books," said Hisham Kassem, an Egyptian journalist who edits the *Cairo Times,* a weekly English-language paper. In 1999, the government intervened to ban some ninety books being sold or taught at the American University of Cairo that have long circulated freely. It has also arrested several journalists for libel, earning it a place on the Committee to Protect Journalists' list of the ten worst enemies of press freedom. "People in Egypt don't read much. We had the misfortune of having the soldiers and television arrive at the same time," Kassem said, referring to the Egyptian revolution of 1952, which installed Colonel Gamal Abdel Nasser. "We have eight daily newspapers for sixty-five million people; the largest has a circulation of 370,000."

The apparently diminishing intellectual freedom may, however, reflect the fact that the government is losing its grip on the movement of information. There are now more than a million satellite dishes in Egypt, with approximately five million TV viewers, almost 10 percent of the population; their numbers are expected to double in the next several years. Moreover, the government has granted unrestricted access to the Internet, albeit to only about 150,000 subscribers. Thus, much of the information that can't be found on newsstands or in bookstores is available on the Web.

The new library is part of the policy of openness, but creating a cultural revival in Alexandria by government diktat from Cairo would seem to be a contradiction in terms. The library project represents an improbable attempt to remake Alexandria into a hub of world culture after the government in Cairo has succeeded in reducing it to a poor provincial city that can no longer even support a daily newspaper. And yet, so far at least, the project's somewhat heavy-handed centralized administration has alienated many of the local cultural institutions that it is trying to revive.

Alexandria's fortunes have generally waxed and waned according to Egypt's up-and-down relationship with Europe. "It's as if there are two different [cultural] winds," said Kamal el-Zoheiry, director of the Greater Cairo Library. "One is from the Mediterranean and the other is from the desert. From the sea, it's nice. From the desert, it's hot." Thus, the state of Alexandria is like a weather vane registering the changing directions of Egyptian society.

There is an eerie quality about contemporary Alexandria. There is perhaps no other city of such size and importance of which so little remains. Almost nothing is left of the ancient city, but the extraordinary natural position.

This site attracted Alexander because of its deep harbors strategically placed at the mouth of the Nile, with the island of Pharos a few hundred yards offshore, sheltering boats against the open sea. The Greeks built a causeway to connect the island to the mainland and on the island itself constructed their famous lighthouse, which is said to have climbed some four hundred feet in the air and whose fire could be seen from seventy miles away.

From this single point, the Macedonian Greeks were able to dominate both the Mediterranean and Egypt, linking the Nile Valley, with its thousand-mile swath of the ancient world's richest agricultural land, with the trading markets of Europe and the Near East. Alexandria grew rapidly into the world's first great metropolis, with a population of about 600,000 people in the three centuries before the birth of Christ. (Centuries later, imperial Rome surpassed Alexandria with a population of about one million.) By contrast, Europe was unable to sustain urban life on this scale until the eighteenth century, when London and Paris reached populations of 600,000.

Alexandria changed hands numerous times. Caesar conquered it in 47 B.C., and his nephew, Octavian, defeated Antony and Cleopatra, reducing Egypt to a Roman province. Queen Zenobia of Palmyra (modern Syria) briefly conquered it, only to provoke a furious Roman counterattack that left much of the city in ruins. In the fourth century it became a great center of Coptic Christianity but in A.D. 641 it was conquered again by the Arabs. Cairo replaced Alexandria as capital under Islamic rule, which looked more to the other Arab lands in the Middle East than to the north and Europe. After the Middle Ages, Egyptian sea trade gradually shrank in importance so that when Napoleon landed in 1798 in his attempt to conquer Egypt, he found a small fishing town of some seven thousand souls with barely a trace of its ancient past.

The pioneering archeologist Heinrich Schliemann, fresh from his triumphant discovery of ancient Troy, arrived in Alexandria in the

1880s with visions of finding the famous alabaster sarcophagus of Alexander the Great and other ancient wonders but left a few weeks later, convinced that the city had nothing to offer. By then, what little was left of the ancient city was being paved over as Alexandria was enjoying a second renaissance as a modern city. Starting in 1805, the pashas of the Ottoman Empire had adopted a conscious strategy of inviting Europeans in an effort to modernize Egypt and stimulate trade. In a matter of decades Alexandria again became a thriving port, the center of Egypt's booming cotton industry, one of the first cities in Africa with electricity, modern plumbing, trams, streetlights, a stock exchange, movie theaters, and newspapers. With Italians dominating the building trade, the city filled up with Italianate villas sprouting palm trees, eclectic fin-de-siècle architecture with both neopharaonic and Western motifs, wide boulevards with art deco palaces, grand squares with magnificent bronze statues, even a bank modeled on the Renaissance Palazzo Farnese, which Michelangelo helped design in Rome. The streets were a curious babel of languages and nationalities, Jews speaking Arabic, Egyptians speaking Greek, Armenians speaking Italian, Syrians speaking a Franco-Arabic patois; men in French suits, English bowlers, and Egyptian galabiyas, smoking waterpipes at the Miramar Café, eating pastries at Pastroudis or Délices, or drinking tea at the Trianon Café of the Metropole Hotel. "Five races, five languages, a dozen creeds," is how Lawrence Durrell described the city in his famous *Alexandria Quartet.*

By the 1950s, there were some 200,000 Europeans in Alexandria out of a population of about 600,000. "The city was beautiful, and so clean that one could have eaten off the streets," the Egyptian novelist Naguib Mahfouz has written about the Alexandria of his youth. "Anything from Europe could be found in Alexandria for half the price, cinemas, restaurants, dance halls. . . ."

Curiously enough, modern Alexandria mirrored the ancient city: both were cosmopolitan cities, early experiments in multiculturalism, with a mixture of Greeks, Egyptians, Italians, and a strong Jewish component. (The builder of modern Alexandria, Mohammed Ali, although a Muslim, was, like Alexander the Great, a Macedonian.) The strange affinities between the ancient and the modern city may help explain why Durrell referred to Alexandria as the "capital of memory." Even though the modern city was almost devoid of ancient ruins and monuments, its inhabitants, through some strange metempsychosis, seemed to be reliving the lives of its ancient inhabitants. E. M. Forster, another writer who lived in Alexandria, wrote that "visions kept coming as I went about in trams or on foot or bathed in the delicious sea." Looking at the Arab fort on the island of Pharos, he "would multiply the height . . . by four and envisage the Pharos [lighthouse] which had once stood on the same site. At the crossing of the two main streets I would erect the tomb of Alexander the Great."

But this world of Forster, Durrell, and others is gone. After Gamal Abdel Nasser's nationalist revolution in 1952, the Egyptian government began confiscating foreign businesses. Anti-European sentiment reached a fever pitch after French, British, and Israeli troops attacked Egypt in an attempt to prevent Nasser from nationalizing the Suez Canal. Nasser responded by expelling all Jews, British, and French en masse. In the following years, most of the other Europeans left because their businesses were confiscated, their bank accounts were frozen, or they were subjected to constant harassment.

Although the city's population has grown to about four million, its European population has gone from 200,000 to something close to zero. With the foreigners went foreign capital, and Alexandria's sidewalks are now broken and crumbling, its streets dirty and poorly lit, strewn with litter, garbage, and potholes. The architecture of the city is like an exquisite corpse in an advanced state of decomposition: crumbling neoclassical pillars, broken windows, Corinthian columns covered in grime, ornamental details chipped away into nothingness, plaster and brick showing under the stucco façades, colors darkened with soot and car exhaust, the ghostly remains of the Italianate structures illuminated by the garish light of neon signs and fluorescent storefronts. The streets are clogged with battered and dented cars honking their horns, the sidewalks crowded with Egyptian street peddlers and beggars—all locked in the ferocious struggle of earning their daily bread.

The literary and historical associations of Alexandria so resonant to Forster and Durrell are either unknown or meaningless to most of the current inhabitants of Alexandria. The city is like the decaying stage set of a play that closed half a century ago, its actors long dead, their place taken by men and women engaged in a drama with a different plot and characters. For a Westerner, visiting Alexandria is a bit like what it must be like for a Muslim to see the Alhambra in Granada, the last grandiose expression of Islamic culture in southern Spain, an isolated set of buildings that were once the center of a now-vanished world.

This sense of loss is probably felt most acutely by Europeans, while for many Egyptians the "cosmopolitan" period provokes mixed emotions. The closeness with Europe led to the British occupation between 1882 and 1922 and many of the statues and buildings of European Alexandria were toppled or torn down during the Nasser revolution. Thus, what is the capital of memory for some is the capital of forgetfulness for others.

Richard Nixon—hardly known as a patron of culture—unwittingly acted as a catalyst to the Alexandria library project. On a presidential visit to the city in 1974, Nixon (presumably after being briefed) asked his Egyptian hosts where the ancient library of Alexandria was. The Egyptians were embarrassed to admit that they had no idea. To make amends, the authorities contacted Mustafa El-Abbadi, a distinguished professor of ancient history at the University of Alexandria, and asked him to draw up a memorandum on the subject.

"The ancient library might be right beneath us," El-Abbadi told me when we met in his study overlooking the eastern harbor in downtown Alexandria. No one knows exactly where the ancient library was, but it was located somewhere within the royal palaces of the Ptolemies, which occupied a vast area near the harbor. Indeed, the lot in front of El-Abbadi's house—now occupied by an old, rusting amusement park—was considered one of the possible sites for the new library. "Perhaps if we dug in the basement, we might find the ancient library," El-Abbadi said, petting his beautiful Siamese cat, Cleopatra, named, of course, after the last of the Ptolemies—to whose three-hundred-year dynasty, El-Abbadi has dedicated most of his career.

El-Abbadi is typical of that rapidly disappearing breed, the Alexandrian cosmopolitan. A small man in his late sixties with cottony tufts of gray hair on his head, he combines a warm sense of Egyptian hospitality with the courtly manners and natty professorial dress of a British university don. Having earned his doctorate in ancient history at Cambridge in the 1950s, he is equally at home in Arabic and English, not to mention French, ancient Latin, and Greek. He is a Muslim with a keen interest in the Greek, Jewish, and Christian history of Egypt. His study—lined floor to ceiling with books on ancient history, the poetry of Milton, Shelley, and Keats—might briefly give you the feeling that you were somewhere in England until a gust of wind blows open the flowered curtains, offering a glimpse of the sea. The brilliant Egyptian sun floods in, tempered by the Mediterranean breeze, introducing a deliciously languid, honey-colored air into the room—a breath of the temperate climate that travelers to Alexandria from the ancient Greeks to the present have all remarked on with enthusiasm.

Hoping to revive the cultural life of the city, El-Abbadi and his university colleagues decided to use Nixon's visit and the sudden interest of the central government as an opportunity to push for a major new university library. But when they approached UNESCO directly, according to El-Abbadi, they were told: "We cannot make agreements with universities. We make agreements with governments." In order to sell it, the project could be presented not simply as a new university library but as the Revival of the Ancient Library of Alexandria, the Bibliotheca Alexandrina, as it is now officially called.

The idea did not really take off, however, until Hosni Mubarak became president of Egypt after the assassination of Anwar Sadat in 1981. French president François Mitterand was apparently influential in persuading Mubarak of its importance. Mitterand spent the waning years of his life building his own massive library—the new Bibliothèque Nationale de France—like an aging pharaoh overseeing the completion of his pyramid. In 1986 the Egyptian government procured UNESCO support for the project, and in 1988 Mubarak laid a symbolic foundation stone.

The following year, UNESCO sponsored a major international competition for a building design, with 524 entries from fifty-eight countries. The jury, composed of Egyptian and foreign architects, selected a bold, modernist concept by a team of young, little-known architects based in Norway. Built like an amphitheater facing the sea, the building has seven graduated floors, each one narrower than the one beneath it, which rise in one enormous open space under the tilting glass roof. The lowest floor, below sea level, will house the books on the ancient past, and each successive level will move forward toward the present.

To raise money for the project, Mubarak summoned a collection of world leaders to join him for the launch at a meeting in Aswan, in southern Egypt—Mitterand's favorite winter vacation resort. There, the assembled company—including Mitterand, Queen Sophia of Spain, Princess Caroline of Monaco, and the heads of most of the Arab nations—assisted in the curious spectacle of sheiks from the oil-rich Gulf States, where even the hint of dissenting information is harshly punished, competing with one another to make the largest contribution to the new universal library. Sheik Zaid of the Arab Emirates stunned the crowd with an offer of $20 million, only to be bested by Iraqi leader Saddam Hussein, who put up $21 million—which, in turn, was topped by Saudi Arabia, which made a lavish gift of $23 million. (Luckily for the Egyptians, Saddam Hussein's $21 million check cleared before the beginning of the Gulf War, which turned Egypt and Iraq into adversaries and drained Iraq's coffers.)

As the plans took shape, El-Abbadi's memorandum on the library gradually grew into a book, *The Life and Fate of the Ancient Library of Alexandria*, which UNESCO published to help promote the project. In the same period, an Italian scholar, Luciano Canfora, published *The Vanished Library*, part of a growing interest in Alexandria and its library.

Ancient Alexandria combined the opulence and grandeur of Egypt with elements of traditional Greek culture. A description survives of a Dionysian procession in Alexandria involving—among many other things—a 180-foot golden phallus, 2,000 golden-horned bulls, a golden statue of Alexander carried aloft by elephants, and an 18-foot statue of Dionysus wearing a purple cloak and a golden crown of ivy and grapevine. As foreigners governing in Egypt, the Ptolemies took on the trappings of traditional Egyptian pharaohs, having themselves declared gods on earth. They even created their own bicultural deity, Serapis, which was represented simultaneously as both a bull and a man, the bull for the Egyptians (who were used to animal gods) and the man for the Greeks, who were used to the anthropomorphic gods of Mount Olympus.

But in the realm of culture, the Ptolemies were anxious to be seen as the rightful heirs of classical Greece. The Alexandria library was probably modeled on the Lyceum in Athens, which was the school and library of Aristotle, who had been tutor to Alexander the Great. According to some sources, it was Demetrius of Phaleron, an Aristotelian intellectual who ruled Athens for a time, who advised Ptolemy Soter to found a major library in order to gather together literature on the different forms of kingship, legislation, and governance in different parts of the world.

The library of Alexandria eventually amassed some 490,000 books written on papyrus—700,000 if you count duplicates. Another 42,000 scrolls were stored in the "daughter library," housed in the Serapeum, the Temple of Serapis. Scholars debate whether there were 490,000 separate works or simply 490,000 scrolls. Longer works were generally stored on multiple scrolls, so that the twenty-four books of Homer's *Iliad,* for example, were probably contained on twenty-four scrolls. In either event, the figure, for the time, was enormous. For instance, the largest library in Europe in the fourteenth century A.D.—the Sorbonne in Paris—had about 1,700 books.

More than a simple collection of books, however, the library of Alexandria was the ancient equivalent of a think tank. According to the Roman geographer Strabo, who visited Alexandria in 20 B.C., the library "was part of the royal palaces, it had a walk, an arcade, a large house in which was a refectory for members of the Mouseion. They formed a community who held property in common with a priest appointed by the kings (and, under the Empire, by Caesar) in charge of the Mouseion." The scholars of Alexandria established the definitive text of Homer by careful philological analysis: comparing all available copies, eliminating additions, forgeries, or poorly copied passages from later editions. But they were also known for abstruse and pedantic scholarship. "Many are feeding in populous Egypt, scribblers on papyrus, ceaselessly wrangling in the bird-cage of the Muses," writes one skeptic of the third century B.C. in a caustic passage remarkably similar to modern satires of academic life.

But learning in Alexandria was hardly limited to scholarly hairsplitting. Eratosthenes, head librarian from 245 to 204 B.C., made the first accurate measurement of the circumference of the earth. (More impressive than the measurement itself is the elegance of Eratosthenes' reasoning. He knew that at noon on the day of the summer equinox, the sun made no shadow in a town in southern Egypt that was located five thousand *stades* due south of Alexandria. Knowing that the earth was round, Eratosthenes measured the curve of the shadow at noon in Alexandria on the day of the equinox and, through the use of geometry, derived the earth's circumference.)

Aristarchus, sixteen hundred years before Copernicus, understood that the earth revolved around the sun. The anatomists Herophilus and Erasistratus, working in the third century B.C., dissected human bodies and understood that the brain was the center of the nervous system and the seat of intelligence. And the engineer Heron of Alexandria, in his books *Mechanica* and *Pneumatica*, laid out the principles of steam power as well as designed machines that showed a full understanding (according to the Oxford *Short History of Science*) "of the cogwheel, of rack and pinion, of multiple pulleys, of transmission of force from a rotating screw to an axis at right angles to it, and to the combination of all these devices with levers."

The level of knowledge at Alexandria was such that the great French historian Fernand Braudel asked in his book *The Structures of Everyday Life* why the Industrial Revolution didn't happen there. One of the reasons, he decided, was slave labor, which diminished the need for labor-saving machinery.

Thus, while the destruction of the library of Alexandria may not have been what prevented the Industrial Revolution from occurring in A.D. 500, it is true that the dispersion of ancient texts resulted in the loss of certain kinds of knowledge for about fifteen hundred years. Gone, too, are hundreds of works of the great Greek dramatists and poets as well as virtually all of ancient history. Only three historians survive from the first five hundred years of Greek historiography, whereas we know, from brief references in later works, of countless books about various ancient peoples—the Chaldeans, the Babylonians, the Etruscans, the Carthaginians, the Egyptians, and the Ptolemies themselves—that almost certainly were in the ancient library but have since vanished.

How the library of Alexandria was destroyed, however, remains one of the great detective stories of antiquity, with many clues but no clear solution. The principal suspects: Julius Caesar, the Christians, and the Arabs. Since the evidence is contradictory, each historian has a favorite culprit, often depending on his nationality or ideology: Edward Gibbon blames the Christians, in keeping with his theory that religion caused the fall of the Roman Empire; Professor El-Abbadi, in his book on the library, blames Julius Caesar and seems particularly concerned to deflect blame from the Arabs; the Italian Canfora seems equally determined to exonerate his fellow countryman, Caesar, and has blamed the Arabs—at least until recently.

The evidence against Caesar would, at first glance, appear to be quite strong. Seneca and Plutarch both wrote that Caesar, after taking Alexandria in 47 B.C., found himself under attack from the sea and torched the boats in the harbor. The fire spread to the shore and, according to Seneca, some 40,000 scrolls were destroyed. (This scene is immortalized on celluloid as Elizabeth Taylor, playing Cleopatra, berates Rex Harrison—Caesar—for destroying her beloved library.) Canfora's book points out that Seneca's text, the closest in time to the event, refers to scrolls in a warehouse. These, he writes, were books probably stored near the docks waiting to be exported. Even if they were in the library, 40,000 scrolls were only a tiny fraction of the 490,000 scrolls in the library. Plutarch reports that Mark Antony compensated

Cleopatra by commandeering 200,000 scrolls from the library at Perg-amon, the other great Hellenistic library of the time, and giving them to Alexandria. Clearly, an important number of books were destroyed in Caesar's fire, but it is also clear that the library, as an institution, was not destroyed, since there are several accounts of work being done there not long after Caesar's day.

The evidence against the Christians is more circumstantial. After Christianity became the state religion of the Roman Empire in A.D. 324, tensions rose in Alexandria between pagans and Christians. In 391, the Christians went on an iconoclastic rampage, destroying pagan idols throughout the city and destroying the Serapeum, the Temple of Serapris, which was also the home of the daughter library. But there is no specific record of their having also attacked the Great Library in the Mouseion.

The last principal suspect is the first caliph of Egypt, who ruled the country after the Arabs brought Islam to North Africa in the seventh cen-tury A.D. The story, told in an Arabic account, is that the new vizier of Alexandria asked the caliph what to do with this enormous library. The caliph is reported to have replied: If the books are in accordance with the word of Allah, we have no need of them. If they are not in accord with the word of Allah, they are dangerous. In either event, destroy them. According to the account, the bathhouses of Alexandria were heated for six months with burning scrolls. El-Abbadi points out, however, that this account dates from the twelfth century, nearly six centuries after the fact, and more likely reflects the hostility generated by the Crusades than actual historical fact. The early Islamic conquerors were distinguished for being unusually respectful of local customs and cultures.

In fact, Canfora, in a pamphlet recently published in French, iden-tifies a new culprit. In A.D. 271, Queen Zenobia of Palmyra captured the city and was then ousted by the Roman emperor Aurelian in a battle that laid waste to much of the old city.

In the end, however, the idea of the burning of the library of Alexandria as a single catastrophic event is probably a myth. There were at least a dozen major libraries in the ancient world—in places like

Pergamon, Antioch, Athens, and Rome—and none of them fared any better than Alexandria because ancient documents, by their very nature, don't last very long. "Papyri rolls were very vulnerable and climate control must not have been very good," said Alan Cameron, a classicist at Columbia University who has written extensively about the poet Callimachus, who is known to have written a vast catalog of the ancient library, which, like so much else, is lost. "I suspect that if you went there in the second century A.D. you might have found broken scraps of papyri where many rolls had been." (The ancient papyri that do survive, such as the Dead Sea Scrolls or the Gnostic gospels, were buried in dry sand or in a sealed tomb.)

Given the extreme fragility of unique manuscripts written on a medium like papyrus, every major disaster—fire, flood, political upheaval, or military invasion—almost certainly involved the loss of books. The works that do survive were generally the most popular texts, which were copied and recopied and eventually found their way onto a more stable medium like parchment, made of tough animal skin, which gradually replaced papyrus as the dominant writing material by about the third or fourth century A.D. Even these works, however, had to be recopied repeatedly. The oldest complete version of Homer, for example, is a medieval copy made in the tenth or eleventh century A.D., nearly eighteen hundred years after it was written. "The relationship between texts that are lost and those that have survived is about forty to one," writes Canfora. "The relationship is even more unfavorable when you consider the countless number of texts of which we have no record."

It was the print revolution in the mid–fifteenth century that made the long-term preservation of large numbers of texts possible. Islam, after lovingly translating ancient Greek works in the first centuries of its existence, turned its back on Western culture. The Ottoman sultan banned printing on pain of death in 1516 in order to keep the power of writing and interpretation in the hands of the Ottoman bureaucrats and of the religious leaders. Thus when Napoleon arrived in Egypt in 1798, he found a country that was almost entirely illiterate and without the technical and military means to resist foreign occupation.

Having missed out on the print revolution, the Egyptian government is determined not to miss out on the new digital revolution.

Like its ancient predecessor, the new library of Alexandria has the feeling of a grand royal project. The library is the most ambitious cultural project undertaken in Egypt during the Mubarak era and it has enjoyed the president's "high patronage" (as one library brochure states). Suzanne Mubarak, the president's wife, is the head of the commission overseeing the completion of the project.

Power in Egypt, as in both pharaonic and Ottoman times, flows clearly from the top down and the library is no exception. A striking example occurred when Mrs. Mubarak visited the library construction site. Looking at the nearly complete building, she suddenly decided that a rather drab hospital next door spoiled the appearance of the library from a certain angle. "That has to go," she said. And the hospital is now gone.

The library reflects the hierarchical nature of the Egyptian government, with one man—a trusted government servant with close links to Cairo—clearly in charge. He is Mohsen Zahran, a professor of architecture at the University of Alexandria and the project manager of the library. Initially, power was supposed to be shared equally by UNESCO and the Egyptian government, but Zahran and the Egyptian government moved ably to limit UNESCO's role and take full charge of the library. The project is governed by a complex dual structure—something called the International Commission for the Alexandria Library Project, based in Cairo, and the General Organization of the Alexandria Library (GOAL), based in Alexandria. The commission, headed by Mrs. Mubarak and the Egyptian minister of higher education, is supposed to oversee the overall direction of the project, while GOAL is responsible for the day-to-day work on the library. While the Egyptians controlled the commission, a UNESCO official from Italy, Giovanni Romerio, was the executive director of GOAL and the project manager of the library, with Zahran as his deputy. But as Romerio quickly discovered in his years in Alexandria, his authority as project manager was more nominal than real because Zahran, while his deputy on GOAL, also sat on the International Commission, which held the real power and the purse strings of the project. "So even though he was supposedly my deputy, he in fact took orders from the minister," Romerio explained. "The Egyptians are very good at creating these diabolic mechanisms where they nominally give control to a foreigner but then undermine it through a complex double structure."

Zahran is a stocky, stolid-looking man with gray hair, a grayish complexion, and a large, dark mole on his left nostril. Although he affected an air of joviality and spoke with lyrical, almost mystical rapture of the new library as "a lighthouse of knowledge," he had a reputation as a suspicious and closed man with a prickly character but also as a tough political infighter who knew how to work the levers of the Egyptian bureaucracy. "He is an apparatchik," said Romerio, now back in Italy. "He would almost tremble with veneration when he spoke about the government, about the ministers, about political power."

Romerio says he found himself constantly being outmaneuvered by his supposed deputy. At one point, Zahran hid the fact that he had gone to the Frankfurt Book Fair to acquire books for the library. "I asked his secretary where he was and with great embarrassment she said she thought he might be home sick," Romerio said. "He was in Frankfurt. . . . He could not tolerate sharing power."

In 1995, after three years in Alexandria, when Romerio reached the standard retirement age of sixty-five, Zahran took over as project manager of GOAL. The Egyptian government showed no interest in either having Romerio's retirement deferred or having another UNESCO official in an oversight position in Alexandria.

Although Zahran's determination and his background as an architect have been important in bringing the library to near completion, he is not considered a man of broad culture, and it is far from clear why he should be flying to the Frankfurt Book Fair and making decisions about the contents of the library. "At the beginning, they ignored the scholars completely," said Professor El-Abbadi. Between 1990 and 1997, there was no committee of academic consultants to help recommend books in their areas of speciality. "It wasn't well supervised at the beginning," El-Abbadi said. In 1997, El-Abbadi and others were invited to form a committee of scholars to advise the library on the formation of its con-tent. But even since then, El-Abbadi has felt very little desire for active input. "So far, they have been concentrating on the building. Dr. Zahran is an architect and he is working night and day on that. He is not a library man."

In its original proposal the library was supposed to be finished in 1995 and have a collection of two million books by the year 2000. The library had still not opened in 2001 and contains somewhere between 250,000 and 300,000 books. To give a sense of scale, Vassar College has a library of 500,000 books, while the holdings of large state univer-sities range from 2.5 million volumes at the University of Kentucky to over 8 million at the University of Illinois at Champaign-Urbana.

Without its spectacular claim of being the "revival of the ancient library of Alexandria," the project would never have received UNESCO support and the "high patronage" of President Mubarak, but its size and high-tech design have already made the library extremely expensive. The cost of the building has tripled over its life from $65 to $192 million and may become prohibitive in the future. And by building such an ambitious building, the Egyptians have locked themselves into high operating costs in perpetuity. The chief architect, Christoph Kappeller, said that it is standard to spend between 10 and 15 percent of the total cost of a building annually to keep it in good working order. Thus, the Egyptians, having spent about $192 million over seven years building the library, will have to spend a similar amount every seven years to keep it running as designed. The entire budget of the University of Alexandria, according to Zahran, is 100 million Egyptian pounds (about $33 million); the library, he said, will need a budget of similar size. Although Zahran insisted that the government will pay whatever is necessary to keep up the library, he acknowledged that there is no actual budget for maintenance or book acquisitions.

The library is in the odd position of having been conceived before the Internet revolution and completed afterward, meaning that it is big-ger and contains room for more printed books than some view as neces-sary. Others consider the timing providential. "I think we are lucky to be starting now rather than five or six years earlier," said Gerald Grunberg, a French librarian whose services as chief consultant have been "donated" to Alexandria by his government. He worked extensively on the new Bibliothèque Nationale in Paris, a high-tech library that has been beset by numerous problems. "There are many things that are much easier to do than when we were doing the Bibliothèque Nationale or the new British Library, during which time there was a complete technological upheaval. We were buying technology that was obsolete in a year. Now, I think there has been a settling or stabilization in the technology."

An intense-looking French intellectual with wire-rimmed glasses, cigarette-stained teeth, and a handlebar mustache, Grunberg is a highly regarded professional in a field that has grown dramatically in complexity and importance during the past decade. If being a librarian once meant filing and retrieving books, it now means operating immensely complicated and expensive information systems, combining knowledge of traditional books and microfilm with that of computers, fiber-optic cables, server networks, elaborate software formats, audiovisual systems, among many other things. With monkish dedication, Grunberg has left his family in France for the past few years in order to bring the Alexandria project to completion. "As a librarian, Alexandria was a myth for me," he said.

Grunberg and the Egyptian managers of the project recognize that they cannot create a universal library. "It makes no sense," said Grunberg. Even the Library of Congress in Washington, the world's largest library, with a stratospheric 119 million items in its collection, is nonetheless selective in its acquisitions. It is the closest thing to the ancient library of Alexandria today and its commitment to quasi-universality is incredibly expensive. Its annual budget is $386 million and it has twenty-eight people in Egypt alone—one of six overseas offices—whose sole job is to scour the world for little-known books and periodicals.

The new library in Alexandria will try to have a good general collection and then several areas of specialization—Egypt, Alexandria, the Middle East, and the Mediterranean—in which it hopes to build world-class collections. The library has made some important acquisitions and received some major gifts. It has acquired, on microfilm, all the papers related to the construction and operation of the Suez Canal, some of which are in France and some in Egypt. The Spanish government has given it microfilm copies of the Arabic manuscripts in the royal library at the Escorial. It has become the custodian of some ten thousand Arab manuscripts from local mosques and is setting up a modern laboratory for the conservation of manuscripts. The library will try to acquire microfilm copies from the major Arab manuscript collections around the world. The Spanish, who are particularly advanced in this area, are placing the Arab manuscripts in Cordoba, Seville, and Granada on CD-ROM and will give them to the library.

Like the ancient library, the new one will try to be more than a book depository. It will have an information systems center, with banks of computers offering on-line access, a large audiovisual library, with equipment donated by Japan, and a planetarium. The plan calls for the creation of a business research center where Egyptian companies will be able to pay for market research to find out, say, about the Brazilian textile industry or current European Community import regulations. In theory, at least, the center could become an income source for the library—although it is an untried concept. The library will also store the historic footage of Egyptian television, which, if managed properly, could, beyond its scholarly value, be licensed to television producers and filmmakers in other parts of the Arabic-speaking world.

But does it make sense to collect all of this in a physical space when it could be made available over the Internet? "Actually, I think it is more important than ever," said Grunberg. "With globalization, there is an enormous need for spaces where one will assemble and conserve the collective memory of a community or of a country. The more globalization we have, the more these sort of places are necessary. It is not a paradox. Take the example of Egypt. It is a country with a great civilization, an extremely rich history, and a strong identity, but because of historical circumstances—the invasion of Napoleon, the British occupation of the country—many of the cultural riches of Egypt are in great museums and libraries overseas. The Alexandria library testifies to a desire to conserve

Egyptian identity. You can't get all of that material on the Internet. In fact, if you look at most of the big national digitization projects, each country tends to favor its own history, to preserve its own roots. The Library of Congress has an on-line project called *American Memories,* and the French have one called *Gallica,* on French civilization. Egyptian history is not going to be a priority for other countries. Collecting things today in this age of technology is not a paradox. If a country like Egypt does not want to be submerged in the cultural production from outside (from the United States, one must say), it must create its own content, constitute its own identity. A place like this could help very much."

At the same time, Grunberg said, "Today's technologies allow Egypt to be very open toward the outside world, to be a crossroads of communication."

But the fact that the new library is an emanation of the Egyptian central government makes it difficult for it to become a place of openness and memory—as became clear before the building even started to rise.

At a certain point, Giovanni Romerio, the former project director, suggested organizing a major exhibition on the Septuagint. Romerio convinced Israeli officials to lend materials about the Dead Sea Scrolls for the show. But when Romerio spoke with the Egyptian minister of higher education, he was told: "This is a Muslim country. Leave the foreign policy to us."

In order to build an international library, Egypt must reconcile itself to the periods of foreign presence in Alexandria. "The Egyptians are proud of only two periods in their history—ancient Egypt and the Arab conquest," said Professor El-Abbadi. "The Greek and Roman period is looked upon in a way as an alien culture." Since the Egyptian revolution the history taught in Egyptian schools has largely ignored the nearly thousand-year European presence in ancient Egypt, skipping from the collapse of the pharaohs to the Arab conquest in A.D. 641, leaving the entire Greek, Roman, and Christian phases of the country's history an unexplored black hole. This year, the Egyptian government reformed the curriculum to include the Ptolemaic period. At the same time, parts of ancient Alexandria are literally emerging from the ground. As the city undertakes a major building boom, construction workers are stumbling on Greek and Roman cemeteries, temples, statues, and pillars from an ancient city that appears to be still surprisingly intact several feet below the sidewalk. Out in the eastern harbor of the city, French archeologists in wet suits have located the underwater remains of what they believe to be the ancient lighthouse of Alexandria, one of the Seven Wonders of the Ancient World.

The city has decided that its past may well be its future—albeit a fantasy version of that past. There are at least six different projects to rebuild versions of the ancient lighthouse of Alexandria, despite our having only rather sketchy ideas of what it actually looked like. One project would build a lighthouse as depicted in a famous eighteenth-century reconstruction—itself half fantasy, half history—but with shops on the lower floors and a revolving restaurant on top. Another plan, sponsored by the French clothing designer Pierre Cardin, involves the futuristic use of laser lights.

The library project, therefore, is part of a much larger cultural shift in which Egypt is both symbolically and physically reappropriating a long-neglected piece of its past. "The Bibliotheca Alexandrina is coming up again," said Zahran. "This proves that there are cycles of history, that things do not disappear forever. They may hide, they may be eclipsed, but they are there for us." But this rediscovery of Alexandria is not without its troubling ironies: the modern city, eager for economic development and new housing, is busily bulldozing and paving over the remains of the ancient city just as it is beginning to reemerge. There is no more dramatic example than the new library itself.

Since the library stands on part of the ancient royal palaces of the Ptolemies, it would have been standard procedure to excavate the site for any ancient remains before building. There was a six-year lag between the designation of the site, which was a vacant lot belonging to the University of Alexandria, and the beginning of construction. "Unfortunately, the Egyptians have no concept of salvage archeology," said Jean-Yves Empereur, the French archeologist excavating the ancient lighthouse and the director of the Centre d'Etudes Alexandrines. The

Egyptian government will call for excavation only when it is obvious that a major archeological site is being damaged. As a result, Empereur and his team at the Centre d'Etudes Alexandrines watch vigilantly over new development in the city while builders often try to hide or destroy what they find in order to avoid costly delays. At a certain point in 1993, Empereur noticed that in the middle of the night bulldozers were beginning to dig the foundation of the library. Empereur called Mohammed Awad, an Egyptian architect who is the head of the Alexandria Preservation Trust, a not-for-profit group that is trying to preserve historic Alexandria. Awad went to see for himself. "The bulldozers were working between one and four o'clock in the morning," Awad said. "They claim they were doing it because there was no traffic around. They were doing it in secrecy."

"Everything we did was done in consultation with the Egyptian Supreme Council of Antiquities," Zahran insisted. "That is a big lie," Awad replied.

When Awad and Empereur went to see Zahran, he reportedly became furious and ended their meeting. After contacting various government ministries, Awad went back to the library site in the middle of the night and, standing on top of a car, videotaped the bulldozers moving earth. He went to the police station and filed a report. Meanwhile, the French newspaper Le Monde ran an article that embarrassed UNESCO and the Egyptian government. A small amount of money was appropriated for an archeological excavation and almost immediately workers uncovered two extraordinarily beautiful Greek mosaic floors. But because the Egyptian government appropriated less than $20,000 for the dig, archeologists excavated only a portion of the site. However, the mosaic work that has been cleaned so far—almost as finely detailed as an oil painting—provides a tantalizing glimpse of what a full and systematic excavation of the area might have revealed. Thus, ironically, the revival of the library of Alexandria could be burying the ancient library once and for all.

Awad was severely reprimanded and subjected to an official inquiry by the university but emerged unscathed—an encouraging sign about the possibilities of dissent in Egypt. Nonetheless, the episode reveals something disturbingly typical about Egypt: that the government seemed far more bothered by the bad press it was receiving than by the fact that an important archeological site was being destroyed.

Another revealing fiasco in the construction of the library involved the loss of an important collection of books. About two years into the project, the University of Alexandria library decided to get rid of fifty thousand or so books it decided it did not need. The obvious thing would have been to give the books to the new library. Instead, the books ended up on the street being sold off for about a dollar apiece. "I could only afford to buy about six hundred," said Empereur. He pulled open a glass case in the library of the Centre d'Etudes Alexandrines. Among the books that Empereur has in his case are numerous eighteenth-century illustrated editions of European accounts of travels in Egypt and the Middle East, many of which belonged to the library of the Egyptian royal family. In London or Paris antiquarian shops, these volumes would have sold for hundreds, if not thousands, of dollars apiece. "They sold about ten thousand. They told me that they had first offered them to the new library but Dr. Zahran said, 'We don't need any old books. We are buying new books.'"

When *Le Monde* published a short article about the dispersion of books in Alexandria, the minister of higher education supposedly called Zahran to protest. Zahran dispatched Grunberg, who was able to salvage twenty thousand books. But the best ten thousand were already gone while the remaining twenty thousand books were not considered worth keeping. Zahran claimed that he never refused the books but that the ten thousand books were lost through a regrettable miscommunication.

Perturbed by the doubts surrounding the project, Zahran insisted that one should not lose sight of its positive potential. "We always think of the problems, of the obstacles. Can we think of the light, of the hope, of the brighter side of the coin? The promise of genius is springing forth once again in Alexandria, and we have to help it. I said 'the promise of genius.' How could you expect a baby to be a genius overnight? It will take time."

Ultimately, however, the success or failure of the new library may depend on the overall direction of Egyptian society. The Egyptian government talks about wanting foreign investment and expertise, privatization, and a pluralistic society. But it had all of these things in Alexandria in the 1950s and systematically destroyed them.

Even though there is a tendency to consider prerevolutionary Egypt as a colony, Egypt had gained its full independence and sovereignty in 1922, and well before 1952 it had begun to take back control of its national institutions. In 1937, the Egyptian government ended the system of "capitulations"—exemption for foreign nationals from Egyptian taxes and laws. And in 1942, it opened the University of Alexandria, where Egyptian and foreign scholars worked together. "There was full cooperation between the foreign community and the Egyptian intelligentsia," said Professor El-Abbadi, whose father taught Islamic history at the university, where he himself took his undergraduate degree in 1953. In the 1940s and 1950s, there were foreign scholars on the faculty and some of the Egyptian professors enjoyed enough of an international reputation to be able to teach overseas.

The Egyptian revolution—in creating a socialist-style command economy and a military police state—concentrated almost all the nation's resources in Cairo and sucked much of the life out of Alexandria. Many Alexandrian businesses actually shifted their headquarters to Cairo because of the number of government permissions needed to operate. Journalists, writers, movie directors, actors, and publishers were virtually all in Cairo. Old cosmopolitan Alexandria was governed by an elected municipal council, which after the Egyptian revolution was replaced by a series of governors, almost all of them retired military men, almost none of them Alexandrians, who allowed the city to fall into ruins a second time.

"What happened afterward was a tragedy, which we still feel badly," El-Abbadi said. Cultural institutions such as museums, foreign schools, and universities were nationalized along with everything else. When El-Abbadi returned with his Ph.D. from Cambridge in 1960, he found a much more dour, monochrome city. Nasser kept Egypt on a war footing, and the stores in Alexandria were covered over with black paper in case of air raids. Alexandria's polyglot society became monocultural and monolinguistic, with schoolchildren taught to memorize the glorious dates of the Egyptian revolution and not much else.

Nasser did help democratize Egyptian society, passing land reform and opening up Egyptian universities to the masses. But he also sacrificed quality for quantity: he promised a place at university to any student who finished high school and a civil service job to anyone who finished university. The result was armies of people with worthless degrees and an enormous state bureaucracy made up of ill-paid, ill-trained civil servants.

Not surprisingly, scholarship also suffered. "As a result of the cultural break with Europe in the 1950s and 1960s, many graduates were educated either locally or in Eastern Europe, where they did not learn the local language and were taught in broken English," El-Abbadi said. "And now the new generations of students are equally handicapped in their knowledge of foreign languages and the standard of research." The University of Alexandria does not have a proper library. "Because of the dearth of books, students depend on textbooks and secondhand books. . . . There is no research material available. We live in isolation, far from all that is going on in the outside world of scholarship and culture. Only those who have the opportunity to go abroad for conferences have a glimpse of what is happening. It is hoped that the library will break the vicious circle of the decline in research."

Zahran's autocratic manner and insistence on total control have alienated some of Alexandria's more important cultural resources. Awad's Preservation Trust has a formidable collection of thousands of photographs, maps, and postcards of the nineteenth and early twentieth century. The new library—if it wants to become the collective memory of Alexandria—should seek to become the storehouse for the collection but instead, because of their confrontation over the mosaics, Awad and Zahran are barely speaking.

While this may seem a purely personal conflict, it has larger ramifications symbolic of the central government's uneasy relationship with

Alexandria and its cosmopolitan culture. Although only in his forties, Awad, like El-Abbadi, is a member of Alexandria's cosmopolitan Egyptian society. Half Egyptian, half Greek, he was educated at British schools in Alexandria and moves seamlessly between Arabic, French, and English.

"In trying to save this cosmopolitan world, I am trying to save myself," Awad said in his office in the crumbling downtown area. "I am one of these people who grew up in this cosmopolitan world, part of this pluralism and this tolerance. Alexandria symbolizes this pluralism, this tolerance, and this multinational society that existed throughout the nineteenth and first half of the twentieth century." Until fairly recently, historic preservation in Alexandria has been an uphill battle.

"This is a more serene period of our history and we are more at peace with our recent past," said Awad. Although he has been extremely frustrated by the neglect and destruction of the architecture of modern Alexandria, he sees the beginnings of a positive change. Before, one could not suggest preserving a former British government building or a Jewish house. "You could not say: 'This is a beautiful building. We must save it.' Now, we can say this. . . .

"Alexandria has always been an open city since its foundation. It's part of our history, but it's also our future. I can only envision a future for this city as an open, international city. And the library project, whether it will work or not, is at least in line with what we see as the future of the city."

A sign of greater openness is the recent return of the statue of a famous and controversial Egyptian figure, the khedive Ismail, an influential nineteenth-century Ottoman pasha who helped modernize Egypt. Known as the "impatient Europeanizer," Ismail introduced the telegraph, the railroad, and gas lighting to Egypt and built much of modern Alexandria and Cairo, including countless schools, libraries, and learned societies, an astronomical observatory, the National Library in Cairo, and the Cairo opera house, commissioning Giuseppe Verdi to write *Aida* for the opening of the Suez Canal. At the completion of the canal, he declared (in French, of course): "Now we are no longer part of Africa. We are part of Europe."

Unfortunately, Ismail's ambitious building program bankrupted the Egyptian treasury, leading to his abdication and the occupation of Egypt by the British, who had lent him most of the money for his public works. As a result, the nationalists toppled the statue of the impatient Europeanizer that the Italian community of Alexandria had dedicated to him with great fanfare in 1938. The statue, showing the khedive in Western dress but holding a sword and wearing an Ottoman fez, was placed right on the Corniche facing the sea, looking north toward Europe. The statue was relegated in 1948 to a place of ignominy in the backyard of the local arts museum. At one point, the government even threatened to melt it down for its bronze and the Italian government offered to buy it back. In 1998, the governor of Alexandria had the statue put back in a prominent place in the city. He did not, however, put it back in its original spot—a move that would have been too politically risky. The Egyptian nationalists reused the base of the khedive's statue—an elaborate Fascist-era monument with white marble classical columns—for a tomb of the unknown soldier and renamed the once-elegant nineteenth-century square in which it stood Tahrir Square, or Liberation Square. And the statue now stands in a busy traffic roundabout facing northeast, roughly in the direction of Turkey.

The Vatican Library Mystery

ONE SPRING DAY in 1997, the studious calm of the Vatican Library—where scholars sit hunched over Egyptian papyri, scrolls of Greek mathematical treatises, and illuminated Renaissance manuscripts—was suddenly shattered by the arrival of several members of the Vatican police. A highly unusual presence in this temple of learning, the Swiss guards closed down and sealed off the library coffee shop, two stores near the Sistine Chapel where Vatican Library merchandise was sold, and an office of the computer giant IBM, used for the digitization of the Vatican's manuscript collection. The employees were led off the premises by the guards as if they were criminals. Several days later, a short, cryptic note appeared in the Vatican newspaper, *L'Osservatore Romano*, announcing that Father Leonard Boyle, a highly respected scholar of the Middle Ages who had been prefect of the library for the past thirteen years, was stepping down from his post.

Coming in the wake of the strange police blitz, Boyle's sudden departure—without a replacement being named—suggested that the prefect had been unceremoniously sacked. The Vatican is an institution that prefers an extremely discreet and low-key approach to conflict and is generally indulgent toward those in its flock who stray.

Priests accused of pedophilia are quietly transferred and large financial settlements made under court seal; when Bishop Paul Marcinkus, the head of the Vatican bank, was implicated in a major financial scandal and Italian prosecutors issued a warrant for his arrest, the Vatican protected him and paid out hundreds of millions of dollars in losses. The Vatican's decision to use such heavy-handed means to discredit Father Boyle, a man who by all accounts had devoted his entire life to the service of scholarship and the Church, was highly unusual and begged interpretation. After all, Boyle, who was seventy-three at the time, was only about a year and a half from retirement. Presumably, the Vatican could have waited to make a change and gently eased him out. Someone evidently wanted to get rid of Father Boyle very badly and may have preferred to do so publicly in order to destroy his reputation.

For the world of international scholarship, the news was genuinely stunning. Boyle enjoyed almost universal respect in academic circles and his tenure as prefect of one of the world's great libraries was considered a total success. At the time, in fact, I was preparing to go to Rome to write about Boyle and the Vatican Library as a striking example of a great medieval library transforming itself into a modern one.

I had met Boyle two years earlier in his wood-paneled office at the library, a crucifix and a photograph of the pope on the wall behind him. A young Italian carrying a sleek laptop computer entered the room. "Excuse me, Father, I have to show you something," he said. Fabio Schiattarella, a representative of the Italian branch of IBM, turned on his laptop and images of the Vatican appeared: we were seeing a prototype of a CD-ROM that IBM was designing of a computerized visit to the library. We moved through shadowy digital chambers, passing through doors representing the different branches of the arts and sciences in what promised to be an almost infinite virtual temple of knowledge. The prototype was part of a much larger and more ambitious project: an IBM-Vatican joint venture to digitize every page of the Vatican's 150,000 rare manuscripts, which range from the oldest surviving copies of the Bible, Virgil's *Aeneid,* and Dante's *Divine Comedy* to the astronomical observations of Galileo and the love letters of Henry VIII to Anne Boleyn.

Boyle, a charming and deeply learned Irish Dominican priest, seemed himself the prototype of a new breed, the twenty-first-century humanist, at home deciphering the monastic script of a tenth-century manuscript or talking about "bits" and "pixels" with a computer engineer. Boyle opened up the traditionally closed and forbidding Vatican Library and restored it to the status it enjoyed in the Renaissance as a great center of international culture and scholarship. He hired women for the first time, relaxed the dress code, opened the library in the afternoons, and started a café where scholars could break for cappuccinos and sandwiches or talk about what they had discovered. In the library café, one scholar said, you could hear the conversation across two millennia between three different eras: the ancient texts in the collection, the Renaissance humanists who collected or copied them, and the contemporary scholars from around the world discussing them animatedly. "Father Boyle's Vatican Library reminded me of Raphael's *School of Athens*," she said, referring to Raphael's famous fresco in the Vatican palace depicting the Renaissance ideal of a community of scholars in which Plato, Aristotle, the Arab philosopher Averroës, and Raphael's contemporary, Michelangelo, are shown discussing philosophy, religion, art, and science.

For many years Boyle lived and worked at the Roman church of San Clemente, which is itself a metaphor for the cultural continuity of Rome. The church is an architectural palimpsest, with three different churches built one on top of the other. The church one enters at ground level dates from the late Middle Ages and the Renaissance; at its lowest level there is both a clandestine Christian church from the first century A.D. and a Mithraeum, a place of worship of the Oriental cult of Mithras, popular in pagan Rome. In one of the excavated subterranean rooms, one can still see a little statue of Mithras slaughtering a bull. Boyle, who dug up archeological remains at the lowest level of San Clemente, appeared to be a living bridge from the Mithraic cult to IBM.

Boyle's sudden dismissal, however, turned a case of medieval manuscripts in cyberspace into a tale of Vatican intrigue reminiscent of

Umberto Eco's *The Name of the Rose*. When I returned to Rome, the scholarly community there was buzzing with conspiracy theories. According to one scenario, Church conservatives wanted to prevent Father Boyle, a highly independent man and suspected "liberal," from taking his place in the College of Cardinals that would elect the next pope. Seven out of the eight former prefects of the Vatican Library in this century have gone on to become cardinals after their retirement. With Pope John Paul II barely able to walk without assistance, many people believe that Boyle's ouster was part of the jockeying for position in anticipation of the next conclave. Since cardinals can vote until the age of eighty, Boyle, if made cardinal, might have been eligible to help elect a new pope. Boyle himself dismissed this theory. "I never wanted to become cardinal," he told me, adding with his characteristic Irish wit, "I'm not interested in some second-rate job—the papacy or nothing!"

Others saw Boyle's undoing in opposition to his policy of openness and modernization at the library. Boyle had clashed with his immediate predecessor, the redoubtable eighty-seven-year-old Austrian cardinal Alfonz Stickler. Cardinal Stickler used to say (and proudly repeated to me): "As long as I am prefect of the Vatican Library, a computer will never cross the threshold!" The computerization of the library's catalog was Boyle's first major initiative after arriving at the Vatican. When Boyle arranged to make seventy-five thousand images from the library available on optical disk, Stickler wrote a scathing report to the Vatican secretary of state. But Boyle won that particular battle: Stickler was himself removed from the position of *cardinale bibliotecario,* or cardinal librarian, the official in charge of overseeing the entire operation of the library. Although Stickler lost his first major confrontation with Boyle, some suspected he might have gotten his revenge in the end.

Moreover, Boyle's freewheeling style—his opening the library to film crews and computer companies, his willingness to send its treasures to exhibitions around the world—gradually rubbed many in the Vatican the wrong way. His critics pointed to the fact that two illuminated pages from among the library's most precious manuscripts, estimated to be worth half a million dollars, turned up stolen on the American art market in 1995. The culprit is believed to have been an American scholar whom Boyle allowed to be alone with the manuscripts, although the pages may well have been stolen long before Boyle's tenure.

As in *The Name of the Rose,* set in a medieval monastery whose library's contents are carefully hidden, there are two very different conceptions of knowledge at work in the Vatican Library—one that views knowledge as power, something to be jealously guarded and meted out as a privilege to a select, trusted few, and a more open mind-set that maintains that knowledge should be disseminated as widely as possible and that everyone is strengthened by the constant and broad exchange of ideas. Boyle is decidedly in the second camp. One day when he was doing archeological work at the church of San Clemente, he uncovered an ancient Roman mosaic. That evening, an older Dominican took him to task for digging up the ancient floor, saying that Boyle should have left it for posterity. To which Boyle replied, "But aren't we also posterity?" Similarly, Boyle felt that the Vatican's fabulous manuscripts were useless unless they were read and used by scholars. "It is a library, not a museum," he said. Throughout his thirteen-year tenure, Boyle did whatever he could to make the library's unique collections available, allowing enormous parts of them to be microfilmed and shared with other libraries and initiating the ambitious and incomplete IBM project. Boyle grasped the spirit of the digital age: that information can be shared infinitely without diminishing the original. Boyle was a digital man in a decidedly analogue world. "Boyle is being punished," said one scholar priest at the Vatican, "for doing what none of his predecessors managed: making the library work."

The situation, however, turned out to be considerably more complex. Many of the reasons for Boyle's sudden dismissal lay buried in the documents in a California courthouse. To finance his ambitious modernization of the Vatican, Boyle committed the library to a bold commercial venture to sell books, jewelry, clothing, souvenirs, films, and CD-ROMs based on the images in the collection, as many museums around the world do. Unfortunately, Boyle got himself and the library into a terrible legal tangle. In 1988, Boyle assigned exclusive worldwide rights to the images in the Vatican Library to a California businesswoman, Elaine Iannessa, who, it turns out, had filed for bankruptcy that same year. The investor she found for the project turned out to be the head of a failed savings and loan. Boyle signed the contracts without having a lawyer examine them and then loaned Iannessa $1.5 million in library funds to help her out of her personal difficulties. Within a few months, they were all in court, and in 1996, after six years of litigation, the Holy See paid out $8.8 million to settle the case and was hit with attorneys' fees of $1.3 million.

Beyond its personal aspects, however, the troubles at the Vatican Library reflected larger problems. The downside of the digital age is that technology is expensive and in today's cost-conscious, commercially minded society cultural institutions are expected to be able to pay their own way. The new commercial pressures strained the Church's efforts to reconcile its religious and cultural mission with the reality of its economic needs. "It's the old problem of trying to serve both Christ and Mammon," one experienced Vatican official told me, asking not to be quoted by name. "Our fundamental mission is religious, but we have economic needs like any other institution. We're better at the first than the latter." The downfall of Father Boyle is a cautionary fable of the dangers of digitization and of an ancient institution's trying to leapfrog into the modern commercial age.

Boyle's mistakes are indicative of an institutional culture at the Vatican that is profoundly distrustful of the world of big business and prefers to trust individuals over large corporations. Boyle, for example, turned down a possible deal with CBS—afraid of embarrassing indirect associations with recording artists like Madonna—but signed a contract with a little-known businessman without even receiving his résumé.

Woefully naïve and inexperienced in business matters, Boyle made several serious blunders, and the Vatican had legitimate reasons for taking the purse strings out of his hands. But the fury with which it booted him out reflected both a legal strategy to disown contracts he signed and a form of payback for his maverick style and fierce independence from the ecclesiastical hierarchy. "I think they are making a scapegoat of Father Boyle," said one high-level lay employee. "Even if the charges against Father Boyle are true, if those were grounds for dismissal at the

Vatican, the place would be empty. The Vatican is like a very complex provincial court of the eighteenth century which is highly informal in its handling of its money."

To understand the reasons for Father Boyle's eventual downfall, one needs to understand something about the institution he led for thirteen years. To reach the Vatican Library, one must pass through the Porta di Sant' Anna, a large black-and-gold cast-iron gate located between St. Peter's Square and the entrance to the Vatican Museum. While millions of visitors pass through St. Peter's and the museum, only a select few are allowed past the colorfully dressed Swiss Guards and into the heart of the Vatican palace. Along sidewalks thick with priests, nuns, bishops, and cardinals, one walks through the massive fortresslike brick walls constructed in the fifteenth century when the popes moved back to Rome after two centuries of the Avignon "captivity." The library is located within an interior courtyard, the Cortile del Belvedere, designed by the great Renaissance architect Bramante. A central part of the popes' plans to create the most brilliant court in Europe, the Belvedere is now used mainly as a parking lot. Julius II, the pope who commissioned Michelangelo's Sistine Chapel and ruled St. Peter's with all the pomp and luxury of a temporal prince, held jousts in the court-yard and even had its vast space filled with water in order to stage mock naval battles for his amusement, just as the Caesars had done in the Roman Colosseum. In the 1580s, a disapproving successor, Sixtus V, put an end to these unholy practices by erecting the current Vatican Library building smack in the middle of the courtyard. Thus the library, from its inception, has found itself in the middle of the conflict between the Vatican's warring religious and secular impulses.

The collection it houses was officially begun in 1451 by the human-ist Pope Nicholas V as a Latin and Greek library for "the common con-venience of the learned" and was a central part of the ambitious project of Christian humanism: to reform society by restoring the ancient learning that had been lost or dispersed during the Middle Ages. "The central conviction of the humanists . . . was the belief that reviving classical antiquity—both pagan and Christian—would bring a new golden age of peace and wealth, flourishing arts and letters, and vibrant religious faith," Anthony Grafton, a professor of history at Princeton, has written.

Fortuitously, the library was founded just two years before the fall of Constantinople to the Ottoman Turks so that many manuscripts that had survived the Dark Ages in the only part of the old Roman Empire that had not been sacked by the barbarians now escaped oblivion by finding their way to Rome.

With a thirst for learning that bordered on rapacity, the popes sent out representatives to buy, copy, or even steal manuscripts across Europe. "The first six books of the Annals of Tacitus, for instance, were stolen from the Monastery of Corvey, and, after various adventures, fell into the possession of Pope Leo with full knowledge of the circumstances," wrote the American bibliophile William Dana Orcutt. "Using the manuscript for copy, these Annals were printed in 1515, and the Pope graciously sent a copy of the printed book specially bound to the abbot of Corvey as a substitute for the original! 'In order that you may understand that the purloining has done far more good than harm,' Pope Leo wrote, 'we have granted you for your church a plenary indulgence.'"

When the popes conquered the city of Urbino, perhaps their most-coveted booty was the legendary library of the duke of Urbino, which included manuscripts illustrated by the great painters Ghirlandaio and Piero della Francesca.

Although the grandiose humanist project of transforming society through the diffusion of Latin and Greek culture may seem naïve today, the humanists and their patrons succeeded in one of the most important cultural salvage operations in history. Many of the works that are fixtures in the Western canon—Plato, Aristotle, Sophocles, and Tacitus—were lost to the West for centuries and rescued because of the bibliomania of the humanists and their patrons within the Church. The development of early modern science was made possible in part through the recovery and copying of key treatises of Greek mathematics, such as the work of the great Archimedes. Indeed, for centuries

Archimedes' work was known exclusively through a single Latin translation commissioned by the papacy in 1269 and jealously preserved in the
Vatican Library. The collection also contains a ninth-century copy of
Plautus that is the only source for twelve of his sixteen comedies. The
manuscript's arrival in Rome helped stimulate the revival of modern
comedy in the Renaissance.

Moreover, the Vatican collection not only preserves the texts of
antiquity but provides an extraordinary record of how they were used
over centuries as European society attempted to refashion itself. The
Vatican has the copy of Virgil that the Renaissance poet Petrarch read
and annotated. A fourth-century Roman history contains marginalia
from major writers of the ninth, fourteenth, and fifteenth centuries.
There is the copy of Euclid's treatise on optics that Piero della
Francesca is believed to have consulted in perfecting the art and science
of perspective.

"The whole tradition of scholarship, the millennial conversation
between texts and readers through which the West has tried to understand its own past, can be overheard in the margins of the Vatican's
manuscripts," Grafton wrote in a catalog on the Vatican collection for
an exhibition that he and Father Boyle organized at the Library of Congress in Washington in 1991.

Because of the collection's importance to world culture, the Library
of Congress offered to undertake an ambitious cataloging project in the
1920s and 1930s. The Vatican accepted, managing to catalog its three
million printed books and to establish a modern conservation laboratory. But to this day the only listings of tens of thousands of manuscripts
are handwritten notations in Latin, Italian, and French. Since the collection grew over the centuries by subsuming numerous other libraries—
of queens, princes, cardinals, and popes—the books are still listed as
part of these different collections, so that one needs to know a considerable amount about the history of the papacy and the library itself to be
able to find what one is looking for. It often takes scholars six months
just to figure out how to decipher the script and understand the arcane
logic of the Vatican's handwritten catalogs. Tens of thousands of items

remain uncataloged or noted in only the most skeletal form, their contents virtually unknown. The seemingly infinite uncharted stacks of the Vatican Library continue to stimulate a considerable amount of fantasy, rumor, and legend.

Many Jewish scholars suspect that thousands of lost Hebrew texts that were supposedly burned during the Inquisition lie secreted among the labyrinthine shelves of the Vatican Library. There is also a deep-seated belief that the Vatican possesses one of the rarest and most important collections of pornography in the world. Until the nineteenth century, most of the collection was kept under lock and key, causing a Spanish priest, Juan Andres, to refer to it as "a cemetery of books, not a library."

Given this long history of secrecy and diffidence toward the outside world, it was a surprise to many when Pope John Paul II chose Leonard Eugene Boyle to head the Vatican Library in May 1984. Boyle, who died in 2000, was a free spirit, every bit as at home with his secular colleagues as with fellow clergymen. Short and delicately built, with jet-black hair and pale skin, he generally had a playful, ironic glint in his eye and a sharp tongue that seemed always ready with a joke, spoken in his distinct Irish brogue. Born in Donegal, Ireland, in 1923, he was initially educated in Gaelic and always remained close to his working-class Irish roots, which gave him an extremely colorful, down-to-earth manner, an irreverent sense of humor, and a stubbornly independent attitude toward authority. People who knew him almost always refer to him as a leprechaun and, although it is a cliché, the dictionary definition—"a small mischievous sprite"—fits him quite well. He once told visitors that there was an ancient Roman badminton court on the grounds of San Clemente, even though the game did not exist in Roman times.

Boyle also, however, had impeccable academic credentials that made him a natural choice as prefect. He had distinguished himself as a medievalist at Oxford, where he specialized in Latin paleography, the art of deciphering ancient manuscripts. Between 1956 and 1984, he taught in Rome and Toronto, published numerous books and articles, and came to know the Vatican collections as well as anyone alive.

Indeed, Father Boyle had become something of a legend in the scholarly community. Perhaps because he was raised partly by an older brother who worked as a policeman, Boyle worked like a detective, treating every tiny detail of a text—the script and abbreviations used by the copyist, the materials and condition of the document—as a clue to its history. He reconstructed the often-adventurous lives of early books that sometimes traveled from one end of Europe to the other, surviving exile, war, and theological disputes, and traced their peregrinations, which reflected the lines of the intellectual and cultural life of medieval Europe. As Boyle began to teach paleography first in Rome and later in Toronto, he told his students that the handwriting of each manuscript has its own "distinct voice" and that they had to be patient enough to allow it to speak to them. The zeal, loving attention, distraction, or growing fatigue of a scribe revealed itself to Boyle's trained eye. In one case, as he traced an increasingly uncertain hand coming to an abrupt halt, Boyle concluded that the scribe had probably grown ill and died in midsentence.

From a careful examination of the famous *Beowulf* codex in the British Museum—the first known example of Old English literature—Boyle was able to establish that it was a copy of an already existing text, thus telling literary scholars that the original *Beowulf* predates the eleventh-century manuscript. Through his scholarly sleuthing, Boyle actually recovered the bones of Saint Cyrus, a ninth-century saint who was buried in San Clemente in Rome and whose remains were stolen by Napoleon's troops during the French occupation of Rome at the end of the eighteenth century. This discovery has made Boyle something of a hero among the Slavic nations, since Saint Cyrus brought Christianity and written language—hence the Cyrillic script—to much of Eastern Europe.

In a scholarly world that can sometimes be petty, narrow, and intensely competitive, Boyle was known as unfailingly generous and encouraging to others, believing that scholarly activity was a vain waste of time if knowledge was not shared as widely as possible.

In the pre-Boyle era, the library had the rather forbidding atmosphere of a strict English boarding school where scholars were afraid they might receive a paddling if they stepped out of line. The vice-prefect's desk was on an elevated dais at the front of the reading room so that he towered intimidatingly over the scholars as they worked, like a headmaster in study hall. One day in the early 1980s when two Italian scholars, conferring over a manuscript, failed to keep their voices down, the vice-prefect called for their library cards and publicly ripped them up, banishing the men from scholarship's Garden of Eden indefinitely. Women's legs and arms had to be well covered, and men were required to keep their jackets on, even in Rome's hot summer months. There were no females among the eighty or so library employees and women scholars felt decidedly unwelcome.

All this began to change with astonishing rapidity when Boyle became prefect on May 24, 1984. Boyle wanted to fulfill Nicholas V's mandate that the library was for "the common convenience of the learned."

"In all the years I had studied in the Vatican Library I had never felt welcome," Boyle told me as he sat in the garden of San Clemente during the summer of 1997, ill and thin as a reed, after the traumatic end of his time as prefect. He appeared to have aged ten years since I had seen him just a year before, and had lost fifteen or twenty pounds from his already slight frame. "I wanted scholars to feel that this was their home." Boyle moved the vice-prefect's desk to a more inconspicuous place in the back of the reading room, relaxed the dress code, hired women, and opened the library café. He doubled the hours of the library, which had been open only in the mornings. Moreover, one of his very first acts was to computerize the library. Because of the respect Boyle enjoyed in North America, GEAC, a Canadian computer company specializing in systems for libraries, offered to donate a mainframe worth about half a million dollars, and Boyle undertook to computerize the card catalog. He also drew up big plans to create a periodical room, to rewire the library so that scholars could use laptops in the reading room, and to install air-conditioning for the protection of the manuscripts as well as for the comfort of the readers.

The only problem was that Father Boyle's vision would cost money and funds were close to nonexistent. The Vatican pays the salaries of the eighty employees who fetch and stack books, write catalogs, work in the preservation and photo laboratories, and run the small publishing department. The library's only discretionary funds are the roughly $500,000 it receives each year from selling postcards and catalogs and charging scholars for photographs, photocopies, and microfilm. That tiny amount is all there is for acquiring books, periodicals, office supplies, and equipment as well as for capital improvements. While the free-spending popes of the Renaissance spared no expense on the library, the current Vatican, understandably, feels it needs to concentrate on its principal religious mandate. "There is no money for culture," lamented Cardinal Stickler, Boyle's predecessor.

Stickler was able to raise the money to build temperature-controlled stacks for the manuscript collection through a commercial arrangement with the German publishing company Belser, which acquired the rights to produce expensive facsimile editions of eighty Vatican manuscripts. The German Council of Bishops put up four million dollars to build the stacks, agreeing to be repaid from the proceeds of Belser's book sales. Although the deal allowed the library to build its stacks, it was a financial disaster for the German bishops. Sales did not go as planned, Belser went bankrupt and was sold to another company, and the bishops had to absorb a considerable loss, taking over and giving away the stock of unsold books. But Stickler emerged unscathed. "I had the German bishops do all the financial arrangements," Stickler explained to me, making the gesture of wiping his hands. With this shrewd, silent gesture I knew why Stickler was in his purple cardinal's robes in a vast, well-appointed apartment on St. Peter's Square with an elderly nun waiting on him while Father Boyle was living in his cell in San Clemente, wearing the same threadbare clothes I had seen him in years earlier.

Although Father Boyle took the fall, it was, in fact, Cardinal Stickler who introduced Elaine Iannessa to Father Boyle and encouraged him to undertake the business enterprise that would prove his undoing.

A native Californian who had sold television advertising and ran her own public relations firm in the Los Angeles area, Iannessa seemed an unlikely partner for one of the world's oldest and most august libraries.

Everything about Iannessa is larger than life: a statuesque woman in her early sixties with a large chest, a helmet of gray-blond hair, bright blue eyes, and a loud, strident voice, Iannessa looks like a soprano in a Wagnerian opera, even though she generally wears a sweat suit and jogging shoes. She speaks in long arias, moving from peals of laughter to thunderclaps of anger. Although she and her husband have no children, she lives on a ranch with two large houses in the San Bernardino Mountains a two-hour drive east of Los Angeles, next door to the equally large Roseanne Barr, the actress. Iannessa is a woman of great energy and optimism with an active imagination and a rather grandiose vision of the world. She originally projected the Vatican rights business to earn a hundred million in profits each year, and when we met in 1997, when her business was at a total standstill, she still insisted it was worth half a billion dollars.

While knowing next to nothing about the Vatican Museum or Library, she had an idea that she might be able to market dolls based on objects in the Vatican collections. Her mother, a devout Catholic, had been a donor to the Church and she herself had helped raise money for a local Catholic school. And through a Salesian father based in Los Angeles, Iannessa was able to set up some meetings at the Vatican in 1987. She first approached the museum, which rejected her proposal. "We said no. I could tell this was going to end badly," said one museum official. She got a much more positive reception from Cardinal Stickler, who, after leaving the job as prefect of the library, had been made cardinal librarian. "Cardinal Stickler told me that when he took over the Vatican Library he had a conversation with Pope Paul VI, who told him: 'Go out and find the money and I will absolve you of everything,'" Iannessa said.

Father Stickler told me that he recalled meeting Iannessa but doesn't remember much about their conversation. "I have several letters from this man who now claims to barely know me," Iannessa insisted indignantly. Indeed, when I visited her in California, she showed me several long letters from Cardinal Stickler that had a warm, personal tone. Most important, she had one, which is filed in court and bears the Vatican seal, in which Cardinal Stickler states "that ELAINE IANNESSA has my authorization to act as my agent to secure a Licensing contract with the

Biblioteca Apostolica Vaticana . . . for the reproduction of the treasures still available for this purpose." Stickler also signed a letter stating that Father Boyle was "the legal representative appointed by the Vatican and has the only legal right to sign contracts binding" the library.

In 1988, Iannessa met Father Boyle and began to develop a business plan. As she got to know the hidden riches of the library, her head began to whir with commercial possibilities: books, CD-ROMs, greeting cards, scarves, T-shirts, jewelry, religious vestments, commemorative coins, and collectible items based on the designs in the Vatican Library.

Father Boyle was both charmed by Iannessa's enthusiasm, warmth, and determination and appalled and amused by her grandiosity and her tendency to confuse and exaggerate the contents of the Vatican Library. "I will say one thing about Mrs. Iannessa; she had a great facility for getting names mixed up, particularly Bramante, Bernini," Father Boyle testified in one court deposition.

But if Iannessa was loose about historical and artistic matters, Boyle was equally careless about business details. Boyle did not want the new venture to be associated with any company that might cause negative publicity for the Vatican. According to Iannessa, along with rejecting CBS and J. C. Penney, he turned down an offer from American Express. "Father told me jokingly, 'They'd probably have a blimp floating over the Vatican, saying "Don't leave home without us,"'" she said. "I think they were afraid to get involved with a large corporation and I think they thought that because I am a woman they could control me. Nobody expected me to be the way I am."

Like many in the Vatican, Boyle felt more comfortable doing business on a personal level: in signing up with Iannessa, he relied on the word of a Los Angeles priest instead of performing a financial background search. Had the Vatican run a credit check on Iannessa, it would have learned that she and her husband had filed for bankruptcy in 1987 and that a bank had foreclosed on their home in Pasadena that same year, precisely the time when she first approached Cardinal Stickler. Boyle not only decided to work with Iannessa but came up with her company name, Cortile del Belvedere.

Boyle seems to have been in a hurry to get the money up front for his library renovations and impatient with the details of the business venture, which he apparently assumed that Iannessa would take care of. This disdain for cumbersome business procedures and diffidence toward large corporations was to prove costly. In 1988, Boyle and Iannessa narrowly escaped entering into a partnership with a man who turned out to be a professional con artist wanted for fraud. "Father was naïve and he was greedy—greedy for the Vatican Library," Iannessa said.

Having narrowly escaped one potential fiasco, Iannessa and Boyle walked into another, with a second investor, Leroy Carver Jr. Iannessa approached Carver because she knew his father, who had run a Rolls-Royce dealership in southern California. A real estate developer who had moved into the banking industry, the younger Carver acquired Escondito Savings and Loan in the early 1980s, renaming it Carver Savings and Loan. In 1989, when Carver and Iannessa first met, Carver's bank had failed and been taken over by the federal government in the savings and loan crisis, at a cost of some $60 million to the American taxpayers.

Nonetheless, Carver appears to have emerged from the failure with his personal fortune intact and was eager to invest in Iannessa's project. Both Boyle and Iannessa say they had a bad feeling about the slick young Carver, but it did not stop them from going forward. In July 1989, Carver flew to Rome and, almost on the spot, Boyle and Iannessa agreed to give him a 40 percent share of the profits of Cortile del Belvedere, in return for a nonrefundable payment to the library of $3 million and $1.5 million in operating capital. After a flurry of faxes between Rome and Los Angeles, Boyle and Iannessa signed an agreement drawn up exclusively by Carver's attorneys. Boyle did not even have them examined by a Vatican attorney. Boyle and Iannessa never waited to receive a copy of Carver's résumé, which they had requested. Had they bothered to look into Carver's past, they would have discovered that Carver's bank had been taken over by federal authorities. "Had this been revealed at the beginning before the contract was signed, Mr. Carver would never have been accepted as a funder," Iannessa stated in a later court filing.

"Elaine to me was a person who had a very good idea, but she was not sophisticated enough to make this thing bulletproof," said Suzelle Smith, the Los Angeles attorney who represented Boyle and the library in the Carver litigation. "The idea was to take the P.R. value of the Vatican Library and the incredibly beautiful things there and cash in on the commercial value. I continue to believe that the idea made all kinds of sense. But she was not a very sophisticated person when she involved herself in this deal, which was bigger than she was."

Within just a few months of their agreement, the relationship between Carver and Iannessa began to sour. Although he was theoretically only a passive investor, Carver took an active interest in the business, something Iannessa initially encouraged. She grew irritated, however, as he peppered her with suggestions, including putting Vatican Library merchandise on a TV shopping network—something she knew Father Boyle would not countenance. Carver insisted that Iannessa needed to move to Rome right away to get the business operating and became increasingly impatient at her delays. At a certain point, Carver and his family drove up to Iannessa's home in Lake Arrowhead and discovered that she had recently moved to much grander quarters—the Casa Felice compound where she still lives. Could it be, Carver wondered, that this expensive new ranch was purchased with some of the $3 million he had given to the library?

Communications between the two became increasingly acrimonious and Carver stopped making monthly payments into the operating account of Cortile del Belvedere. Iannessa, insisting that he had breached their contract, rescinded their agreement. In February 1990, just six months after their original agreement, Carver sued.

In the course of the litigation, Carver was able to confirm his suspicions about Iannessa's newfound wealth. Just a few days after Father Boyle received the $3 million from Carver, he made a wire transfer to Iannessa of $1.5 million. The very next day, Iannessa purchased her new home with one million in cash. Carver had been careful to put into the contract a clause that stated that "neither CDB [Cortile del Belvedere] nor Iannessa has received nor will receive any commission, brokerage fee, finder's fee or other compensation of any kind from the U.S. $3 million which is being provided to BAV [Biblioteca Apostolica Vaticana] as its nonrefundable licensing fee under paragraph 5 of the 1989 License Agreement."

The $1.5 million payment appeared to be in violation of the agreement, and in his lawsuit Carver's attorneys referred to it as an under-the-table "kickback." Iannessa and Boyle explained that he gave the money to her purely as a loan, to be paid back with interest. "There was nothing in the contract that says I couldn't take a loan," Iannessa said. "The man was in the savings and loan business. His attorneys wrote the contract. If he didn't want me to take a loan, he should have put it in the contract. I paid back the loan. It was a legal loan." (In 1994, Iannessa paid back the $1.5 million principal, but not the interest.)

While Boyle's conduct may seem hard to understand, it makes more sense when seen in the context of the culture of the Vatican. Boyle may have felt that the only way he could modernize the library was to take matters into his own hands, rather than go through the slow-moving Vatican bureaucracy. "There is a principle here: sometimes it is easier to ask forgiveness for something that is already done than to ask permission," said one retired Vatican official who spent his career handling contracts for the Church. Boyle was impatient to get the Cortile del Belvedere project off the ground and get the money to build his periodical room. He saw the apparent ease with which Carver wrote out a check for $3 million and assumed that Iannessa would have no trouble repaying the $1.5 million when the business began to take off as everyone seemed to feel sure it would.

Although the Vatican later accused Boyle of acting without authority, when Carver filed his lawsuit Boyle consulted with the secretary of state and was told to handle the matter himself.

Unfortunately for Boyle, the litigation process appeared to strengthen Carver's hand. Boyle handed over all his correspondence with Iannessa, some of which had an incriminating air to it. Father Boyle granted Iannessa a loan based on a single handwritten letter, which stated:

Dear Father,

This letter will serve as my "note" to you. . . . May I borrow back $1.5
million from your share. This will be used to pay back some of the monies I have
borrowed over the years to keep this project afloat. . . . I just don't think it is right
for me to leave with all the bills behind me. . . . I can't feel good about it. . . .

I will repay you immediately from the sale of the first license. Thank you
Father, I prefer to keep this between you and I, Father.

Iannessa misled Boyle by stating that the money was to be used to
repay debts and never told him that she intended to buy a house. This
deception and her insistence that he keep the matter secret gave the
whole business the appearance of wrongdoing. The fact, however, that
Boyle didn't know what the money was to be used for testifies to his good
faith, and if there was nothing improper in his granting her a loan, then
it shouldn't matter how she spent the money. Technically, the library
might have had a strong case, but Boyle and his lawyers worried about
how it would look in court.

"The whole thing was naïve enough to appear like collusion," Boyle
said when I asked him about the loan. "If I were an ordinary member of
a jury I might have thought it looked bad, too."

The litigation dragged on for six years. As a trial date drew near,
Boyle began to push for a settlement. At this point, however, the cost of
a settlement had gotten considerably higher. Carver's $3 million, had
he invested it elsewhere, might have doubled and he had accumulated six
years of legal bills, which he included in the cost of settlement. Unable
to come up with that kind of money, Boyle had to go to his superiors
within the Vatican, who were alarmed to discover that they were facing a
potential economic disaster. The office of economic affairs took over
the litigation, hired its own lawyers, and pushed for a settlement. In the
spring of 1996, the Holy See agreed to pay Carver $8.8 million, with
Iannessa agreeing to pay the Vatican back half of the amount.

Given the size of its loss and the amateurish way that Boyle handled
the Carver-Iannessa matter, it is understandable that the Vatican
insisted on taking control of the legal-economic side of the library.

Boyle was asked to step down as head of the library. He asked his superiors to set the date of his departure for May 24, 1997, the thirteenth anniversary of his arrival as prefect, so that his early retirement would not give rise to gossip and scandal. Then, on the eve of his departure, the Vatican, without informing Boyle, carried out its police blitz at the library and announced that Boyle was stepping down—casting a heavy cloud of suspicion over him.

But the violence with which the Vatican pulled the plug on Cortile del Belvedere may have been another major mistake. Despite the disaster of the $8.8 million settlement, the business that Boyle and Iannessa created began to bear fruit during the years of the litigation.

In 1992, Iannessa succeeded in selling book rights for half a million dollars to Turner Publishing, which produced a lavishly illustrated family Bible that sold very well. A company called Intensity Religious in Los Angeles paid nearly $1.5 million to produce religious garments, bronze figurines, and greeting cards. Ecco bought the rights to make scarves; 1928 started making Vatican Library costume jewelry. A Canadian company, Illuminated Films, paid $3 million for film and CD-ROM rights.

"They produced things of very good taste that are selling in Neiman Marcus, Marshall Field's, and the finest emporia in the United States," Boyle said. Boyle was, in fact, a considerable asset to the new business. "If somebody was looking for a certain kind of image, he knew exactly what would be right, because nobody knows that collection like Father Boyle," Iannessa said. "All of our licensees love him." Father Boyle could not prevent his puckish sense of humor from getting the better of him. He told one licensee that a silver hammer in the Vatican Library with which the pope breaks the seal of a door at St. Peter's in celebrating the Jubilee Year was actually used to tap the pope's body when he was on his sickbed to tell whether he was dead or alive. The licensee, who was Jewish and unfamiliar with Catholic ritual, went around repeating the story until Iannessa told him Father Boyle was only joking.

Boyle and Iannessa also set up shops in the Salone Sistina—a part of the Vatican palace near the Sistine Chapel that belongs to the library. At the time they were closed down, the two library sales counters had been on the way to earning $1 million, according to sales figures Iannessa showed me. The Vatican Library received 40 percent of all proceeds, with the manufacturers and Iannessa each receiving 30 percent. In the last six years, Iannessa has sold seventeen sublicenses for a total of more than $7 million. Half of the money has gone to the Vatican Library. When added to Carver's original $3 million, the Cortile del Belvedere venture looks like less of a bad deal. "The boutiques in the library were going like houses on fire, and they are only a small part of it," Boyle told me. There were good reasons to suppose that the Vatican Library would have more than made up the money it lost in the litigation settlement, particularly since Iannessa had agreed to pay half of the $8.8 million.

"The people at the Vatican started to talk about Boyle as a crook and an embezzler until I marched in with all the documents," Iannessa said. "Every penny we made can be accounted for and these various licenses paid for the rewiring of the library, the new registration desk, the air-conditioning system, the Barberini periodical room," Iannessa said.

By closing up the Cortile del Belvedere selling booths and denying access to its sublicensees, the Vatican may have killed the goose that laid the golden egg—as well as set off a second round of litigation that could cost millions more. While the Vatican Museums have had difficulty creating similar licensing arrangements, the library, which no one imagined had much commercial potential, may in fact, because of its hundreds of thousands of drawings and designs imbedded within its manuscripts, be something of a gold mine in terms of the selling of images. "The museum has a souvenir industry; we turned it into a licensing industry," Iannessa said. "I sold a fantasy to everybody because there was something there. Now they want to take it over."

The Vatican took the position that Iannessa's contracts are invalid since Boyle had no right to make binding agreements for the library. "If I tried to sell you the dome of St. Peter's, would you buy it?" Monsignor Francesco Salerno, a legal expert with the Vatican's office of economic affairs, asked me when I called. Salerno was given principal responsibility for reorganizing the library's business and defenestrating Father Boyle, and he was rewarded with a promotion to bishop for his efforts.

"This litigation has nothing to do with the Vatican Library. A certain person made a series of unauthorized contracts, but they are not binding on the Vatican Library," he said angrily. "If you knew Vatican law you would know that the books in the library belong to the pope and the Holy Father alone. No one else has the right to dispose of them." Salerno refused, however, to discuss the case in detail or to meet with me. "I know you journalists, I know you Americans. You're not interested in the truth, you're just interested in throwing mud at the Church," he said with vehemence.

"That's going to be a hard sell, to say that Father Boyle didn't have the authority," said Suzelle Smith. "After all, [Boyle] organized a show with the Library of Congress and nobody said he shouldn't do that. The stores were operating right down the corridor from the Vatican Museum." (Smith had her own reasons for taking this position: the Vatican had refused to pay Smith's firm, Howarth & Smith, the $1.3 million in legal bills it racked up fighting the Carver litigation.)

One of the things that made the dispute difficult to resolve is that in 1994 Father Boyle, without getting any more money from Iannessa, extended her contract for another thirty years, meaning that she would have control of the Vatican Library until the year 2048. At the time, the business appeared to be taking off, no settlement money had been paid, and so extending the contract seemed to him a good deal for all concerned. "I own the Vatican Library! And there's nothing they can do about it," Iannessa said. "As long as Father Boyle was there, I would never have done anything against them, but now I am going to sue them for fraud"—which she subsequently did. And despite Monsignor Salerno's posturing, the Vatican eventually settled its suit with Iannessa, at further expense to the Church.

The way in which the Vatican treated Father Boyle and its efforts to discredit him were part of a legal strategy, to make him appear like a rogue priest, equivalent to a con man offering to sell the dome of St. Peter's, so that the Holy See could walk away from the contracts he had signed. Indeed, at the time Boyle died of heart troubles in 2000, the Holy See had brought charges against him in Vatican court, although there is no evidence that, for all his mistakes, he ever misappropriated any money for himself.

It is difficult now to see Father Boyle's dismissal as part of the plot to prevent his voting at the next papal conclave, but papal politics may have influenced the way he was treated. In his tenure as prefect, Boyle did little to cultivate powerful friends and made numerous enemies in the Vatican hierarchy. He had, for example, flatly refused a request from the Vatican Secretariat of State that he ban from the library a scholar who had published a book that embarrassed the Holy See. At another point, he had resisted (unsuccessfully this time) when the pope gave away a precious Aztec manuscript from the library's collection as a gift to the president of Mexico. Could this lack of deference to authority explain his treatment? I asked him. Hesitant between his abiding loyalty to the Church and a desire to defend his good name, Boyle replied cryptically: "You are free to draw whatever conclusions you like."

Lost in all the controversy surrounding his departure is the fact that Boyle succeeded, to a remarkable degree, in fulfilling his grand vision for the library. Scholars in the newly wired, air-conditioned reading room tap along quietly at their laptop computers. His project to computerize the library's three million printed books is complete. Far more than a mere computer card catalog, the Vatican system has a powerful search engine that is a genuine research tool. For example, one scholar explained that she was able to reassemble the library of an important seventeenth-century artist on the basis of a handwritten inventory of books. Because there was no standard way of listing titles, names, or spellings in the seventeenth century, it would have been close to impossible to track down the books in a paper card catalog. But even with one or two accurate words from the title and part of the author's name, she was able to identify most of the books in a couple of weeks at the Vatican. Moreover, through Boyle's generosity and imagination, the Vatican agreed to use its mainframe computer to link the catalogs of most of the major scholarly libraries in Rome, forming a consortium called URBS. Now a scholar at any one of these libraries can identify the books he or she needs throughout the city from one computer terminal. In effect, he has modernized scholarship not just at the Vatican but in the city of Rome as a whole.

The last piece of unfinished business, however, remains the ambitious IBM project, which was on hold, in part because of the Iannessa litigation, in part for economic reasons. Boyle had initiated the joint venture with IBM in 1994 as a pilot project. The company digitized some twenty thousand images at high resolution, creating an initial database. But the creation of such high-quality images is a slow and expensive process. It takes between one and two minutes to scan a single page and it took two years of work to digitize the twenty thousand images. And these represent the contents of about 150 of the 150,000 manuscripts in the library. At this rate, it would take some two hundred years to complete the project. Nor have IBM and the library figured out how the project would be financed. Selling other libraries the rights to use the images could run afoul of rights that Iannessa has already sold. "[The Vatican] has already taken in about seven million dollars from my licenses," she said. "They think you can just take people's money, spend it, and then rip up the contracts and sell new licenses. That's not the way the world works."

But the pilot project of twenty thousand images has created a tantalizing glimpse of what the future may hold. A scholar can call up a manuscript and pore over it page by page, as in the library, and with the magnification powers of the computer, in some cases seeing things that might escape the naked eye. In 1996, Boyle and IBM put together an exhibition that showed the extraordinary potential of the new medium for enhancing the value of the Vatican Library. They digitized a series of illuminated musical manuscripts and you could listen to the music as you followed the notes on the page.

Although a pioneer of the digital library, Boyle remained, even after his downfall, confident that digitization would enhance rather than diminish the status of actual books and libraries. He noted the way in which the IBM technicians were seduced and humbled by their contact with the Vatican's extraordinary manuscripts. Jorge Luis Borges tells the story of a barbarian who, while laying siege to Ravenna during the collapse of the Roman Empire, sees the enormous beauty and richness of its civilization, suddenly switches sides, and begins to defend the city from destruction. Boyle seemed to feel the same thing would happen with the computer and the Vatican Library. When he was negotiating with an IBM executive about financing the digitization, the man asked him, "What are you prepared to put up?" Father Boyle recalled. "And I said, 'I'm not putting up anything. I've got 150,000 manuscripts. That's bigger than IBM any day.'"

When I last saw Boyle in the fall of 1998, he had just returned from the hospital after a bad case of bronchitis that had been nagging at him since the time of his resignation. He looked even smaller and more fragile than he had the previous summer. Nonetheless, he saw his own private misfortune within a bigger picture about which he remained optimistic. "The library is 550 years old and it will survive this, too," Boyle said. While he himself was defeated, the vision he traced for the library has now been embraced by many in the Vatican who initially resisted it. A number of those who were skeptical about digitization were now impatient to get rid of Iannessa so they could proceed with IBM. "In using electronic media, we are just being our age, just as Nicholas V was, carrying on the tradition of the library as a library of the human spirit," Boyle said.

Are We Losing Our Memory? or
The Museum of Obsolete Technology

I N A TEMPERATURE-CONTROLLED laboratory in the bowels of the vast new National Archives building outside Washington—nearly two million square feet of futuristic steel and glass construction—an engineer cranks up an old Thomas A. Edison phonograph. A cylindrical disc begins to turn and from its large wooden horn we suddenly hear the scratchy oompah-pah of a marching band striking up a tune at a Knights of Columbus parade in July of 1902.

Nearby sits an ancestor of the modern reel-to-reel tape recorder; it's the very machine that recorded President Harry Truman's famous whistle-stop speeches as he traveled the country by train during his legendary come-from-behind victory in the election of 1948. Instead of capturing sound on magnetic tape, the device stored its data on coils of thin steel wire as fine as fishline. Now some of the wire has rusted, and it occasionally snaps when it is played back through the machine.

This laboratory, in the Department of Special Media Preservation, is a kind of museum of obsolete technology where Archives technicians try to tease information out of modern media that have long vanished from circulation. But the laboratory is more than a curious rag-and-bone shop of technologies past; in many ways, it offers a cautionary vision of the future. The problem of technological obsolescence—of fading words and images locked in odd-looking, out-of-date gizmos—is an even bigger problem for the computer age than for the new media produced in the first half of the twentieth century.

One of the great ironies of the information age is that, while the late twentieth century will undoubtedly have recorded more data than any other period in history, it will also almost certainly have lost more information than any previous era. A study done in 1996 by the Archives concluded that, at current staff levels, it would take approximately 120 years to transfer the backlog of nontextual material (photographs, videos, film, audiotapes, and microfilm) to a more stable format. "And in quite a few cases, we're talking about media that are expected to last about twenty years," said Charles Mayn, the head of the laboratory. Decisions about what to keep and what to discard will be made by default, as large portions will simply deteriorate beyond the point of viability.

Mayn is a tall, thin man with gray hair, a soft-spoken, gentle manner, and the neat, understated, conservative dress of a computer engineer of the 1950s—the time of his youth. A self-described "science weenie," he is more comfortable fiddling with the interior of a machine than talking about himself. He plays down his own considerable ingenuity in rebuilding or reinventing many of these machines, rigging up pieces of the original items with modern parts in order to get them to play back intelligible sounds and images. His particular laboratory is dedicated to "dynamic media"—things with moving parts such as audio and video players. In his spare time, Mayn has been known to scour junk shops and yard sales in the Washington area, looking for old castaway Dictabelts or movie projectors that have been consigned to the dustbin of history.

A short distance down the laboratory workbench from the Edison phonograph are some eighteen-inch glass discs, precursors of the long-playing vinyl record—rapidly becoming a relic itself. The U.S. army used the disks to record enemy radio broadcasts throughout World War II. They play on a machine called the Memovox, which has a turntable that changes speed as the record plays, slowing down to compensate for the quicker rotation of the disc as the stylus approaches the center, so that the needle always moves at a constant speed in relation to the groove in which it sits. It was an ingenious invention, but it didn't catch on, perhaps because it required rather complex internal machinery. A glass disc—marked "Germany, October 24, 1941, 11:55 p.m."—lies shattered on its turntable. "Luckily, the glass generally breaks in fairly clean pieces so we are often able to put them back together," Mayn explained. The Archives possesses some seventy thousand of these foot-and-a-half military recordings, each of which has a playing time of about two hours. It would take a researcher who worked without interruption for eight hours a day approximately forty-eight years to listen to this collection in its entirety. "A lot of them may contain a lot of nothing, airwave noise, shortwave whistles, but you may have to listen to the whole thing to figure that out," Mayn said.

On the wall are the internal organs of a film projector from the 1930s; the old heads have been mounted to play together with modern reels. "Twenty-eight different kinds of movie sound-tracking systems were devised during the 1930s and 1940s, trying to improve the quality of sound tracks," Mayn explained. "Most of them are unique and incompatible." This particular one used something called "push-pull" technology, in which the sound signal was split onto two different tracks. The technology was meant to cancel out noise distortion, but the two tracks must play in near-perfect synchrony. "If it is played back properly, it is better than a standard optical track, but if it is played back even a little bit improperly, it is far, far worse," Mayn said. In the mid-1980s at a theater in downtown Washington, he was able to actually use this reconfigured projector to show several reels of push-pull film containing the trial of top Nazi leaders at Nuremberg. And the lab has transferred some eighteen hundred reels of push-pull tape onto new negatives.

Potentially, the computer age appears to offer the historian's Holy Grail of infinite memory and of instant, permanent access to virtually limitless amounts of information. But as the pace of technological change increases, so does the speed at which each new generation of equipment supplants the last. "Right now, the half-life of most computer technology is between three and five years," said Steve Puglia, a preservation and imaging specialist whose laboratory is just down the hall from Mayn's. In the 1980s, the Archives stored 250,000 documents and images onto optical discs—the cutting edge of new technology at the time. "I'm not sure we can play them," said Puglia, explaining that they depend on computer software and hardware that is no longer on the market.

In fact, there appears to be a direct relationship between the newness of technology and its fragility. A librarian at Yale University, Paul Conway, has created a graph going back to ancient Mesopotamia that shows that while the quantity of information being saved has increased exponentially, the durability of media has decreased almost as dramatically. The clay tablets that record the laws of ancient Sumer are still on display in museums around the world. Many medieval illuminated manuscripts written on animal parchment still look as if they were painted and copied yesterday. Paper correspondence from the Renaissance is faded but still in good condition while books printed on modern acidic paper are already turning to dust. Black-and-white photographs may last a couple of centuries, while most color photographs become unstable within thirty or forty years. Videotapes deteriorate much more quickly than does traditional movie film—generally lasting about twenty years. And the latest generation of digital storage tape is considered to be safe for about ten years, after which it should be copied to avoid loss of data.

Digital technology—based on incredibly precise mathematical coding—either works perfectly or doesn't work at all. "If you go beyond the limits of the error rate, the screen goes black and the audio goes to nothing," Mayn said, "and up to that point, you don't realize there are any errors. Analogue technology"—used on vinyl records or electromagnetic tapes—"deteriorates more gracefully. The old wax cylinders of the original Edison phonograph sound faded and scratchy, but they are still audible." Mayn picked up some tiny plastic digital audiotapes that fit neatly in the palm of his hands. "People love these things because they are so small, compact, and lightweight and store tons of data, but as they put larger and larger amounts of data on smaller and smaller spaces, the technology gets more precise, more complex, and more fragile." He bends the little data tape in his hand. "We have a lot of these from the late 1980s and even the mid-1990s that can't be played at all."

The National Archives and Records Agency (NARA) was created during the 1930s on the optimistic premise that the government could keep all of its most vital records indefinitely, acting as our nation's collective memory. Now, as it drowns in data and chokes on paper, the agency is facing the stark realization that it may not be able to preserve what it has already has, let alone keep up with the seemingly limitless flow of information coming its way.

The numbers are so huge as to be almost comical. The Archives is currently custodian to 4 billion pieces of paper, 9.4 million photographs, 338,029 films and videos, 2,648,918 maps and charts, nearly 3 million architectural and engineering plans, and more than 9 million aerial photographs. Storage consumes nearly half its budget so, ironically, the more information it keeps the less money it has to spend on making it available to the public. Because other government agencies are generally not required to hand over their records for permanent storage for some thirty years, the Archives is only just beginning to grapple with the extraordinary explosion of information over the last generation.

Space has been a problem at the National Archives from before it opened on November 8, 1935, in a grand neoclassical structure on Pennsylvania Avenue, down the street from the White House. That building was supposed to have a handsome internal courtyard, but the nation's first archivist had the space filled in for more stacks. These, too, quickly proved inadequate, so the high-ceilinged floors were chopped in half, creating twenty-one short floors of stacks. An archivist much over six feet tall would risk a concussion navigating this rabbit warren of seemingly identical corridors and shelves. Here you can see the information explosion in tangible terms. Six rows of shelves on a single floor hold all of the documents generated by the U.S. Supreme

Court in its first 140 years of life, while it takes the rest of the floor, the equivalent of about half a city block, to house the papers from the last sixty years. One term of the Supreme Court now generates as much paper as forty years did in the early nineteenth century.

With nowhere left to store all the paper, the Archives built new headquarters in College Park, Maryland, which opened in 1994. Although the third-largest government building and about half the size of the Pentagon, Archives II is already approaching its storage capacity. Despite predictions some twenty years ago about the paperless office, most government agencies are still printing out their computer files and producing more paper than ever. Each year, on average, the Archives receives about 1.5 million cubic feet of new records, of which about one-third are kept for storage. At this rate, the space for paper records at Archives II is expected to run out by 2003—less than ten years after its opening.

In theory, computer technology should be more helpful with the storage of textual documents than with the audio and video records of Mayn's dynamic media lab. But so far, it has only compounded the problem. In 1989, a public interest group trying to get information about the Iran-contra scandal successfully sued the White House to prevent it from destroying any electronic records. The result is that all federal agencies must now preserve all their computer files and electronic mail. Because government offices use different kinds of computers, software programs, and formats, just recovering this material has proved to be a logistical nightmare. It took the National Archives two and a half years (and its entire electronic records staff) just to make a secure copy of all the electronic records of the Reagan White House. And it may take years more to make most of them intelligible. "They are gibberish as they currently stand," said Fynette Eaton, who worked at the Archives' Center of Electronic Records before moving over to the Smithsonian Institution.

The beauty of digital technology is that it reduces everything to a series of zeroes and ones—a simple, seemingly universal mathematical language—but unless one has the software that gives meaning to those zeroes and ones, the data is meaningless. The problem of deciphering Egyptian hieroglyphs may look like child's play compared with recovering all the information on the hundreds of major software programs that have been discarded during the astonishing transformations of the computer revolution.

The losses from the first decades of the digital age are likely to be considerable. The federal government, with its multitude of departments, agencies, and offices, is a dense thicket of incompatible computer languages and formats—many of them old and obsolete. Many of the records of the National Military Command Center are stored in a database management system (known as NIPS) that IBM no longer supports and that the National Archives has difficulty translating into readable form. The Agent Orange Task Force has been unable to use herbicide records written in the NIPS format.

For several years a disturbing rumor has circulated that the data from the United States Census of 1960 has been lost. According to the story, the information lies locked on obsolete thirty-six-year-old computer tapes that can no longer be read by today's machines. The Archives continues to reassure the public that the material has been safely copied to more modern media, but because census data must be kept private until seventy-two years after its collection, the rumor will probably persist until independent researchers can view the material for themselves in the year 2032. Meanwhile, later census surveys are still at risk. "Bureau of Census files prior to 1989 threaten to eclipse the NIPS problem," the Archives reported to Congress a few years ago. "The Bureau reported to us . . . that they have over 4,000 reels of tape, containing permanently valuable data, which are difficult, if not impossible to use because they are in CENIO (Census Input/Output) format or because the files have been compressed on an ad hoc basis." Each computer tape can store seventy-five thousand pages of information so that, if the data cannot be recovered, the Census Bureau might lose up to 300 million pages of data.

Because of the problems posed by reconstructing obsolete hardware and software, the Archives issued an order that government agencies were free to print out their e-mail onto paper for permanent storage. The Archives may be faced either with mountains of computer data it cannot interpret or an avalanche of paper of unprecedented volume. But Scott Armstrong, a journalist who helped bring the initial White House e-mail suit, has protested the Archives' directive. "It makes no sense," said Armstrong. "If your basement were flooded, the first thing you would try to do is turn off the flow of water, and then start worrying about mopping up. The Archives are doing the exact opposite. They are already drowning in paper, but they are still telling people to print out their records onto paper. If the government had dedicated the energy it has spent fighting the e-mail lawsuits into modernizing its record-keeping operations, it would have gone a long way to solving its problems."

Although "the era of big government is over," as President Clinton declared, the era of big government data banks is only just beginning. Ken Thibideau, the head of the Electronic Records Division at the Archives, insisted that Armstrong and others underestimate the immense technological difficulties in trying to recover e-mail from thousands of different government computers. Between 1989 and 1996, the Electronic Records Division took in twenty-five thousand new records. The e-mail from the Reagan-Bush White House suddenly buried it in an avalanche of 200,000 electronic files, just as the State Department prepared to hand over 1,250,000 electronically stored diplomatic cables. And this represents just the tip of the iceberg—the period from 1972 until 1975. Since then, the State Department has been averaging about a million messages a year. Meanwhile, in recent years, the White House has been pumping out an average of six million electronic files a year.

These expected additions could well lead to a crash of the Archives' computer system. "We designed a new system to handle maybe ten thousand messages a year. You cannot scale up our system to deal with a million messages a year," Thibideau said. His office ran an experiment, trying to copy one single storage tape of the Clinton e-mail. The Archives' computer churned and ground for some fifty hours but failed to copy the entire tape. "We can normally copy a whole tape with up to 200 megabytes in about ten or fifteen minutes," Thibideau explained. The reason the computer had so much trouble with the White House tape is that e-mail systems are not designed with long-term storage in mind. Given the state of current technology, the computer insisted on treating each individual e-mail message as a single file that had to be opened and closed in order to be copied from one tape to another. It takes far longer to copy a hundred thousand one-page messages than to copy a thousand one-hundred-page messages even though they may use up the same amount of space on the tape.

Thibodeau said the Electronic Records Division was looking at sophisticated storage devices coming onto the market, but these present problems of their own. "There's a new kind of tape that can hold two hundred times the volume as the kind of data tapes we are using, in the same plastic cartridge we use," Thibideau said. "So it would be great in terms of space. But as we talk to people who use this technology, we have not talked to anyone who has successfully taken the tape out of the silo and read it on a different machine." The extreme precision and miniaturization of the new technology is such that each machine produces tapes that are unintentionally customized to fit the particular alignment of the laser beams that encode and read information. It's as if you were stamping a record with grooves that were thousands of times smaller than on an LP and using a stylus that needed to land just right in order to play back the record. "When you get to these highly dense media, your tolerance for error is extremely small," said Thibideau. "A slight misalignment of the head is sufficient to guarantee that you will never read the tape other than on a machine that has the same misalignment. And if you are in the archive business, if we can't take a tape from another system and read it on ours, then it's no good."

Ironically, the downsizing of government has actually magnified the information crisis. "When a government agency downsizes, usually the first thing they do is get rid of the record keepers and clean out the storage closet," Mayn said. "We suddenly get a call telling us to pick up a trailer-sized truckload of records." When the Pentagon closed

Northrop Air Force Base, it decided to turn over its huge motion picture storage warehouse to the Archives, doubling in a single stroke the Archives' video holdings. At the same time, the Archives is having to do more with fewer resources. Factoring in for inflation, the budget of the Electronic Records Division has fallen by about 15 percent and its personnel have been cut by 10 percent during a period when the volume of new data has increased tenfold. The staff of Mayn's dynamic media laboratory has been cut from sixteen to nine in the last decade. Everyone seems to want to keep everything, but nobody wants to pay to keep it.

The problem, in Mayn's view, is that nobody inside or outside government is making the tough decisions about what to keep and what to discard. "I'm not a historian, but personally I have my doubts about some of the stuff we are trying to keep," Mayn said. "Do we really need hundreds of different films on the workings of the M1 tank?" he asked. "I can see keeping a few as a sample, but I'm not sure we need the entire collection." At the height of the Vietnam War, the Pentagon routinely sent hundreds of men with cameras out into the jungles and the battlefields to film the combat. "Each of these people was told to shoot hundreds or thousands of feet of film," Mayn said. While much of this film is of genuine historical interest, the total quantity would take several lifetimes for a technician to copy or for a researcher to study. Because much of this material will eventually deteriorate beyond the point of intelligibility, Mayn believes that the choice of what to keep will be made by default. "We will keep those things that researchers happen to have requested and that get copied onto new media," he said.

The sorting out of the information explosion may resemble the process that determined the books we now possess from antiquity. The works of authors such as Homer and Virgil survived intact because of their enduring popularity and the multiple copies that were made at different times. But many of the works we regard as fixtures of our culture (including Plato) were lost for centuries and are known to us only because of a copy or two that turned up in medieval monasteries or in the collections of Arab scholars. Some works of undoubted greatness did not survive at all: Sophocles is known to have written some 120 plays, of which we possess only nine.

There is not likely to be a modern Sophocles in the databases of the Department of Agriculture or the Census Bureau. The greater risk, instead, is of such a vast accumulation of records that the job of distinguishing the essential from the ephemeral becomes more and more difficult. The Archives of the future may resemble the "Library of Babel" that Jorge Luis Borges imagined nearly sixty years ago, an infinite library that contained every conceivable book in the universe. There were books that consisted purely of a repetition of a single letter of the alphabet and others in which all the pages except one were blank. The discovery of an intelligible sentence was cause for jubilation. Eventually, after many centuries, the librarians of Babel were driven to despair in their unfulfilled quest for a coherent, complete book.

Writing and the Creation of the Past

1. WHAT IS THE PAST?

Some might argue that, in a strict sense, it doesn't exist. The past is only the memory or residue of things that now exist in the present moment, a mental construction that—cleaned up or embellished—often serves the needs of the current moment instead of corresponding to any historic "truth." "History is bunk," Henry Ford said, expressing a common view in the United States, which thinks of itself as a new, future-oriented society of self-made people and has a pragmatic suspicion of excessive preoccupation with the past. And yet, perhaps because we live in a time of such rapid change, history holds an extraordinary power to stir up emotions. Native Americans and white supremacists fight over the bones of a frozen corpse from ten thousand years ago, each believing it to be their rightful ancestor. The construction of a Wall Street skyscraper is abandoned when workers uncover a graveyard of Colonial-era African slaves. American school boards come to blows over the depiction of the nation's Founding Fathers, women, and minorities in history textbooks. Rarely do debates evoke so much passion as those over, say, the nature of the Vichy government in France or the wartime conduct of former Austrian leader Kurt Waldheim. The citizens of the former Yugoslavia have given recent testimony to their willingness to kill and die to avenge defeats in battles fought in the fourteenth century and have used the systematic erasing of historical memory—destroying libraries, archives, and monuments—as a means of regaining control over Bosnia.

The dream of Islamic fundamentalism—however fictive—is to return the Muslim world to the first community of believers at the time of the Prophet Mohammed and of the first four caliphs. Societies that fail to deal adequately with their past seem, like people, to become ill. The crucial importance of history is evident in a country like Russia. Why has such a powerful country, with a highly educated population and vast natural resources, been in a prolonged state of paralysis, while other former Communist states such as Poland, Hungary, and the Czech Republic have done so much better? The answer, in part, lies in their very different histories. Why did Communism in China, which set about to wipe the slate of history clean and create an entirely new society, end up reproducing so many features of the centralized bureaucracy of the imperial dynasties it wanted to dismantle? For something that doesn't exist, the past is extremely powerful. As William Faulkner wrote: "The past isn't dead. It isn't even past."

However, since the past is also a mental and social construction, it too has a history, which varies from one culture to another and has changed over time. I have tried in this book to describe various aspects of our relationship with the past as well as the ways in which it is shifting under the pressures of the profound technological changes under way in the world. Perhaps the biggest common thread in these chapters is the profound effect that writing and other information technology have had on the recording of history and our relationship with the past.

2. FROM ORAL CULTURE TO WRITTEN CULTURE

Writing is a relatively recent invention of human history, appearing just five thousand years ago and ushering in the first great information revolution. Despite the importance of writing, oral culture remained the dominant form of communication until the last two centuries, when the Industrial Revolution made global mass literacy possible. Even today, only a small fraction of the approximately sixty-five hundred languages spoken around the world are written down, and about a third of the world's population is still nonliterate. But by now, most traditional cultures live as minorities within larger, literate societies and our particular time in history will probably witness the disappearance of the last few pockets of "purely" oral societies in the world.

For many years, there was a tendency in Western scholarship to dismiss all oral testimony as nothing but old wives' tales. But recent archeological work has begun to reevaluate the foundation myths of many societies. Recent excavations on the Capitoline Hill in Rome appear to confirm important elements of the traditional tales of the city's founding in the eighth century B.C. And DNA research supports the claim of a small population of black South Africans whose oral tradition insists that they came from Israel centuries ago, by showing a strong genetic similarity between them and modern-day Jews.

In one sense, traditional societies are more burdened by the past. Much of their mental energy—as in Kitawa (chapter 6)—must be taken up by learning and memorizing the traditions, oral poetry, and incantations of their ancestors. But oral cultures are often wrongly thought to be entirely tradition-bound and unchanging. The fact that nothing is written down actually allows them a certain freedom from tradition that written cultures lack. British colonial officials dutifully recorded that in the foundation myth of a certain region of Africa the kingdom's founder had seven sons, which corresponded to the seven territories of the land. When the British came back sixty years later, they were surprised to learn that the local people now insisted that the mythic founder of their kingdom had had five rather than seven sons. When the British pulled out the written document to prove their point, the locals insisted that it was simply mistaken. In the intervening decades, the political situation had changed and the area was now divided into five and not seven territories. The oral tradition responded by changing the myth, while nonetheless maintaining (and no doubt believing) that it was immutable and unchanging.

Even though many oral cultures practice ancestor cults, in many ways they are more present-minded than written cultures. It is interesting to note that the people of Kitawa—like those of many other oral societies—have no past tense in their language. This, of course, does not mean that they have no sense of the past: their language has other ways of indicating the past and the distant past. But in a world in which there is no means of recording dates or events, a precise accounting of past centuries becomes difficult if not impossible. People whom Giancarlo Scoditti interviewed would, for example, refer to founders of their clan as their grandfather or grandmother, as if these people had lived relatively recently. For oral societies, the distant past is necessarily an indistinct continuum. Many American Indian tribes dispute the notion that their ancestors migrated from Asia across the Bering Strait, insisting their people have lived in their current homeland since time immemorial. Many Malagasy believe that their forebears have always lived in Madagascar even though archeological data suggests that they began settling the island less than two thousand years ago.

3. THE TECHNOLOGY OF WRITING

History as we understand it begins with writing. The act of writing in some sense separates us from the past by making it an object outside ourselves, a tablet carved in stone or a carefully painted hieroglyph.

Writing is a technology that is invented to serve very specific needs that arose in a particular moment of history. Whether in the Middle East, China, or the Indus Valley, writing was the product of the first large-scale agricultural societies. The agricultural surplus allowed the creation of trading networks, requiring communication and record keeping between people at a distance of space and time. And, not surprisingly, many of the first known examples of writing document commercial transactions in which people were exchanging wheat and barley for heads of sheep and cattle. Writing permitted a centralized state government to control a vast, unified territory. It is perhaps no accident that one of the earliest surviving Egyptian hieroglyphic texts is the famous Narmer Palette, which celebrates the conquests of King Narmer, who is thought to have unified northern and southern Egypt.

Scribes enjoyed special prestige in ancient Egypt and, even then, the Egyptians understood that control of the dominant media meant political power. One ancient Egyptian invocation states: "Thou shalt be scribe there and keep in order those who may perform deeds of rebellion . . . against me." Indeed, the anthropologist Claude Lévi-Strauss wrote in *Tristes Tropiques* that writing had primarily served as a device for the enslavement and control of mankind. After the Normans conquered England in 1066, among the first things they did to consolidate their rule was to commission a vast written census of every man, woman, and piece of livestock. The inhabitants understood the power that this document gave the new rulers, labeling it the *Domesday Book.*

Writing, however, also was seen by many of the societies that first adopted it as having magical properties—the ability to stop time and preserve things for eternity. The Egyptians were so convinced of the power of their hieroglyphs that to write something was actually to give it life. Thus, when they drew the symbol of the serpent, they generally left it with a gap in the middle of its back, as if the snake, complete, would jump off the wall and bite someone. (The Jewish tradition of leaving one letter of the name of God blank testifies to a similar belief in the power of the written word.)

Although writing has been used as a device of social and political control, widespread literacy also created a critical attitude toward tradition that is recognizably modern. It is far easier to scrutinize and question a written text than one recited in a rhapsodic near-trance as the Greeks appear to have done during performances of Homer's epics. "The spread of writing checked the growth of myth and made the Greeks sceptical of their gods," Harold Innis, the Canadian economic historian (who was the mentor of Marshall McLuhan), has written. "Hecataeus of Miletus could say, 'I write as I deem true, for the traditions of the Greeks seem to me manifold and laughable,' and Xenophanes that 'if horses or oxen had hands and could draw or make statues, horses would represent forms of the gods like horses, oxen like oxen.'" Thucydides quotes Pericles as saying: "We do not need the praises of a Homer, or of anyone else whose words may delight us for the moment but whose estimation of facts will fall short of what is really true."

The invention of the alphabet—made by the Phoenicians and refined by the Greeks—was almost as revolutionary as that of writing itself. It allowed the extraordinary variety of human speech to be represented in a phonetic code of little more than twenty symbols that even a small child could learn in just a few weeks. The extreme ease of the Greek alphabet is partly why Greek became the common language of so much of the Mediterranean world from Turkey and Syria in the east to Spain and North Africa in the west. The ancient library of Alexandria was, in many ways, the ultimate expression of this extraordinary expansion of Hellenistic literary production. Alexandria fused two of the great civilizations of the ancient world and joined the software of the Greek alphabet and the hardware of papyrus. It thus was hardly an accident that the largest library of antiquity, with its 490,000 books, was a Greek library located in Egypt.

The availability of a vast number of texts in one place helped to create a bookish culture that had a distinctly modern cast to it. Alexandrians already thought of earlier Greek authors—Homer, Hesiod, Herodotus, and Aeschylus—as ancient. They were interested not just in creating new works of literature but in studying and preserving the past, engaging in the systematic pursuit of grammar, bibliography, and philology. In order to establish the authenticity of texts, these scholars engaged in intense philological analysis, producing studies such as "Words Supposed to Be Unknown to the Ancients," one of the many works in the library of which we have a title but no text. The library culture of the Alexandrians created a strong sense of the past, accompanied by a sense of their own "lateness" and modernity.

The ancient library—and the multiplication of texts—not only created a highly self-conscious literary culture but was also important to the scientific research of Alexandria. Scholars such as the great Archimedes traveled to Alexandria to consult the library. The scientific revolution of Alexandria was not merely the result of brilliant speculative minds; one generation of scholars built upon the knowledge and works of others.

Archimedes' brilliant mathematical works on such highly sophisticated topics as the geometry of conic surfaces were built upon the foundations of Euclid's *Elements of Geometry,* produced in Alexandria.

But many of these gains remained temporary because of the dispersion of texts and the vulnerability of manuscript culture. Thus, certain advances made at Alexandria in the third century B.C. were already lost just a few centuries later.

4. PRINT AND THE DISCOVERY OF THE PAST

The invention of moveable type printing was the central event that transformed our ability to preserve the past and transmit knowledge from generation to generation. In many ways, print shaped our ideas about the past. "The past is a burden we owe to printing," Eugene Rice and Anthony Grafton, historians of the Renaissance, have written. In certain ways, it was not until print that the past became truly past, became a dead letter on the page rather than the work of a live hand. Before the invention of print, even the most illuminated minds had only a sketchy sense of chronological history. Without the extraordinary documentation and record keeping that print makes possible, it becomes very difficult to keep close track of dates and events. For example, the Italian poet and scholar Petrarch believed that manuscripts of ancient texts that he saw written in Carolingian script (adopted in medieval France) were actually ancient Roman. Since the number of texts that any single individual encountered was necessarily small and almost all of them were copies of copies of copies, distinguishing an ancient text from a recent one was not simple. In a sense, because almost all ancient texts were copied by medieval hands, chronological boundaries were necessarily blurry. Similarly, people in fifteenth-century Italy were convinced that the Baptistry of the Florence cathedral was an ancient building even though it was actually built between the eleventh and the thirteenth century. Thus, in only a few hundred years exact knowledge of its origins had already been lost. Because the Baptistry is octagonal and early-fifteenth-century architects were convinced that the octagon was an ancient form, it had to be ancient. To our eyes, the

Baptistry, with its white and green marble, looks nothing like an ancient building. But the Florentines—before the invention of engraved prints—had almost no means, other than traveling to Rome or other Roman cities, of seeing ancient buildings. It is easy for people in our age to forget how limited the access to knowledge was in an era in which there might be only a single, unique manuscript of a given book. Scholars of the law had to travel from one end of Europe to the other to consult the Justinian Code, the principal codex of Roman law, the single copy of which was jealously held in Ravenna. Before print, the paucity of copies meant that many fundamental works were, for all intents and purposes, nonexistent. Dante, the greatest poet of the Middle Ages, never read Homer, the greatest poet of antiquity. (There were but a handful of texts of Homer in all of Europe and no translations.) Knowledge of ancient Greek had dwindled to almost nothing along with the number of Greek texts available.

Print was invented in the early 1450s, just at the time the Ottoman Turks conquered Constantinople, the last great storehouse of ancient Greek learning. Thus, in an extraordinarily fortuitous coincidence, ancient Greek scholars and texts began to move from East to West precisely at the moment when Western Europe was in a position to give them a much broader audience through the technology of print. With the availability of so much information, the periodization of history, which is so much a part of our modern sensibility, began to take hold. Thus, Erasmus, one of the first major authors of the print era, was able to demonstrate, through intensive philological analysis, that the passages in the New Testament that referred to the Trinity were added to the original text in the fourth century A.D., when debate was raging in the Church over the question of Trinitarianism. He was able to do so by showing that the text used Greek words that were simply not in use during the first century A.D., when the rest of the Gospels were drafted. This would not have been possible without the flood of new books printed in Greek in the second half of the fifteenth century.

This kind of critical consciousness is a result not of print per se but of the widespread availability of texts. The scholars of Alexandria, with their vast library, were doing the same kind of philological analysis when they tried to establish the most authentic text of Homer and compiled lists of "Words Supposed to Be Unknown to the Ancients." And the Italian humanist Lorenzo Valla, just a few years before the invention of print, used similar methods to prove that the Donation of Constantine—a Latin text in which the Roman emperor supposedly gave the lands of central Italy to the Catholic Church—was a medieval forgery rather than an authentic ancient text. Valla's comparative analysis benefited from the dramatic increase in Latin texts in the late Middle Ages. Print increased this capacity exponentially: it is estimated that some twenty million books were printed in the first fifty years of the print era, far more than had been copied in the previous hundred years of writing.

5. THE CULTURAL CONSEQUENCES OF PRINT

In the medieval period, many people had the impression that history, rather than being progressive, was a continual falling away from the golden age represented by Periclean Athens and imperial Rome. In an important sense, the nature of manuscript culture encouraged this view: texts themselves deteriorated with each passing generation as each new copy unwittingly introduced new errors. All the great scientific texts of antiquity—such as Ptolemy's *Geography,* Pliny's *Natural History,* and Vitruvius's *De architectura*—lost their accompanying illustrations in the course of the centuries. Petrarch coined the term *dark ages* to refer to his own time (the fourteenth century), not to the early Middle Ages. But print was one of several innovations that convinced Renaissance men that in some ways they were actually superior to the ancients. Francis Bacon wrote, "We should note the force, effect, and consequences of inventions which are nowhere more conspicuous than in those three which were unknown to the ancients, namely, printing, gunpowder, and the compass. For these three have changed the appearance and state of the whole world."

The invention of print itself became a kind of dividing line that distinguished the modern period from medieval and ancient times.

The modern progressive sense of history, the notion that each generation builds upon the knowledge and achievements of the past, owes much to the invention of print. While manuscripts got worse with each round of copies, one of the great satisfactions of print was that publishers could produce several editions of a work, each new one correcting errors or updating material contained in the previous ones. Early publishers even solicited readers to send in corrections so that later editions could be improved. "The Power which Printing gives us of continually improving and correcting our Works in successive Editions appears to me the chief advantage of that art," wrote the English philosopher David Hume. As Elizabeth Eisenstein, a historian of the print revolution, has written, "Typographical fixity is a basic prerequisite for the rapid advancement of learning."

Print ensured that discoveries did not get lost. In recent decades, it has been fairly well established by historians that Norse seafarers such as Leif Eriksson "discovered" America long before Columbus. But the Norsemen's discovery was recorded on only a few scraps of parchment and was quickly forgotten, and thus did not lead to successive voyages that made the colonization of America an enduring reality. By contrast, Columbus's letter to the king of Spain describing his trip was published throughout Europe within two years of his return. This guaranteed that other ships from Europe would begin exploring the new territories.

The permanence of print meant that scientists and technicians could build on past breakthroughs, while broadcasting their own innovations through journals and newspapers with increasing rapidity. It gave scientific work real traction, leading to the extraordinary boom of the Industrial Revolution.

6. PRINT AND THE CULT OF ANTIQUITY

Curiously, this growing sense of progress and modernity that print helped to foster went hand in hand with the cult of antiquity and an increased interest in the past. People began systematically digging up ancient statues in Italy and elsewhere in the fifteenth century precisely at the same time that they began trying to dig out and publish lost ancient texts.

The effects of print on our relationship to the past are multiple and complex. On the one hand, print made the past much more present and available; on the other hand, the creation of the first museums was, in some way, a sign that ancient works could be collected because the past was now past. In the Middle Ages and Renaissance, artists and patrons thought nothing of dismantling ancient buildings in order to make new ones. Even in the seventeenth century, the leading architects used the Colosseum as a marble quarry for their own works. The changing attitude toward the past is reflected in the evolution of the restoration of ancient works of art, as I explored in chapter 2 on art conservation in China. Up until relatively recently, in the West as in the East, the prevailing tendency was to rebuild ancient works and try to make them as good as new. Perhaps because there was still a sense of continuity between past and present, Gianlorenzo Bernini thought nothing of altering ancient sculptures and saw himself as being in direct competition with ancient works of art. But as systematic archeology began and the outlines of the modern world emerged, the past seemed to recede and the ancient object became precious and untouchable. A turning point in this history is at the beginning of the nineteenth century when Lord Elgin brought the sculpted frieze of the Parthenon back to London but, at the insistence of the neoclassicist sculptor Antonio Canova, the broken and missing parts were left as they were found. Thus, between the time of Bernini and the time of Canova, something important happened in our attitude toward the past. The antiquarian culture of neoclassicism, by placing the past on a pedestal and in a museum, saw it as truly past.

In a whole series of fields, print had the paradoxical effect of first glorifying the ancients and then overthrowing their authority. In the first century of print, the revival and publication of ancient texts was seen as fundamental to the advancement of science. Thus, in the late fifteenth century, the brilliant German mathematician and astronomer Johannes Regiomontanus sought to serve the cause of science not by setting up a laboratory but by learning Greek and starting up a printing press. He prepared a meticulous new Latin translation of Ptolemy's *Epitome,* the greatest known work on planetary theory, which was printed in 1496. Although Ptolemy's work was based on the mistaken notion that the sun revolved around the earth, its precise calculations and rigorous mathematical methods taught a generation of new astronomers like

Copernicus, who then overthrew Ptolemy by introducing the heliocentric universe. The publication of Copernicus's *De revolutionibus orbium coelestium* (1543) would not have been possible without the publication of Ptolemy, even though it rendered Ptolemy obsolete.

The same thing happened in the fields of geography, physics, botany, and medicine, in which ancient authors were first lifted onto a pedestal and then knocked off within a few generations. In some cases, the very act of publication—by exposing works to close scrutiny—revealed their imperfections. In republishing Pliny's *Natural History*, the Italian botanist Niccolò Leoniceno corrected some five hundred errors he found—errors in botany as well as errors that had crept into the text through centuries of copying and recopying.

The publication of Ptolemy's *Geography* was an important factor in stimulating Christopher Columbus's voyage to America, even though that discovery definitively revealed the limitations and errors in Ptolemy's knowledge of the world.

"Between 1550 and 1650 Western thinkers ceased to believe that they could find all important truths in ancient books," Anthony Grafton writes. He goes on to describe how the Jesuit José de Acosta realized, as he traveled across the Equator in South America, that Aristotle's descriptions of the Torrid Zone were completely mistaken. The ancients had insisted that anyone passing through the region would be burned to death, while de Acosta found himself suffering from a sudden chill. "What could I do then," he wrote, "but laugh at Aristotle's Meteorology and his philosophy?"

Thus, print, within a century of its invention, had the extraordinary effect of bringing about first a rediscovery and then an eclipse of the ancients.

7. PRINT AND SECULAR CULTURE

The overturning of scientific authority figures such as Aristotle, Ptolemy, Galen, and Pliny and Erasmus's philological debunking of the doctine of the Trinity were evidence of a critical mode of thinking that is inherent in print culture. Putting large numbers of books into the hands of individual readers tends to empower them by offering alternative sources of knowledge to received authority. (It is for this reason that the Catholic Church vehemently opposed the translation from Latin into the vernacular of the Bible and why the Ottoman sultans banned the printing press on pain of death in 1516—condemning their empire to a period of long, slow decline.) It is widely accepted by historians that the print revolution gave wings to the Protestant Revolution of Martin Luther. There had been previous rebellions against the central authority of the Church—many of the ideas of the Reformation were present in the works of Jan Huss and John Wycliffe, who had made the first English translation of the Bible. But the church was able to snuff out Wycliffe and Huss because they were not able to circulate their ideas. In 1517, Luther's famous theses were printed throughout Europe within fifteen days.

The sociologist Max Weber and others have noted the close ties between the rise of capitalism and the Protestant ethic—with their common emphasis on the individual and on self-discipline. Others have noted the contribution of the print revolution to the Reformation, but there are also organic ties between print and capitalism. Printing in Europe—unlike writing on clay tablets or papyrus—was from the beginning both a technology and a commercial industry.

Because print was a lucrative business as well as a technology, printers kept looking for new markets to supply with an ever-increasing number of books. The effects of this were arguably more radical than the computer revolution in today's world. Because printing was a business and not just a technology, the search for larger and larger markets led to a democratization of reading and changes in the nature of readers as well as in the nature of the books published.

Changes in quantity led to changes in quality. In the first fifty years of print (1450 to 1500) 77 percent of the known books that survive were written in Latin and the vast majority were religious in character. Half a century later, although the number of religious books did not decline, they were greatly outnumbered by a flood of classical texts as humanist culture began to dominate. Since most of the humanist books were also written in Latin, however, the next wave of publishing involved opening up publishing to those who spoke only their native language. Thus, in the seventeenth century there was an explosion of books in the vernacular tongues of Europe.

The increased number of books changed the type of person who read and possessed libraries. In their seminal work *The Coming of the Book*, the French historians Lucien Febvre and Henri-Jean Martin survey wills that left substantial libraries in France. In the period between 1480 and 1500, they found twenty-five, twenty-four belonging to clergymen and one to a lawyer. In the period between 1551 and 1600, the proportions were dramatically reversed: they found inventories belonging to seventy-one lawyers and twenty-one clergymen.

This change reflected, clearly, the rise of a literate bourgeois class. Moreover, the size of libraries had grown significantly. In the late fifteenth century, a good-sized personal library consisted of fifteen to twenty books. By 1550, private libraries of more than five hundred volumes were not uncommon. Ordinary merchants and lawyers suddenly had the access to knowledge that only a prince or an archbishop could have hoped for a mere fifty or a hundred years earlier—just as in our day the Internet has given the individual access to knowledge that only a large corporation or library might have had a decade or two ago.

The fact that tradesmen and professionals now had the same information as the aristocracy led them, almost inevitably, to demand the same rights as well. Alexis de Tocqueville wrote that the French Revolution occurred because the French population had already become much more equal: "The farther down the eighteenth century we come there is a corresponding increase in the number of royal edicts . . . which apply the same rules in the same manner to all parts of the governed. . . . Not only did the provinces resemble each other more and more, but in each province the men of different classes, at least all those who ranked above the common people, become more and more alike, despite the differences in rank."

8. WRITING, READING, AND DEMOCRACY

In fact, writing has been linked to democracy from the time of ancient Athens. The ancient Greeks insisted that their rulers post their laws in written form so that the citizens might scrutinize the work of those who governed. Literacy was a requirement of citizenship in Athens and a means for citizens to hold their leaders accountable.

The growth of print and the emergence of the newspaper greatly expanded literacy, with unsettlingly democratizing effects. As one conservative critic wrote disapprovingly in 1663, "A public Mercury makes the multitude too familiar with the actions and counsels of their superiors, too pragmatical and censorious, and gives them, not only an itch, but a kind of colourable right and license to be meddling with the government."

While literacy has, at times, been used as a bar to exclude the illiterate from exercising power, reading and writing have generally been a form of empowerment. There are good reasons why the slaveholders in the United States made it a crime to teach slaves to read. Frederick Douglass, who went to great lengths to learn to read—despite his master's strict prohibition—saw it as an essential step in his eventual liberation. In fact, in very broad terms, the expansion of literacy has gone hand in hand with the enfranchisement of wider and wider spheres of society. And the sense of historical context that comes with literacy is a part of the feeling of enfranchisement; knowing where you have come from is important to forming an idea of where you want to go.

9. TELEVISION—PRO AND CON

So, now that print has been dethroned by various electronic media, especially television, as the world's principal source of information, what has happened to this equation? According to the technological optimists, nothing has changed, at least not for the worse. By reaching more people, television and other electronic media should simply extend the benefits of more information to more people.

To some extent, in some parts of the world, this has been true. The transparency of the television age has made it much harder for governments to practice the crudest forms of discrimination and oppression. The images of Southern police officers firing water cannons and siccing dogs on civil rights protesters in the United States may have had a greater impact on galvanizing public opinion against segregation than any newspaper stories. The televised images of Boris Yeltsin standing defiantly on a tank in front of the Russian parliament building during the attempted coup of 1991 (shown on CNN) helped rally support around the world. President George Bush, who initially reacted to the coup with a tepid statement that indicated he was prepared to accept the new Soviet rulers, suddenly changed course. Yeltsin demanded that Bush do two things: telephone him and make a statement of support on television.

Yeltsin has argued that the Soviet generals lost because they were staging an old-fashioned coup that failed to reckon with today's technology. They naturally took over the TV stations and removed Mikhail Gorbachev from all outside contact. But they did not shut down the satellites of CNN and other international media; they did not shut down the phone lines that were busily spreading information via fax and the Internet. "The middle-aged coup plotters simply could not imagine the extent and volume of the information," Yeltsin said. "Instead of a quiet and inconspicuous coup executed party style, they suddenly had a totally public fight on their hands. The coup plotters were not prepared—especially psychologically—for an atmosphere of complete publicity."

But the revolutionary effects of television go well beyond loosening the grip of national governments and helping to end the Cold War. Studies of communities into which television was introduced, from Germany and Bulgaria to rural Canada, show astonishingly profound changes in people's daily habits and social patterns. After the introduction of television they do less of practically everything: less reading, less visiting with friends, less cooking, less cleaning, less traveling, less going to church, less going to dances or to the movies, even less sleeping and less talking. The two things people do more of are shopping and eating.

These studies have been adumbrated in an interesting way by Harvard political scientist Robert Putnam, whose *Bowling Alone* examines the decline of civic engagement in America. Putnam is struck by the dramatic decrease in participation in a whole series of social and civic activities—PTAs, rotary clubs, union membership, political parties, voting, bowling leagues, and bridge and chess clubs. Putnam initially suspected other major social trends—the increased number of women in the workplace, increased mobility, the growth of the role of government—but as he got further into his research he controlled for all kinds of factors, including age, economic class, race, gender, and geographic location. The one common denominator, the one clear correlation with low civic participation—in every type of activity—was high levels of TV watching. Putnam's index of civic engagement shows a decline of about 50 percent in the last twenty-five years.

Against those who suggest that people's activities have simply shifted—from bowling leagues to health clubs—Putnam notes that many activities have declined in absolute terms: the percentage of married people who have dinner together has declined between 20 and 30 percent. Voting has declined by about 20 percent from the early 1960s, from 63 to 49 percent between 1960 and 1996.

Putnam's work is confirmed by a major study coming from a completely different direction. Researchers at UCLA have been examining the attitudes and behavior of incoming college freshmen for thirty years and have found dramatic changes. In the late 1960s, developing a meaningful philosophy of life was these students' top value, endorsed as an "essential" or "very important" goal by more than 80 percent of them. Being very well-off financially, on the other hand, lagged far behind, ranking fifth or sixth. Since that time these two values have basically traded places.

The authors of the study conclude that an increase in conservative and materialistic values "were associated with the number of hours per week that students watched television during the past year. . . . The more television watched, the stronger the endorsement of the goal of being very well-off financially, and the weaker the endorsement of the goal of developing a meaningful philosophy of life. While such cor-relations obviously cannot prove causation, they raise some interesting possibilities."

Because television—at least as it has been set up in the United States—is a system for delivering advertising, it is hardly surprising that its "content" should create a materialistic culture that is favorable to the sale of consumer goods. As Edmund Burke once said, "Let a man only tell you his story every morning and evening and at the end of a twelve-month he will have become your master." Commercial television has been telling its story every morning and evening for the last fifty years.

Putnam also found that high levels of civic participation—voting, being active in the community—were closely linked to newspaper reader-ship. That result, too, should not be too surprising, since the two are correlated historically.

This participation was initially restricted by race and gender, but from the mid-nineteenth to the mid-twentieth century both voting and newspaper reading became virtually universal. "The reach of this news across class lines was remarkable," Thomas Leonard writes in his history of American newspapers. "A government survey after World War I showed that for low- and medium-income white families in urban American, more than nine in ten took a paper. . . . Half of those news buyers slipped away in the low- and middle-income groups by the 1970s. . . . This century ends with only an economic elite showing the loyalty to newspapers that was once shared by blue-collar workers, small farmers and clerks."

The feeling that people took control of their own world both by reading about it and participating in it was not a hollow illusion.

Conversely, during the age of television, people have dropped out of the political process, newspaper reading has become an elite phe-nomenon, and we have experienced a sharp increase in the gap between rich and poor.

Reading is not less important than it was. On the contrary, it is per-haps more important, but it has become more of an elite activity. Com-petition for top schools is more intense than ever and educational level has become a much greater determinant of future income. But the average SAT score in verbal aptitude has dropped dramatically from 1960, when it was 477 (on a scale of 800) to a mere 427 by 1996.

Increasingly, our society is divided into an informed minority that understands how to protect its interests and a passive but alienated majority that receives its news from television, feels that it has little control of its destiny, and has dropped out of the political process. Distrust of government has grown dramatically during this same time span. In 1964, despite the assassination of John Kennedy and the protest marches of the civil rights movement, 76 percent of Americans said they trusted their government to do what is right most of the time. By 1996, that figure had dropped to 27 percent. Despite increased education levels, fewer Americans today can name their own congressmen than forty years ago. It is difficult to trust what you don't know. Overall newspaper circulation dropped by 57 percent between 1948 (the time television began to be a factor in U.S. life) and 1998. The percentage of people under thirty-five who read newspapers regularly has dropped from 67 percent to less than 30 percent since 1965.

Television has created a flat, two-dimensional world of an eternal present—in which everything, whether it is depicted in the present or the past, appears to be happening now. In historical representation, it is generally impossible to distinguish the fictional details from those based in historical fact, and past and present are often conflated and confused. When President Jimmy Carter was having trouble getting Congress to approve the return of the Panama Canal, the announcement that movie actor John Wayne approved of returning the canal to Panama suddenly turned the tide in the treaty's favor. Although Wayne had never fought in a foreign war and had no expertise in foreign policy, it was as if, in the public mind, he had become an amalgam of all the roles he had ever played—as if he had really fought the Spanish at the Alamo, shot Indians at Fort Apache, defeated the Japanese on the sands of Iwo Jima, and been a Green Beret in Vietnam. The lack of a real command both of history and of events of the present leaves people distrustful and withdrawn.

10. THE INTERNET AND FRAGMENTATION

The birth of the Internet and the explosion of information would seem to offer a possible way out of the lowest-common-denominator nature of television culture. The Internet, so far at least, is dominated by words and not images and has brought about a significant revival of reading and writing. Potentially, it threatens to break the monopoly of large network broadcasters and media by allowing everyone to be his or her own publisher. In many ways, the Internet is the fulfillment of the dream of the founders of the Great Library of Alexandria—the universal library that contains all useful and important knowledge from all cultures and all historical eras. Genealogy Web sites rank just after pornography sites as the most popular venues on the World Wide Web—and the Mormons have already placed the names of 400 million dead souls on-line—suggesting that the desire for finding one's historical roots ranks just after erotic pleasure among humankind's deepest needs.

The ability to read publications on-line from India, Kenya, Manila, or Buenos Aires is a fabulous resource that genuinely makes the world much richer and more varied. In its first years, the Internet was itself a kind of modern version of Raphael's *School of Athens,* a grand international forum of intellectual exchange in which scientists and scholars from Seattle to Singapore traded papers, ideas, and equations. The use of the Internet as a place of free exchange of ideas remains very strong, but in the last several years it has been flanked by a commercial twin: the Internet as marketplace.

When I was working on the chapter on Giancarlo Scoditti and the island of Kitawa, I did an Internet search for Bronislaw Malinowski's *Argonauts of the Western Pacific,* which was out of print at the time. Within seconds, I found a whole range of possible copies, from a 1910 first edition with original plates for several hundred dollars to a beat-up paperback with a stain on the cover for $4.95 and almost everything in between, with offerings from bookshops from London to California. Within a week, I had my copy (the beat-up paperback). It is impossible not to be impressed by the mechanism. The Internet had performed as a perfect marketplace, matching supply and demand among people who otherwise would have no access to one another, in a mutually beneficial exchange.

Technology, as I have tried to argue, is not neutral and the fact that the dominant technology of our age—and that of the immediate future—is knitting the world into an ever more perfect marketplace has profound cultural consequences, just as writing and print did.

Marshall McLuhan understood that electronic technology has a fragmenting effect on our culture. Print, by contrast, promoted linguistic and cultural standardization: the daily newspaper (or even the nightly newscast) had to be prepared for millions of different people with vastly different interests. The Internet is the realm of the tailor-made. Rather than make do with the people who live in their neighborhood, people now can find like-minded souls on the Internet—beekeepers can speak with beekeepers, astronomers with astronomers, etc. But this also creates a balkanized universe where people seek out and associate only with those who think as they do.

Already, the Internet makes it possible for people to assemble their own daily newspaper that collects news on the subjects that interest them and leaves out material that doesn't. But one of the chief virtues of the daily newspaper is that it exposes you to a little bit of everything: in flipping the pages to find your favorite section, you stumble upon a science story or a piece of local news that intrigues you or a contrary opinion that annoys or surprises you. Because the general-interest newspaper has to provide something for everyone, it is written broadly for the needs of hundreds of thousands of different readers, and to read it is to stand in a common space, like a crowded public square that you must share with others. By contrast, the self-designed Internet newspaper amplifies our existing tendencies rather than challenges them. It is what information guru Nicholas Negroponte enthusiastically calls "The Daily Me." By learning about our likes and dislikes, our tastes and buying habits from our on-line behavior, advertisers are working hard to figure out ways to tailor their advertising to each single Internet user rather than waste money on people from demographic groups or economic categories that would not be interested in a particular product.

The notion of "The Daily Me" is antithetical to traditional historical consciousness, which takes us out of ourselves into the world of what Ralph Waldo Emerson called "the not-me," a world where we connect with others in a common history. In a medium of communication that caters specifically to our individual needs, the citizen is replaced by the consumer. This trend continues the erosion of common space that goes back several decades but picked up steam with the advent of the computer and of television.

There are major potential political consequences, as Cass Sunstein, a professor of law at the University of Chicago, observes in his recent book *Republic.com*. The general newspaper or even the evening newscast usually feels an obligation to reflect several different viewpoints and has a moderating effect on people's opinions. Sunstein cites studies indicating that, in the political realm, people "surf" between political sites that reflect their own views: the Web serves as a kind of echo chamber that tends to make their views more extreme.

11. THE INTERNET AND DISINTERMEDIATION

One of the principles that people versed in the Internet invoke most often is called disintermediation—the capacity to bypass traditional intermediaries in order to get what you want for yourself. Rather than pay a stockbroker a commission, you can buy stocks yourselves. Rather than go to a bookstore, you can order on-line. Some people see the Internet as the ultimate form of democracy, allowing people to vote on issues directly thereby bypassing their elected officials.

Television has already pushed us a good ways in this direction. Before television, political parties in the United States acted as the intermediaries that chose candidates at party conventions. State primaries were used to test the public mood but the final decisions were made by party bosses. The growth of primaries and television went hand in hand: in an age in which people could watch candidates via satellite as they campaigned hundreds or thousands of miles away, people insisted on picking their own leaders. This may have had a democratizing effect on our political life, but it has also had a series of unintended consequences.

During a recent election, Reuven Frank, the former head of NBC News, noted that in his day covering a convention posed considerable technical difficulties but there was a great deal of news—behind-the-scenes jockeying to support this or that candidate or this or that plank in the party platform. Now, he said, with handheld cameras and satellite TV you can cover everything but there is no story left. The last time there was any real uncertainty about the choice of candidate in a major party was 1968. Increasingly, a convention is a televised pageant to rally support for the candidate on the part of the viewers back home, not an event where important business is to be conducted. Indeed, in the year 2000 ratings for the conventions were at an all-time low and many network newsmen complained that they were tired of covering what had become nothing more than party infomercials.

Thus, by going over the heads of local political leaders, television emptied the event of substance and meaning. It seems to empower the ordinary citizen by doing away with the party bosses and the smoke-filled rooms. But it also empties out the collective, common space of direct participation that Putnam's research shows in decline, the political club or organization. In one sense it brings politics closer, right into the living room, but in another sense it takes politics farther away. With television, the cost of elections has skyrocketed to such a point that only candidates with high name recognition and huge war chests can run for office, making officials much more subject to monied interests. Thus the ordinary citizen-viewer feels less and not more powerful—a fact that may help account for the apathy and lower voter turnout.

12. THE INTERNET AND THE PERFECT MARKETPLACE

The Internet, as I indicated above, is, among other things, a perfect marketplace, bringing together supply and demand in almost seamless fashion. A perfect marketplace has many advantages—raspberries in winter, Neapolitan buffalo mozzarella in Manhattan, Hawaiian pineapple in

Berlin, seventeen kinds of coffee, two million books a computer key-stroke away—but it also puts pressure on all sorts of pockets of inefficiency in our lives that we value.

When I first went to live in Italy in 1980, I remember being struck by how restaurants would simply close their shutters for the entire month of August, turning away thousands of potential customers with a sign that said, "On vacation until September." From a strictly business point of view, closing at the height of the tourist season makes little sense, but it is an expression of the idea that there are more important things to life than making money. A perfectly efficient market—where rent is strictly calibrated to the maximum earning capacity of a business—will not tolerate this kind of attitude. And globalization is putting pressure on such practices. There is a big push in Europe to liberalize store hours, to promote the competition of American-style supermarkets with smaller, family-owned stores. There are obvious advantages for consumers, but there will be an inevitable loss of color, of personal idiosyncrasy, and regional flavor in the standardization that will come.

Just as computer-generated market research made it possible to pick apart the subscribers of general-interest magazines, to distinguish lucrative from unlucrative readers, so a series of cultural institutions—universities, museums, publishing houses, television news stations—that were once comparatively immune to the pressures of the market now must live under increasingly close financial scrutiny. Until recently, for example, it was an accepted practice in book publishing that best-selling books would partially subsidize the so-called serious books that the pub-lisher felt a cultural duty to publish. Publishing houses were generally family-owned, often by men who had made or inherited their fortunes in other businesses, and were generally content with modest profits. In the last thirty years, most of the major publishers have been bought up by larger corporate conglomerates that apply much stricter economic control. With the increased ability to track profit and loss, each book is expected to earn its keep (and each editor his or hers) or face elimina-tion. Many of the new corporate owners work in newer industries that are used to much higher profits. Traditionally, in many older industrial businesses, a profit margin of 5 to 10 percent was respectable. Book publishing is a slow, labor-intensive industry in which each book must be individually prepared and sold practically one copy at a time. It is weighed down by material costs, paper, printing, storage, shipping, and the return of unsold books from bookstores, all of which eat into profits. Alberto Vitale, the former president of Random House, the largest publishing group in the United States, has often said that in a good year—a year when the cost of paper doesn't skyrocket and you have several major best-sellers—a book publisher can expect to make a profit of about 5 percent.

In television—which sells something immaterial over the waves—the cost of broadcasting a show to one person or a billion people is essentially the same. "This is a business where if you're a birdbrain you have a 35 percent profit margin," Barry Diller, the head of USA Networks, has observed. Many of the corporate owners of book publishing expect the same performance from books.

Traditionally, universities were operated on the rather paternalistic principle that the professors and the administration knew what an educated young man and woman should know. This principle was challenged during the 1960s with demands of political relevance and calls for the curriculum to better reflect the growing diversity of American society. Requirements were dropped—requirements for science, history, foreign languages—to accommodate courses specifically designed for African Americans, Hispanics, women, Jews, and homosexuals.

Many of these changes filled long-standing gaps and made universities more varied and interesting, but they have also gone together with universities' adoption of a consumer model of operation. Students "shop" for courses, teachers are judged successful by the numbers in their classes, students judge their professors through "teaching evaluations," a device borrowed straight from the consumer world. Negative evaluations can seriously harm the career of a young professor and are sometimes used by students as a negotiating lever to bargain for lighter workloads, more entertaining assignments, and, above all, higher grades. Since their parents are paying a fortune to send them to college,

many American students behave like entitled consumers who have purchased a very expensive product: they expect a good grade, fun courses,
and not to have to do the work if they don't feel like it.

Because the university operates more like a business, eliminating
departments and courses with low enrollment, higher compensation has
begun to be more closely pegged to the departments that are the most
lucrative: business and the sciences. Nationally, in 1976, a newly hired
assistant professor teaching literature earned $3,000 less than a new
assistant professor in business. In 1984, that gap had grown to $10,000
and by 1996 it exceeded $25,000.

The number of faculty in the liberal arts has declined from one in
six to one in thirteen. And with the decline of the prestige of humanistic
disciplines, there has been a decline in the quality of the students pursuing graduate degrees in those fields. The average score on the Graduate
Record Exam—the main test for admission to graduate programs—in literature declined by 60 points (out of 800) between 1965 and 1992,
while scores in the sciences generally were unchanged.

If the humanities departments at our universities function as our
collective historical memory, then it would be hard not to conclude that
we are putting few of our resources into that part of life.

Although we pay lip service to living in a global, interdependent
world, Americans are, in many ways, becoming more insular. Foreign
language requirements at many schools have been lifted, and while 16
percent of all students were taking a foreign language in 1960, that percentage has dropped by more than half.

The terrorist attack of September 11, 2001, exposed how dangerous
this cultural neglect could be. Intelligence reports sent by foreign governments to the FBI and the CIA were ignored because almost no one at
the agencies reads foreign languages. A quite specific warning from
French police on the eve of the attack went unread and untranslated.
"Not a single Iran desk chief during the eight years that I worked on Iran
could speak or write Persian," wrote a former CIA agent recently. "Not a
single Near East Division chief knew Arabic, Persian, or Turkish, and
only one could get along even in French."

13. HOMOGENIZATION

To its champions, globalization was supposed to bring about an increased sense of interdependence and multiculturalism. And yet world culture has never been so homogeneous: in Brazil, 70 percent of the songs played on the radio are in English; the figure is 80 percent in Germany. In Japan it is 50 percent. The six major record companies control more than 95 percent of the American market and more than half of the European markets.

The increased globalization of film has made Hollywood the second-largest export industry—after airplane manufacturing—in the United States. But the need to find movies that will work on a world-wide scale has tended to favor big action movies with lots of violence and special effects that can be easily comprehended by audiences from Buenos Aires to Manila. Thus, virtually all of the one hundred highest-grossing films in movie history are American, and the list is topped by ones like *Jurassic Park, Armageddon,* and *Robocop.* Making these types of movies, often for more than $100 million, is something only the major Hollywood studios can afford. And with so many millions riding on a single film, studios play it safe with action and violence. Indeed, an increase in violence has gone along with increased global markets.

In the original movie *Death Wish,* which came out in 1974, a mere 9 people die, while in the 1988 sequel the vigilante crusader for justice kills 52. The initial *Robocop* movie, released in 1987, involves 32 killings, while *Robocop II* has 81. *Rambo* goes from a body count of 62 to 106 by *Rambo III.* The *Die Hard* series progresses from eighteen to an incredible 264 deaths between its first and second incarnations.

While our cultural products are becoming more global, our own culture is in some ways becoming more provincial: foreign coverage has dropped from nine to six minutes during the average nightly newscast in recent years. In 1960, for every hundred students in college, sixteen enrolled in foreign languages. In 1970, it was twelve, and by 1995, with a global economy in full swing, fewer than eight.

The high-tech economy is characterized by a fundamental paradox. On the one hand, it empowers the individual by giving access to both information and a potentially infinite audience through the Internet. Each of us has our own library, our own newspaper, publishing house, and broadcasting studio in our own computer. And yet, at the same time, the technical possibility of reaching a world market has dramatically increased the power of those with a truly global reach. Thus, movie stars with proven box office appeal receive $25 million a movie; baseball players able to draw a large television audience sign contracts for $250 million. In an age of fragmentation, the products with proven box office appeal are more valuable than ever. And the dramatic rise in the cost of producing entertainment with proven mass appeal favors increased concentration—hence the mergers in broadcasting, movies, publishing, and Internet companies. Thus, there is a struggle between the forces that empower and dwarf the individual. The inexpensive digital camera may have made it much cheaper to make a movie, but other technological forces—the dazzling special effects used in most big action movies designed for the global marketplace—have dramatically escalated the cost of movies.

14. END

Fragmentation, depoliticization, the decline of newspapers and reading, the personalization of media, the decline of the humanities, the replacement of the citizen with the consumer are consequences of electronic technology's gradual replacement of print as our preeminent medium. If print was the technology that helped create our sense of history—the complex sense of periodization and cause and effect—television is a flat world in which everything occurs in a consumer present.

But there are, perhaps, reasons to be optimistic. Despite the creation of virtual worlds, reality still matters. A recent study showed that the biggest single factor in the neurological development of young children was the number of words they heard each day. The more someone talked or read to a child during its first three years of life, the more neurons grew. But the words had to be spoken by a live human being, some-one with an emotional attachment to the child; the brains of children left in front of a TV didn't develop as fully.

Although virtual communities establish useful human bonds, if they entirely replace real human communities they will not last. Tech-nologies have changed dramatically in the last ten thousand years, but human nature is relatively constant. The need for community, physical closeness, personal contact, and affection has not disappeared even if our lives have been considerably restructured. Sociologists have closely studied people's moods while performing various activities throughout their day and found that subjects reported very low levels of satisfaction and self-esteem when they were asked how they felt during or after watching television. The growing levels of distrust of government are a sign that the disengagement from politics is producing widespread dis-satisfaction and alienation whose consequences are unpredictable. Our need for meaning in life is tied up with a sense of our place in history, and if new technologies do not fulfill their potential to enhance this sense, there may be a backlash.

If the gap between rich and poor continues to grow, there will be a reaction. People may rediscover politics and use new technology to organize politically in powerful new ways. (The signs that this has already begun to happen are evident in the recent anti-globalization protests in Seattle and Genoa, whatever one may think of their aims or their means.) If people continue to feel that they are losing control of their lives and that they are losing their cultural traditions, they will work to regain control, using technologies in ways that we have not yet imagined.

Acknowledgments

I would like to thank the American Academy in Rome, where I lived between 1990 and 1993, and whose community of scholars and artists— constantly concerned with studying and interrogating the past and the present—provided the environment in which this book gestated. The Alicia Patterson Foundation awarded me a generous grant to begin working systematically on this topic in 1995. I also want to thank Vassar College and the Gladys Krieble Delmas Foundation for inviting me to teach a semester at Vassar. By encouraging me to organize a course around the subject of "The Future of the Past," they forced me to do a lot of the background reading that gave the book historical context. I also owe a great debt to the editors of *The New Yorker*, who saw the potential in what were initially little more than vague hunches and sent me all over the world to explore them.

Perhaps my deepest gratitude, however, is to the many people who became the central characters of this book—Mark Lehner, Michele Cordaro, Malcolm Bell, V. B. Mishra, Patricia Wright, Giancarlo Scoditti, Mohammed Ibrahim Warsame (Hadrawi), Reginald Foster, and Leonard Boyle. Their passions are the driving force of this book.